SHAKER DESIGN

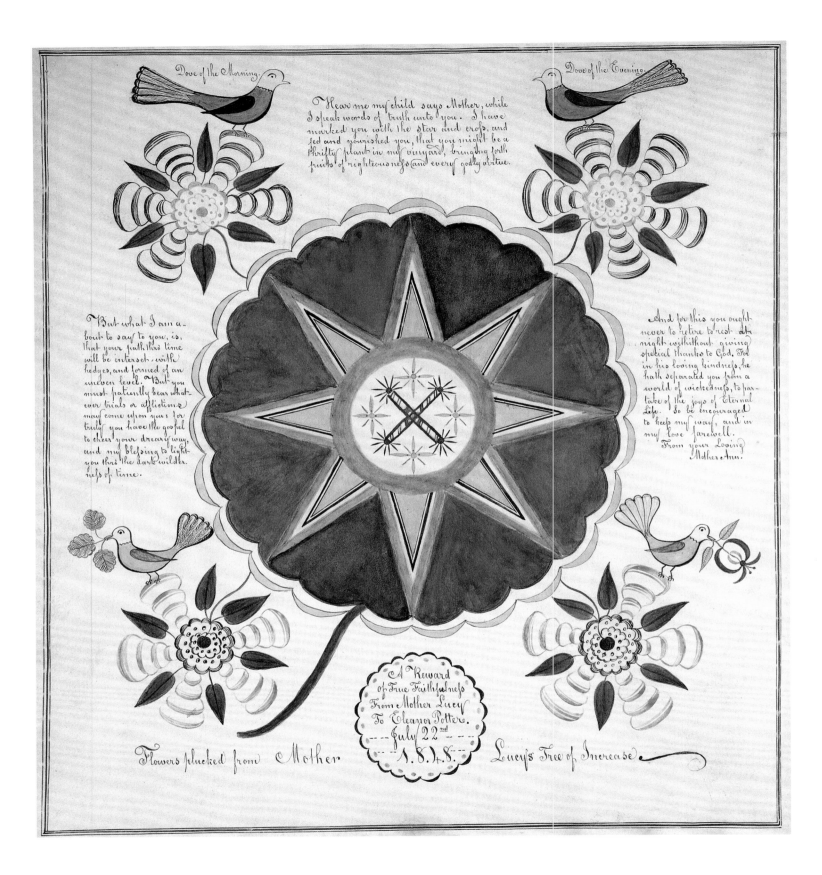

Dove of the Morning.

Dove of the Evening.

Hear me my child says Mother, while I speak words of truth unto you. I have marked you with the star and cross, and fed and nourished you, that you might be a thrifty plant in my vinyard, bringing forth fruits of righteousness and every godly virtue.

But what I am about to say to you, is, that your path this time will be intersect with hedges, and formed of an uneven level. But you must patiently bear whatever trials or afflictions may come upon you; for truly you have the gospel to cheer your dreary way, and my blessing to light you thro' the dark wilderness of time.

And for this you ought never to retire to rest at night without giving special thanks to God. For in his loving kindness, he hath separated you from a world of wickedness, to partake of the joys of Eternal Life. So be encouraged to keep my way, and in my love farewell. From your Loving Mother Ann.

A Reward of True Faithfulness From Mother Lucy To Eleanor Potter. July 22nd 1.8.4.8.

Flowers plucked from Mother Lucy's Tree of Increase.

Shaker Design

Out of This World

Jean M. Burks, Editor

Jean M. Burks
Robert P. Emlen
Jean M. Humez
M. Stephen Miller
Sumpter Priddy
Kory Rogers
Gerard C. Wertkin

Published for the
Bard Graduate Center for Studies in the
Decorative Arts, Design, and Culture, New York
and the Shelburne Museum, Shelburne, Vermont
by Yale University Press, New Haven and London

This catalogue is published in conjunction with the exhibition *Shaker Design: Out of This World*, held at The Bard Graduate Center for Studies in the Decorative Arts, Design, and Culture from March 13 through June 15, 2008. The original version of the exhibition entitled *Out of This World: Shaker Design Past, Present, and Future*, at the Shelburne Museum, Shelburne, Vermont, ran from June 16 through October 28, 2007.

Exhibition curator: Jean M. Burks
Project coordinator at the Bard Graduate Center:
Earl Martin
Editor: Barbara Burn
Coordinator of photography: Alexis Mucha
Catalogue production: Sally Salvesen, London

Director of Exhibitions and Executive Editor,
Exhibition Catalogues, Bard Graduate Center: Nina
Stritzler-Levine

Catalogue and jacket design: Sally Salvesen
Printed and bound: Conti Tipocolor SpA, Italy

Library of Congress Cataloging-in-Publication Data
Burks, Jean M., 1949-
  Shaker design : out of this world / Jean Burks.
     p. cm.
  Includes bibliographical references and index.
  ISBN 978-0-300-13728-6 (alk. paper)
  1. Shaker decorative arts. 2. Decorative arts—
United States—History—19th century. 3. Shakers.
I. Title.
  NK807.B84 2008
  745.088'2898--dc22

2007051415

Endpapers: George Kendal (b. 1813). Detail, *Plan of the First Family, Harvard,* 1836. Pencil, ink, and watercolor on paper. Fruitlands Museums, Harvard, Masschusetts.

Half title page: Sarah Collins taping a chair seat, 1930s. Mount Lebanon, New York. Courtesy Hamilton College, Burke Library, Clinton, New York.

Frontispiece: Polly Ann (Jane) Reed (1818–1881). *Gift Drawing: A Reward of True Faithfulness From Mother Lucy to Eleanor Potter,* 1848. New Lebanon, New York. Ink and watercolor on paper. Collection American Folk Art Museum, New York, Promised gift of Ralph Esmerian P1.2001.302. Photo: Gavin Ashworth, New York.

Contents page: Joshua H. Bussell (1816–1900). Detail, *The Shaker Village at Alfred, Maine,* 1845. Pencil, ink, and watercolor on paper. Library of Congress, Washington, D. C.

The exhibition *Shaker Design: Out of This World* is organized by the
Shelburne Museum in Shelburne, Vermont, in collaboration with
the Bard Graduate Center. Major support for the exhibition has
been provided by Chittenden Bank and The Americana Foundation,
with additional support from Thos. Moser, Inc., The Charles Engelhard
Foundation, the Vermont Wood Manufacturers Association, The
Oakland Foundation, Jane and Gerald Katcher, and John and Kathryn
Wilmerding Heminway

Funding for the catalogue has been provided by Furthermore: a
program of the J. M. Kaplan Fund, Jane and Gerald Katcher, and
Thos. Moser

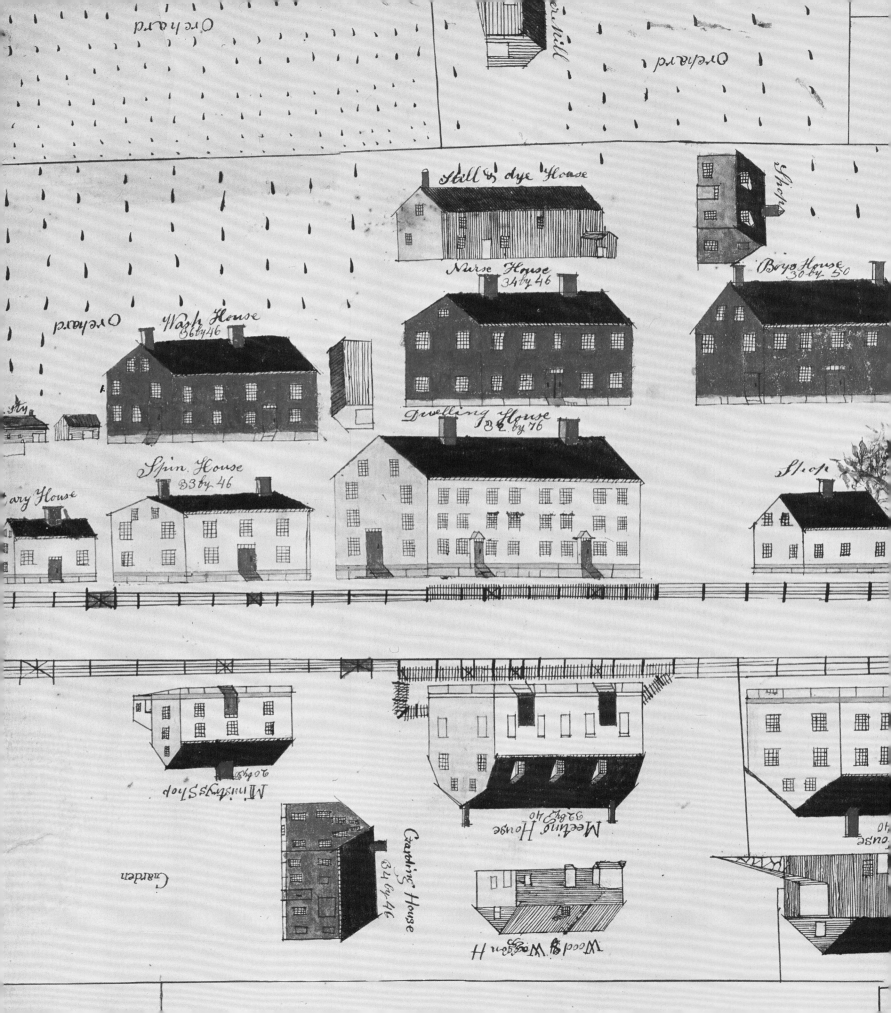

Orchard

Orchard

Still & dye House

Shop

Boys House
30 by 50

Orchard

Nurse House
34 by 46

Wash House
36 by 46

Dwelling House
84 by 76

Sty

Spin House
33 by 46

ary House

Shop

Ministry's Shop
26 by 43

Meeting House
32 by 40

Garding House
34 by 46

house
40

Garden

Wood & Waggon H

CONTENTS

The Angels sound aloud their trumpets in praise and thanksgiving to thee, because of the burden thou hast borne, the tribulation and sorrow thou hast felt, & the grief which has fallen upon thee. Yet never hast thou murmured against me, but daily cried, Thy will, O Lord, not mine, be done. Therefore I say, let thy mirth be like unto Pharaoh's daughter, and thy rejoicing be exceeding great; for lo! the Angels in Heaven rejoice over thee, & thou art my delight, and my pleasure; the holy anointed of my choice, in whom I do place trust; to whom I have given the keys of my kingdom, upon whom I have placed my anointing oil, and into whose hands I have given my wisdom, to direct, protect and guide my people in time. Therefore mark thou the signs, and observe the times, for lo! I come quickly. cunning are my devices, and crafty are my proceedings. As peals of thunder I roar, and as gentle breezes I gather. I return unto my Kingdom, bearing thee upon my wings, and placing thee at the right hand of my eternal Throne, forever to reign: joining thy praises with my holy Seraphs, and with thy eternal Parents above, within the courts of Eternal Wisdom, & feasting upon my Eternal love.

Instruction of Holy Wisdom

Asenath
April 21st

Clark
1844

Well done my good and faithful Servant, come and dwell in my glory for ever

The Bard Graduate Center is pleased to contribute this publication to the literature on American material culture and international design history. Shaker design, which has garnered international acclaim, was derived in part from the requisites of religious devotion. It was also in large measure shaped by an astute understanding of and insight into the needs of American life outside the Shaker communities, especially during the nineteenth century. This volume examines the way in which religious life of the Shakers and their interactions with the secular world enabled the creation of many magnificent objects and goods of exceptional quality.

Despite the steady decline of the Shaker communities during the twentieth century, they have left a remarkable legacy. In a sequence of fascinating essays, the authors of this volume provide a greater understanding of the motivations behind Shaker design as it emerged inside the communities and in response to secular life in the United States. Another important contribution is a better understanding of ways in which Shaker furniture has endured in modern and contemporary international design.

It has been a great pleasure to have the Shelburne Museum as a collaborator on this project. I am tremendously appreciative that Stephan Jost, director of the Shelburne Museum, brought this project to my attention and that we agreed to jointly publish a catalogue on Shaker design. I would like to thank the Board of Trustees of the Shelburne Museum for their ongoing commitment to this important subject and to the preservation of their unique Shaker artifacts. Jean Burks has brought incomparable expertise and knowledge to shaping the content of this volume and to the outstanding checklist of objects for the exhibition that accompanies it.

The Shelburne Museum received generous support for the exhibition from the Chittenden Bank and The Americana Foundation, and additional support from Thos. Moser, Inc., The Charles Engelhard Foundation, the Vermont Wood Manufacturers Association, The Oakland Foundation, Jane and Gerald Katcher, and John and Kathryn Wilmerding Heminway. Furthermore: a program of the J. M. Kaplan Fund, and a truly remarkable benefactor of scholarly catalogues on design history, Jane and Gerald Katcher, and Thos. Moser provided funding that made possible the realization of this publication.

Polly Jane Reed (1818–1881). *Gift Drawing for Aseneth Clark, The Word of the Lord Almighty Jehovah, To a Daughter of his Everlasting Love*, 1844. New Lebanon, New York. Ink and watercolor on paper, Collection of Bob and Aileen Hamilton.

I am grateful to the catalogue authors, Jean M. Burks, Robert P. Emlen, Jean M. Humez, M. Stephen Miller, Sumpter Priddy, Kory Rogers, and Gerard C. Wertkin, for their insightful contributions to this publication. Bruce White took photographs of the installation at the Shelburne Museum that will enable readers to better understand the truly surprising range of colors associated with Shaker design, as well as contributing other magnificent photographs for the catalogue. Barbara Burn was a superb editor and also provided considerable assistance and support. In addition to overseeing production of the catalogue in London, Sally Salvesen created a beautiful design for this publication that complements the elegance and refinement of Shaker design. Alexis Mucha has skillfully dealt with the challenge of coordinating the photography orders. Many institutions assisted with gathering photographs for the catalogue essays including the American Society for Psychical Research, American Folk Art Museum, Canterbury Shaker Village, Christie's Images, Colonial Williamsburg Foundation, Dansk Kunst Industrimuseet, Fruitlands Museum, Hancock Shaker Village, Carl Hansen, Fritz Hansen, Henry Francis de Pont Winterthur Museum and Library, Historic New England, the Library of Congress, Moooi, Museum of Fine Arts, Boston, the New York Public Library, New York State Museum, Philadelphia Museum of Art, Schiffer Publishing, the Shaker Museum and Library, Skinner Inc., and the United Society of Shakers.

The exhibition *Shaker Design: Out of This World* includes an outstanding group of objects. I would like to express a heartfelt debt of thanks to the individuals and institutions who provided loans for the exhibition and who offered assistance in this regard. Lending institutions include American Society for Psychical Research, American Folk Art Museum, Berkshire Athenaeum, Canterbury Shaker Village, Fruitlands Museum, Hancock Shaker Village, Hightower Group, Museum of Fine Arts, Boston, Philadelphia Museum of Art, the Shaker Museum and Library, and the United Society of Shakers. Individuals, both lenders and those who offered assistance with assembling this exhibition, include Tetsu Amagasu, Christian Becksvoort, Robert and Katharine Booth, Douglas Brooks, Leonard Brooks, Sabrina Buell from Matthew Marks Gallery, Jennifer Carroll-Plante, Maria Ann Conelli, Elliot Davis, Andrew D. Epstein, Renee Fox, Christian Goodwillie, Jerry Grant, Bob and Aileen Hamilton, Stacy Hollander, Jane and Gerald Katcher, Patrice Keane, Sharon Duane Koomler, William Laberge, the McGuire Family Furniture Makers, Roy McMakin, M. Stephen and Miriam Miller, Thomas Moser, Ann-Marie Reilly, Kathleen Reilly, John Keith Russell, the Sabbathday Lake Shakers, David Schorsch, Elaine Smith and Jeff Clark, Ellen Spear, Michael Volmar, and Wittus Fire by Design.

At the Bard Graduate Center, the exhibition department directed the editorial production of this volume. Earl Martin coordinated many aspects of this publication and facilitated organization of the exhibition at the Center, applying his administrative skills and understanding of design and the decorative arts. Han Vu provided extensive technological support, including filming and then creating the digital DVD that accompanies the exhibition, and using his knowledge to enhance our production efforts in many ways. Ian Sullivan designed a wonderful installation for the exhibition at the Bard Graduate Center. Sarah Fogel, the in-house registrar, assisted with the assembly and dispersal of the exhibition. Olga Valle Tetkowksi helped to keep the exhibition department office operating during the production of this catalogue. Other staff members at the Bard Graduate Center assisted in invaluable ways with realization of this project, including Susan Wall and Brian Keliher, who raised funds for this publication and the exhibition; Tim Mulligan and Hollis Barnhart spearheaded the publicity campaign; Rebecca Allan, with the assistance of Laura Rau and Benjamin Miller, organized a marvelous array of educational programs and tours; Lorraine Bacalles, with the assistance of Cassandra Rosser and Lisa Bright, provided financial and administrative support; John Donovan and the facilities staff of the Bard Graduate Center ably attended to the needs of the gallery; Chandler Small and the security staff of the Bard Graduate Center facilitated the complex task of gallery security.

I am grateful to all of the staff and faculty of the Bard Graduate Center for their outstanding professionalism and contribution to the remarkable growth and success of this institution over the past fifteen years.

Susan Weber Soros
Director
Bard Graduate Center for
Studies in the Decorative Arts,
Design, and Culture

Shelburne Museum is honored to collaborate with the Bard Graduate Center for Studies in the Decorative Arts, Design, and Culture on this important exhibition and publication of one of our nation's seminal design legacies. With the study of American design at the core of our institutions' missions, this partnership made perfect sense.

Shelburne Museum, founded by Electra Havemeyer Webb in 1947, has long had strong connections to Shaker design. One of the most distinctive of the museum's thirty-nine exhibition buildings is a large shed built in 1840 at the Shaker community in Canterbury, New Hampshire. Moved to Shelburne Museum in 1951, this unornamented commercial structure defines the northern edge of the museum's campus and displays much of the museum's extraordinary collection of nineteenth-century hand tools.

Every project has a visionary and a leader. Jean Burks, senior curator of Shelburne Museum, conceptualized, articulated, and organized this exhibition. Her knowledge, connoisseurship, and good grace have made the project possible. The exhibition during its tenure at Shelburne (June 16– October 28, 2007) set a new standard of excellence and introduced Shaker design and culture to tens of thousands of visitors from all fifty states and more than two dozen countries.

No exhibition of this scale can be accomplished without a large team of willing co-conspirators. First and foremost, I extend our warmest thanks to the dozens of generous lenders acknowledged by Jean in her introduction to this publication.

This exhibition would not have been possible without the financial support of many generous individuals, foundations, and corporations, to all of whom we are deeply grateful.

Shelburne Museum trustee Bruce Lisman and museum friends Donna and Marvin Schwartz made lead gifts to the project. Major support was from The Americana Foundation and Chittenden Bank. Additional support was from The Charles Engelhard Foundation, Carlie and Neal Garonzik, John and Kathryn Wilmerding Heminway, Jane and Gerald Katcher, The Oakland Foundation, The Vermont Wood Manufacturer's Association, Thos. Moser Cabinetmakers, Shaker Workshops and David Webster. We cannot thank our supporters enough for bringing this ambitious endeavor to life.

A member of the museum's curatorial staff, associate curator Kory Rogers, contributed his unique expertise on contemporary design; Polly Darnell ensured that all the text was correct; and Douglas Oaks and Todd Townsend designed an elegant exhibition with sub-

Round Barn at Shelburne Museum. The Round Barn serves as both visitor center and unique gallery space for special exhibitions.The rare 80-foot-diameter Round Barn was constructed in East Passumpsic, Vermont, in 1901 after a Shaker design. Round barns, designed for economy of labor, were first built by Massachusetts Shakers in 1826 and re-introduced by a national farm magazine in 1896. The Round Barn was moved to Shelburne Museum in 1985–86.

stantial support from Chris Kent, Donna Kennedy, Bob Furrer, and Rick Gage.

Cathi Comar efficiently led the collections management team and tracked countless loan details, with assistance from Katherine Taylor-McBroom, Sara Craig, Nick Bonsall, and Suzanne Zaner.

It was truly comforting to have Rick Kerschner and Nancie Ravenel on hand as highly trained conservators. Lois Nial kept us on budget, and Rick Peters and Jessica Gallas designed, planted, and maintained a stunning Shaker garden outside the gallery at Shelburne Museum.

Our imaginative and hard-working education staff, Renee Compagna, Claire Robinson-White, and Hannah Weisman, developed high-quality programs for our visitors and also created a complementary hands-on exhibition about the Shakers for children, with help from Samantha Bellinger and Katelyn Ziegler. All during the season, the museum's guides helped the public enjoy and understand the exhibition. Finally, we all slept better knowing that the museum security force, led by Tim Delisle, Rob Baker, and George Nichols, was doing its job.

I would like to extend a special word of thanks to our dedicated trustee Frances von Stade Downing, who encouraged this dynamic collaboration. Under the leadership of Susan Weber Soros and director of exhibitions Nina Stritzler-Levine, great things are happening at the Bard Graduate Center.

Finally, a sincere thanks to the past, present, and future members of the United Society of Believers in the First and Second Appearance of Christ. Without their faith and insight, we would be unable to share their story and designs with the world.

Stephan F.F. Jost
Director
Shelburne Museum

Introduction

JEAN M. BURKS

TENSIONS WITH "THE WORLD"

Shaker Design: Out of this World, the title of the exhibition at the Shelburne Museum in Vermont and at the Bard Graduate Center in New York, was chosen to reflect the spiritual, intellectual, and visual components of Shaker design over time. The Shakers exist simultaneously in parallel worlds—an inner world bound by deeply religious customs and conventions and an outer world open to complete freedom of artistic expression. The phrase "Out of this World" suggests several different concepts that, when taken together, help define the Shaker aesthetic.

From the perspective of the Shakers themselves—beginning in the eighteenth century and continuing to the present day—Believers have lived, worked, and worshiped in villages built apart from their rural neighbors, literally "out of this world". However, the Shakers have remained economically connected to the World, as the Shakers referred to non-Believers, through a variety of commercial activities, which they carefully forged and fostered over the years.

In another sense, Shaker design is firmly rooted in and derived from nineteenth-century popular approaches to design and decoration. These approaches, taken "out of this world," were modified to reflect the Believers' religious orthodoxy, which dominated every aspect of their daily life. Although the sect embraced the principles of neoclassical form, for example, they rejected the fanciful ornamental schemes and surface decoration that permeated American decorative arts from 1790 to 1840.

From a purely visual standpoint, Shaker objects are perceived by the general public as "beautiful," or simply "out of this world." This attraction was noted in 1947 by Sister Jennie Wells at the time the community in Mount Lebanon, New York, was closed:

> Most of our visitors these days are antique collectors and all they're interested in is buying up what little fine old handmade Shaker furniture we have left. Why, those people would grab the chairs right out from under us if we'd let them. Our furniture is very fashionable all of a sudden you know. . . . We've always been told how beautiful our things are. I don't say they aren't but that isn't what they were meant to be. . . . All our furniture has ever meant to be was strong, light and above all, practical.1

It is ironic that the furniture was consistently removed from Shaker surroundings—or taken out of their world—to be embraced by the world of non-Believers.

To this very day, the enduring principles of the Shaker aesthetic have had a strong resonance outside the Shaker community, from Scandinavian design of the 1930s to contemporary design. It is not surprising that at least one distinguished collector of Shaker furniture and lender to this exhibition also acquires examples of Scandinavian design and of the furniture made by Japanese-American woodworker George Nakashima (1905–1990). The inspiration that Shaker furniture had on both is discussed in Chapter 7 in this volume.

The artifacts, images, and products fashioned

Installation view, Shaker Design: Out of this World, Shelburne Museum, Shelburne Vermont, June 16–October 28, 2007. Photo: Bruce White.

by the Shakers for home use or for sale during their two-hundred year history indicate that the Believers have interacted with society on many levels and consciously accepted and rejected specific aspects of Worldly culture and design. It is this ongoing and changing tension between the Shakers and the World that has defined their aesthetic and is examined for the first time in this exhibition and the accompanying catalogue.

HISTORIOGRAPHY

Much of the early literature on the subject of Shaker design offered a perception of the Believers from a particular standpoint. Beginning in the 1930s, written and visual interpretation of Shaker interiors conveyed the impression of a sect that had rejected the World and created an alternative worldview. The photographs of Shaker spaces taken by William F. Winter (1899–1939)[2] reinforce the single-minded opinions that the antique dealer and author Edward Deming Andrews (1894–1964) expressed about the Believers in his many books on the subject of Shaker design.[3]

Over the last fifty years, the Shakers have continued to fascinate collectors, historians, and curators from a variety of perspectives. The installations and accompanying catalogues conceived by June Sprigg[4] during the 1980s emphasized the beauty of Shaker design by displaying objects as pieces of sculpture, an approach that influenced subsequent exhibitions. John Kirk's analysis of the "Shaker look" in several publications[5] dating from the 1990s is based primarily on a visual response to Shaker furniture in comparison to fine or conceptual art. My research, which spans the last two decades, has taken a different approach, which is to focus primarily on a technical examination of hundreds of pieces of furniture in an effort to determine the physical characteristics that identify a specific Shaker community of origin.[6]

The design and cultural issues addressed by this exhibition and the accompanying catalogue were first raised in 1987, when I went to Canterbury Shaker Village in New Hampshire as curator of col-lections. After the death of one of the remaining four Shaker women at the community, the 6,000-square-foot, twenty-two-room dwelling house in which she resided came under the care of the museum for which I worked. It became my responsibility to sort, evaluate, and catalogue the contents of the building, which was filled from floor to ceiling with a surprisingly wide variety of artifacts. I discovered painted Shaker furniture from New England and a large assortment of what appeared to be early-nineteenth-century, non-Shaker varnished case pieces, as well as elaborate sewing accessories; a booklet containing colorful drawings; and diaries kept by Shaker sisters during the 1940s. The diaries revealed, among other things, that hordes of antique dealers had descended on Canterbury to purchase the nineteenth-century furnishings offered for sale by the remaining sisters, all of which appealed to the contemporary taste of twentieth-century collectors.

The first question this repository suggested was: to what extent did this vast assortment of objects represent the material culture—the values, ideas, and attitudes—of the communal society known as the Shakers? But my immediate attention was diverted from exploring this question while I focused on examining and identifying the distinguishing characteristics of Shaker furniture that had been produced in the nineteen different communities from their earliest days of settlement in the United States to the middle of the twentieth century.[7] In 1995, several books and curatorial positions later, I came to the Shelburne Museum, where as curator of decorative arts I was responsible for one of the largest and most distinguished public collections of nineteenth-century painted furniture. In the meantime, during the first few years of the twenty-first century, several scholars undertook groundbreaking research on related topics that interpreted original Shaker paints and pigments through scientific analysis; explored the role of women in the Shaker religion; provided new insight into the "gift" drawings; identified the wide range of commercial products sold to the World; and rediscovered and defined the so-called "Fancy" style in America. Thanks to the information that resulted from this new research, it became possible to assemble many pieces of the Shaker material culture puzzle together in one place.

THE COMPLEXITY OF SIMPLICITY

The Shaker aesthetic is an outer expression of an inner belief system, but it also reflects the logistical needs of a communal way of life in which the principles of utility, order, honesty, and cleanliness are highly valued. Shaker literature uses the term "simple" in a variety of diverse sources from the eighteenth and nineteenth centuries. The word *simplicity* has, over the years, become pedestrian to the point of losing its meaning, and when applied to three-dimensional Shaker objects displayed as minimalist pieces of sculpture, the term is particularly misleading. Its use in this publication relates directly to Shaker terminology and belief. Manuscripts dating as early as 1790 present such precepts as: "Plainness and simplicity in both word and deed is becoming [to] the Church and the people of God."[8] The exposition of the views of the United Society expressed in the 1823 work publication entitled *A Summary View of the Millennial Church* provides insight into the Shakers' governing virtues, including simplicity, which is defined as

> A real singleness of heart in all our conversation and conduct. . . . Its thoughts, words and works are plain and simple. . . . It is without ostentation, parade or any vain show, and naturally leads to plainness in all things. In all the objects of its pursuit, in all the exercise of its power, in all its communications of good to others, it is governed solely by the will of God and shows forth its peculiar singleness of heart and mind in all things.[9]

The concept is reiterated in the lyrics of the familiar tune "'Tis the gift to be simple," which suggests that simplicity grows from an inner realization of the purpose to which one has been called by God[10] and takes on a more concrete expression in the 1845 Millennial Laws, which forbid the manufacture of any articles that are superfluously wrought.[11] As the Shakers strove for simplicity in

both spiritual and secular matters, they achieved this goal through strict rules permeating every aspect of their society that were far from simple. The Shaker leadership structure was fully established by the 1820s, following the founding of the nineteen major Shaker communities. At this time, a hierarchical governance system was in place, its authority deriving ultimately from appointments said to have been made by founder Ann Lee (1736–1784).

The physical layout of each village and the processes that required communal neatness, consistency, and order were relatively complex. Order implies control, which was implemented by the establishment of rules that shaped the spirit and practice of communal living. The specialized function, design, and placement of the various structures—meetinghouses, dwelling houses, and workshops—to conduct religious, domestic, business, and educational, activities within each community, as well as the required gender division to establish physical and social patterns, far surpassed those found in military, health-care, or other institutions in the outside world.

Initially, the Shakers' ecstatic dances were an extemporaneous expression of their faith, but by the early nineteenth century the routines became elaborate ritual. The movements and patterns were codified, strictly choreographed, and meticulously rehearsed, and Believers relied on wooden or metal cues embedded in the meetinghouse floor to ensure uniformity. Thirteen new forms of worship were used at Canterbury in the 1830s and 1840s, and these were given colorful names, such as "Winding March," the "Cross and Diamond," "Moving Square," and "Celestial March," which convey images of the Believers performing the dance.[12]

Seemingly simple daily activities were also strictly regulated. Community chores were identified and carefully programmed on a rotating basis to insure that both pleasant and grievous jobs were shared equally among Believers. Family deacons and deaconesses responsible for the smooth operation of domestic affairs scheduled the brethren to take turns at farming, tailoring, and blacksmithing, while sisters were assigned shifts in the kitchens, laundry, and sewing shop. Even familiar actions and behaviors were legislated under the section of the 1845 Millennial Laws entitled "Miscellaneous Rules and counsels," in which Believers were advised: "When we kneel, all should kneel on our right knee first; when we clasp our hands, our right thumbs and fingers, should be above our left, as uniformity is comely."[13]

The rules governing Shaker behavior centered on celibacy, a choice that was not without serious consequences. Although denying sexuality is, in one respect, a simple option that avoids the secular complications of "messy interpersonal negotiations,"[14] such a decision necessitated an entire range of intricate behaviors that were restricted in the 1845 Millennial Laws. Among other things, brothers and sisters were forbidden from shaking hands, passing each other on the stairs, or sitting closer than five feet at singing meetings.[15] Clearly, there is a real dichotomy between the complex regulations that govern Shaker behavior in order to achieve spiritual simplicity and the use of the word *simple* to describe their material products.

FURNITURE DESIGN

The Shakers themselves have, almost from their American beginnings, understood the importance of interacting with the World's people and valued this relationship as central to their survival. This ongoing communication is no less evident in the evolution of their furniture. The continuity of Shaker life freed Believers from the whimsical vagaries of worldly fashion, yet their designs were not created in a vacuum. Since no one is born a Shaker, adult converts who were familiar with or trained, either formally or informally, in worldly woodworking traditions brought their taste and technical skills with them when they joined the community. They worked from what they knew, using ideas, forms, and patterns that were within their physical and intellectual reach. The geographical and social distance between urban and rural areas often results in a simplification of overall forms and decorative details, as country cabinet-

makers tend to produce a more basic pared-down or vernacular interpretation of upscale urban fashions using local, available materials. This was certainly true for the craftsmen who brought their talents and tastes into the Shaker population when they converted. Within the community, acceptable designs seem to have been perpetuated by traditional apprenticeship programs. Several sources documenting Shaker domestic life[16] indicate that children raised within the society were indentured to skilled Shaker craftsmen in order to learn various trades, such as woodworking. In this respect, the concept of appropriate design and taste was passed from one generation to the next. Shaker journal entries, as well as written directives called "circulars" emanating from the central ministry to the outlying communities and surviving letters documenting "general meetings," indicate that orders were issued on a variety of temporal matters. However, it is not known how much authority secular leaders delegated to the individual craftsmen who produced furniture in accordance with Shaker beliefs. Were the cabinetmakers free to interpret the principles of the spoken or written word in their furniture or were all aspects of their work subject to the scrutiny and approval of the family deacon as well as answerable to a higher authority?[17]

Much of the previous scholarship on the Shakers has focused on their peculiarity rather than on their continuity with their surrounding cultural environment. Shaker forms must be evaluated in relation to other contemporary expressions of the period in America rather than always in isolation. Many misconceptions about their material products stem directly from this restricted view. Between the years 1790 and 1820, neoclassicism in furniture design was introduced to America by the English furniture makers George Hepplewhite (*The Cabinet-Maker and Upholsterer's Guide*, 1788) and Thomas Sheraton (*The Cabinet-Maker and Upholsterer's Drawing Book*, 1791). Their designs, disseminated through published pattern books and imported high-style furniture, were warmly accepted by Americans, who were aware of the ideological ties between their new republic and classical Greece and Rome. The restrained decoration of English neoclassical furniture provided designers with an opportunity to embody those philosophical ideals in allegorical symbols of abundance and fertility (cornucopias, baskets of fruit, and garlanded putti); elements borrowed from Greek and Roman architecture (urns, fascia, and dentils) and classical figures.

Because of its connection with the developmental period in America's history, this new style has been called Federal.[18] The importance of plainness and permanence to emerging America was eloquently expressed by the statesman Gouverneur Morris, who advised George Washington in 1790: "I think it of very great importance to fix the taste of our country properly, and I think your example will go very far in that respect. It is therefore my wish that everything about you should be *substantially good and majestically plain, made to endure*"[19] — ideas that reflect the rational, truth-seeking intellectual movement called the Enlightenment, which originated in Europe but which also influenced the leaders of the American colonies in both the religious and political spheres. There are few worldly American designs that embody this philosophy in woodworking more than Federal furniture.

Is it mere coincidence that the Shakers readily incorporated these neoclassical forms and the ideals they represented in their newly founded communities? The Believers' plain and functional furniture was the inevitable result of two compelling forces—a worldly cultural environment embracing the new Federal style, combined with a theology that demanded a physical statement of simplicity based on community ideals and institutional needs. The elegance of proportion, emphasis on rectilinear lines, preferences for surfaces emphasizing the natural grain of the wood, and reliance on finish rather than ornament are all consistent with fashionable neoclassical principles. However, the Shakers eliminated the sophisticated expression of classically ordered elements, such as the application of moldings, turnings, reeding, and fluting and the reliance on all veneer or inlay work. But it

is the banishment of all embellishment—especially the popular Worldly motifs relating to fertility or to the classical pantheon of deities that were understandably anathema to this celibate, monotheistic Christian sect—that clarifies the Shakers' interpretation of the neoclassical aesthetic.

The end result is the emergence of "classic" Shaker design, which characterized the period from 1820 to 1850.[20] The Shakers pared down their furniture in a way that gives it a timeless quality. They removed all of those elements of adornment that they saw as distracting in worldly design and created an essential, "simple" form that today could be described as minimalist. As Peter Dormer astutely noted: "Ornament is an evolutionary activity, it grows from decade to decade and each new style carries with it hints and reminiscences of the old. Ornament is a carrier of values which may be antithetical to the doctrines of a new aesthetic or ideological movement. . . . Ornament got banned by the Shakers and Modernists because it was too talkative."[21] It is this plain strictness, with the restraint and moderation that was always a critical part of the Shaker ethos, that continues to appeal to enthusiasts today.

This publication serves as both a catalogue of an exhibition and as an examination of the cultural and societal context for Shaker design in a series of essays written by authors who each bring a different background, area of expertise, and approach to Shaker scholarship.

Robert P. Emlen, university curator and senior lecturer in the Department of American Civilization at Brown University, analyzes the architecture and the village planning of the Shakers' physical world. M. Stephen Miller, lender, author, and collector of Shaker ephemera, presents his research on the Shakers' business activities and their dealings with the commercial world. Dr. Jean M. Humez, chair of the women's studies department at the University of Massachusetts at Boston, is a religious scholar rather than a design historian and suggests a surprising new perspective on the gender tension between the male and female leadership within the Shaker world. Gerard C. Wertkin, director emeritus of the American Folk Art Museum, the author of numerous publications, and a friend of the Sabbathday Lake Shakers, shares his expertise on the vivid forms of religious expression that make up the Shakers' spiritual world. Sumpter Priddy III, material culture specialist, consultant to museums and collectors, and author, provides new insight on the "Fancy" world as a dramatic counterpoint to the Shaker aesthetic. Kory Rogers, associate curator at the Shelburne Museum with a particular knowledge of contemporary design, offers an innovative vision of the Shakers' self-perpetuating style, which continues to inspire others both nationally and internationally.

These authors provide multiple viewpoints which, taken together, offer the most current insight into the dynamics behind the many Shaker worlds of design; past, present, and future.

ACKNOWLEDGMENTS

This exhibition would not have been possible without the assistance of many dedicated individuals who offered help, advice, and direction from its inception to its successful completion. First and foremost, I am grateful for the generous cooperation and support of the distinguished private collectors, dealers, and institutions who shared the objects under their stewardship with the public at the Shelburne Museum and the Bard Graduate Center. This exhibit depended heavily on collaboration with and contributions of: Robert and Katharine Booth, Douglas Brooks, Leonard Brooks, Sabrina Buell from Matthew Marks Gallery, Maria Ann Conelli, Elliot Davis, Andrew D. Epstein, Renee Fox, Christian Goodwillie, Jerry Grant, Bob and Aileen Hamilton, Stacy Hollander, Jane and Gerald Katcher, Patrice Keane, Sharon Koomler, William Laberge, the McGuire Family Furniture Makers, Roy McMakin, M. Stephen and Miriam Miller, Thomas Moser, Ann-Marie Reilly, Kathleen Reilly, John Keith Russell, the Sabbathday Lake Shakers, David Schorsch, Elaine Smith and Jeff Clark, Ellen Spear, and Michael Volmar.

Staff members at both institutions were key participants in this endeavor. At the Shelburne Museum, Director Stephan Jost provided artistic freedom, abiding confidence, and continuing encouragement; exhibition preparers Douglas Oaks and Todd Townsend designed and implemented a stunning installation; Polly Darnell, archivist and librarian, made sure that our gallery guides and label texts were both informative and accurate; and at the Bard Graduate Center, Han Vu, digital designer, created the remarkable video to accompany the exhibition.

Finally, I want to thank Susan Weber Soros, Director of the Bard Graduate Center a respected colleague and former graduate school classmate for the rewarding opportunity to collaborate with the Bard Graduate Center on this exciting project and for encouraging me to seek as high a level of quality as possible in this publication.

1   Mel Byars, *The Design Encyclopedia* (London: Laurence King; New York: Museum of Modern Art, 2004): 678.

2   See Schorsch, David A., *The Photographs of William F. Winter, Jr. 1899–1939* (New York: David A. Schorsch, 1989); also William F. Winter, "Shaker Portfolio, a Picture Record of an American Community," *US Camera Magazine* (March/April 1939).

3   Edward Deming Andrews, *The People Called Shakers* (New York: Oxford University Press, 1953); idem, *Shaker Furniture: The Craftsmanship of an American Communal Sect* (New York: Yale University Press, 1937).

4   June Sprigg, *Shaker Design*. Exh. cat. (New York: Norton and Whitney Museum of American Art, 1986).

5   John T. Kirk, *The Shaker World: Art, Life, Belief* (New York: Harry N. Abrams, 1997); Jerry V. Grant, 'Forty Untouched Masterpieces of Shaker Design," *The Magazine Antiques* 135, no. 5 (May 1989): 1226–37.

6   Timothy D. Rieman and Jean M. Burks, *The Complete Book of Shaker Furniture* (New York: Harry N. Abrams, 1993); idem, *The Encyclopedia of Shaker Furniture* (Atglen, Penn.: Schiffer Publishing, 2004).

7   Ibid.

8   Joseph Meacham, "Collection of Writings Concerning Church Order and Government, Copied Here by Rufus Bishop in 1850" (1791–96): 42, 45, Western Reserve Historical Society, Shaker Collection, Cleveland, Ohio, VIIB: 59.

9   Calvin Green and Seth Youngs Wells, *A Summary View of the Millennial Church . . .* (Albany: Packard & Van Benthuysen, 1823): 296, no. 12; 299, no. 25; 297, no. 17.

10 France Morin, "Simple Gifts," *Heavenly Visions: Shaker Gift Drawings and Gift Songs* (New York: The Drawing Center): 27.

11 "The Millennial Laws of Gospel Statutes and Ordinances Adopted to the Day of Christ's Second Appearing. Revised and reestablished by the Ministry and Elders, October 1845." Reprinted in Andrews, *The People Called Shakers* (1963): 282.

12 Henry C. Blinn, *The Manifestation of Spiritualism among the Shakers, 1837-1847* (East Canterbury, N.H., 1899): 31.

13 Reprinted in Andrews, *The People Called Shakers* (1963): 287.

14 This interesting and appropriate phrase resulted from a discussion with a psychologist visiting the exhibition in Shelburne during the summer of 2007.

15 Reprinted in Andrews, *The People Called Shakers* (1963): 267.

16 See Rieman and Burks, *Complete Book of Shaker Furniture* (1993): 50.

17 Ibid., 28–30.

18 Charles F. Montgomery, curator and author, may have been the first to coin the phrase in his landmark publication *American Furniture: The Federal Period in the Henry Francis du Pont Winterthur Museum* (New York: The Viking Press, 1966): 10, introduction. He states that "'Federal furniture' is appropriate for these pieces. In Philadelphia, and perhaps elsewhere, furniture was made by 'The Federal Society of Cabinetmakers,' and many pieces of the period were carved or inlaid with the American eagle, symbol of the Federal union."

19 Gouverneur Morris, quoted in Charles F. Montgomery and Patricia E. Kane, eds., *American Art: 1750–1800 Towards Independence* (Boston: New York Graphic Society, 1976).

20 Although this exhibition focuses on classic Shaker furniture, Shaker design was not static but evolved over time. After the Civil War, Victorian motifs started to appear on simple forms, a transformation in design reflecting the fact that the Shakers were an extremely progressive sect. For them this later furniture represented an optimistic revival of spirit, bringing their society into a new era and hopefully attracting new converts. Although not as aesthetically pleasing to 21st-century taste, the Victorian era of Shaker design is a valid part of the study of their material culture and is discussed in greater detail throughout *The Encyclopedia of Shaker Furniture.*

21 Quoted in Stephen Bowe and Peter Richmond, *Selling Shaker: The Commodification of Shaker Design in the Twentieth Century* (Liverpool: Liverpool University Press, 2007): 154.

Fancy Work Department Float,
Parade, 4th of July, 1916.
Canterbury, New Hampshire.
Collection of Canterbury
Shaker Village 25-P30, 1-PN156.

1736   Shaker leader Ann Lees is born, the second of eight children of a Manchester blacksmith. In Shaker usage, her name is later changed to Lee.

1742   Ann Lee is baptized in the Church of England.

1747   According to Shaker tradition, a religious society is formed in Bolton and Manchester, England, under the leadership of Jane and James Wardley. They are derisively called "Shaking Quakers" or "Shakers" for their exuberant worship style. In the early nineteenth century the Shakers adopted as a formal title the United Society of Believers in Christ's Second Appearing.

1758   Ann Lee enters the Wardley group.

1762   Ann Lee marries blacksmith Abraham Standerin, with whom she has four children.

1772   Ann Lee and other Shakers are imprisoned for interrupting religious services at Christ Church, Manchester. During Lee's imprisonment, she experiences a series of revelations. Her visions and skill as a spiritual mentor caused the Shakers to acknowledge Lee as their leader and to confer on her the title Mother Ann. She teaches that celibacy and confession provide a fuller way to live a Christian life.

1774   Under Ann Lee's leadership, a group of eight followers depart for America in May, arriving in New York City on August 6. The Shakers live and work quietly for the next few years.

1776   Several members lease and later purchase land just north of Albany in a town called Niskeyuna, later known as Watervliet. The Shakers begin their communal life here, and it serves as their base of operations for several years.

1780   The Shaker community first comes to public attention in America because of their pacifist views at the time of the American Revolution.

1781–83   Ann Lee and her followers conduct their first missionary trips through New York and New England. Many conversions are made and the seeds of later Shaker settlements are planted.

1784   After several exhausting years of preaching and missionary work, Ann Lee dies on September 8 at Niskayuna. One of Lee's English followers, James Whittaker, succeeds her as leader of the Shakers.

1786–87   First meetinghouse built at New Lebanon, New York (twenty-four miles southeast of Albany.) It features gambrel roof construction, which allows large unbroken spaces suited to the Shaker dance or "march" in worship. Meetinghouses in most of the eastern Shaker communities are modeled after the one built at New Lebanon.

1787   James Whittaker dies, and American-born Joseph Meacham assumes leadership. Meacham brings Believers together into the first formally organized Shaker community at New Lebanon, a process known as "gathering into Gospel Order." New Lebanon becomes the "mother" community and a model for other Shaker communal settlements, as well as the seat of leadership for much of Shaker history

1787   Niskeyuna, later Watervliet, New York, becomes the second Shaker village formally brought into the Gospel Order.

1788   Joseph Meacham selects Lucy Wright to join him as his companion in the Shaker hierarchy or ministry, thus formalizing the place of Shaker women within the leadership of the Society.

1789   New Lebanon account-book records indicate that chairs are sold to other Shaker communities and to non-Shaker customers as early as 1789.

1790   The Shakers publish their first statement of faith, *A Concise Statement of the Principles of the Only True Church According to the Gospel of the Present Appearance of Christ* (Bennington, Vermont).

1790   Large-scale manufacture of staved and bound wooden vessels (cooper ware) begins at New Lebanon and continues until about 1830.

1790   The community at Hancock in western Massachusetts (near Pittsfield) is founded; it is about five miles east of New Lebanon.

1791   A Shaker community is founded at Harvard, Massachusetts, about thirty-five miles west of Boston.

1792   A Shaker community is established at Tyringham in western Massachusetts, a few miles southeast of Hancock and New Lebanon.

1792   The Shakers found a community at Enfield, Connecticut, on the former homestead of Joseph Meacham.

1792   The community at Canterbury, New Hampshire, is established with the building of the community's meetinghouse.

1793   The Shaker community at Enfield, New Hampshire, is established.

1793   A Shaker community is formally organized and a meetinghouse built at Alfred, Maine.

1793   The Shirley, Massachusetts, community is established forty miles west of Boston, near the Harvard community.

1794   A second community in Maine is formally organized on what was then known as Thompson's Pond Plantation and later became part of the town of New Gloucester. This community is also known as Sabbathday Lake.

1794–95   New Lebanon Shakers begin cultivating and selling garden seeds, a leading source of income for this and later many other Shaker communities. It is thought that the Shakers introduced seeds in individual paper packets for small-scale or home gardeners at this time. Before

now seeds were only sold to farmers on a wholesale basis.

1795–99   The New Lebanon and Hancock communities experience a five-year period of dissent and rebellion, in part a reaction against Lucy Wright's leadership of the Society.

1796   Joseph Meacham dies.

1798   The flat broom, one of the Shakers' most famous inventions, is introduced by Theodore Bates of the Watervliet community.

1800   A lucrative packaged-seed industry begins at Shirley and Harvard, Massachusetts.

1800   The United States census records 1,373 Believers living in Shaker villages.

1805   Three Shaker missionaries, John Meacham, Issachar Bates, and Benjamin S. Youngs, travel from New Lebanon to Ohio and Kentucky, where they preach the Shaker faith to people caught up in a widespread frontier revival.

1805   Union Village, the first western Shaker community, is founded near Lebanon, Ohio (thirty miles northeast of Cincinnati). Union Village becomes the center of western Shaker leadership and the parent of the new Ohio communities.

1806   In December 1806, the community at Pleasant Hill is founded just southwest of Lexington, Kentucky.

1806   The Watervliet, Ohio, community (named after the New York settlement) is founded just south of Dayton.

1807   South Union, the longest-lived Shaker community in the west, is founded about ten miles west of Bowling Green, Kentucky.

1807   Richard McNemar, an important leader of the frontier revival and one of the first western converts to the Shaker faith, writes *The Kentucky Revival* (published in Cincinnati), the first bound Shaker book. The following year he publishes a pamphlet, *A Concise Answer to the General Inquiry Who or What are the Shakers*, an early defense of Shakerism.

1808   Benjamin Seth Youngs writes *The Testimony of Christ's Second Appearing*, one of the earliest Shaker theological works. It was first printed in Lebanon, Ohio, and was reprinted two years later at Albany, New York.

1810   The Shaker community at West Union, Indiana, is founded. A short-lived community, it closes in 1827.

1812   Thomas Brown publishes *Account of the People Called Shakers: Their Faith, Doctrines, and Practice.*

1816   Shaker leaders Rufus Bishop and Seth Youngs Wells compile *Testimonies of the Life, Character, Revelations and Doctrines of Our Ever Blessed Mother Ann Lee, and the Elders with Her. . . .*, the earliest account of the life and teachings of Ann Lee based on the memories of her first followers.

1816   The Pleasant Hill, Kentucky, community begins cultivating silkworms to support a small-scale silk industry at that community.

1820   The Harvard, Massachusetts, community begins a successful dried herbs industry, which continues until about 1910.

1820–50   Period in which much of what is now called "classic" Shaker furniture, with its simple and spare forms, is produced.

1820s–30s   The "Fancy" aesthetic dominates the interiors of most Americans. The plain furniture and lack of decoration in Shaker interiors can be seen as a rejection of this popular style.

1821   Lucy Wright dies in February.

1821   After Wright's death, the Society's leadership codifies its precepts and bylaws as *Orders and Rules of the Church at New Lebanon: Millennial Laws or Gospel Statutes & Ordinances.* These are revised several times, in 1845, 1860, and 1887.

1821   The Order of Physicians and Nurses is established, beginning at New Lebanon.

1822   The Shaker community of White Water, Ohio, is established about twenty miles west of Cincinnati.

1822   The North Union, Ohio, community is founded near Cleveland.

1822   The first large central dwelling house, the Center Family, is built at South Union, Kentucky. Similar buildings for communal living are constructed at other Shaker communities during the 1820s and 1830s.

1823   Seth Youngs Wells and Calvin Green publish *A Summary View of The Millennial Church*, a major Shaker document that further explains and refines the Society's beliefs and Mother Ann's teachings for the Shakers, as well as those in the outside world.

1826   A Shaker community is established at Sodus Bay on the shores of Lake Ontario in Wayne County, New York.

1835   The Canterbury, New Hampshire, community issues its first bound herb catalogue.

1837–38   After the Shaker leadership agrees to sell the Sodus Bay community to speculators interested in building a canal, this community moves about ninety miles southwest, to Groveland in Livingston County, New York.

1837   Beginning of a period of revival during which members at various communities experience visions and revelations. This period, which extended into the 1850s, is known as the Era of Manifestations by Believers. During this time, large numbers of gift songs and messages and more than 200 gift drawings were created.

1837–41   The Great Stone Dwelling, the largest Shaker dwelling ever constructed, is built at Enfield, New Hampshire. Still standing, it encloses 30,000 square feet.

1840s   The first wrinkle-resistant fabric is perfected by the Sabbathday Lake Shakers.

1840   By about 1840, the population of the eighteen principal Shaker communities peaks at an estimated 4,500 Believers.

1840   *A General Statement of the Holy Laws of Zion* records the revelations given by New Lebanon Shaker Philemon Stewart, who was said to be speaking for the spirit of James Whittaker. It is one of the most important of several statements of rules and codes of conduct given under divine revelation during the Era of Manifestations.

1842   Charles Dickens visits the New Lebanon Shakers and writes an unflattering description of the people, architecture, and interiors he encounters.

1842   A revelation received by Philemon Stewart instructs the Shakers to create a place for outdoor worship, called a

Feast Ground, at each community. These holy areas are created at communities throughout the country.

1845   In October the *Millennial Laws, or Gospel Statutes and Ordinances* are released. This document, revising the 1821 version, is one of the most important set**s** of rules and guidelines given during the Era of Manifestations. The *Millennial Laws* of 1845 contain detailed rules regarding design, construction, and care of furniture, among other detailed regulations.

1852   Brother George O. Donnell's metal ball-and-socket mechanism, or tilter, for chairs is submitted to the United States Patent Office.

1861   The United States Post Office changes the name of the station at New Lebanon to Mount Lebanon. The community is identified by this name after 1861.

1863   The mass-production chair industry starts at Mount Lebanon. It is very successful and continues until the business is finally closed, about 1940.

1875   Two fires at Mount Lebanon destroy eight structures and necessitate major rebuilding and new furnishings.

1875–76   The community at Tyringham, Massachusetts, declines to the point that the leadership at Mount Lebanon decides to sell it. The remaining Shakers at Tyringham move to Enfield, Connecticut, after their community closes.

1876   Shaker products and inventions are featured at the Philadelphia Centennial Exhibition. Both Shaker production chairs and an improved washing machine patented by Brother David Parker are given awards.

1877   The first metric dry measures made in the United States are manufactured at the Sabbathday Lake Shaker workshops.

1888   The last of the Shaker seed industries comes to an end at the Mount Lebanon community.

1889   The North Union, Ohio, community disbands, and its twenty-seven remaining members are relocated to the Watervliet or Union Village, Ohio, communities. In the early twentieth century one of the first "garden city" suburbs in the United States, Shaker Village, later called Shaker Heights, is developed on the North Union site.

1890s   Shaker trustees Emeline Hart and Lucy Ann Shepard establish a business at Canterbury, called Hart & Shepard, which designs, produces, and markets cloaks and sweaters.

1892   The Groveland, New York, community closes because of financial difficulties, and the remaining members and much of the furniture are transferred to Watervliet, New York.

1893   Mrs. Grover Cleveland wears the Shaker-designed and made "Dorothy" cloak to her husband's inauguration.

1900   Shaker leaders decide to disband the Watervliet, Ohio, community and move its members and their belongings to Union Village.

1904   Canterbury Shakers install battery telephones throughout their village.

1908   Canterbury Shakers purchase their first car, a Reo.

1908   Facing dwindling numbers, the community at Shirley, Massachusetts, closes, and remaining members move to the nearby Harvard community. The Commonwealth of Massachusetts purchases Shirley as the site that is used first for a school and later for a state prison.

1910   The Canterbury Shakers install an electrical powerhouse.

1910   The Pleasant Hill, Kentucky, community closes as an active religious society. The land and buildings are deeded to a local merchant, who agrees to care for the twelve remaining members until their death. The last Pleasant Hill Shaker dies in 1923.

1912   The Union Village, Ohio, community is sold to the United Brethren Church, now part of the United Methodist Church, for use as a facility for retired ministers, missionaries, and their families. The agreement states that the remaining seventeen Shakers may reside in the office building for ten more years, from 1913 to 1923.

1916   An automobile garage is constructed at Sabbathday Lake.

1916   The White Water, Ohio, community is sold, and the remaining Shakers are relocated to Mount Lebanon and Hancock.

1917 The Enfield, Connecticut, community is closed. The six remaining members and their possessions relocate to the Mount Lebanon community.

1918 The last five sisters remaining at Harvard, Massachusetts, move to Mount Lebanon, and the Harvard community is sold. The trustees' office building, built in 1794, is purchased by Clara Endicott Sears in 1920 and is preserved at the Fruitlands Museum.

1920s By the 1920s, membership declines at Mount Lebanon, and Sisters Sarah and Emma Neale oversee the selling of furniture and other Shaker objects to collectors, including Faith and Edward Deming Andrews and John S. Williams.

1922 Last of the western communities, the South Union, Kentucky, society is disbanded, and the land, buildings, and furnishings are sold at public auction.

1923 As membership declines at Enfield, New Hampshire, sections of the community are sold in 1889, 1913, and 1918. By 1923 the entire community is closed, and the remaining eight members have moved to Canterbury, New Hampshire. In 1927 the Shakers sell the site to the Missionaries of Our Lady of La Salette.

1927 A Shaker chair is sold at auction in Copenhagen, Denmark, where it catches the eye of Kaare Klint, director of the furniture and interiors department at the Royal Academy of Fine Arts. This chair serves as inspiration to Klint and his students, including some of the most important Danish designers of the twentieth century.

1931 The Alfred, Maine, community is sold to the Brothers of Christian Instruction and the remaining twenty-one members move to Sabbathday Lake.

1931 The Sabbathday Lake community opens a small museum and library.

1933 Leading Shaker scholar, collector, and dealer Edward Deming Andrews publishes his first Shaker book, *The Community Industries of the Shakers*.

1935 The Whitney Museum of American Art mounts the first major exhibition of Shaker furniture, *Shaker Handicrafts*.

1937 *Shaker Furniture: The Craftsmanship of an American Communal Sect*, by Faith and Edward Deming Andrews is published by Yale University Press. It is also published in Danish in 1937 and exerts an important influence on Danish design.

1938 After parts of the Watervliet community are sold in 1915, 1919, and 1924, the final section is closed in 1938, and the remaining three sisters and their possessions move to Mount Lebanon.

1943 Danish designer Hans Wegner's J-16 Rocker combines Shaker elements with characteristics of Windsor seating.

1947 After 160 years of leadership the Mount Lebanon, New York, community closes and the remaining six members move to Hancock, Massachusetts.

1947 Danish designer Børge Mogensen finds inspiration in Shaker design as expressed by his J39 chair and a trestle table introduced in 1947.

1950 The Shaker Museum and Library at Old Chatham, New York is founded by John S. Williams in collaboration with the Shaker leadership of the time. This is the first public museum dedicated to preserving the life, work, art, and religious history of the Shakers.

1953 Oxford University Press publishes Edward Deming Andrews's seminal work *The People Called Shakers*.

1956 The Shaker Historical Museum is established in Shaker Heights, Ohio (formerly the site of the North Union community), to house the Shaker Historical Society's collection of Shaker furniture and artifacts.

1960 The Hancock, Massachusetts, community is closed, and the buildings and surrounding 900 acres are sold to a group of Shaker enthusiasts, collectors and scholars who form the not-for-profit corporation that eventually becomes Hancock Shaker Village. The museum opens to the public on July 1, 1961.

1961 A nonprofit organization, Shakertown Inc., is formed to purchase and restore the remaining buildings and land of the Pleasant Hill, Kentucky, community. In 1968 the site is opened to the public as a living-history museum.

1969 Canterbury Shaker Village museum at the Canterbury, New Hampshire, community is founded.

1977 The Shaker Heritage Society is formed to preserve the first Shaker settlement site and Shaker community at Watervliet, New York.

1984   Documentary film *The Shakers: Hands to Work, Hearts to God* by Ken Burns is released.

1986   The landmark *Shaker Design* exhibition is presented at the Whitney Museum of American Art.

1986   A museum is opened at the Enfield, New Hampshire, community.

1989–91   The Hamilton County Parks District purchases land and buildings formerly belonging to the White Water, Ohio, Shaker community. The buildings are stabilized and a non-profit organization is formed in 2001 with the goal of restoring and opening the buildings to the public.

1990, 1992 The last Shaker sisters die at the Canterbury, New Hampshire, community. The site still operates exclusively as a museum today.

2002   The Shaker Museum and Library board of directors votes to construct a museum within the shell of the Great Stone Barn at the North Family site in New Lebanon, New York. Once the largest stone barn in America, it was ravaged by fire in 1972. The museum hopes to preserve the barn and other historic structures, to move the library, and to reunite the museum collection, drawn largely from the New Lebanon community.

2007   The Sabbathday Lake Shakers transfer the development rights of their 2,000-acre property to a land conservation trust, insuring the preservation of their village in its traditional form.

2008   Three Shakers remain at Sabbathday Lake, where they continue to work and worship in the traditions of the community.

The Shaker World

1

Shaker Villages and the Landscape of "Gospel Order"

ROBERT P. EMLEN

On an August evening in 1856, the New York journalist and illustrator Benson John Lossing had a quiet but memorable introduction to a Shaker village. Lossing had taken the train up the Hudson River Valley to visit the Shaker community at New Lebanon, New York, for an article he was writing for *Harper's New Monthly Magazine*.[1] Strolling into the rural village in the soft light of early evening, he recorded his impressions of first encountering the landscape of Shaker life:

> As I walked into the village, serenity and peace seemed to pervade the very air. . . . It was a Saturday evening. The weekly toil of the community had ceased, and a Sabbath stillness brooded over the populous town. Immense dwellings filled with men and women, and extensive workshops supplied with choicest implements, lined the one broad street. Order and Neatness there held high court with a majesty I had never before seen. The very dust in the road seemed pure.[2]

Benson Lossing's rhapsodic impression of the community at New Lebanon was not an unusual reaction among visitors to Shaker villages. By the middle of the nineteenth century, a host of writers had remarked in innumerable letters, journals, and published articles on the extraordinary appearance of Shaker villages. Some were impressed by the size and extensive improvements to the landscape. Some wrote about the magnificence of individual buildings. Some, like Lossing, were taken aback by the manifest sense of neatness and consistency they found so unexpectedly in a rural village. A

common thread in these travelers' accounts, however, is the persistent observation that Shaker communities in the middle of the nineteenth century had a distinctive appearance of prosperity, unity of design, and orderliness that set them apart from their neighboring farms and villages. This appearance was a manifestation of the distinctive thought, belief, and behavior that governed life in a Shaker community.

The Believers themselves called this way of life "living in Gospel Order." They chose to withdraw from what they called "the World," and to create communal families in which spiritual brothers and sisters committed to a radically different way of life. The Shakers were communards who shared their property and tried to subdue their individual identities. They were pacifists and celibates who modeled their lives after the example set by Jesus, laboring to rise above what they saw as the corrosiveness of the basest human instincts. They eschewed the distractions and needless complications of the Worldly life outside their serene communal villages. They aspired to perfection in the conduct of their everyday lives, believing that the works of their hands revealed the purity in their hearts. The remarkable appearance of the villages they designed and built was a natural expression of this commitment to order every aspect of their lives according to the dictates of the gospel.

At the height of the Shaker experience in America, there were eighteen principal Shaker communities stretching from Maine to Kentucky. By 1794 Believers had founded communal societies in New York, Massachusetts, Connecticut, New

Facing page:
Joshua H. Bussell (1816–1900). Detail, The Shaker Village at Poland Hill, Maine, 1850. Pencil, ink, and watercolor on paper. The Shaker Library, Sabbathday Lake, Maine.

3

Fig. 1-1. Attributed to Joshua H. Bussell (1816–1900). *Shaker Village, Canterbury, N.H.,* ca. 1850. Pencil, ink, and watercolor on paper. Henry Francis du Pont Winterthur Museum, Winterthur, Delaware, Edward Deming Andrews Memorial Shaker Collection, SA 1535.

Shaker artist Joshua Bussell's watercolor painting of the community at Canterbury, New Hampshire, pictures a hill-top village of brick and wooden buildings painted in drab colors, with only the meeting-house painted white.

Hampshire, and Maine. By 1822 they had established their western communities in Ohio, Indiana, and Kentucky. Each of these Shaker villages was composed of individual groups the Believers called "families," which were identified with their own group of buildings within the village.

In the 1780s, as the first Believers began to gather into communal living, nascent Shaker villages were indistinguishable from the home farms of their non-Shaker neighbors. As those first converts committed themselves to this new way of life, they donated their property to their common good. Those who had the most suitable farms welcomed like-minded converts to live and work in whatever buildings were already on the land and to farm those fields that were already cleared. When the property of later converts was donated for the benefit of the community, it would be sold or traded to acquire adjacent land as it became available. In time the landscape was transformed as Shaker villages grew to encompass scores of buildings on thousands of acres. At first, however, as Shaker communities became established on the land, the Shakers' sense of place was based more in the spirit and conviction of communal life than on any distinctive appearance of the built environment.

With the great ingathering of converts to the faith in the late eighteenth century, the Shaker villages grew to accommodate this greater population. In 1800, after the last of the eastern Shaker societies was formally organized, the United States census recorded 1,373 Believers living in Shaker villages.[3] At about the same time, a new generation of leaders in the Shakers' central ministry began to consider, and advocate, the usefulness and the need for consistency of thought, word, and deed in these newly formed residential communities. One consequence of these two trends—the development of Shaker-built villages large enough to support great numbers of Believers, and the Shakers' simultaneous inclination toward more regularized behavior and appearance in this life—was a new look on the land. In those regions where the Shakers' ministry took hold, Shaker villages began to assume this distinctive cultural identity.

SHAKER MEETINGHOUSES

The most prominent manifestation of this new order in Shaker villages was the construction of houses of worship specially designed for a religious society that expressed their faith through dance.

The gambrel-roofed design of their first meeting-houses allowed Shaker housewrights to build wide-open meeting rooms supported by trusses from the rafters downward, which resulted in large spaces unbroken by the partitions or columns that would have impeded this ecstatic religious exercise. The first of these meetinghouses was built in 1786–87 at the Shakers' central ministry in New Lebanon, near enough to the old Dutch settlements of the Hudson River Valley that the local people would have been familiar with the old-world architectural convention of gambrel-roofed construction. When the new meetinghouse at New Lebanon was finished, Moses Johnson, the Shaker housewright who oversaw its construction, was charged with the responsibility of raising an identical building for the Shaker society at Hancock, Massachusetts, in 1787. After that Brother Moses moved on to the Shaker village at Watervliet, New York, and then to the society at Enfield, Connecticut. By 1794 he had overseen the construction of Shaker meetinghouses of the same design in all ten of the eastern Shaker communities.[4]

Contemporary accounts reveal that these first Shaker meetinghouses were eye-catching for their brilliance, as well as for their distinctive architectural form. Not only was their gambrel-roofed construction unusual in eighteenth-century New England, but their white color made them stand out in a land of drably painted buildings. In 1795 the Salem, Massachusetts, minister and diarist William Bentley visited the Shaker community at Shirley, Massachusetts, where he recorded that "We first viewed the meeting House, which drew our attention, because beautifully painted white on the sides & even on the roof. The doors were green. Within, the woodwork is painted a deep blue, & the seats are of a chocolate colour"[5] (fig. 1-1).

A generation later, those distinctive buildings still had the power to impress. In 1831 Nathaniel Hawthorne visited the Shaker community at Canterbury, New Hampshire, and the next year used his first impression of the hilltop community in his short story "The Canterbury Pilgrims" as the

dialogue of Worldly visitors approaching the Shaker village. "'Is that white building the Shaker meeting house?' asked one of the strangers. 'And are those the red roofs of the Shaker village?' 'Friend, it is the Shaker village,' answered Josiah, after some hesitation."[6]

Three years later, Hawthorne again employed that first impression of the Canterbury Shaker village for an essay in *The American Magazine of Useful and Entertaining Knowledge,* a short-lived journal he edited in order to support himself in his first years as a struggling writer. "As you approach the Village," he wrote, "the first object is the Meeting House on the right, the only white building in the village, which stands a few rods from the road, at the head of a large open lawn."[7]

Even today the three surviving examples of those white eighteenth-century meetinghouses illustrate how these buildings—the spiritual center of each community—were sited, designed, and painted in such a way to be the focus of attention in the nascent Shaker villages. Their prominent appearance on the rural landscape was also the first visual characteristic by which a Shaker community could be distinguished from its neighbors. Moreover, the similarity of these ten original buildings linked the appearance of all the Shaker communities in the east. They were the harbinger of a growing penchant for order and regularity in Shaker life.

VILLAGE ORDER

In 1819 Professor Benjamin Silliman of Yale University remarked on this orderliness when he passed through the New Lebanon Shaker village while journeying on horseback to Toronto. "The utmost neatness is conspicuous in their fields, gardens, courtyards, out houses, and in the very road; not a weed, not a spot of filth, or any nuisance is suffered to exist. Their wood is cut and piled, in the most exact order; their fences are perfect; even their stone walls are constructed with great regularity."[8]

Trained as a natural scientist, Silliman was accustomed to observing and recording the physical world. Trained also as a lawyer, he may have intuited in the remarkable tidiness he encountered at New Lebanon the human motivation for order and control. Julie Nicoletta has written that the Shakers desired "to create villages as orderly communities with buildings that would control behavior and shape men, women, and children into proper members of the Shaker community."[9] As Shaker villages took form and grew in population, it became increasingly clear that community life should conform to universal standards of extraordinary regularity. They regarded the blessings of their communal life as a spiritual gift, and they spoke of this union of souls as "being in the gift," or "living in the gift." In a series of homilies he wrote for impressionable youth living in Shaker communities, Elder Elisha Blakeman admonished young Shakers "never to try to run on ahead before the main body of good Believers, and above all, never fall back, but keep close up and be in the gift." On the spiritual obligation of Shakers to be orderly in daily life, he wrote: "Order is the creation of beauty. It is heaven's first law, and the protection of souls. Keep all things in order, as keeping the laws of heaven; and keep the order of Zion, that heaven may protect you."[10]

In the practice of Shaker faith, Believers did not distinguish between the ordinary experiences of daily life and their contemplation of the spiritual realm. Because their faith informed every aspect of their earthly existence, from exalted worship to mundane tasks, their daily lives were regulated by the dictates of gospel order. John Kirk has written that

> Any establishment housing large numbers of people must create physical and social patterns, and the Shakers added to this a theological understanding that pushed their needs to lengths not known in the military, penal institutions, hospitals, or other such temporal institutions. . . . This unity facilitated spiritual development, created guidelines for actions, and, like order in the army or elsewhere, it made things look neat.[11]

The Shakers meant to be neat, orderly, and regular, but not only for the efficiency of managing large numbers of people living together. More than that, gospel order in community was an expression of their spiritual aspiration to live a heavenly life on earth. In the middle decades of the nineteenth century, when Shaker communities had reached their mature forms, this gospel order was apparent in every aspect of Shaker life. It was the state of grace the manifestations of which so impressed all those visiting journalists, diarists, and letter writers. It is what gave Shaker villages their distinctive appearance. Noted a visitor to the Shaker village at Sabbathday Lake, Maine, in 1855:

> One of the first characteristics that strikes the visitors at the Shakers, is the perfect neatness that is apparent in every thing that surrounds him. Both in doors and out it is a feature not to be mistaken—a virtue that no one can easily disregard. If cleanliness is akin to religion, as has been asserted, then certainly are the Shakers a most religious people. Their costume is as neat as it is unique, and everything about their dwellings betokens the same regard to cleanliness.[12]

By about 1840, the population of the eighteen principal Shaker communities peaked at an estimated 4,000 to 6,000 Believers.[13] By then the defining characteristics of Shaker villages had been established, and although the specific features of their fields, buildings, roadways, or millponds would continue to evolve, no more growth was needed to accommodate additional members. The landscape plan of each community was now essentially in place, although the Shakers might continue to purchase adjacent farmland and construct larger farm buildings in their ongoing quest to be efficient land managers and modern farmers. As these villages evolved into the equivalent of small towns, the largest containing scores of buildings on thousands of acres, Shaker artists created illustrated maps to document the structures and landscapes of their extensive properties. These Shaker village views were not intended to be ornamental or decorative,

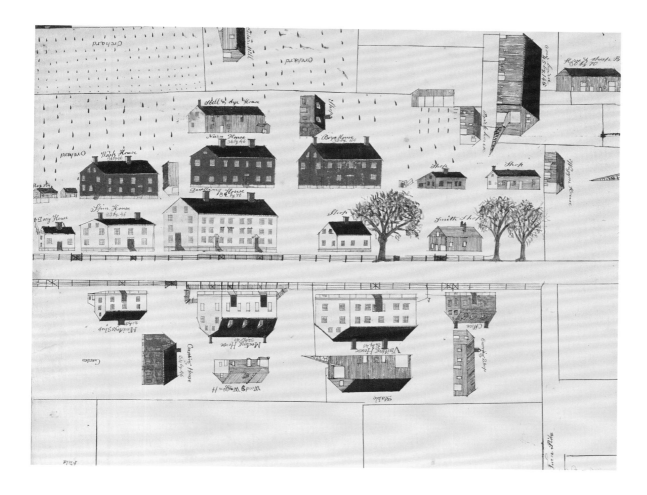

Fig. 1-2. Joshua H. Bussell (1816–1900). *The Shaker Village at Alfred, Maine,* 1845. Pencil, ink, and watercolor on paper. Library of Congress, Washington, D. C.

In 1845 Joshua Bussell drew the buildings of the Shaker village at Alfred, Maine, clustered together and flanking the public road that passed through the center of the village.

but first and foremost to be working documents for community planning. Consequently they can be studied today as evidence of Shaker communities at the height of their population and prosperity.

Brother Joshua Bussell's plan from about 1848 of the Shaker village at Alfred, Maine, illustrates how Shaker villages were designed to be linear, their buildings laid out in rows flanking a public highway (fig. 1-2). The model of the "one broad street" Benson Lossing admired as he passed through the center of the New Lebanon Shaker village was replicated in most other communities, providing, as Dolores Hayden has noted, "possibilities for growth afforded by a linear plan."[14] After visiting the village at Canterbury, New Hampshire, Hawthorne wrote to his sister, "I walked to the shaker village yesterday, and was shown over the establishment . . . [which] is immensely rich. Their land extends two or three miles along the road, and there are streets with great houses painted yellow and topt with red; they are now building a brick edifice for their public business, to cost seven or eight thousand dollars."[15]

In the earliest years, the close proximity of these buildings to the highway was a matter of convenience, although it also provided an opportunity for the Shakers to demonstrate to occasional passersby the material benefits of life in the community and the conscientious work ethic of its inhabitants (fig. 1-3). In most communities, the Shakers sited their most prominent buildings— their meetinghouses, dwelling houses, community office, and in time their schoolhouses—where they could be admired by the public, where they could serve as a public testament to the high standard of Shaker life and as impressive evidence of divine favor for their conduct and beliefs (fig. 1-4).

Fig. 1-3. Attributed to Joshua H. Bussell (1816–1900). *The Shaker Village at Alfred, Maine*, ca. 1848. Pen, ink, and watercolor on paper. Museum of Fine Arts, Boston, Massachusetts, gift of Dr. J. J. G. McCue, 1978.461.

In Joshua Bussell's view of the Shaker community at Alfred in about 1848, he depicted a stage coach carrying Worldly travelers along the public road through the village. This visual access gave passersby a first-hand impression of the Shakers' prosperity and penchant for neatness.

Fig. 1-4. Peter Foster (b. 1803). *Diagram of the South Part of Shaker Village, Canterbury, N.H.*, 1849. Pencil, ink, and watercolor on paper. Library of Congress, Washington, D.C.

As it passed through Canterbury Shaker village, the road to Loudon, New Hampshire, was prominently flanked by Shaker buildings, including the community's large brick office. The Shakers maintained their section of the town road, which artist Peter Foster proudly noted was a grand 3½ rods, or almost 58 feet wide.

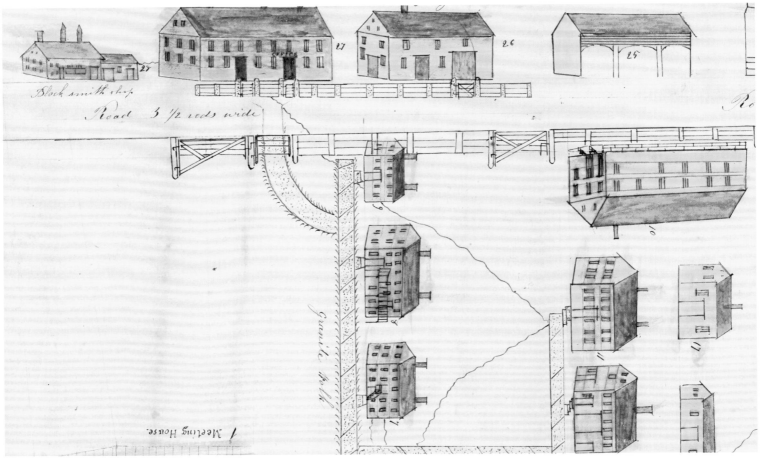

Fig. 1-5. David Austin Buckingham (1803–1885). *A Delineation or View of the Village Called the Church Family*, 1838. Pencil and ink on paper. New York State Museum, Albany, H-1930.14.1.

At Watervliet, New York, Brother Austin Buckingham pictured Shaker buildings clustered together in an open landscape and illustrated a stone bridge the Shakers built across the creek that flowed through the village.

Shaker villages were not unusual because their buildings were sited close to the road. That was common practice in early America, where the constant benefit of easy access was valued and the occasional appearance of strangers in the dooryard was not necessarily a cause for concern. What made Shaker villages distinctive was the anomaly of neighborhood density in a rural setting. The proximity of their buildings served the Shakers' purposes in facilitating communication and efficient access in community life. In the neighboring farms of the northeast, some Yankee farmers linked their main houses to their barns with woodsheds and outhouses so they could tend to farm chores without having to step outside in inclement weather. But the nuclear families on these neighboring farms did not need to relate to each other in the same way that Shaker families did. For better or worse, the close arrangement of their buildings meant that the many residents of a Shaker village were able to stay in constant visual contact with one another. The efficiencies of a village of unusually close buildings could help cement solidarity among the gospel kindred. As with so may other facets of their material lives, the appearance of a Shaker village was the manifestation of the thought within the community (fig. 1-5).

STONE STRUCTURES

One of the amenities that distinguishes the Shaker village at Canterbury, New Hampshire, is a stone watering trough made by Brother Micajah Tucker in 1831 and placed at a fork in the road at the bottom of the hill travelers had to ascend to reach the community (fig. 1-6). The trough was a boon to the Shakers on whose land it stood, as well as to strangers on the public road passing through the village. Not only did it supply refreshment to man and beast, but it also served as a public statement about the Shakers' concern for their fellow human beings and as a conspicuous example of their high level of craftsmanship. Cut from solid granite, the trough was connected with underground pipes to a hilltop spring hundreds of yards away. The investment of time it took to hollow a basin out of a

Fig. 1-6. W. G. C. Kimball. *Stopping for a Drink.* Stereopticon photograph, ca. 1870. Canterbury Shaker Village, Inc., Canterbury, New Hampshire.

The stone watering trough at Canterbury made by Brother Micajah Tucker in September 1831 was a local landmark throughout the nineteenth century in the countryside north of Concord, New Hampshire. It represented the care and dedication of Shaker craftsmanship and the concern the Shakers felt for the well-being of man and beast.

block of granite six feet square and to excavate a trench so deep that the water line supplying it would be protected from freezing during a New Hampshire winter was obvious to any nineteenth-century traveler who passed that way. In addition to providing comfort for all, this public amenity represented the value the Shakers placed on perfecting their lives here on earth.

The granite water trough was such a fine piece of work and was set in such a prominent location along the road to Loudon that it became well known in its day. It certainly caught the eye of Nathaniel Hawthorne, who used it as the central metaphor in his 1832 short story "The Canterbury Pilgrims."

> The summer moon, which shines in so many a tale, was beaming over a broad extent of uneven country. Some of its brightest rays were flung into a spring of water, where no traveler, toiling as the writer has, up the hilly road,

beside which it gushes, ever failed to quench his thirst. The work of neat hands and moderate art was visible about the blessed fountain. An open cistern, hewn and hollowed out of solid stone, was placed above the waters, which filled it to the brim, but by some invisible outlet were conveyed away without dripping down its sides. Though the basin had not room for another drop, and the continual gush of water made a tremor on the surface, there was a secret charm that forbade it to overflow. I remember that when I had slaked my summer thirst, and sat panting by the cistern, it was my fanciful theory that nature could not afford to lavish so pure a liquid, as she does the water of all meaner fountains.[16]

Hawthorne's extravagant description of this block of stone in 1832 may sound a bit florid to modern ears. With the advent later in the nineteenth century of mechanized stone cutting and hard steel tools, it became relatively simple to shape granite for architectural elements or sculptural figures, and it is easy now to forget what a great investment in labor once went into working with this hardest of New England materials. The stone had to be quarried from a ledge, transported, and then dressed by hand with chisels that dulled after a few stokes and required constant resharpening. Sculpting granite was beyond the abilities of ordinary folk in early America because it required such a great investment of specialized labor. In Shaker villages, however, great investments of specialized labor were commonplace.

There, daily work was an expression of faith. Believers consecrated their labor to the needs of community life, keeping in mind the admonition to perfection from founder Mother Ann Lee, who told them to do all their work as though they had a thousand years to live and as if they might die tomorrow. This enormous resource of dedicated volunteer labor created the village landscape of excellent craftsmanship and assiduous maintenance that so distinguished the Shakers from their neighbors. The appearance of even the most prosperous farms down the road suffered by comparison with Shaker villages, where the Believers could concen-

trate on exacting tasks, knowing that their gospel brethren and sisters would provide the support needed for them to achieve excellence in their work. The stone trough on the road to Canterbury Shaker village was only one of countless grace notes encountered in a Shaker village.

Nathaniel Hawthorne's reading public envisioned the stone watering trough in "The Canterbury Pilgrims" as a metaphor for the tension between freedom and control, as the spring water surged right to the rim but never quite escaped its bounds. For those traveling the road through the Shaker village, however, the object lesson of a large block of granite transformed into a domestic artifact was fraught with another kind of symbolism. It served as a concise public statement about how the Shakers subdued the raw material of the natural world and shaped it into a tool for serving the needs of a civilized people. The Shakers labored constantly to subjugate the primitive forces and unruly materials of daily existence so they could bring rational order to the rough and irregular. "Improving" on the natural landscape was one more way of regulating all manner of unkempt things—including, by extension, their behavior. With the discipline of spiritual labor they brought gospel order to the natural world around them.

One of the striking features of nineteenth-century Shaker villages was the stone walls that lined the roads of the community. Every farm family in early America had to demarcate their land, contain their livestock, and clear their fields of loose rocks. Stacking these stones at the edges of fields solved all three of these problems. Despite their gravity and mass, however, stone walls can be damaged by collisions with falling trees and large errant cattle, or they can be gradually exploded by ice, which expands when water is trapped between or below the rocks. The backbreaking, finger-bruising, exquisite work of laying durable walls straight and high, using just the irregular pieces of stone that come to hand, is a special skill, and it was viewed in early America as a manifestation of the landowner's pride, competence, and diligence.

The Shakers' stone walls were hallmarks of their

which extends into the edge of Pittsfield.   They sprung up in this town about 1780.   Some persons about that time began to visit mother Ann and the elders at Escuania, near Albany.   Approving of the tenents of the Shakers, they immediately set up their meetings according to the customs of that sect.   They built their meeting-house in 1784.

Shaker Village in Hancock.

Fig. 1-7. John Warner Barber (1798–1885). *Shaker Village in Hancock,* ca. 1839. Wood engraving from Barber, *Historical Collections: Being a General Collection of Interesting Facts of Every Village in Massachusetts* (Worcester, Mass.: Dorr, Howland & Co., 1839): 74. General Research Division, The New York Public Library, Astor, Lenox, and Tilden Foundations.

The illustrator and gazetteer John Barber pictured a long stone wall at the Shaker village at Hancock, Massachusetts. In the background is the conical roof of the Shakers' famous round stone barn. The road through the center of the village is now Massachusetts State Route 20.

villages. Lining the public roads leading to the village and often visible before the buildings came into view, these elegant stone structures prepared visitors for the gospel order they would encounter in the heart of the community (fig. 1-7). Many were the travelers who had tried their own hands at laying up field stone, and many were the admiring remarks they recorded after visiting Shaker villages. While visiting the community at Shirley, Massachusetts, in 1795, the Reverend William Bentley noted that "the walls are excellent & high & upon a horizontal line, & straight as they can be laid."[17] Even though the walls were built along hilly ground, the uneven topography below was made to conform when Shakers brought the top of the stone walls up to a consistently flat and level surface. Transforming the rough refuse of their fields into these straight, true, useful structures must have seemed at times a transcendent experience to the Shakers. That which has the greatest use, they said, has the greatest beauty.

The granite outcroppings of New England provided the source for the large finished slabs of stone the Shakers used for sidewalks. The New Hampshire politician and newspaper publisher Isaac Hill was a great proselyte for the cultivation of the rural landscape, and when he visited the Canterbury Shakers in the summer of 1840, he took particular note of the stone sidewalks laid there:

> A great convenience about the dwellings of the first family is their stone walks by which they pass high and dry from house to house in rainy weather, and when the mud or snow is deep. These walks are made of large rocks with a flat and smoothed surface. A venerable Shaker, Michael [Micajah] Tucker, aged seventy-six years, prepares and lays down these stone walks alone: he goes to a distant field, splits and hews the rough granite, takes a yoke of oxen, and alone loads, brings them home and lays them down in their proper place. They are so adjusted to the ground that the frost has no unfavorable effect; and under the operations of the old man's hammer and chisel they are made a walk three and a half to five feet wide, smoother than the common brick sidewalks of the cities.[18]

In a region where early springtime mud has a serious impact on landscape maintenance, travel, and the cleanliness of building interiors, these paved granite walks were an extraordinary benefit to the community. On his 1849 plan of the Shaker village at Canterbury (fig. 1-8), Brother Peter Foster took special note of these walks. His drawings of the buildings there are rudimentary, but he took great pains to illustrate the paved pathways connecting the major structures, portraying the shapes of individual stones and distinguishing their surfaces from the adjacent ground with pen stokes to represent paving blocks as edging. Here was a brilliant example of the efficiency of communal labor. Clearly, the Canterbury Shakers valued this amenity enough to give Elder Micajah Tucker the support he needed as he quarried this stone from the ledge, dressed it in the field, carted it to the site, and laid it, like the adjacent stone walls, straight

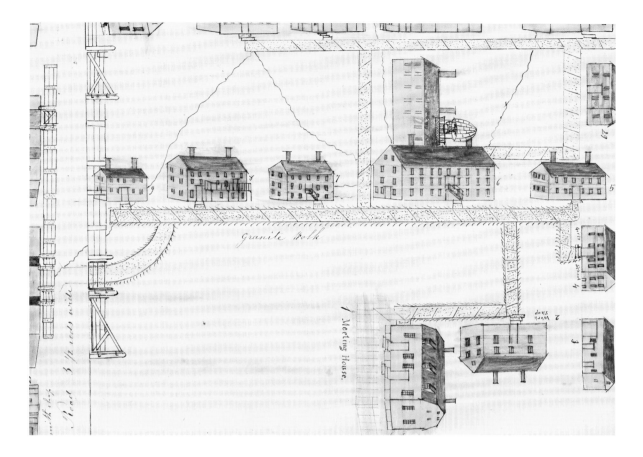

Fig. 1-8. Peter Foster (b. 1893).
*Diagram of the South Part of
Shaker Village, Canterbury, N.H.,
1849.* Pencil, ink, and watercolor
on paper. Library of Congress,
Washington, D.C.
   In his 1849 drawing of the
Canterbury Shaker village,
Brother Peter Foster took pains
to illustrate the granite walk-
ways and gate posts in the
Church Family.

and true. Sidewalks of large blocks of finished granite could be found in the more prosperous cities of
nineteenth-century America, where the public
funding of such civic amenities might be justified to
serve a concentrated urban population. These
labor-intensive stone sidewalks, however, were virtually unknown in the rural villages of mid-nineteenth-
century America, and visitors to Shaker villages
who gratefully stepped out of the mud and walked
these paths could not help but be impressed by
this display of extraordinary resources and motivation in Shaker life.

   Peter Foster illustrated another use for the granite quarried on Shaker lands on his drawing of the
village at Canterbury. Along the road, where gates
opened into fields, yards, and walks, are illustrations of large stone gateposts. Anchored deep in
the ground, these stone posts were stable enough
to support the extended weight of the wide
wooden gates that swung open from the road into

Shaker lands. Gates suspended from great stone
posts would not lean and sag as gates inevitably do
when suspended from ordinary wooden posts. Like
the water trough at the bottom of the hill, the
solidity and intransigence of the granite mass of
these stone posts served as yet another visible
public demonstration of the quality of work, and
thus the quality of life, in a Shaker village (fig. 1-9).

   Shaker craftsmen, like every other rural resident
in early America, used local materials in their work.
In the Berkshire Mountains of western Massachusetts,
marble was often used for building stone. After a
visit to the Hancock Shaker village in 1828 James
Fenimore Cooper wrote: "I have never seen, in any
country, villages so neat, and so perfectly beautiful,
as to order and arrangement, without, however,
being picturesque and ornamented, as those of the
Shakers. At Hancock, the gate-posts of the fences
are made of white marble, hewn into shape and
proportions."[19] Five miles to the west, in Columbia

County, New York, John W. Barber reported that at New Lebanon: "Their stone walls and other fences are constructed with the utmost regularity and precision, and their gateposts are of massive marble columns, of many tons weight."[20]

In the bluegrass country of central Kentucky, granite and marble were unknown. The distinctive color of grasses growing there was caused by limestone deposits lying not far beneath the surface. At Pleasant Hill, the Shakers mined this limestone from a riverbank quarry on their land, whose sedimentary deposits yielded soft flat blocks easily shaped for wall stone, gate posts, paving slabs, or architectural elements. Laid in horizontal courses and capped with a row of stones stacked vertically, the limestone walls erected at Pleasant Hill demonstrate how the Shakers employed discrete vernacular building traditions and local materials to create the same orderly landscape that their gospel kindred were building in distant Shaker villages to the east (fig. 1-10). Referring to Canterbury Shaker village, Scott Swank has written:

The eastern Shaker achievement in stonework lies less in stone buildings than in stone's comprehensive application throughout the communities. At Canterbury the Shaker accomplishments in stone are seen in foundations or sill blocks, walkways, steps, gateposts, walls, drains, bridges, dams, culverts, and tombstones. Whether rough cut or dressed, the ubiquitous stonework conveys a message of permanence. Like the peg rail of Shaker interiors, the ribbons of stone that demarcate the Shaker community identify a Shaker space.[21]

SHAKER BUILDINGS

The form and function of the buildings the Believers erected were among the great defining characteristics of a Shaker village. The materials the Shakers used to construct these buildings were no different from those of their neighbors, which were made from the same timber and the same stone available to everyone in the region. But the Shakers' buildings were different from their neighbors' in design, in quality, in size, and in number. The cumulative appearance of these characteristics in a village created under a central control and by people with a penchant for consistency was striking. Whether or not visitors could articulate the differences, invariably they saw that Shaker villages just looked different.

Over the years the Shakers shaped and articulated their ever-evolving notions of gospel order in a set of rules they called the Millennial Laws, which the lead ministry circulated among the communities. A sense of the design aesthetic they valued in the mid-nineteenth century can be seen in the 1845 revision of these admonitions.

Section IX: Concerning building, painting, varnishing, and the manufacture of articles for sale:

1. Beadings, mouldings and cornices, which are merely for fancy may not be made by Believers.

2. Odd or fanciful styles of architecture, may not be used among Believers, neither should any deviate widely from the common styles of

building among Believers, without the union of the Ministry.

3. The meeting house should be painted white without, and of a blueish shade within. Houses and shops, should be as near uniform in color, as consistent; but it is advisable to have shops a little darker shade than dwelling houses.

4. Floors in dwelling houses, if stained at all, should be of a reddish yellow, and shop floors should be of a yellowish red.

5. It is unadvisable for wooden buildings, fronting on the street, to be painted red, brown, or black, but they should be of a lightish hue.

6. No buildings may be painted white, save meeting houses.

7. Barns and back buildings, as wood houses, etc., if painted at all, should be of a dark hue, either red, or brown, lead color, or something of the kind, unless they front the road, or command a sightly aspect, and then they should not be of a very light color.[22]

These formal dictates for order and consistency in Shaker life should be taken with a grain of salt. Handed down from the central ministry at New Lebanon, they were observed to greater or lesser degrees depending on how reasonable they were thought to be by the Believers living in individual

Fig. 1-10. Photograph by Paul Rocheleau of Shaker village at Pleasant Hill, Kentucky, ca. 1994.

At Pleasant Hill, the Shakers used local limestone and local masonry construction techniques to build their stone walls. The "soldier" course of stones set on edge on the top row were supposed to discourage cattle from jumping over the wall.

communities. In Maine, for instance, Brother Joshua Bussell's illustrated maps of the Shaker village at Alfred consistently show that many buildings were painted white in addition to the meetinghouse. The admonition against odd or fanciful styles of architecture, however, seems to have resonated with the Shaker aspiration for simplicity. Shaker buildings still standing today, starting with the gambrel-roofed meetinghouses of the 1780s and 1790s and continuing through the antebellum era, have plainer lines than neighboring farm buildings down the road. They tend to be symmetrical, with simple moldings used for door and window casings, and without modillion blocks or brackets to support the raking eaves of their overhanging roofs. From the vast dwelling houses and barns to their modest workshops and farm dependencies, Shaker buildings from this period really do reflect their builders' conscious attempts to simplify contemporary styles in architecture and the awareness that the plain life can be achieved holistically, in material as well as spiritual form.

By the 1820s and 1830s, Shaker communities were well enough established that Believers were able to construct large central dwelling houses to accommodate as many as one hundred members of the spiritual family under one roof. The size and quality of these dwellings made them an anomaly on the rural landscape. Many were the biggest and finest buildings in their region, and often they were the biggest anyone in the region had ever seen. The relative grandeur of these central dwellings was made possible by economies of scale, by the concentration of capital and purchasing power in Shaker communities, by the availability of so much of the building material from Shaker lands, by the efficiency of communal labor, and by the availability of virtually unlimited free labor of a workforce committed to creating something as close to perfection as humanly possible.

The sheer size of a Shaker dwelling house was a function of communal life. As they gathered into gospel order, the Shakers found that bringing all the members of the spiritual family into a central building to worship, dine, and sleep strengthened the bonds of community. As the New York journalist Charles Nordhoff noted on his 1873 visit to the Mount Lebanon Shakers (in 1861 the name of the community there was changed from New Lebanon to Mount Lebanon), "the peculiar nature of their social arrangements leads them to build very large houses."[23]

Another reason that the Shakers built large dwelling houses was to provide separate accommodations for sisters and for brethren. Separation of the sexes was fundamental to life in a Shaker community, where Believers renounced sexual conduct and led celibate lives. One side of a Shaker dwelling was occupied by the sisters and the other was occupied by the brethren. To emphasize the idea that the genders were separate but equal, there were duplicate doorways leading to duplicate stairways within the house. Separate walks led out through separate gates in the fence and across the street to a meetinghouse with the same paired entrances. This pleasing architectural redundancy allowed the sisters and the brethren to live among one another and yet keep from close physical contact. It was a constant visual reminder of the duality of Shaker life, both in this world and in the next. One consequence, however, was that it added to the size of a Shaker dwelling house.

In their first years of living in community, the Shakers slept in the increasingly cramped rooms of whatever farmhouses already stood on the land. As their numbers grew, they expanded existing dwellings and built more houses until they had the means to construct the large modern institutional buildings that drew them together in spirit and place. The first of these great institutional buildings was begun by the Centre Family at South Union, Kentucky, in 1822, followed by the Centre Family at Pleasant Hill Kentucky in 1824. Because these communities were founded later than the eastern Shaker villages, the western Shakers could anticipate the growth of their own communities along the model already being achieved by the eastern societies. Instead of building what they could foresee would be more interim houses to shelter their families, Shakers in the west began to construct their new large central dwellings sooner than their gospel kindred did in the east.

It was difficult for Shakers in the distant western villages to build communities in the same spirit and in the same appearance as those in the east. The great distances from the central ministry at New Lebanon made communication difficult in the early nineteenth century, and despite their regular efforts to share information in both directions, the same seeds the Shakers planted in New York and New England grew differently in the soil of Ohio and Kentucky. Ever striving for gospel unity, in 1823, the year before construction began on the Centre Family's central dwelling, the Shaker ministry at Pleasant Hill wrote to the central ministry at New Lebanon to ask for guidance in designing their village to reflect the appearance of the parent community: "The Word comes from the East say [New Lebanon] is the most beautiful place there is on Earth . . . & if I dare use so much freedom as to ask anything of a temporal nature it would be to ask for a map of that place, Buildings, gardens, Orchards, etc."[24] Consistency was valued and promoted, not only within the social structure of individual villages, but also as a way of linking all of the Shaker communities of nineteenth-century America.

The cultural environment resulting from the distances among Shaker villages was not the only factor that gave them their regional identities. Natural resources varied from site to site, dictating how a design might be realized in the local environment. "Uniformity is comely," the Shakers said, and in 1818 the South Union Brother Benjamin S. Youngs, laboring to live in the gift while facing the realities of local culture, discussed the challenges of creating a common appearance in a letter to the central ministry.

> It would seem that what is wisdom & prudence with one people in a certain situation, is not always wisdom & prudence with another people in another situation. Countries and climates, people & laws, manners & customs, local situations & circumstances, advantages and disadvantages peculiar to each—all are

> different—and each requiring a different method of arrangement from the other in the line of outward economy. . . . This is much the case with us in regard to building materials— we are much put to it for a little building timber, as it is extremely scarce here . . . but good building stone of different kinds & the best kind of materials for brick, we have convenient & in plenty.[25]

Four years later, in 1822, the South Union Shakers began building their large central dwelling of brick, unlike the framed wooden dwellings then in New Lebanon or anywhere else in the eastern Shaker communities. The following year, the Pleasant Hill Shakers started construction of their new dwelling house using the same limestone they quarried to build their stone fences and walks (fig. 1-11).

Inside these western Shaker dwellings, their architects designed amenities to respond to the physical environment of the American South. Their chimneys were set into exterior walls to help dispel heat from cooking during the summer months. The ceilings could be as much as twelve feet high, to allow summer heat to rise above the living spaces of the rooms. Their buildings had wide central hall-

Fig. 1-11. Photograph by Bret Morgan of the Centre Family dwelling at Pleasant Hill, Kentucky, 1994.
In 1824 the Centre Family at Pleasant Hill constructed a new dwelling house of limestone. Although its design followed the established form of communal dwellings in the east, the Pleasant Hill Shakers used local materials in its construction, including this soft rock, which they were able to saw from their riverbank quarry.

Fig. 1-12. Stereopticon photograph of the Shaker community at Enfield, New Hampshire, ca. 1872. Photograph by C.E. Lewis. Historic New England, Boston. Digital ID 001571

The Enfield Shakers' great stone house was the largest Shaker dwelling ever built. Constructed between 1837 and 1841, it replaced the antiquated 1794 wooden dwelling house in the foreground.

ways to increase ventilation from the outside.[26] The form of the exterior, however, followed the function of the same spiritual life present in every Shaker village. The crisp symmetry of the buildings' facades reflected the neoclassical taste for balance so popular in early nineteenth-century America, but it also indicated the equality of women and men in Shaker life.

By 1830 the Church Family at Hancock, Massachusetts, had outgrown their old dwelling house and were ready to build a new central dwelling large enough to accommodate almost one hundred Believers. Using stone from their own quarry, brick from their clay pits, and timber from their own woodlots, they raised a three-story brick structure containing rooms for food preparation, dining, worship, and sleeping. By the following year, when they completed the interior woodwork and plastering, the new dwelling house had become a remarkable presence on the landscape. "The work is all done," reported Hancock Elder William Deming in 1832. "There is none to excel it in this country."[27] In what had become a hallmark in Shaker villages, the size of the building and the quality of the craftsmanship drew crowds of visitors, not only travelers passing through the village, but also the curious public, who went on outings to the Shaker village specifically to admire the new dwelling house. By 1835 the Hancock Shakers were obliged to publish a special notice informing the public that they could no longer oblige the hundreds of visitors a year "who call upon us and 'wish to see the house.'"[28]

The largest Shaker dwelling ever constructed was built at Enfield, New Hampshire, where, by the mid-1830s, the Church Family had long since outgrown its 1794 dwelling house (fig. 1-12). Imagining a new dwelling so large that it would serve the community's needs for all eternity, and so grand that it would make a powerful public statement about the blessings of a Shaker life, Enfield trustee Caleb Dyer spent three years researching comparable domestic institutional architecture in northern New England. Realizing that there were limits even to the consecrated ingenuity of Shakers builders, he hired the local architect Ammi Burnham Young to assist with the design for a family dwelling to be made of granite from the quarry on Shaker land. Young, who had recently designed two dormitories at nearby Dartmouth College and two more academy buildings in central New Hampshire, and was about to begin work on the Vermont statehouse in Montpelier, obliged the Enfield Shakers with plans in a simplified Greek Revival style for a four-story dwelling house 100 feet long by 58 feet in width. Constructed to the Shakers' designs during the summer and fall of 1837 by a crew of specialized stone masons from Boston, it immediately became a local sensation and was often cited as the most expensive building in New Hampshire after the state house in

Concord.[29] The newspaperman Isaac Hill, who seemed to be constantly roaming the state in search of progressive trends to report in his *Farmer's Monthly Visitor*, made special note of what he called a "Grand Edifice." Even while it was under construction, he wrote of the Enfield Shakers' great stone dwelling: "The best dwelling house in the state is now erecting on their premises. . . . Although their carpenters and principal masons are hired . . . the cash expense has been lessened by their ability to furnish excellent lumber and granite bricks from their own premises and by their own hands."[30]

VILLAGE ORGANIZATION

In the linear Shaker villages, the most prominent buildings were found in a row along the public road. Some of them were intended for public use; the trustees' office, for example, where business with the World was transacted, was meant to be the visiting public's portal to the community. In most cases, the meetinghouse fronted on the road, both to provide easy access for Worldly visitors and to concentrate them at the public road and away from private family buildings. In later years, the same was true of Shaker schoolhouses, which also served as district schools for the other children of the neighborhood. Other structures on this first row of buildings—the large central dwellings or the workshops and residences of members of the Shaker ministry—were not intended to be accessible to visitors but were sited in prominent locations so the public, including potential converts, could observe the high quality of life in Shaker villages.

There were times when this public exposure wore too heavily on the Shakers, who could tire of constant scrutiny. In 1842, when Charles Dickens stopped at New Lebanon, he found that public religious services had been suspended, and when he wrote his sour description of the Believers there, he was forced to rely on a commercial print showing Shakers dancing.[31] At Enfield, New Hampshire, the Church Family breathed a sigh of relief when

construction of the great stone dwelling was completed. Even though they set a large date stone with the year 1837 carved in the gable of the dwelling to catch the attention of passersby, they confided in a letter to the central ministry at New Lebanon "our dooryard is constantly annoyed with the presence of the world."[32]

Buildings of secondary and tertiary importance and the more private structures in a Shaker village tended to be aligned along a lane running parallel to the public road but set back a little distance. Following the invisible line that divided the meetinghouse and the dwelling house into a side for the sisters and a side for the brethren, the workshops and agricultural buildings along this back street were similarly grouped by gender, with the sister's shops nearer the laundry and the brethren's shops nearer the barns (fig. 1-13). As this community plan was first being established, the emphasis the Shakers meant to place on the prominent buildings flanking the public road can be seen in the village views they made in the second quarter of the nine-

teenth century. These depict the front row of buildings highlighted in bright, light colors and the inner range of buildings painted in drab browns or grays to diminish attention and leave them less conspicuous or accessible to the public.[33]

The Shakers' barns were some of the largest constructed in rural America during the antebellum period, and although they were some of the community's most notable buildings, their function generally required that they also be sited back and away from the main road. On his 1840 visit to the Shaker village at Canterbury, Isaac Hill was impressed with the Church Family's cow barn. "The principal barn of the family, it is believed, is the largest building of the kind in the state; it is 200 feet in length, 35 feet in width, and 22-feet posts."[34] Fourteen years later at Enfield, New Hampshire, a visitor admired "perhaps the most expensive barn in America," a slate-roofed structure 250 feet long.[35] On his 1872 visit to Mount Lebanon, Charles Nordhoff noted the Shakers' 1858 stone barn.

As you drive up the road from Lebanon Springs, the first building belonging to the Shaker settlement which meets your eye is the enormous barn of the North Family, said to be the largest in the three or four states which near here come together, as in its interior arrangements it is one of the most complete. This huge structure lies on a hillside, and is two hundred and ninety six feet long by fifty wide, and five stories high, the upper story being on a level with the main road and the lower opening on the fields behind it.[36]

LANDSCAPE IMPROVEMENT

Improving the land made its operation more efficient and convenient, but it also gave the landowner a sense of control over the natural environment. The Shakers were more determined to dominate the land than even their most progressive farming neighbors, as by doing this they helped subdue the natural spirit of unpredictability and uncertainty they guarded against constantly in themselves. The distinctive organization and extensive resources of Shaker communities provided them with unique reasons and abilities to undertake these extraordinarily large construction projects. Building on this scale was more common in cities, where the concentration of population and capital made it more practical to construct large municipal or industrial buildings. But in the countryside, the very size and extent of the Shakers' modifications to the landscape were unparalleled and became some of the most distinguishing features of a Shaker village.

Illustrated maps made by Shaker artists in the 1830s and 1840s picture landscapes divided into grids of fields, orchards, yards, pastures, and woodlots (fig. 1-14). These Shaker village lands were assembled incrementally as neighbors became converted to the faith and donated their farms, or as the Shakers purchased adjacent property. This pattern of acquiring adjacent land went on until individual Shaker villages grew to encompass thousands of acres. In 1874 Nordhoff reported that, in aggregate, Shaker villages occupied nearly 50,000 acres.[37]

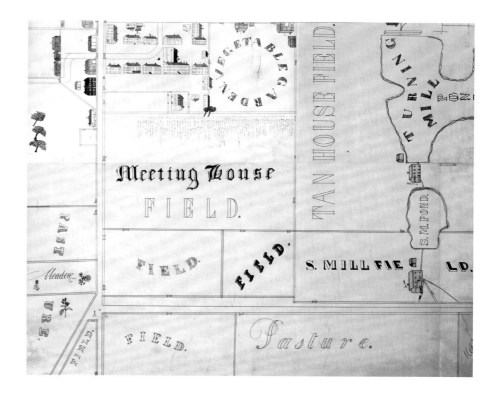

By combining individual farms, the Shakers created enormous properties, whose sheer size alone set them apart in appearance from their neighbors. But because the Shakers labored under a moral imperative to further "improve" their combined land holdings, their villages assumed a unified appearance of neatness and regularity. Developed and managed under a central authority, the landscape of Shaker villages was consistently orderly. At Canterbury in 1840, Isaac Hill visited with the aged Brother Peter Ayer, who was busy transforming a rocky field into a landscape of gospel order (fig. 1-15).

> It was a mile from the road, and contained a hundred acres, being a purchase made by the first family some twenty years ago, and upon it had been a house and barn, the last of which is still standing in the midst of a beautiful apple orchard of several acres containing more than one thousand bearing trees. The face of this hundred acres was hard and full of rocks, as was nearly every rod of the several thousand acres owned by the three Canterbury families. The orchard itself seemed to be but a mass of rocks. At this place "solitary and alone,"

Fig. 1-14. Henry C. Blinn (1824–1905). *Plan of Canterbury,* 1848. Pencil, ink, and watercolor on paper. Canterbury Shaker Village, Inc., Canterbury, New Hampshire.

Henry Blinn depicted the open lands of the Canterbury Shaker village as an orderly grid of fields and pastures. He was the community's printer, and his enjoyment of the different typefaces from his print shop is evident in the way he lettered the labels on his map.

Fig. 1-15. "Shaker Village." Stereopticon photograph attributed to W. G. C. Kimball, ca. 1855–59. Canterbury Shaker Village, Inc., Canterbury, New Hampshire.

When the Shakers farmed rocky soil they constructed substantial stone fences with the debris they removed from the ground. They built their best stone walls along the public byways in prominent view of passersby. This early photograph shows the Shaker village at Canterbury, New Hampshire.

excepting one stout, faithful yoke of oxen as his assistants, Peter Ayer had worked among the rocks two entire seasons, taking up the old and crooked stonewalls and laying over new walls in a direct line, digging out and piling up immense masses of stones in piles the size of a common haystack.[38]

Wherever there was a Shaker village, there seemed to be a written account of how, by tenacity, hard work and a dedication to a greater purpose, Believers had transformed rough fields into orderly lands suitable for cultivation. In his visit to the Mount Lebanon Shakers, Charles Nordhoff noted: "In their farming operations they spare no pains; but, working slowly year after year redeem the soil, clear it of stones, and have clean tillage."[39] The Shakers labored in the knowledge that they were

building for eternity and that there would always be time enough to create order out of chaos.

In this aspiration they were guided early on by the admonition of Father Joseph Meacham, who exhorted the Shakers at Harvard, Massachusetts, to plant their fields and gardens in straight rows. This appearance of regularity would be a form of "preaching to the world for they admire the beautiful outward order of the people of God."[40] Not only would the Shakers have the quiet satisfaction of order in their lives, but the public display of this order would also serve them well in religious proselytizing and public relations.

It was not just the improved soil and straight rows of crops that gave Shaker villages such an admirable appearance. The large new lots they created from small properties became unified under a comprehensive plan of land management. As Isaac Hill noted at Canterbury, the Shakers purchased the hundred-acre farm with buildings standing on it, but as they began to integrate the property with the greater Shaker community, they dismantled those structures and stored the building materials for eventual reuse. As they enlarged the fields and rebuilt the stone walls surrounding them, the Shakers also transformed the topography. With rocks they cleared from the fields they filled in low or wet patches, which they then covered with topsoil to level out the ground.

In their never-ending effort to improve the land, the Shakers could marshal the manpower to move the course of streams to better advantage for farm irrigation, mill waterpower, providing domestic drinking water or watering the stock. At the Church Family at Enfield, New Hampshire, the Shakers diverted a brook to prepare the construction site for their great stone dwelling, digging a new channel to redirect the stream precisely where they wanted it. Then they dug drainage ditches to lead the rainwater gathered by the gutters and downspouts away from their stone house. They filled the ditches with the loose stones they had gathered from clearing the hard New Hampshire soil and covered them over with stone slabs. Buried below the finished lawn, these underground channels conveyed the rainwater shed from the roof of the vast new building over to the new bed of the stream they had relocated.

In his 1836 plan of the village at Harvard, Massachusetts, Brother George Kendal illustrated the ditches the Shakers dug to drain the swampland around Bennett's Brook. Labeled on his map as a "Water Course," these drainage and irrigation channels appear unnaturally straight and true (fig. 1-16). Marshaled into orderly canals, they bore little resemblance to the meandering stream the Shakers found there when they acquired the site.

Wetlands and stream beds in every Shaker village were excavated, channeled, and dammed to create reservoirs or mill ponds. The eighteen-acre "Lower Shaker Lake" in the present-day city of Shaker Heights, Ohio, was once a mill pond in the North Union Shaker village. In 1836 the Shakers there excavated a marsh and dammed Doan Brook to impound water for turning the water wheels powering their saw mill and grist mill.

Nowhere was the landscape more extensively altered for harnessing water power than at the Canterbury Shaker village, where during his visit in 1840, Isaac Hill was endlessly fascinated with the transformation of this land for industrial use. In his lengthy article for the *Farmer's Monthly Visitor* he marveled at:

> the artificial water power created by the first family at an almost incredible amount of labor and expense. The Shaker village is situated at the high point near the sources of the Suncook River running into the Merrimack from the northeast, and above the mill seats found upon the stream. Here, where no natural stream ever ran, they have created a more permanent water power than can be found within the distance of ten miles.[41]

After listing the mills the Shakers built along this waterway for carding wool, sawing wood, milling flour, manufacturing pails, finishing woven woolen fabric, tanning leather, and threshing grain, Hill went on to describe how the Shakers had harnessed the water to power them.

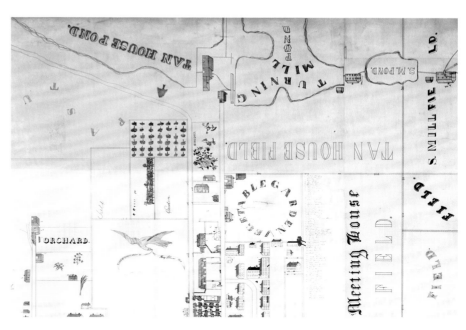

Fig. 1-16. George Kendal (b. 1813). *Plan of the First Family, Harvard*, 1836. Pencil, ink, and watercolor on paper. Fruitlands Museums, Harvard, Masschusetts.

The blue lines marked "water course" and "ditch" in George Kendal's 1836 plan of the Shaker village at Harvard, Massachusetts, represent efficient drainage and irrigation channels the Shakers there created out of meandering streams and wetlands.

Fig. 1-17. Henry C. Blinn (1824–1905). *Plan of Canterbury* (detail), 1848. Pen, ink, and watercolor on paper. Canterbury Shaker Village, Inc., Canterbury, New Hampshire.

In every Shaker village, Believers drained bogs and channeled streams into an integrated system of mill races and storage ponds to direct the water they needed to power their mills.

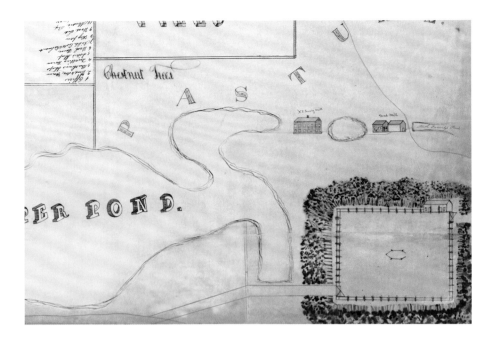

Among the most recent improvements here, is the erection of an excellent Mill situation upon a small stream, but one which is never dry. During the great drouth of last season when all the mills in the vicinity were obliged to suspend operations for want of water, this one was kept in constant use, doing service for a large region of country round about, proving of great convenience to all. The Mill is built in the most thorough and substantial manner— has three run of stones, and its machinery is of the most perfect kind, with all the modern improvements, producing the most beautiful Flour, Meal, &c, and is doing its work so admirably that it is visited by all the Farmers from a great distance.[43]

Fig. 1-18. Henry C. Blinn (1824–1905). *Plan of Canterbury,* 1848. Pencil, ink, and watercolor on paper. Canterbury Shaker Village, Inc., Canterbury, New Hampshire.

In the early 1840s, each Shaker community created an identical spiritual "Feast Ground" for outdoor worship. Sited on hillsides away from the village centers, these were meticulously landscaped features amidst rough unimproved lands. In 1848 Brother Henry Blinn pictured the Feast Ground located out beyond the mill ponds at Canterbury, New Hampshire.

Above the last described mills in the extensive range of pasture lands belonging to the Shakers are the larger artificial ponds which they have created with great perseverance and labor. The masses of stone and gravel removed and brought together for the purpose of forming these reservoirs stand there as permanent evidence of the industry and hard labor of this enterprising people.[42]

On the illustrated map he drew of Canterbury Shaker Village in 1848, Henry Blinn pictured these mill streams and ponds, descending the hillside in a long procession (fig. 1-17). The townspeople who came to saw their lumber, grind their grain, and marvel at the Shakers' accomplishments liked to say that the Shakers had made such productive use of the falling water that it was all worn out by the time it reached them downstream.

Because the waterways that collected the water to power these mills were assiduously maintained by the boys of the Shaker village, however, they were often the most reliable industrial operations for miles around, and the neighbors made good use of them also. The 1855 account of the Shaker village at Sabbathday Lake, published in the *Augusta Rural Intelligencer* reported that:

SHAKER MEETING GROUNDS AND CEMETERIES

Up the hill beyond the mills Henry Blinn illustrated a peculiar feature on the landscape of Canterbury Shaker village, although it was unique to all Shaker villages in the 1840s and 1850s. On his map, a green plain enclosed by a rail fence and a perimeter of trees appears with a heptagonal structure in the center (fig. 1-18), but no reference in the numbered key on his map identifies the spot. Intentionally hidden from public view, this was a sacred meeting ground for Shaker worship, constructed in 1842 during the Shaker era of spirit manifestations. Every Shaker community was commanded by the central ministry to build these open-air meeting grounds according to a common design, which required extensive earthmoving operations to create a large, level lawn on rough and unimproved ground. Many years later Henry Blinn described the efficiency of communal labor in creating the worship site, or as the Shakers would call it, the spiritual "Feast Ground."

Several of the societies selected a place in the woods or fields to be used for divine worship. At Canterbury, the place was designated "Pleasant Grove," and was situated about three-fourths of a mile northeast of the Church Family. All who were able to assist in the work of clearing the land and preparing the place for religious gatherings, were expected to contribute the labor of a few days. The printers, after obtaining some hoes and shovels, were soon found among the zealous laborers. A building, 40 feet long, 15 feet wide, and one story high, was built for the protection of the people if it should happen to rain during the time of the meeting. In 1847, a marble slab was purchased, six feet long, three feet wide, and three inches thick. This was placed in the center of the enclosure. On one side of the marble was engraved the name of the place and the date of erection, while on the other side was an extended message or spiritual exhortation to those who visited the sacred place. . . . The stone was erected, beautiful evergreens were planted around the place, and meetings were held frequently for several years. Subsequently, these meetings were discontinued, and the house, fence, and marble slab were removed by the writer [fig. 1-19].[44]

Today all that remains of the broad open-air meeting grounds so meticulously constructed by the Shakers are incongruously leveled plains, now overgrown from disuse, found back in remote areas of Shaker villages. Encountering this landscape of gospel order hidden in the rough uplands of Shaker property is as mysterious today as it was in the middle of the nineteenth century. In 1853 a correspondent for the New York *Illustrated News* reported that

> recently two gentlemen from town went over to survey some lands for the [Canterbury] Shakers, and in the vicinity of the ponds, in a retired spot, they found a square enclosure of about half an acre, surrounding another octagonal enclosure, with a low fence and locked gate; within was a white marble stone five or six feet high, bearing an inscription from Scripture about a fountain, and denouncing any who should pollute the water or deface the stone. Nearby was a spring of water covered with a rock. They could learn nothing from the Shakers except that it was consecrated ground.[45]

In contrast to the deliberately obscured locations of their spiritual Feast Grounds, the Shakers' cemeteries were placed in publicly visible spots in the community, often along the main road, like the cemeteries in neighboring towns. However, the precepts of Shaker life dictated that the Believers' cemeteries would look quite different from those of their neighbors. The town and farm cemeteries of early America were filled with grave markers notable for their variation in styles, materials, and size. On these non-Shaker markers commemorative inscriptions relate Worldly accomplishments and family associations, with carved pictorial allusions to Christian iconography or neoclassical imagery. Shaker gravestones reflect none of these concerns. Mirroring the conformity of life in community, the Shakers' markers tended to be consistent in appearance. Terse inscriptions, including only the name or just initials of the deceased and his or her life dates, were cut on stones of a uniform size and color. This regularity was most precisely achieved when the Shakers at Mount Lebanon and at Harvard, Massachusetts, placed iron markers at each grave site, indistinguishable except for the

Fig. 1-19. David R. Lamson (1806–1886). *Mountain Meeting.* Wood engraving from Lamson, *Two Years Experience Among the Shakers* (West Boylston, Mass.: published by the author, 1848): frontispiece. Shaker Museum and Library, Old Chatham and New Lebanon, New York.

The spiritual Feast Ground at Hancock, Massachusetts, pictured in 1848 by David Lamson, contained a marble tablet inscribed with sacred text, and a shelter with separate doors for the sisters and the brethren. Lamson lived with the Hancock Shakers from 1843 to 1845.

Fig. 1-20. Michael Freeman. Photograph ca. 1987 of the Shaker cemetery at Harvard, Massachusetts.

The conformity of Shaker life is symbolized by cast-iron grave markers filling the burying ground at Harvard, Massachusetts. Except for individual names and dates, the markers are precisely alike in appearance, in the same way that the Shakers tried to appear in life.

names and dates cast into the metal (fig. 1-20). In the twentieth century the individual markers were removed from many Shaker cemeteries and replaced with a single monument emphasizing the communal nature of Shaker life, but also allowing for ease in maintenance. In the rows of original markers that survive today at several Shaker villages, including Watervliet, New York, or at the Second Family at Enfield, New Hampshire, the scores of slate or marble stones bear no imagery,

no expressive shapes, and no epitaphs, reflecting the Believers' intention to be "in the gift," in death as well as in life.

* * *

The physical pattern of Shaker villages persisted over time, even as the communities evolved. The landscape plan was established early on, and when the Shakers constructed new buildings to replace

obsolete or damaged structures, they often located the new ones on the same sites as the buildings they replaced. For example, the 1824 meetinghouse at Mount Lebanon or the 1883 dwelling house at Sabbathday Lake logically belonged where their predecessors stood because of the existing rhythm of the surrounding structures. When new occasions called for new buildings—an electrical power house at Canterbury in 1910 or an automobile garage at Sabbathday Lake in 1916, for instance—the form and function of these structures reflected the new times, but they were sited in a landscape plan established a century or more earlier.

Today the landscape of gospel order can be readily recognized at Sabbathday Lake, Maine, the sole remaining active Shaker community, more than two centuries after the village was laid out. The distinctive architecture of community buildings clustered together in an orderly landscape of well-maintained pastures, fields, and orchards presents an appearance unlike any of the neighboring villages in southern Maine. Indeed, some of the sense of separateness and intimacy that characterized all Shaker villages in the nineteenth century was restored to Sabbathday Lake in 2005, when the state Route 26 was rerouted to a bypass highway, diverting thousands of vehicles a day from the old public road that runs through the center of the

village. In 2007 the Shaker family there transferred the development rights of their 2,000-acre property to a land conservation trust, insuring the preservation of their village in its traditional form.

As their numbers dwindled in the years following the Civil War and throughout the twentieth century, the Shakers closed all the rest of their communities save Sabbathday Lake. The sites of these other seventeen principal Shaker villages have met with various fates over time. At North Union, Ohio, Believers established their community in rural lands just north of what would become the city of Cleveland, and by the early twentieth century, the former Shaker village was obliterated by suburban sprawl. In the last half century, several Shaker sites have been turned into museum villages, whose mission is to maintain their historical appearance. Others were acquired by residential institutions—schools, prison farms, religious institutions or retirement communities—whose comparable requirements for communal living have allowed some of the Shaker landscape to survive in recognizable form. Although the present-day inhabitants of these sites may not themselves know the grace that imbues the daily experience of a community of Believers, the Shakers' commitment to a perfect life persists in the vestiges of their village landscape of gospel order.

1.   [Benson John Lossing], "The Shakers," *Harper's New Monthly Magazine* 15 (July 1857): 164–77. See also Don Gifford, ed., *An Early View of the Shakers: Benson John Lossing and the Harper's Article of July 1857* (Hanover, N.H.: University Press of New England, 1989).

2.   Lossing, "The Shakers" (1857): 166.

3.   "Census Data for Eastern Communities," Appendix C in Priscilla Brewer, *Shaker Communities, Shaker Lives* (Hanover, N.H.: University Press of New England, 1986): 228–38.

4.   For the construction of these meetinghouses, see Edward Deming Andrews, *A Shaker Meeting House and its Builder* (Pittsfield, Mass.: Shaker Community, 1962); Marius Peladeau, "The Shaker Meetinghouses of Moses Johnson," *Antiques* 98 (October 1970): 594–99; and Robert P. Emlen, "Raised, Razed, and Raised Again: The Shaker Meetinghouse at Enfield, New Hampshire," *Historical New Hampshire* 30, no. 3 (Fall 1975).

5.   William Bentley, *The Diary of William Bentley, D.D.*, vol. 2 (Salem, Mass.: The Essex Institute, 1907): 150.

6.   Nathaniel Hawthorne, "The Canterbury Pilgrims" (1832). Reprinted in Hyatt H. Waggoner, ed., *Nathaniel Hawthorne: Selected Tales and Sketches* (New York: Holt, Rinehart and Winston, 1970): 466–71.

7.   [Nathaniel Hawthorne], "The Village of the United Society of Shakers, in Canterbury, N.H.," *The American Magazine of Useful and Entertaining Knowledge* 2 (November 1835): 133.

8.   Benjamin Silliman, *Remarks Made on a Short Tour Between Hartford and Quebec in the Autumn of 1819* (New Haven: S. Converse, 1820): 42.

9.   Julie Nicoletta, "The Architecture of Control: Shaker Dwelling Houses and the Reform Movement in Early-Nineteenth-Century America," *Journal of the Society of Architectural Historians* 62, no. 3 (September 2003): 352.

10.   [Elisha Blakeman], *The Youth's Guide in Zion and Holy Mother's Promises* (Canterbury, N.H.: The United Society, 1842).

11.   John Kirk, *The Shaker World: Art, Life, Belief* (New York: Harry N. Abrams, 1997): 83–84.

12.   ["Pilgrim"], "The Shaker Community," *The Augusta Rural Intelligencer* 1, no. 37 (15 September 1855): 293.

13.   William Sims Bainbridge, "Shaker Demographics 1840–1900: An Example of the Use of U. S. Census Enumeration Schedules," *Journal for the Scientific Study of Religion* 21, no. 4 (1982): 352–65.

14.   Dolores Hayden, *Seven American Utopias: The Architecture of Communitarian Socialism, 1790–1975*, (Cambridge, Mass.: MIT Press, 1976): 77.

15.   Letter from Nathaniel Hawthorne to Louisa Hawthorne, 17 August 1831; quoted in Seymour L. Gross, "Hawthorne and the Shakers," *American Literature* 29 (January 1958): 458.

16.   Nathaniel Hawthorne, "The Canterbury Pilgrims," in *The Token and Atlantic Souvenir* (Boston: Charles Bowen, 1832): 153.

17.   Bentley, *The Diary of William Bentley*, vol. 2 (1907): 153.

18.   Isaac Hill, "The Shakers," *Farmer's Monthly Visitor* 2 (31 August 1840): 113; reprinted in T. E. Johnson, ed., "Canterbury in 1840," *Shaker Quarterly* 4 (Summer–Fall 1964): 85.

19.   James Fenimore Cooper, *Notions of the Americans, Picked up by a Travelling Bachelor* (Philadelphia: Carey & Lea, 1828).

20.   Barber, John Warner and Henry Howe, *Historical Collections of the State of New York* (New York: S. Tuttle, 1841): 120.

21.   Scott T. Swank, *Shaker Life, Art, and Architecture: Hands to Work, Hearts to God* (New York: Abbeville Press, 1999): 202.

22.   The Millennial Laws of 1845 are transcribed and published in Edward Deming Andrews, *The People Called Shakers: a Search for a Perfect Society* (New York: 1953), 243–89. For a discussion of the history and evolution of the Millennial Laws, see Theodore E. Johnson, ed., "The 'Millennial Laws' of 1821," *Shaker Quarterly* 7 (Summer 1967): 35–58.

23.   Nordhoff, Charles, *The Communistic Societies of the United States* (New York: Harper & Brothers, 1875): 156.

24.   Letter from Brother Samuel Turner for the Ministry at Pleasant Hill, Kentucky, to the Ministry at New Lebanon, New York, 1 May 1823. Collection of the Western Reserve Historical Society, quoted in Robert P. Emlen, *Shaker Village Views: Illustrated Maps and Landscape Drawings by Shaker Artists of the Nineteenth Century* (Hanover, N.H.: University Press of New England, 1987): 12.

25.   Letter from Benjamin S. Youngs, South Union, Kentucky, to the ministry, elders, and deacons at Lebanon, and Hancock, 26 February 1818. Western Reserve Historical Society Library Shaker Collection, IV:A-52. Quoted in Kirk, *The Shaker World* (1997): 51.

26.   For a discussion of regional variations in Shaker architecture, see Julie Nicoletta, *The Architecture of the Shakers* (Woodstock, Vt.: The Countryman Press, 1995).

27.   Letter from elder William Deming to elder Benjamin Youngs, January 1832. Quoted in John Harlow Ott, *Hancock Shaker Village: A Guidebook and History* (Hancock, Mass.: Shaker Community, Inc., 1976): 73.

28.   "Public Notice" (Pittsfield, Mass.: Daniel Goodrich, William Deming, and Joseph Wicker, trustees for the Shaker Community at West Pittsfield, Mass, 1835).

29.   Robert P. Emlen, "The Great Stone Dwelling of the Enfield, New Hampshire, Shakers," *Old-Time New*

England 69 (Winter–Spring 1979): 69–83.

30. Isaac Hill, "A Grand Edifice," *The Farmer's Monthly Visitor* 1, no. 9 (20 September 1839): 142.

31. Robert P. Emlen, "The Shaker Dance Prints," *Imprint: The Journal of the American Historical Print Collectors Society* 17, no. 2 (Autumn 1992): 14–26.

32. The Ministry at Enfield to the Ministry at New Lebanon, 13 November 1839, manuscript collections of the Western Reserve Historical Society, Cleveland. Quoted in Emlen, "The Great Stone Dwelling" (1979).

33. For an extended discussion of these Shaker-made village views, see Emlen, *Shaker Village Views* (1987).

34. Isaac Hill, "The Shakers," *The Farmer's Monthly Visitor* 2, no. 8 (June 1840). Quoted in *Shaker Quarterly* 4 (Summer–Fall 1964): 85.

35. "A Barn," *Ohio Farmer and Mechanics Assistant* (15 July 1854): 1, 109.

36. Nordhoff, *Communistic Societies* (1875): 154.

37. Ibid., 117

38. Hill, "The Shakers" (June 1840): 87.

39. Nordhoff, *Communistic Societies* (1875): 149.

40. Clarke Garrett, *Spirit Possession and Popular Religion: From the Camisards to the Shakers* (Baltimore: Johns Hopkins University Press, 1987): 227.

41. Hill, "The Shakers" (June 1840): 49.

42. Ibid., 53.

43. ["Pilgrim"] "The Shaker Community" (1855): 292.

44. Henry C. Blinn, "Autobiographical Notes," in *In Memoriam: Elder Henry C. Blinn 1824–1905* (Concord, N.H.: The Rumford Press, 1905): 28.

45. "Rambles Among the Shakers," *Illustrated News*, New York, 29 October 1853, p. 245.

2

Faith, Form, and Finish:
Shaker Furniture in Context

JEAN M. BURKS

We are not called to be like the world; but to excel them in order, union and peace, and in good works—works that are truly virtuous and useful to man, in this life.

Father Joseph Meacham[1]

The Shaker aesthetic that evolved from the 1820s through the 1850s resulted from the intersection of religious beliefs with Worldly design traditions. Classic Shaker furniture as it emerged in the early nineteenth century combined two themes: the vernacular interpretation of the prevailing neoclassical aesthetic and the elimination of unnecessary decorative details associated with the so-called Fancy style (see Chapter 6 in this volume). Because no one was born a Shaker, early craftsmen were trained in the World before converting to the faith, and they brought their skills, tastes, and awareness of current techniques with them into the community. These cabinetmakers influenced the direction of Shaker design during its formative stages, although the end result was always tempered by spiritual considerations.

SHARING SPACE

My Mother is a Joiner Wise
She builds her spacious dome
And all that trace her sacred ways
Will find a happy home

Shaker Hymn[2]

The Shakers saw their homes as the closest thing to heaven on earth, which meant that their goal was to shape the actual physical environment of the village after the traditional concept of heaven as the realm of infinite space. Since the meeting-

house was the most sacred place in the entire village, it is natural that this large hall was as open as possible. Although no contemporary structures existed to satisfy their way of life and their religion, the Shakers borrowed aspects of existing architectural styles and modified them. The construction of the first eastern Shaker meetinghouses in the 1780s combined the elements of English gambrel roofs with exposed, closely spaced beams, which were common in Dutch buildings. They created an interior structure without pillars that left the first floor an open area, a necessity for Shaker worship, which included dances that were an integral part of the religious meeting. The 1824 New Lebanon meetinghouse measured 44 by 32 feet of unencumbered area and was fitted with movable benches for the accommodation of both the Shakers and their visitors (see fig. 2-2).

The Shakers developed an innovative use of all available square footage within their structures, which they organized into distinctive patterns that were differentiated according to function. This resulted in a Shaker system of efficient design that was characterized by a profusion of built-in storage units and a repetition of peg rail units.[3] Built-in closets and cupboards were uncommon in single family New England houses, but the Shakers made the most of every inch of available space in each building. The most impressive example of Shaker built-in storage is the 1837 attic in the Canterbury Church Family dwelling house. This 35-foot-long room is equipped with two long storage areas under the eaves that contain 6 walk-in closets, 14

Fig. 2-1. Miniature Hanging Cupboard over Drawers, 1860–80. Canterbury, New Hampshire. Paper label affixed to inside of door with printed initials: N.W.R. Pine, cherry, iron, and brass hardware with traces of chrome yellow paint. Andrew D. Epstein. Provenance: John Keith Russell Antiques, Inc., South Salem, New York. Photo: Bruce White.

cupboards, and more than 100 drawers designed to house off-season bedding, clothing, and crockery.

The Shakers further regulated their lives through an extensive classification system of numbers and letters to indicate the location of stored items. All buildings were assigned letter designations, such as "D" for dwelling house, and each room, closet, and drawer was numbered, as recorded in several manuscript booklets in the collection of the Canterbury Shaker Museum Archives. This system would make it possible for a sister to be instructed to store a blanket for the summer in drawer 85, room 8, Building D. The 1837 Great Stone Dwelling at Enfield, New Hampshire, was fitted with 860 drawers, which eliminated the need for a box or a chest anywhere in the house[4]; the dining room in the same building was equipped with "cupboards and drawers which occupy the whole side of the room on either side."[5] The church family dining room at the

Hancock community had 369 drawers, 245 cupboards, and more than 100 full-sized doors.

The communal nature of the Shaker way of life gathered together into gospel order many people who shared one home to live as a unified family under Christ. From a practical standpoint, it made sense to eliminate any unnecessary furnishings that would require funds or time to maintain, move, or clean. To conserve space, Shaker furnishings were designed to hang from or be built into walls and to satisfy several needs at once or to be easily portable. Pegboard, placed about six feet above the floor, was a ubiquitous feature of nearly every Shaker dwelling house or workshop room and eliminated the need for free-standing furniture that took up valuable floor space. The miniature cupboard over drawers in figure 2-1 is an unusual, scaled-down version of a free-standing Shaker cupboard over a case of drawers. Although this tiny cupboard was clearly designed to hang from a peg

rail, its exact purpose—whether in the dwelling house or the workshop—is unknown.

From a functional standpoint, the Shakers' communal organization also demanded furniture that met the needs of many brothers and sisters living together. Large, centrally positioned tables in monasteries and baronial halls were part of the European medieval tradition, and similar trestle tables, which were originally intended to be dismantled and stowed away at the end of the meal, were adapted by the Shakers for communal dining. The typical Shaker table had the same basic support system and overall size (measuring up to twenty feet) in order to seat a large group of people, but the medial stretcher was moved from its position just above the floor to just beneath the top so that diners had more leg room (fig. 2-3). These tables were not taken apart but were given a permanent location in the family dining room. Thomas Brown, a member of the Watervliet, New York, community wrote in 1812: "The brethren and sisters generally eat at the same time at two long tables placed in the kitchen, men at one end and women at the other, during which time they sit on benches and are all silent."[6] The short length of this table, measuring only six feet, suggests it may have been designed specifically for use of the four ministry leaders who ate apart from the family brothers and sisters.

The design of the distinctive chairs in figure 2-4 is derived from eighteenth- and nineteenth-century American Windsor chairs, which are characterized by turned spindles; splayed, swell-tapered legs with four rungs; and shovel-shaped, undercut plank seats. They are strong, lightweight, and utilitarian, providing support for the lower back yet low enough to be pushed underneath the table and out of the way when not in use. According to written Shaker documentation on the history of the Canterbury community:

Fig. 2-3. Trestle Table, ca. 1830. Watervliet, New York. Cherry and curly maple. Courtesy John Keith Russell Antiques Inc., South Salem, New York. Photo: Luigi Pelletieri.

Instead of chairs at the dining table, the first Believers used long benches which accommodated some four or five persons each. They were not convenient, especially if one was obliged to leave the table before the others were ready. All were under the necessity of sitting just so far from the table. Elder Micajah Tucker (1762–1848) of the Canterbury, New Hampshire community who was an excellent wood workman has now (1834) furnished the dining hall with chairs very much to the satisfaction of the family generally. At this date [1892] they are all in good order."[7]

SETTING UP STRUCTURE

Order is the creation of beauty. It is heaven's first law, and the protection of souls. Keep all things in order, as keeping the law of heaven
The Youth's Guide in Zion[8]

Fig. 2-4. Attributed to Micajah Tucker (1764–1848). Dining Room Chairs, 1834. Canterbury, New Hampshire. Birch and pine with red stain. Canterbury Shaker Village, Inc., Canterbury, New Hampshire, 1982.113. Photo: Luigi Pelletieri.

The Shakers embraced gospel order as a guiding principle that permeated every aspect of their daily lives and determined the physical organization of their community, the execution of their dance worship, and the acceptance of their hierarchical governance structure. The spiritual order of the community was reflected in the actual layout of each village, which was divided into several different families or "orders" (novitiate, junior, and senior) of up to one hundred people, each order based on progressive levels of commitment to the Shaker faith in terms of spiritual development and physical possessions.

Unlike the layout of neighboring towns, where individual houses were often spaced to provide privacy, Shaker structures were arranged closely together according to function. Although there was no universal village plan, the meetinghouse was often placed near the dwelling house, and the

barns were usually adjacent to the brethren's workshops. However, hierarchical concerns or common sense called for the segregation of certain members. The children brought in by parents who joined the community, as well as the orphans raised by the United Society, lived with their caretakers separately from the fully covenanted adult members. The elderly and infirm were secluded in the infirmary building, where they could recuperate from illness while protecting the rest of the community from contagious disease. The four ministry elders and eldresses occupied their own apartments, dining room, and workshops apart from the family as a whole. This segregation prevented the leaders from mingling with the rank-and-file members and perhaps developing friendships that might promote favoritism. Neutrality was important for them, because the ministry had the final authority in resolving domestic matters.

Dance affirmed and celebrated that each Believer had a communal rather than an individual relationship with God, and it was therefore a powerful symbol of order in the Shakers' cultural system. Early dance was ecstatic and individualistic, and any believer could spontaneously express himself or herself with whirling, jumping, and falling to the floor. In the early nineteenth century, discipline, order, and organization were imposed on worship practices, and the most irregular and charismatic aspects of Shaker dance were standardized. Group marches and dances were introduced by the central ministry at New Lebanon and circulated to all the other communities. Brothers and sisters were instructed to perform set patterns, which they rehearsed in evening practice sessions to guarantee proper harmony and order. No detail was omitted.

At the Canterbury, New Hampshire, community, a remarkable survival of this precision is visible in the red pine floor of the meetinghouse. As the dance formations became increasingly intricate, the Shakers embedded cues made of wooden plugs or copper tacks in the dance floor. These cues form five rows of markers, some straight and others in flaring lines, presumably to keep the brothers and sisters in unison at all times. In this sense, there is

a parallel between the regimented choreography of Shaker dance and the ritual of daily life. The Believers also controlled circulation through the village with solid devices such as granite walks, steps with iron railings, and stone walls, all of which strictly regulated the passage of people from one place to another.

The Shakers created a clear and functional hierarchical structure to administer the spiritual, domestic, and commercial needs of each community. More specifically, the Millennial Laws of 1845 provide an extensive outline of the General Organization of Society, that is, the community structure of different families and the system of governing by the ministry, elders, and deacons as originally formulated by Father Joseph Meacham in the 1790s. This document also defined the responsibilities, roles, and duties of various leadership levels within the Shaker community.

According to Father Joseph's organizational structure, supreme authority over the whole United Society of Believers was vested in the central or lead ministry at New Lebanon, made up of two elders and two eldresses who received their inspiration directly from Mother Ann. These leaders appointed the branch ministries consisting in turn of two elders and eldresses serving several outlying societies, which were usually grouped into bishoprics, determined by geographic proximity. Each community contained several families of up to one hundred individual members who were to "acknowledge and look to their [family] Elders as their lead and protection, in all things." Hence, the government of all spiritual matters was entrusted to the eldership, who received their orders directly from the lead ministry at New Lebanon. The temporal affairs of each family were the specific realm of the deacons, generally two of each sex, who took their instructions from the family elders. It was their responsibility to see to "the domestic concerns of the family in which they reside" and to manage the daily work of the family. Four trustees were selected to oversee each family's finances and business transactions with the World's people. Believers were instructed to consult the proper authority for the specific tasks. In this way, gospel order was maintained throughout the Shaker society, and appointments always moved from head to foot.[9]

Their dedication to order as a guiding principal finds physical expression in the design of their furniture, whose form is determined by the concepts of balance, pattern, hierarchy, and scale. Balance entails a state of equilibrium between opposing forces. Symmetry, the distribution of equivalent forms and spaces on either side of a vertical or horizontal axis, is the most common method for achieving balance. Bilateral symmetry, in which the parts on either side of the axis are mirror images of each other, is central to most eighteenth- and nineteenth-century Worldly furniture. For example, in a chest of drawers, a sideboard, or a cupboard, the case is divided visually by a vertical axis or center-line in which each half mirrors the other. Although

some Shaker furniture follows this common pattern, other Shaker cabinetmakers regularly moved away from this rigidly held aesthetic and developed many asymmetrical forms, which can achieve balance by presenting equivalent but nonmatching forms on either side of a vertical or horizontal axis. Unbridled by Worldly fashion, customer whim, or the traditionally conservative apprenticeship system, Shaker craftsmen were able to create furniture to suit the community's specific needs, which often involved developing new combinations and layouts to suit the task.

Counters and sewing desks are the most prominent examples of asymmetrical arrangements seen in Shaker work furniture. Often built as long horizontal cases, they present a highly organized though asymmetrical layout with different shapes placed on either side of the center of the piece. In a counter built by Grove Wright (fig. 2-5), for

Fig. 2-5. Attributed to Grove Wright (1789–1861). Counter, ca. 1830. Hancock, Massachusetts. Curly maple, cherry, and pine, with bone escutcheons. Bob and Aileen Hamilton. Photo: David Hollinger.

example, a bank of four short drawers is juxtaposed opposite a wider bank of three drawers, occupying one-third and two-thirds of the case, respectively. The opposing sections are balanced successfully, despite the different horizontal dimensions given to each half. The arrangements of unequal parts are organized around an imaginary visual centerline rather than a rigidly placed, geometrically accurate centerline. Maine and New Hampshire sewing desks regularly display an asymmetrical layout. The example in figure 2-6 has a lower storage unit containing two unequal banks of three drawers—probably designed to hold specific implements—while the gallery above is fitted with a central door flanked by six short drawers. The unidentified maker of the striking washstand in figure 2-7 skillfully exploited the asymmetrical balance between the large single door and bank of three short drawers punctuated by solid walnut knobs.

One of the most asymmetrically balanced pieces is the cupboard-over-drawers-over cupboard shown in figure 7-11. The original Shaker piece first appeared in an exhibition at the Whitney Museum in New York City in 1986 and was illustrated in the accompanying catalogue. Almost twenty years later, physical examination by furniture historian John Kirk revealed that the piece had always been turned upside down.[10] When the piece is right side up, it is clear that, although the four central drawers are asymmetrically placed in relationship to the centerline, they take up about half the height of the piece when taken together with the small cupboard below, creating a pleasing visual balance to the single large cupboard above.

Pattern involves the repetitive use of similar shapes, forms, or spaces to create unity and organization within a design. The most common configuration is found in cases of drawers, with the

Fig. 2-6. Attributed to Henry Green (1844–1931), Sewing Desk, ca. 1860. Alfred, Maine. Birch and pine, with red paint and porcelain and metal pulls. Courtesy John Keith Russell Antiques Inc., South Salem, New York. Photo: Luigi Pelletieri.

Fig. 2-7. Washstand, ca. 1830. Enfield, New Hampshire. Pine with walnut knobs, yellow paint and steel catch. Robert and Katharine Booth. Photo: Don Roman.

Fig. 2-8. Washstand, ca. 1830. Hancock, Massachusetts. Cherry and pine with red wash. Robert and Katharine Booth. Photo: Don Roman.

reiteration of similar elements. In one arrangement, each drawer in a single bank is smaller than the one below it. Drawers can also be graduated in sets, or more commonly in pairs, decreasing in size from bottom to top. In other cases, none of the drawers is graduated. The alternation of two doors with three raised panels across the façade of the wash-stand shown in figure 2-8 reflects an awareness of pattern and results in an unusual yet harmonious rhythm that avoids the monotony of a flat surface.

The position of parts and their importance in terms of function, shape, or size relative to the overall arrangement defines the hierarchy of a piece (see fig. 2-2). In most Shaker storage units consisting of a cupboard over drawers, greater importance is given to the single door by centering it at eye level above a bank of drawers. This combination is probably the norm in Shaker furniture design.

Scale refers to the size of an object relative to its surroundings, which includes other objects, the object's users, and the space it inhabits. In Shaker furniture, the dimensional relationship of a piece to its immediate space ranges from a diminutive seven-drawer case made at Hancock (fig. 2-9) to the 860 built-in drawers found in the Church Family dwelling house at Enfield, New Hampshire. Because of the institutional requirements of communal living, Shaker furniture often grew to monumental size and proportions not seen in Worldly design. Tailoring counters ranging from six to twelve feet long and four feet wide, trestle tables spanning over twenty feet in length, meetinghouse benches measuring 162 inches (see fig. 2-1), and washstands over five feet long (fig. 2-8) to accommodate several members simultaneously were not uncommon in Shaker dwelling-house, workshop, or meetinghouse spaces.

Fig. 2-9. Sewing Case, ca. 1830. Hancock, Massachusetts. Cherry and pine with wrought iron and brass. Robert and Katharine Booth. Photo: Don Roman.

THE PURSUIT OF PERFECTION

> Anything may, with strict propriety, be called
> perfect, which perfectly answers the purpose
> for which it was designed. [and therefore was
> pleasing to God.] A circle may be called a
> perfect circle, when it is perfectly round; an
> apple may be called perfect, when it is per-
> fectly sound, having no defect in it; and so of
> a thousand other things.
>
> Calvin Green and Seth Y. Wells[11]

Believers trying to create a heaven on earth as part
of their daily routine strive for perfection in all
things temporal. The need to make the connection
between the heavenly and earthly spheres and integrate both worlds is clearly expressed in several of
the Shaker spirit drawings (see Chapter 5 in this
volume). In the Shaker written explanation and key
entitled "Explanation of the Holy City with its
Various Parts and Appendixes pointed Out," completed in 1843, the author, Father Adam, explains
that the plan of the City of the New Jerusalem is a
perfect pattern of the high City in the Heavens,
which is right over this, the Holy City on Earth
Mount Lebanon.[12]

From the beginning, the New Lebanon ministry
established a pattern for all Shaker settlements to
follow in the areas of theology, religious practice,
and architecture. In each community, the Believers'
devotional services were conducted in the meetinghouse, which assumed a place of central importance. The leadership determined that all
meetinghouses should have a uniform appearance
and selected Moses Johnson (1752–1842), one of
the original signers of the Enfield, New Hampshire,
covenant and a carpenter by trade, to take charge
of framing the building at the center of the Shaker
faith. With the help of brethren from the New
Lebanon community, he designed and constructed
the first meetinghouse—a two-and-a-half-story
building measuring 44 feet wide by 32 feet deep
with a gambrel roof, dormers, single shutters, and
double doors for the brothers and sisters, as well
as separate entrances for the four ministry leaders,
who occupied the second-floor apartments. The

building was painted white; its interior woodwork
was colored a Prussian blue—an expensive pigment reserved exclusively for use in religious
spaces—with yellow-ocher floors. This building
established the style of Shaker religious architecture; between 1785 and 1794 Brother Moses reproduced nine, and possibly ten, other churches in
Maine, New Hampshire, Massachusetts,
Connecticut, and New York, after the original
pattern.

Perfection required patterns in their work as well
as in their faith. Elder Benjamin Smith, a talented
woodworker at Canterbury, was "conscientious that
all his handwork should keep close to the perfect
pattern of the Master Workman—who drew his
affection in early days."[13] The Shakers' dedication
to perfection is found in their love of patterns and
precise measurement. The only way to create a
perfect circle was to use a specific instrument, such
as a compass, in the same way that yardsticks were
highly regarded as accurate measuring tools.
Consequently, the Shakers made simple rulers from
beautiful pieces of wood, including tiger maple, in
varying lengths, with hand-stamped increments to
perform specific tasks, such as tailoring.

Patterns played an important part in the workshops and were developed to ensure uniformity in
a variety of materials and products, both for sale
to the World's people and for home use. The
Shakers at Sabbathday Lake, Maine, anticipated
progressive trends by adapting to the introduction
of the metric measures in the United States in
1877, a system that appealed to them because it
was so logical and exact. That same year, they
began to mass-produce wooden dry measures,
ranging from a capacity of one-tenth of a liter to
twenty liters, for sale to the World (see fig. 3-15).
Metrics were very much in keeping with the Shaker
ethic of applying the latest, most scientific
Worldly ideas to their own industries. Another
example of this dedication to precision is the very
successful production furniture business at Mount
Lebanon that commenced in the 1860s. The
acceptance of machine technology and standardization of parts made assembly-line replication

possible. The Shakers even numbered the chairs they made and advertised in their yearly catalogues according to size, ranging from 0 (the smallest) to 7 (the largest).

Templates enabled the Believers to make exact duplicates of many objects—from tinware to oval boxes, cloaks, bonnets, baskets, and furniture. Three cabriole leg forms, which match those on surviving tripod stands, were discovered in the eaves of the 1815 carpenters' shop at the Pleasant Hill, Kentucky, community during the twentieth-century restoration of the building. In his journal, Brother Maurice Thomas of Kentucky Hill recorded that on Wednesday, October 15, 1817, "Micajah Bernett and my self made some patterns,"[14] a pos-

sible reference to templates for furniture parts such as these.

The chest in figure 2-10, with its unusual combination of shallow and deep drawers, was found in 1988 at the Canterbury Shaker village, in the basement of a building where the community's thriving textile industry was located during the twentieth century. Shaker trustees Emeline Hart (1834–1914) and Lucy Ann Shepard (1836–1926) had established a business called the Hart and Shepard Company during the 1890s to protect the Shakers' commercial interests from Worldly imitators. They successfully designed, produced, and marketed their famous cloaks and Ivy League letter sweaters for sale to the World (see figs. 3-23, 3-25). The

Fig. 2-10. Case of Drawers, ca. 1840. Canterbury, New Hampshire. Pine with red paint. Canterbury Shaker Village, Inc., Canterbury, New Hampshire, 1988.498. Photo: Bill Finney.

shallow drawers are ideally suited to store flat pieces and the deep drawers to hold bonnets, suggesting the chest was originally designed specifically for this purpose in the mid-nineteenth-century. When this case was found by the Canterbury Shaker Village Museum after the last sister died, the chest still contained a large number of paper patterns, some cloak fabric, and related materials that were used in the textile business.

THE TEST OF TIME

> Do all your work as though you had a thousand years to live on earth and as you would if you knew you must die tomorrow.
>
> Mother Ann Lee[15]

For the Shakers, a day's work was viewed in terms of productivity and fulfillment, rather than the length of time spent. To avoid rushing, the Shakers economized on time by establishing a definite daily schedule. Diary and journal references provide insight into the daily routine, which is described by one man in his manuscript entitled "Narrative of Four month's residence among the Shakers at Watervliet":

> the hours for rising were 5 o'clock in the Summer, and half past 5 in the Winter [a half hour earlier in some communities]—the Family all rise at the Toll of the Bell, and in less than ten minutes, vacated the Bed Rooms;—the Sisters, then distributed themselves throughout the Rooms, and made up all the Beds, putting every thing in the most perfect order, before Breakfast;—the Brothers proceeded to their various employments, and made a commencement for the day; the Cows were milked, and the Horses were fed. At 7 o'clock the Bell rang for Breakfast, but it was ten minutes after, when we went to the Tables. After Breakfast, all proceeded immediately to their respective employments, and continued industriously occupied until ten minutes to twelve o'clock, when the Bell announced dinner. Farmers then left the field, and Mechanics their

Shops, all washed their hands, and formed procession again, and marched to Dinner.... Immediately after Dinner, they went to work again...and continued steady at it until the Bell announced Supper.... At eight o'clock all work was ended for the day.[16]

Believers also were given time to develop several specialized job skills. If a brother had experience in a certain trade, he devoted the major part of his time to perfecting it and, if qualified, he assumed responsibility for that workshop. Brethren were also encouraged to master two or more callings in the belief that "If you improve in one talent, God will give you more."[17] This diversified approach not only prevented boredom, but it also enabled the community to be less dependent on the contributions of a few key members of the society. For example, in addition to woodworking, Richard McNemar of Union Village, Ohio, was a printer, a composer, and a preacher; Henry DeWitt of Mount Lebanon was a shoemaker and a bookbinder; and Henry Blinn of Canterbury was a dentist, a beekeeper, a teacher, and an historian. The life of Brother Isaac Newton Youngs epitomizes the varied occupations pursued by one individual, as recorded in his "Biography in Verse":

> I'm overrun with work and chores
> Upon the farm or within doors
> Which every way I turn my eyes;
> Enough to fill me with surprise.
> Of tayl'ring, Join'ring, farming too,
> Almost all kinds that are to do,
> Blacksmithing, Tinkering, mason work,
> When could I find time to shirk?
> Clock work, Jenny work, keeping school
> Enough to puzzle any fool.
> An endless list of chores and notions,
> To keep me in perpetual motion.[18]

Released from the vagaries of fashion or the demands of the marketplace, the Shakers faced no pressures to hurry their work. Shaker account books kept primarily by the family deacons and trustees record more than just a summary of hours spent on a specific task. Brother Isaac Newton

Youngs, a clockmaker, was acutely aware of exactly how he spent his time:

> October, 1816. Finished a cheap kind of time-piece, having made it in about 22 hours.

> July 1820. 4th. Finished a striking clock. No. 8. I began it in May 1819 & worked at it by little at a time & I reckon it took me about 40 days to make the clock & case.

> I meant to have written some useful remarks in this book from experiments. But alas time flies & I am no more in time![19]

Brother Isaac refers to his timepiece as cheap—not in the cost or quality of materials—but in the amount of time he spent creating it.

It is not surprising that this fascination with time finds physical expression in the design and construction of clocks and watches. Shaker brothers at Mount Lebanon and Watervliet, New York, produced wall and floor clocks for their own use, as well as for the Believers at other communities. Placed primarily in halls, these timepieces insured the punctuality that was essential to orderly communal living. Although the brass works are similar to those made by Worldly clockmakers, the pared-down design of the cases reflects the Shakers' religious beliefs. Constructed of local woods and free of costly veneers, inlay, and brass embellishments, Shaker timepieces bear little relation in form to high-style examples, which were usually characterized by broken-arched bonnets, ogee bracket feet, and elaborate moldings. The most severe examples of Shaker clocks are rectangular boxes fitted with only one hole cut to receive the glass covering the dial. The surface treatment is also carried out in accordance with the Millennial Laws, which strongly prohibit the use of "superfluously finished or flowery painted clocks,"[20] as seen in the Worldly example shown in figure 6-20. The Believers consciously rejected the fantastic rather than functional paint-decorated façade, which is a distinguishing characteristic of the Fancy style.

SHUNNING SUPERFLUITY

> All work done, or things made in the Church for their own use ought to be faithfully and well done, but plain and without superfluity. … Plainness and simplicity in both word and deed is becoming the Church and the people of God. Order and conveniency and decency in things temporal.
>
> Joseph Meacham[21]

It is only through spiritual simplicity that derives from self-understanding that the Believer may real-

Fig. 2-11. Side Chair with Tilters, ca. 1850. Mount Lebanon, New York. Figured maple, cane seat, and pewter tilters. Andrew D. Epstein; formerly collection of Edward Deming Andrews and Faith Andrews. Photo: Andrew Epstein.

Fig. 2-12. Freegift Wells
(1785–1871). Armless Rocker, ca.
1830. Watervliet, New York.
Stamped on proper left front
post: FW. Maple and yellow
paint and tape seat. Andrew D.
Epstein. Photo: Andrew Epstein.

ize his basic Christian right and responsibility of self-fulfillment. Shakers value human fulfillment highly and believe that man fulfills himself by being nothing more nor less than himself.[22]

The objects that the Shakers made and used also reflect this philosophy. Dining surfaces were set without textiles, centerpieces, or fancy china, according to Mother Ann's advice to her followers: "Never put on silver spoons for me nor tablecloths, but let your tables be clean enough to eat on without cloths and if you do not know what to do with them, give them to the poor."[23] It is clear from Hervey Elkins's 1853 description of the dining hall

in the Enfield, New Hampshire, Great Stone Dwelling that "the tables, without cloth are furnished with white ware."[24] Instead of relying on the elaborately decorated ceramics that were produced abroad and widely imported into this country (see fig. 6-34), they purchased plain white ironstone from England.

In reference to furniture, "beadings, mouldings and cornices which are merely for fancy may not be made by Believers," as stated in the Millennial Laws.[25] Early and classic Shaker furniture exhibits restrained decorative elaborations on structural forms, such as a rounded table edge or a turned chair pommel (figs. 2-11, 2-12). Moldings were used in moderation, both at mid-case and on the cornice, and these are relatively small and simple, consisting primarily of quarter-round or bull-nose-shape elements. This guiding principle finds physical manifestation in some lift-top boxes that are fitted with a single board pine plank (fig. 2-13). Either integral or applied, the edges are square and are not enhanced with the addition of complex molded pieces, as is often found in Worldly pieces of the same period.

The stand in figure 2-14 is remarkable both for its pared-down design and for its documentation. This type of pedestal table, made up of a simply turned shaft without beading, a round top, and arched spider legs devoid of moldings, is adapted from a Sheraton prototype. Constructed of solid cherry, the Shaker stand retains its original varnish finish. Portable stands like this one probably held candles initially; according to the 1845 Millennial Laws, one of every two stands should be provided for the occupants of every retiring room.[26] By the 1850s, however, the stands may have served to support lamps and probably also migrated into sewing rooms, seed shops, and kitchens. Stamped on the rectangular cleat beneath the circular top of this stand are the names Sister Aseneth and Elder Sister Ruth, the latter probably a reference to Ruth Landon (1776–1850), who was appointed first female in the parent ministry at New Lebanon. Sister Aseneth Clark (1780–1857) was her assistant. This stand must have been made in 1837 for these two leading figures, who likely shared a retiring room in the meetinghouse.

The drawers and doors of most Shaker built-in and free-standing furniture are fitted with simply turned hardwood pulls. During the period of revival and inspiration known as the Era of Manifestations or the Era of Mother's Work (see Chapter 5 in this volume), strict adherence to the Millennial Orders became increasingly important. According to an entry in the *New Lebanon Ministry Sisters' Journal* on Saturday, July 4, 1831, cabinetmaker "David Rowley has been employed for several days in taking out Brass knobs and putting in their stead wood knobs or buttons (on furniture). This is because brass ones are considered superfluous, thro spiritual communication."[27]

CREATING CLEANLINESS

> Clean your rooms well; for good spirits will not live where there is dirt. There is no dirt in heaven.
>
> Mother Ann Lee[28]

For Mother Ann Lee, the meaning of the Lord's command to sweep clean was for the brethren and sisters to cleanse their hearts of the stains of sin.

Fig. 2-13. Box, ca. 1830. Alfred, Maine. Pine with green paint and iron hinges. Courtesy John Keith Russell Antiques Inc., South Salem, New York. Photo: Luigi Pelletieri.

Fig. 2-14. Attributed to Samuel Humphrey Turner (1775–1842). Tripod Stand, 1837. New Lebanon, New York. Stamped on underside of cleat: SISTER ASENETH ELD.S RUTH 1837. Cherry with varnish. Robert and Katharine Booth. Photo: Don Roman.

Fig. 2-15. Bed, ca. 1840.
Harvard, Massachusetts. Maple,
pine, and paint. Courtesy John
Keith Russell Antiques Inc.,
South Salem, New York. Photo:
Luigi Pelletieri.

Spiritual purity was literally expressed in physical hygiene. During the Era of Manifestations, purification rituals were introduced in which bands of Shakers wielding invisible brooms marched through the community dwelling houses and workshops miming spiritual spring cleaning.[29] The Hancock sweeping gift, performed in 1843, raised the everyday activities of Shaker sisters to the level of spiritual activity.[30]

According to a visitor to the Watervliet, New York, community, certain days were set aside for scrubbing the brethren's workshops "by sweeping the walls, and removing every cobweb from the corners and under the workbenches, and washing the floors clean by scrubbing them with sand. By doing this they would remove all the devils and wicked spirits that might be lodging in the different buildings; for where cobwebs and dust were permitted to accumulate, there the evil spirits hide themselves."[31] It is not surprising that the most famous Shaker invention—the flat broom, which proved to be far more efficient than the round broom then in use—was introduced by Theoodore Bates of Watervliet in 1798.[32]

The distinctive design of the Shaker chair evolved from the Shakers' dual position of being in the World and yet separate from it. They refined the New England ladder-back form by eliminating the decorative turnings on the posts and stretchers and often substituting a woven wool or cotton seat for the traditional splint or rush. The resulting design is an outward expression of the Shakers' internal concepts: simplicity, utility, perfection in craftsmanship, and above all cleanliness. Ladder-back chairs were routinely suspended upside down from peg rails to prevent dust from settling on the seat. Some other early chairs were fitted with rattan cane (fig. 2-11), a natural fiber that was appealing to the Shakers because, unlike upholstered material or fabric, it resisted insect infestation. Woven cane also contributes to the physical and visual lightness, delicacy, and portability of Shaker seating furniture. To promote ease of cleaning, beds in retiring rooms were fitted with wooden wheels to make them easily moved (fig. 2-15).

It is not surprising that unlike Worldly dwellings, Shaker interiors were equipped with a minimum number of textiles such as curtains, quilts, or carpets, because they were hidden receptacles for dust, which could be injurious to health if inhaled. Charles Nordhoff described his impressions of the Shakers rooms that he visited in 1874 as follows:

> if there is a stove in the room, a small broom and dust-pan hang near it, and a wood-box stands by it; scrapers and mats at the door invite you to make clean your shoes; and if the roads are muddy or snowy, a broom hung up outside the outer door mutely requests you to brush off all the mud or snow. The strips of carpet are easily lifted, and the floor beneath is as clean as though it were a table to be eaten from. The walls are bare of pictures; not only because all ornament is wrong, but because frames are places where dust will lodge. The bedstead is a cot, covered with the bedclothing, and easily moved away to allow of dusting and sweeping. Mats meet you at the outer door and at every inner door. The floors of the halls and dining-room are polished until they shine.[33]

Laundry buildings express better than any other

Shaker structure the Believers' desire for cleanliness and order, which are at the heart of their religious beliefs. At Canterbury, the unpredictability of New England weather necessitated the remodeling of the 1796 structure so that washing could be done on a regular schedule. In 1854 a steam-drying room was installed on the second floor above the Shaker-made washing machines below, which used water for cleaning as well as mechanical power. A 16-horsepower steam engine powered the washing machine, including the wringers and the dumbwaiter that hauled the wet clothes upstairs to wooden racks, where steam pipes from the boiler below did double duty to dry them. The sisters then ironed and sorted clothes and household textiles upstairs for the entire family of several hundred individuals.

Ventilation, bathing, and sanitation promoted cleanliness along with good health. The Shakers valued fresh air and introduced innovative ventilation systems into their dwelling houses and workshops. As a common practice, the lower sash of each exterior window was raised several inches to permit the insertion of a strip of solid wood that allowed air circulation between the now-separated upper and lower sashes while preventing a direct draft.[34] Interior windows had adjustable transoms made of wooden slats that allowed air to move between rooms.

The connection between the symbolic cleansing of the soul and the actual washing of the body was expressed by one of Mother Ann's followers from England when he preached: "What is cleansing the hands . . . but the confession of sin?"[35] The Shakers immediately recognized the correlation between baptism and bathing, and they promoted washing as part of their regular routine. They paid careful attention to hygiene and developed sanitary plumbing systems in their communities by various ingenious means. They moved fresh running water long distances through log or iron pipes, directing it up from springs below or down from mountains above for drinking, washing, and bathing. The seriousness of the water issue and the Shakers' determination to keep improving their municipal

distribution system can be seen in Peter Foster's 1849 map, which documents the Canterbury community's water lines.[36]

For spiritual as well as practical reasons, disease was regarded as an offense to God, and cleanliness, as well as good health, was deemed a necessity. Consequently, the Believers had a strong commitment to preventive and palliative health care that far surpassed that of most towns and villages in the United States. A state-of-the-art infirmary, staffed by the most knowledgeable brethren and sisters, was a standard feature in each community. It provided a quiet place to isolate sick members in order to help prevent the spread of contagious diseases. By the middle of the nineteenth century, the infirmary was probably the most modern facility in the village. The patients at Canterbury were the first Shakers to have access to an up-to-date water closet, which was built in the upstairs hall of their infirmary in 1852.[37] Well-stocked with medicines and equipment for the comfort and restoration of ailing patients, the infirmary was designed to ensure the quality of life of aging individuals. As a result of progressive medicine and compassionate health care, it is not surprising that the Shakers outlived their Worldly contemporaries, often reaching the ages of eighty, ninety, and even one hundred years.

DEFINING FUNCTION

> These people are strict utilitarians in all they do. The first inquiry is, "will it be useful."
> David R. Lamson[38]

Although the Shakers were unaware of the aesthetic implications of Louis Sullivan's doctrine of "form follows function," their literature contains such phrases as "beauty rests on utility. That which has in itself the highest use possesses the greatest beauty."[39]

From a spiritual standpoint, the Shakers avoided decoration and ornament in material goods because it encouraged the sin of pride, which could turn the Believers' thoughts from worship to Worldly possessions. Brother Hervey Elkins wrote in 1853 that "an arbitrary inhibition rests upon statuary, paintings, watches, jewelry of all kinds, knives of more than two blades, sofas, divans, musical instruments, and whatever gorgeous appendage would serve to feed vanity and pride, more than subserve the practical utility of civilized life."[40]

An important motive in building a functional piece of furniture presumably often involved adapting old forms and developing new combinations over time. These include small work stands with push-pull drawers that could be accessed on either end to accommodate two sisters working simultaneously (fig. 2-16). Small pieces of specialized work furniture intended for the sisters' sewing activities have drawers and doors of various sizes, numbers, and layout supported on square tapering or turned legs. Some diminutive sewing cases, such as the one in figure 2-9, are equipped with a drop leaf in the back and a swing-out forged iron support attached to the rear rail that allowed for the extension of the work surface. The two pull-out battens

contained within a pine housing on either side of the front may have been designed to hang additional sewing accoutrements or finished products. Other more massive sewing desks from New Hampshire and Maine, including the one in figure 2-6 that provided both storage space and expandable surface area for textile activities, were regularly fitted with large rectangular pull-out boards in front to facilitate cutting large pieces of material.

The Shaker trustees who oversaw all business dealings with the World were entrusted with all financial recordkeeping activities for the community. According to the Millennial Laws, "Writing desks may not be used by common members, unless they have much public writing to do. But writing desks may be used as far as is thought proper by the Lead."[41] The monumental secretary in figure 2-17 represents an expansion of the Worldly desk and is designed with dual cupboards containing shelves above; double drop leaf writing surfaces enclosing pigeonholes; and three long drawers below to provide identical workspace for both users.

At first glance, the placement of the small central drawer in the four-by-two-foot box (fig. 2-18) appears to be a later addition, but on closer inspection, one can see that it is part of the original construction. Although one might expect to see a flat bottom when lifting the lid, instead there is a tunnel with the built-in drawer extending the full depth of the case. The presence of the exterior lock indicates it was clearly designed for a specific—yet still undetermined—nineteenth-century purpose.

THE PURSUIT OF PROGRESS

> We have a right to improve the inventions of man, so far as is useful and necessary, but not to vain glory, or anything superfluous.
> Father Joseph Meacham[42]

Forms, fashions, customs, external rules all have to bow to the fiat of evolution and progress toward that which is more perfect. This need not alarm the most conservative

Fig. 2-16. Push-Pull Stand, ca. 1830. Hancock, Massachusetts. Cherry and pine. Robert and Katharine Booth. Photo: Don Roman.

Fig. 2-17. Double Trustees' Desk, ca. 1850. Probably Watervliet, New York. Cherry and pine with yellow paint. American Folk Art Museum, New York, 2004.8.1. Photo: Andy Duback.

Believer. For unless we keep pace with the progress of the universe our individual progress will be an impossibility. We shall be whirled off at some side station and relegated to the limbo of worn-out superannuated and used-up institutions.

Oliver Hampton
Union Village, Ohio, 1887[43]

The opinions expressed by Father Joseph Meacham (d. 1796) and Oliver Hampton (1816–1901) almost a century apart confirm that the Shakers were always searching for new technologies to simplify their lives and streamline their work, unlike the Amish, with whom they are often confused. Throughout their history, the Shakers have embraced spiritual, social, and mechanical progress in every aspect of

their daily work and worship. Brethren and sisters were constantly striving for perfection on an individual basis, as well as trying to make their communities mirror heavenly ideals on earth. Believers were also forward-looking in their approach to social reform. Mother Ann taught that God was both Father and Mother, which led to the belief that men and women were equal in leadership and responsibility in Shaker communities (see Chapter 4 in this volume). This was clearly an innovative concept in the eighteenth century, at a time when women could not own property and legally were regarded as the possession of men. During the nineteenth century, Eldress Dorothy Durgin (1825–1898) of Canterbury, New Hampshire, was a proponent of pioneering reforms, including the introduction of musical instruments into the faith. Eldress Mary Antoinette Doolittle of Mount Lebanon edited the Shaker newspaper—whose title she changed to *Shaker AND Shakeress*—during the 1870s. The Believers were also far ahead of their time during the Civil War in their support of racial equality and pacifism, as well as in their condemnation of capital punishment at the turn of the twentieth century.

Everything, from their physical plant to the products the Shakers invented and sold to the World or made for themselves, reflects an interest in mechanical progress. Brother Elisha Myrick of Harvard explained this philosophy when in 1855 he wrote that "every improvement relieving human toil or facilitating labor [gives] time and opportunity for moral, mechanical, scientific, and intellectual improvement and the cultivation of the finer and higher qualities of the human mind."[44]

Although most rural barns were built to support individual family units, Shaker families were larger and required more massive buildings to house agricultural activities than their Worldly counterparts did. The Shakers enlarged the standard two-story rectangular structure to accommodate the larger herds that were essential to their communal economy, and they introduced innovative designs that reflect their pursuit of efficiency and commitment to progress. Shaker barns were a marvel of ingenuity,

whether they were constructed with ramps at either end so hay wagons could pass through and out in quick succession, or equipped with trap doors behind each stall to collect manure, or fitted with troughs of constantly running water from which the cows could drink at all times.

The workshops for brethren and sisters were also supplied with state-of-the-art equipment designed specifically to suit their needs. Carpenters had machinery for matching boards with tongue-and-groove joints invented by Brothers Henry Bennett and Amos Bishop in 1828 probably for use on flooring and siding. An improved lathe with a screw feeder to turn broom handles more efficiently was introduced by Brother Jesse Wells in 1805, and weavers of splints and work baskets were supplied with tools devised by Brothers Daniel Boler and Daniel Crossman. The seed shops had presses for printing seed bags and herb packages, as well as the machinery for filling them.[45] The sisters' textile work was enhanced through the use of Shaker-made steam-iron stoves and commercially produced power looms, as well as hose and sweater knitting machines.

Throughout their history, the Shakers believed in sharing their inventions with the World. These included what appears to be the first wrinkle-resistant fabric, perfected by the Sabbathday Lake Shakers in the 1840s.[46] They placed cotton or wool fabric into a special press with paper that had been treated with zinc chloride and then they applied heat and pressure. The resulting fabric was shiny and smooth on the top side and was also water-resistant. According to folk legend, Sister Tabitha Babbitt of Harvard devised the circular saw in 1810; however, there is no documentation to substantiate this popular myth.[47] Brother Alonzo Hollister of Mount Lebanon lent his heated, airtight container used in the making of sugar to a visitor named Gail Borden, who conducted experiments in the Shakers' workshops, and this eventually led to his formula for condensed milk.[48]

Unfortunately, Worldly businessmen took advantage of the Shakers' generosity and profited from their ingenuity. In order to protect their own inter-

ests, the Believers patented some of their major contributions, such as Sister Emeline Hart's revolving oven in 1876 and David Parker's water-powered commercial washing machine in 1858 and his sarsaparilla lozenges in 1866.[49] However, the Society was reluctant to invoke government protection, which they regarded as a necessary evil at best, preferring to rely on the inherent quality in Shaker-made goods to attract consumers. Consequently, the number of Shaker ideas that were patented is small in relation to those that were freely shared. Perhaps the best-known example of Shaker ingenuity is Brother George O. Donnell's metal ball-and-socket mechanism or tilter for chairs submitted to the United States Patent Office in 1852 (fig. 2-19).

Fig. 2-19. George O. Donnell (1823–w.1852). Patent Model for Button Joint Tilter, 1852. New Lebanon, New York. Bird's eye maple and tape, with brass tilters and ferrules. Jane and Gerald Katcher. Photo: courtesy of David A. Schorsch and Eileen M. Smiles.

Fig. 2-20. Armed Rocker, ca. 1830. Canterbury, New Hampshire. Maple or birch, cherry with red wash, varnish and wool tape. Bob and Aileen Hamilton. Photo: David Hollinger.

The Shakers often took the realities of human behavior into consideration when making design decisions. They recognized the natural tendency for Believers to tip their straight chairs back on the rear posts and took pains "to prevent wear and tear of carpets and marring of floors caused by the corners of the back posts"[50] by adding tilting buttons or swivel feet to the hind legs. They introduced this ingenious device attached to the rear legs to allow "the chairs [to] take their natural motion of rocking backward and forward while the metallic feet rest unmoved: flat and square on the floor or carpet."[51] Although the wooden tilter is common in Shaker full-size chairs, the pewter variation found in figure 2-11 is rare.

Furniture made for community use also reflects the Shakers' attitude toward adaptation, improvement, and change. Whereas fabric tapes were used in the eighteenth and nineteenth centuries for garters, clothing ties, apron strings, and carpet bindings, the idea of weaving cloth strips together to form a seat probably originated with the Shakers about 1830 (fig. 2-20). Unlike rush or wooden splint seating, these woven seats had the advantage of being colorful, comfortable, durable, and easy to install. The tape is carried over a wooden frame in two layers with a filling of horsehair in between, which results in a firm, buoyant seat.[52] The earliest tapes were woven of homespun, home-dyed wool in a variety of colors on two- and four-harness looms. These fabric tapes, called "listing" by the Shakers, were intertwined to create precise designs in checkerboard, basket-weave, or herringbone patterns. By 1860 the progressively minded Shakers purchased commercially produced cotton tapes for their own use, which were readily available from the World.

The design of the sewing table in figure 2-21 consists of a table base with three drawers supported on square tapered legs; this part of the table dates to 1830, but the gallery above, which consists of six narrow drawers fitted with commercially made porcelain rather than turned wood knobs, was added in 1881. (The middle drawer is inscribed: "Made by Andrew Barrett Feb 1881.") This is evidence of how the Shakers modified existing forms to serve current needs. Particularly interesting are the small brass pins protruding from the table apron on the sides and the back. One theory regarding their use is that they supported a fabric workbag underneath—a practice that was popular during the Federal period in America. A second possibility is that a piece of material was suspended between the pegs to protect the seamstress from winter drafts. Although the society's written rules discouraged the Shakers from marking their work or their possessions, many pieces carry inscriptions giving the name of the craftsman, the date of manufacture, and the name of the user. Apparently, the Worldly tradition of signing persisted among some Shaker craftsmen, who, as converts, brought their skills, tools, and habits with them into the community. Inscriptions might reveal

Fig. 2-21. Andrew Barrett (1836 or 1837–1917). Sewing Table (1830) with Add-On (1881). New/Mount Lebanon, New York. Written on top middle drawer: Made by Andrew Barrett Feb 1881. Cherry (table); cherry and pine, with porcelain knobs and brass pins (gallery). Bob and Aileen Hamilton. Photo: David Hollinger.

the identity of the maker or user, clarify the function of a particular piece of furniture, or specify its location. According to the Holy Orders of the Church, "Ye shall not print your name on anything whatever; that others may hereafter know the work of your hands."[53] However, this rule was apparently not always followed. Cabinetmakers and owners from many communities often identified themselves in a variety of materials, including pencil, chalk, ink, paper labels, or metal stamps. These stamped rather than handwritten letters are found on a small group of unrelated Shaker pieces, including chairs made by Freegift Wells of Watervliet (fig. 2-12), a tripod stand attributed to Samuel Turner of New Lebanon (fig. 2-14), and a number of woodworking tools.

Outward signs of progress continued throughout the twentieth century and into the present. The Canterbury Shakers installed battery phones throughout their village in 1904; purchased their first car, a Reo, in 1908; had electricity in 1910.[54] At this writing, the last active community at Sabbathday Lake sells their herbs on the Internet.

TEACHING TRUTH

> Be what you seem to be, and seem to be
> what you really are, and don't carry two faces
> under one hood.
>
> Father James Whittaker[55]

Shaker commercial products made for the world became widely known for exceptional quality as the sect developed a reputation for honest business dealings, trustworthiness, and fairness (see Chapter 3 in this volume). This philosophy was expressed repeatedly by Shaker leaders at various communities. Simon Atherton, Trustee at Harvard (1829–1898), summarized this viewpoint with the motto "A good name is better than riches,"[56] while Daniel Orcott advises his brothers and sisters at Enfield, Connecticut: "Your name is your only reliable capital and when that is blasted by dishonesty, your character is ruined."[57] Whether they were selling seeds or food products, the Shakers deliberately kept "the top, middle, and bottom layers

equally good in every basket or barrel of fruit or vegetable" sent to market under their name.[58] To guarantee the consistent excellence of the seeds that they raised, packaged, and sold to the World, the Shakers of Hancock, Mount Lebanon, and Watervliet stated the following in 1819:

> We, the undersigned, having for sometime past felt a concern, lest there should come loss upon the joint interest, and dishonor upon the gospel, by purchasing seeds of the world, and mixing them with ours for sale; and having duly considered the matter, we are confident that it is best to leave off the practice, and we do hereby covenant and agree that we will not, hereafter, put up, or sell, any seeds to the world which are not raised among believers (except melon seeds).[59]

The same commitment to integrity is expressed by Brother Orren Haskins, in 1887, who urged his fellow Believers to avoid Worldly styles when designing Shaker-made articles:

> Why patronize the out side world for gugaws in our manufactures, when they will say we have enough of them abroad? We want a good plain substantial Shaker article, yea, one that bears credit to our profession & tells who and what we are, true and honest before the world, without hypocrisy or any false covering. The world at large can scarcely keep pace with it self in its stiles and fassions which last but a short time, when something still more worthless or absurd takes its place. Let good enough alone, and take good common sense for our guide in all our persuits, and we are safe within and without.[60]

The Shakers dedicated themselves to spiritual honesty in their confession of sins, which is reflected in their devotion to "truth to materials."[61] Consequently, no marbling, graining, or trompe l'oeil appear; only natural wood or solidly painted surfaces are visible. More specifically, Elder Giles Avery of Mount Lebanon called the "dressing" of plain pine furniture "with the veneering of bay wood, mahogany or rosewood" deception and placed it in the same category as cheating.[62] The magnificent tailoring counter in figure 2-5 embodies the Shakers' attitude toward honesty of construction. Rather than using a carcass of inexpensive wood faced with costly veneer to reduce costs according to Worldly practice, the Shaker craftsman constructed the case and drawer fronts entirely of carefully selected tiger maple. The deliberate choice of solid figured woods for the exposed surfaces reveals the maker's commitment to authenticity. In fact, from the 1830s on, some communities often preferred a varnish finish like this rather than a pigmented paint or stain to reveal the natural grain of the walnut or cherry beneath. The resulting look consciously echoes that of nineteenth-century Worldly furniture. The overall quality of this tailoring counter raises the question of whether such an exceptional piece of work furniture was designed and constructed specifically for the ministry shop for the Church Family elders or eldresses working there.

The presence of the bone escutcheons on three drawers indicate that locks were used. Given the Shaker communal style and the openness of their living arrangements, it may seem contradictory that many pieces of Shaker furniture—including those that have never left the last two communities at Canterbury, New Hampshire, and Sabbathday Lake, Maine—are fitted with locks. On the surface, this practice may seem contradictory, as Shaker societies were built on mutual trust. However, an examination of key Shaker documents reveals that the leadership made a sharp distinction between public and private possessions and formulated its policy based on the specific contents under consideration. According to the Holy Orders of the Church written in 1841:

> 1. Ye shall not have, in the dwelling house, any locks and keys, by which ye may close any thing, that another may not open it.
>
> 2. Ye shall not lock nor in any way fasten or cause to be fastened, any cupboards, drawers, chests or writing boxes, belonging to individuals.
>
> 3. But where publick stores are kept, let the doors, chests, drawers or cupboards be

secured by locks and keys; they shall be kept locked and by no means carelessly left open or unsecured.[63]

It is apparent that certain circumstances required increased reliance on locks for security purposes. One such influencing factor might have been the annual influx of what Believers called "winter Shakers"—people who, when cold weather approached, professed a desire to become members "with empty stomachs and empty trunks, and go off with both full as soon as the roses begin to bloom."[64] As these potential converts came and then left each community, the Believers' possessions were increasingly at risk. Locks may have been installed at that time to protect both individual belongings and the community's stores from non-covenanted members. There were, however, exceptions to these rules, as stated in the Holy Orders: "Ye shall not lock your cupboards, chests or tool boxes, at the shops, except by the counsel of the 'Elders'"[65] Although the application of locks for private possessions was forbidden, these fastening devices may have been considered necessary to secure these drawers, which may have held special tools or materials for the tailoring trade.

THE CREATION OF COLOR

To the twentieth-century eye, the colors on Shaker built-in and freestanding furniture appear surprisingly bold. Chrome-yellow washstands (fig. 2-7), lipstick-red desks (fig. 2-6), apple-green chests (fig. 2-13), and Prussian blue woodwork survive in private and public collections, although scientific evidence shows that very few extant pieces of colorful Shaker furniture have undisturbed finishes today. Most of this disruption was certainly intentional on the part of the Shakers themselves, who removed or renewed the finish on their furniture over time so that it would remain neat and clean. Later owners, influenced by the Arts and Crafts and Colonial Revival movements, which emphasized natural materials, deliberately stripped original paint surfaces to reveal the uncolored wood below.

Whether embellished or left plain, Shaker furniture was invariably treated with a protective finish.

In a manner generally consistent with Worldly practice, the Shakers used paint, stain, and varnish in various combinations on both freestanding furniture and built-in storage units from the late eighteenth century through the early twentieth. In selecting paint to finish their work, Shaker craftsmen were continuing the long Anglo-European tradition of applying paint to protect the surface of the wood, to create a neat and clean appearance, and to add visual interest to the furniture and its room setting.

The selection of a particular color was based on its expense, availability, and preference, and in this respect the furniture reflected the taste of the Shakers' rural neighbors. Because of its low cost, various shades of red served as the traditional paint color for barns and other large-surface exteriors; it also represented a logical choice for Shaker-made freestanding and built-in units. As a result of advances in paint technology, manufacture, and distribution, however, a variety of new and brighter colors became available by the early 1800s.

Paint, simply defined, is made up of dry pigment that is dispersed in a liquid binder that solidifies and supports the pigment on a hard surface. It was this durable, opaque finish in bold red, yellow, blue, and green colors that coated most early Shaker furniture. It is becoming increasingly evident that the Shakers' living spaces were indeed very colorful compared to our world today. Since the existing surfaces have been so severely altered over time, we can only visualize what these interiors may have looked like by reading Shaker journals or descriptions written by visitors to the various communities. More recently, serious scientific paint analyses of Shaker furniture using advanced scientific methods, including cross-section microscopy, have enabled conservators such as Susan Buck not only to discover the various colors preserved in multiple paint layers but also to detect infinitesimal deposits of pigment trapped in wood grain. This new level of accuracy is significant because original pigments change over time, which alters their perceived color values for twenty-first-century observers, and because the surfaces of many pieces have been intentionally altered over time, both by the Shakers as well as non-believers.

After examining about sixty pieces of furniture and interior woodwork over a period of several years, Buck notes: "The Shakers were using the same pigments and binding materials for their furniture and architecture as decorative painters in the World. What appears to distinguish Shaker painted objects is the use of quite pure, intense paint colors over solid surfaces, unrelieved by decorative geometric or floral patterns."[66] Some of the color pigments, such as chrome yellow, were used alone, whereas others were combined to modify the more basic hues. Worldly Americans used chrome yellow, which may have suggested a more costly gilded surface to them, as a background for more decorative "fancy" painting on top of it. The Shakers, however, used bright yellow pigment on their furniture independently as a solid coat of both interior and exterior paint.[67]

Susan Buck uses the term *varnish* to describe a clear coating[68] "often applied over stained or painted surfaces to protect them, to add a measure of gloss and to produce a rich, saturated color on the surface."[69] Shellac, derived from a resin secreted by the lac insect of the Coccidae family, was readily available from India as early as 1737 in a variety of grades and colors. However, scientific analysis of the painted and varnished surfaces examined, reveal no evidence of an original shellac coating.

By the 1830s, written and physical evidence suggests the Shakers introduced into their repertoire transparent colored stains (which have a greater proportion of the liquid carrier to the dry pigments), which were not so commonly used in American country furniture of the same period. Thinner pigments may have satisfied the same practical and aesthetic needs as opaque paints and simultaneously allowed some of the wood's grain to show through. According to "the order as it respects painting and varnishing," written in 1841: "Ye shall have the stain in your dwelling house, an orange color; and your Shops the same, only a shade darker, your floors in the dwelling house shall be, of a redish [sic] yellow; and these at the shops of a yellowish red, not too dark."[70] Surviving evidence for this staining policy is found in William Deming's description of the 1832 Church Family dwelling house at Hancock. The building contained colorful built-in units consisting of pine cases, 240 pine cupboard doors stained yellow, and 369 butternut drawers stained red.[71] The 1837 addition to the Church Family dwelling house at Canterbury includes a third-floor attic with six walk-in closets, fourteen cupboards, and one hundred drawers, covered with a thinly applied oil-bound paint,[72] which reveals rather than conceals the grain of the pine beneath.

The Shakers used bold colors to define both specific pieces of furniture or architectural spaces. This too is illustrated in William Deming's description of the 1832 dwelling house: "And I think we may say it is finished from the top to the bottom, handsomely stained inside with a bright orange color. The outer doors are green. The outside of the house is painted with four coats of a beautiful red. The plastering is covered with a coat of hard finish & is a beautiful white."[73] Today the third floor built-ins retain the most nearly original surface in the building—drawers and case frame stained red ocher and red lead beside chrome yellow double cupboards and interior woodwork in the room.[74] The floor is painted yellow ocher.

In comparison with the other Shaker communities, the Maine Shakers made greater use of pigment, staining as well as painting their pieces. According to oral tradition,[75] Elder Henry Green (1844–1931) used the coloring from cochineal bugs as a medium for obtaining the bright red color on his sewing desks (fig. 2-6). The striking effect of this pigment was often heightened with an extremely glossy finish. The custom of staining the case and finishing the drawer fronts in clear varnish, seems to have been particular to both Alfred and Sabbathday Lake. The simply but solidly built box in figure 2-13 displays a transparent green color not found on other Shaker furniture.

Another finish option besides paint for both

Shakers and Worldly Americans was a shiny or matte finish. In order to protect the wood and give it a glossy surface, craftsmen applied either varnish or shellac over a colored stain or raw wood. It is difficult to distinguish between the two finishes, although references in Shaker journals suggest that varnish was the most common method of treatment.[76] A visitor writing about the interior woodwork of the great stone dwelling under construction at Enfield, New Hampshire, in 1840, noted that "the paint is very smooth and glossy. Elder Orville says they finished it by dipping the paint brush in boiled oil just as the paint is drying, and brush it over. By this means the oil becomes a varnish which looks elegantly when dry."[77] By the 1860s a common look was that of naturally figured wood with a clear varnish finish (fig. 2-6).

The issue of applying either a matte or glossy finish was apparently of some concern to the mid-nineteenth-century Believers. The Millennial Laws state: "Varnish, if used in dwelling houses, may be applied only to the moveables therein, as the following, viz., Tables, stands, bureaus, cases of drawers, writing desks or boxes, drawer faces, chests, chairs, etc. etc."[78] Conversely, according to the Holy Orders of the Church: "These are the things upon which ye shall in no wise use Varnish: The wood work of your dwelling house and Shops; drawers and cupboards . . . chests."[79] By 1861 the more conservative Believers expressed their opposition to the increased use of varnish on surfaces. "There is a great proclivity in this, our day, for fixing up matters very nice, & the varnish has to go on to the cup-boards, drawers &c. & the paint on to floors, everything has to be so slick that a fly will slip on it."[80]

John Kirk writes extensively about the symbolism and theological significance of the use of particular colors.[81] Unfortunately, virtually no written evidence exists as to how much the Shakers' theology and religion influenced their understanding of color. Less still is written about how this understanding actually directed their use of specific pigments. Was ministry language regarding the color of the meetinghouse's "Prussian blue" woodwork or red or yellow cupboards based on theological wording or shop terminology? John Kirk quotes Elder Calvin Green, a missionary and author (d. 1871), in discussing the symbolic nature of color:

> I will here state that I have ever observed Green color, in vision, to be a sign of an increase. All things in a growing state are green. Red, always denotes sufferings—tribulations. White, represents clean, purified from the stains of sin—accepted. Blue, represents heavenly. Azure blue, or peach blow color represents Love. Gold, denotes pure—rich in goodness. Silver, when spiritually seen, represents Union, for it is common currency.— Every color has its peculiar meaning, & to such as understand, all such appearances are instructive.[82]

In another document, Calvin Green states: "However, black is considered as a destitution of all colors. Hence, as colors are the glory of the natural world, and are the reflecting rays of light, therefore black is put to represent a destitution of all light and glory both in a natural and spiritual sense."[83]

It has only been about a decade since the first serious and scholarly scientific analysis was conducted on Shaker furniture finishes. Even though most of the research has been done on Mount Lebanon and Canterbury furniture, the following conclusions can be related to other communities: (1) Strong opaque finishes were favored on most early pieces of furniture and residential trim.; (2) multiple contrasting colors were used in many interior trim paint schemes against white plastered walls; (3) contrasting paints and/or washes were applied to furniture as early as 1830 and regularly by the 1870s; and (4) varnish was used as a transparent surface to allow the wood figure to show through and appeared to be the favored finish in the latter part of the nineteenth century, probably by 1875.

The Believers' plain and functional furniture was the inevitable result of two compelling forces—a theology demanding a physical statement of gospel simplicity and a Worldly cultural environment that embraced the forms of the new neoclassical style, which was characterized by elegance of proportion and rectilinear lines. These ideas were also expressed in the reliance upon finish rather than on carved, three-dimensional ornament, and a desire either to emphasize the natural grain of the wood enhanced with varnish or to conceal plain lumber with solid but colorful pigments. In the transmission of design, geographic distance between urban high-style centers and rural areas often resulted in a simplification of overall forms and surface treatment. Country cabinetmakers tended to produce a more basic, pared-down interpretation of upscale fashions, and these were for the most part the craftsmen who brought their talents and tastes into the Shaker population when they converted to the faith. The intersection of these spiritual and secular forces resulted in classic Shaker furniture.

1. As quoted in Flo Morse, *The Shakers and the World's People* (Hanover, N.H.: University Press of New England, 1987): 124.

2. As quoted in June Sprigg, *By Shaker Hands* (New York: Knopf, 1975): 76.

3. Scott T. Swank, *Shaker Life, Art and Architecture* (New York: Abbeville, 1999): 39.

4. Eldress Nancy E. Moore, "Journal of a Trip to Various Societies Sept. 1854–Oct.1854." Western Reserve Historical Society, Cleveland. Quoted in Sprigg, *By Shaker Hands* (1975): 72.

5. "Journal of a Trip to the Eastern Societies," 1843, Mount Lebanon, New York, Shaker Museum and Library, Old Chatham, N.Y., MS. 12744, pp. 42–43.

6. *Account of the People Called Shakers: Their Faith, Doctrines, and Practice* (Troy: Parker and Bliss, 1812): 360.

7. Henry Blinn, "Church Record, Canterbury, 1784–1897." Canterbury Shaker Village Archives, 764, p. 247.

8. *The Youth's Guide in Zion, and Holy Mother's Promises.* Given by inspiration at New Lebanon, N.Y., 1842. Quoted in Morse, *The Shakers and the World's People* (1987): 123.

9. "Millennial Laws of Gospel Statutes and Ordinances Adopted to the Day of Christ's Second Appearing. Revised and reestablished by the Ministry and Elders, October 1845." Reprinted in Edward Deming Andrews, *The People Called Shakers* (New York: Dover, 1953): 256–57.

10. See June Sprigg, *Shaker Design* (New York: Whitney Museum of American Art, 1986): 26–27; and John T. Kirk, "Reappraising an Upside-down Shaker Masterpiece," *The Magazine Antiques* (March 2004): 88–91.

11. *A Summary View of the Millennial Church, or United Society of Believers (Commonly Called Shakers)* (Albany; Packard & van Benthuysen, 1823): 320.

12. First Father Adam, "The Holy City" (16 March 1843), New Lebanon, N.Y. Pictured in *The Shakers: Their Arts and Crafts* (Philadelphia Museum Bulletin 57 [Spring 1962]): 95.

13. *The Manifesto* 29, no. 9 (September 1899): 134.

14. "Journal of Maurice Thomas," 1 January 1816–31 December 1817" (part 2, p. 162), Wednesday, 15 October 1817, in the library of the Filson Club, Louisville, Ky. Quoted in Timothy D. Rieman and Jean M. Burks, *The Complete Book of Shaker Furniture* (New York: Abrams, 1993): 334.

15. Quoted in Colin Becket Richmond, *A Collection of Shaker Thoughts* (Oneida, N.Y.: Colin Becket Richmond, 1976): 47.

16. Quoted in Edward Deming Andrews and Faith Andrews, *Work and Worship* (Greenwich, Conn.: New York Graphic Society, 1974): 199.

17. Quoted in Richmond, *A Collection of Shaker Thoughts* (1976): 34.

18. Isaac Newton Youngs, "Biography in Verse" (1837): 129–34. Andrews Shaker Collection, Winterthur Museum, Winterthur, Del., 1010.

19. "Clock maker's journal with remarks and observations, experiments, beginning in 1815. New Lebanon, 1815–35." Western Reserve Historical Society, Shaker Collection, Cleveland.

20. "Millennial Laws" (1845): 282.

21. "Collection of Writings Concerning Church Order and Government, Copied Here by Rufus Bishop in 1859" (1791–96): 42, 45, Western Reserve Historical Society, Cleveland, VIIB: 59.

22. Theodore E. Johnson, "Life in the Christ Spirit: Observations on Shaker Theology, Being in Substance Remarks Delivered at the Shaker Conference, Hancock, Massachusetts, September 7, 1968," *Shaker Quarterly* (Fall 1968). Reproduced in Morse, *The Shakers and the World's People* (1987): 182, 184.

23. Seth Youngs Wells, compiler, *Testimonies of the Life, Character, Revelations and Doctrines of Mother Ann Lee*, 2nd ed. (Albany, N.Y.: Weed-Parsons Printing Company, 1888), as quoted in Sprigg, *By Shaker Hands* (1975): 82.

24. *Fifteen Years in the Senior Order of Shakers* (Hanover, N.H.: Dartmouth Press, 1953): 25.

25. "Millennial Laws" (1845): pt. 3, sec. 9.

26. Ibid., pt. 2, sec. 10.

27. Quoted in Edward Deming Andrews and Faith Andrews, *Shaker Furniture* (New York: Dover, 1937): 19.

28. As quoted in Sprigg, *By Shaker Hands* (1975): 107.

29. Jean M. Humez, ed., *Mother's First-Born Daughters* (Bloomington: Indiana University Press, 1993): xxiv.

30. Ibid., 218–19.

31. John Humphrey Noyes: *History of American Socialisms* (Philadelphia: Lippincott, 1870; reprinted New York, Dover, 1966): 610; quoted in Sprigg, *By Shaker Hands* (1975): 110.

32. Anna White and Leila Taylor, *Shakerism: Its Meaning and Message* (Columbus, Ohio: Fred Heer, 1905): 314; also quoted in Sprigg, *By Shaker Hands* (1975): 12.

33. *The Communistic Societies of the United States from Personal Observation* (New York: Harper, 1875, reprinted New York: Dover, 1966): 136–37. Quoted in Sprigg, *By Shaker Hands* (1975): 113.

34. Sprigg, *By Shaker Hands* (1975): 117.

35. Henry C. Blinn, *The Life and Experience of Mother Ann Lee* (Canterbury, N.H.: Published by the Shakers, n.d.): 17.

36. Swank, *Shaker Art, Life and Architecture* (1999): 137.

37. Ibid., 87.

38. *Two Years' Experience among the Shakers* (West Boylston, Mass: David, Lamson, 1848): 17.

39. Andrews, *Shaker Furniture* (1937): 21.

40. *Fifteen Years* (1953): 29.

41. "Millennial Laws" (1845): pt. 3, sec. 4.

42. As quoted in Morse, *The Shakers and the World's People* (1987): 133.

43. *The Manifesto* 17, no. 3 (1887): 57–58. Quoted in Robley Edward Whitson, ed., *The Shakers: Two Centuries of Spiritual Perfection* (New York: Paulist Press, 1983): 143.

44. "A Diary Kept for the Use and Convenience of the Herb Department." 31 December 1855 (manuscript) as quoted in Andrews, *The People Called Shakers* (1953): 114.

45. Edward Deming Andrews, *The Community Industries of the Shakers* (Charlestown, Mass.: Emporium Publications, 1971): 40–44. Facsimile reprint of the *New York State Museum Handbook* 15; White and Taylor, *Shakerism* (1905): 314.

46. Beverly Gordon, *Shaker Textile Arts* (Hanover, N.H.: University Press of New England, 1980): 27.

47. See Andrews, *The Community Industries of the Shakers* (1971): 42.

48. See *Dictionary of American Biography* (New York: Charles Scribner's Sons, 1964): 457–58.

49. See Andrews, *Work and Worship* (1974): 157–58.

50. United States Patent Office specification, 2 March 1852, no. 8771.

51. Ibid.

52. Gordon, *Shaker Textile Arts* (1980): 130.

53. "An Extract from the Holy Orders of the Church, February 18th. 1841," p. 63, Andrews Shaker Collection, Winterthur Museum, Winterthur, Del.

54. Sprigg, *By Shaker Hands* (1975): 171.

55. As quoted in Morse, *The Shakers and the World's People* (1987): 184.

56. This statement is printed on various product packages and inserts from the Harvard community.

57. As quoted in Richmond, *A Collection of Shaker Thoughts* (1976): 3.

58. Eldress Anna White, as quoted in Elmer R. Pearson and Julia Neal, *The Shaker Image*, 2nd ed. (Pittsfield, Mass.: Hancock Shaker Village, 1994): 50.

59. "An Ancient Witness," *The Shaker Manifesto* 11, no. 2 (February 1881): 45.

60. "Reflections, 1887," Mount Lebanon, Western Reserve Historical Society, Cleveland, VIIA:8.

61. Constantin Brancusi, as quoted in "The Truth in Materials" by Grace Bakst Wapner, *www.chronogram.com/issue/2000/04/lucid.htm*.

62. Quoted in Sprigg, *By Shaker Hands* (1975): 156.

63. "An Extract from the Holy Orders of the Church," p. 55.

64. Nordhoff, *The Communistic Societies of the United States.* Quoted in Morse, *The Shakers and the World's People* (1987): 113.

65. "An Extract from the Holy Orders of the Church," p. 56.

66. Susan Buck, "Bedsteads Should be Painted Green: Shaker Paints and Varnishes," *Old-Time New England* (Fall 1995): 22.

67. Ibid., 31.

68. Susan Buck, "Interpreting Paint and Finish Evidence on the Mount Lebanon Shaker Collection," *Shaker: The Art of Craftsmanship*" (Alexandria, Va.: Art Services International, 1996): 56.

69. Buck, "Bedsteads Should be Painted Green" (1995): 21.

70. "An Extract from the Holy Orders of the Church," p. 77, no. 128.

71. Letter from William Deming, Hancock to Benjamin S. Youngs, South Union, 8 January 1832, in "Copies of Letters from Different Communities from South Union for the Ministry," Western Reserve Historical Society, Cleveland, IVB:35.

72. Susan Buck, "Shaker Painted Furniture: Provocative Insights into Shaker Paints and Painting Techniques," *Painted Wood: History and Conservation* (Los Angeles: Getty Conservation Institute, 1994): 145.

73. Deming to Youngs, 8 January 1832.

74. Christian Goodwillie, "Coloring the Past: Shaker Painted Interiors," *The Magazine Antiques* (September 2005): 80–87.

75. Brother Theodore E. Johnson, "The Last of Mother's Children in the East," lecture given at the Metropolitan Museum of Art, New York, 27 March 1982.

76. See June Sprigg, *Shaker: Original Paints & Patinas*, exh. cat. (Allentown, Pa.: Muhlenberg College for the Arts, 1987): 14, n. 10. Jerry Grant, former assistant director of the Shaker Museum and Library, Old Chatham, N.Y., who has done extensive research on Shaker furniture, recalls only one reference to shellac in his readings in Shaker journals and that was "varnish with shellac."

77. Henry Cummings, "A Sketch of the Life of Caleb M. Dyer," *Enfield Advocate* 30 (December 1904).

78. "Millennial Laws," in Andrews, *The People Called Shakers* (1953): 286.

79. "An Extract from the Holy Orders of the Church," p. 78.

80. 1 May 1861, "A Domestic Journal of domestic Occurrences Kept Originally by Joseph Bennet, and then by Isaac Crouch, Nicholas Bennet, Isaac N. Youngs, and John M. Brown," Church Family, Mount Lebanon, Western Reserve Historical Society, Cleveland, VB: 63-71.

81. John Kirk, *The Shaker World: Art, Life, Belief (*New York: Abrams, 1997): 129–55.

82. Calvin Green, "Biographic Memoir of the Life and Experience of Calvin Green." Copy by Alonzo G. Hollister (1861–69). Western Reserve Historical Society, Cleveland, VI:B-31.

83. Calvin Green, "Discourses," Library of Congress, 76 33–34. A note added by Alonzo Hollister explains that this was taken from Green's "Discourses Illustrating the System of the Gospel."

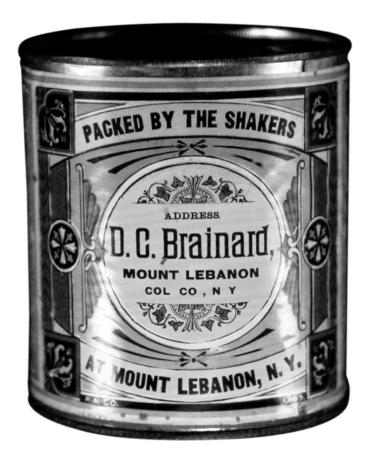

3

Designed for Sale:
Shaker Commerce with the World

M. STEPHEN MILLER

An overarching legacy of the Shakers, and one that continues to this day with the remaining Believers, is their consummate skill as problem solvers. The popular image of the United Society of Believers in Christ's Second Appearing—their formal name—is of a life characterized by piety, celibacy, orderliness, simplicity, and craftsmanship. Although this is certainly accurate, the historical ability of the Shakers to address and overcome challenges of every sort accounts above all else for more than two hundred years of their success as a communal society in America.

When a band of eight English émigrés arrived in New York City in 1774, it was on the eve of America's colonial rebellion against the country they had just left. Led by the charismatic Ann Lee—whom they called Mother—and apolitical to their core, this small group of religious dissidents was already facing the challenge of maintaining political neutrality in a time of extreme unrest. They nevertheless managed to survive for a few years, scattered in and around New York City, until their only wealthy member bought a piece of swampland a short distance north of Albany, New York, in a town then called Niskeyuna (later known as Watervliet). Here they gathered together, cleared the land, and established a self-contained community. They led a marginal existence at first, to be sure, but their mission to establish Christ's Kingdom here on earth was under way.

Shaker historians consider the year 1780 a watershed for the movement, since this is when they began their ministry in America and welcomed many seekers who were disaffected with their own faiths. The border area between New York and Massachusetts was a hotbed of evangelical revivalism at the time of the American Revolution, and news of the small group of Believers quickly reached these New Lights and drew them to Niskeyuna. However, the enthusiastic worship practiced by the "Shaking Quakers" (as they were first known) was characterized by "ecstatic movement," trancelike states, speaking in tongues, and a woman leader, all of which elicited a hostile reaction from the outside world (or the World, as the Shakers called it). As a result, they were met with responses that ranged from rejection by their neighbors and the imprisonment of their leader, Ann Lee, to occasionally severe physical abuse. In spite of it all, the millennial vision of the United Society of Believers persisted.

The Shakers essentially pattern their lives on that of Jesus—a life of piety, brotherly love, modesty, celibacy, communal work and shared possessions, pacifism, and the regular confession of sin. They believe that these goals can be accomplished only by living together and immersing themselves in the purest form of communism—giving according to their abilities and taking according to their needs, with no claims of individual ownership of anything. At first, their greatest challenge in living communally was to establish a system of giving and taking for which no pattern then existed, at least in America. The Shakers met and prevailed over this challenge—or, more accurately, series of challenges—in unique ways, and they have done so repeatedly over the course of their long history.

By the mid-1780s, after the deaths of Mother

Facing page: String Bean Can, ca. 1890. Mount Lebanon.

Fig. 3-1. These wine labels are a sample of the many varieties put up at New/Mount Lebanon between the 1850s and 1890s. At first, excess fruit from the orchards—such as apples and plums—were used. Later in the century, many types of berries were cultivated primarily for this purpose.

Ann Lee and her brother William and the end of the American Revolution, it became imperative that the Shakers separate themselves from the World if their vision of a Christian life was to be realized. With the death in 1787 of the last of the English-born Shaker leaders, Father James Whittaker, the church came under the guidance of two American-born leaders: Father Joseph Meacham and Mother Lucy Wright. The organizational scheme they established—beginning with the formation of villages, or communities, of Believers living apart from the World—still survives to a large extent at the last active site, which is located in Sabbathday Lake, Maine. For 220 years, their plan has allowed Believers to live a "Christlife" in their own sacred space.

In 1787 a group of neighboring farms in New Lebanon, New York, were combined to form the first fully organized Shaker community in a process the Shakers called "gathering into Gospel Order." The

community's name remained New Lebanon until late in 1861, when the group was granted its own post office and the name was changed to Mount Lebanon.[1] Not long after New Lebanon was established, Watervliet became fully organized, to be followed soon afterward by communities in Massachusetts (four), New Hampshire (two), Maine (two), and Connecticut (one). Within each village, membership was divided into communal "families," which were organizational rather than biological units.

Early in the nineteenth century, the Shakers expanded their communal societies into what was then the western United States. The first of these was Union Village, Ohio, which was started in 1805. In that year, Lewis and Clark had not yet returned from exploring the new Louisiana Territory, and Ohio itself had been a state for only two years. Union Village eventually grew to be the largest of the Western communities, its membership for a time surpassing even New Lebanon's. Three more communities were added in Ohio, two in Kentucky and one in western New York State. For a relatively brief time, there were also Shaker villages in Indiana, Georgia, and Florida, but each of these was, in the end, an unfortunate failure—the latter two draining valuable resources of money and people in the late 1800s. In all, there were eighteen long-lived communities.

Each Shaker community was in actuality a small (or not so small) farming collective.[2] Although separated from the World, every Shaker village was also dependent on the World for a wide variety of goods. In other words, every community strove to be self-sustaining to the largest extent possible, but it was apparent from the very beginning that an economic system was needed to help support their communal way of living. It simply was not possible to nourish the Shakers' spiritual vision without providing for certain necessities. This essay will examine how the Shakers addressed this challenge.[3]

From the earliest times, Shakers were well equipped to supply themselves with all manner of agricultural goods,[4] but they lacked foodstuffs that were not part of the farm culture in the Northeast: sugar, salt, coffee, tea, and some alcoholic beverages (fig. 3-1).[5] They also had to obtain from the World all of the metals they used for construction and crafts, including brass, copper, iron, tin, and tin-plated iron. They also needed glassware, ceramics, brick (although some communities were able to make their own), cotton cloth, and thread. This list of materials, some of which could be done without in the early years, became crucial as an industrial base for the Shaker economy developed. From the very beginning, their blacksmiths needed iron, for example, to forge tools and farm implements for sale to neighbors, and glass bottles and ceramic jars were essential for sending medicinal herbs and prepared medicines to market after about 1830.

This essay began with the assertion that the Shakers were and are consummate problem solvers. Their response to the challenges of supporting their communal way of life has traditionally operated on three levels. If there was a solution already available—one that could be found in the World—they improved upon it. If there was an approximate solution at hand, also in the World, they used innovation to adapt it to their particular needs. And if there was no solution to be found because the problem was a new one, they invented one. Improvement, innovation, and invention—this has been the Shaker way.

Although our concern here is the development of the Shakers' communal industries, we must not lose sight of the fact that the Shakers existed, and continue to exist, for the purpose of living their vision of the Christlife. For them work and worship are inseparable, and they have never existed for the purpose of "making things." In their spiritual existence, work itself is a form of secular worship. Most of the World knows the Shakers today (and probably did a hundred years ago as well) for their crafted products—chairs, oval boxes, fancywork, sweaters, sewing carriers, and furniture—but these are in fact by-products of communal living. Nevertheless, without the economic base that we call the communal industries, the Shakers' religious society could never have been sustained.

The people who joined the Shakers in the eighteenth century, men and women alike, brought with them the skills, talents, and work experiences they had already developed living in the World. For women, this invariably meant domestic work, such as kitchen gardening, food preparation and preservation, housekeeping and laundering, textile production, and the making and mending of clothes. In addition to these chores, some women were expected to rear and educate the girls and young women in their charge (as some brethren did with the boys and young men.) This may strike us in the twenty-first century as restrictive and gender-biased, but in 1790, when a married woman's legal standing was essentially that of property, these were accepted women's roles.[6] It must be pointed out, however, that as the model of leadership roles within communities developed at the end of the eighteenth century, women and men were assigned separate but equal responsibilities. Thus there were elders and eldresses, deacons and deaconesses, and so forth. Yet by the end of the nineteenth century, a radical demographic shift left women virtually in charge of their communities!

Men who joined the Shakers, on the other hand, had usually been farmers or tradesmen in the World. In the early years of communal living, they were able to use their excess farm products or handmade objects either as exchange goods in a largely barter-based economy or for sale to local merchants. About 1790, so far as we know, the first true Shaker industry developed: the systematic propagation of garden seeds exclusively for sale. Earlier, all sales of seeds were conducted on a wholesale basis to buyers who lived close by; the Shakers now designed a plan to bring this commodity to distant markets on a retail basis. They are widely acknowledged today as being the first to accomplish this.[7] Interestingly, several Shaker communities have taken credit for initiating this ahead of their peers: New Lebanon and Watervliet, New York; Enfield, Connecticut; Hancock, Massachusetts; and Alfred, Maine (although this last was not organized until 1793). The documentary evidence that survives, however, supports New Lebanon's claim as "first among equals," starting their business in 1794.[8]

THE LEGACY OF NEW LEBANON

An examination of the various products the Shakers made for sale over a period of some two hundred years will show just how central a role New Lebanon played in this process. It is important to consider why this was so. From the very beginnings of the Shaker experiment in communal living, New Lebanon was the seat of the central ministry, the highest authority for the entire movement. This continued to be the case even as seven long-standing communities were established in the West. As the leader, New Lebanon usually established standards, rules, and the overall pattern for communal living that the other villages were expected to follow.[9] The ministry continued to be located at New/Mount Lebanon until that community closed in 1947. Then it was located in Hancock (until 1960) and later Canterbury, New Hampshire (until 1990), and it is now at Sabbathday Lake in Maine.

Another factor in New Lebanon's hegemony was its size. Except for a very brief period, New Lebanon was by far the largest community.[10] It also comprised eight families whereas Hancock, the next largest village in the East, had only six. Yet size and organizational influence are still not sufficiently important to account for why it seemed that all roads led to and from New Lebanon. I believe that two other interrelated factors must be considered—the focus of early Shaker scholarship on New Lebanon and the pattern of early Shaker collecting. Both activities began in the late 1920s and were the dominant paradigm by the 1940s.

The volume of surviving materials written, printed, prepared, marketed, and crafted by Shakers at New Lebanon not only exceeds that of any other community, but in some instances—such as garden seeds—it is also greater than that of all the other communities combined! This is true in part because New Lebanon probably produced more records, journals, pamphlets, ephemera, and hand-crafted goods (except perhaps fancy goods) than any other community. It is also significant that the community was still largely intact from the 1920s into the early 1940s, when private collectors and institutions in the World took an interest in preserving the remnants of what was largely believed to be a vanishing culture.

At the forefront of these scholarly and collecting efforts were Dr. Edward Deming Andrews and his wife, Faith, who first established the Shakers as a field of study.[11] Working separately and together, they gathered up all kinds of "remnants" and wrote articles, exhibition catalogues, and books devoted to Shaker history, industries, music, art, furniture, and design. As important as this was at the time, their efforts were limited by their nearly exclusive focus on the materials obtained at New Lebanon. The legacy of New Lebanon is therefore dominant in most Shaker studies, including the present publication.

SHAKER SEEDS

One of the Shakers' most significant commercial initiatives was their garden seed industry, especially as it was carried out at New Lebanon. The other communities generally followed the patterns for production and marketing that were established here. In fact, this particular industry served as a template for commercial success in general. It demonstrated to Believers that they were capable of relative self-sufficiency, which would insure the survival of their movement. For many decades afterward, thanks to the initiation of many other successful business ventures, the Shakers did more than survive; they thrived.

Their formula for commercial success in the World was as basic as this: Find a product that was needed and not otherwise readily available; make it convenient for consumers to buy and to use; and make it better than anybody else did. It was this last point—quality—that probably set the Shakers apart from their competition. Assuring quality at a fair price was an important part of their formula. Yet price was not even a prime factor, since their seeds were generally more expensive than those sold by their competitors, although in the beginning, there were no competitors for retail sales. Until the 1790s, garden seeds were sold mainly to farmers and always in bulk form, put up in sacks or barrels. The Shakers' innovation of packaging seeds in individual paper envelopes filled the needs of consumers who wanted to plant modest kitchen gardens for home use (fig. 3-2).

Shaker seed envelopes were made readily available in the retail marketplace, usually at general stores scattered throughout rural areas, and they offered the consumer a wide choice of vegetable seeds and an impressive number of varieties. In the mid-1830s, the date of the earliest known surviving printed seed list from New Lebanon, there are six varieties each of beets, peas, beans, and cabbages, plus seeds for twenty-three other vegetables.[12] By the 1840s, planting instructions were printed on each envelope, since it was assumed that users would not be familiar with cultivation methods. Another important innovation, possibly unique for the time, was that Shaker seed envelopes were branded. Almost all consumer goods are branded today with visual devices, such as specific colors combined with distinctive typography, trademarked names, or corporate or product logos that could be immediately recognized by the buying public. For the Shakers, "D.M." was printed on each seed package, the initials of New Lebanon's beloved first trustee or business manager, David Meacham Sr. Although he died in 1826, the invocation of his legacy of trustworthiness and fairness implied a guarantee of quality for a wide range of products at New Lebanon (and sometimes at its sister community of Watervliet) throughout the nineteenth century. "D.M." was used on seed envelopes until the business closed there in 1888 and on other products until even later.

The garden seed business was a true industry in that it required a careful orchestration of efforts by many hands on many levels. Each step was crucial in the overall process, and there were multiple steps. Bringing the product from farm to market involved four distinct areas of endeavor: the fields, the barns, the shops, and the World. Each area was precisely coordinated with the others in order to assure the best possible result.

In the fields, the soil had to be cultivated and fertilized in the spring to receive the parent seed.

Once the seeds were planted, the plants had to be weeded, thinned, and watered to insure optimal growth. Some plants do not produce offspring seed during their first growing season and have to be dug up and stored in barns and root cellars until the following spring. Known as biennials, these plants can be eaten after one growing season, but they do not flower and set seed until the second summer.[13] They include such basic species as onions, beets, carrots, radishes, turnips, and cabbages. As every list of Shaker seeds indicates, these vegetables constituted at least half of all the seeds offered for sale. The final field chore was harvesting. For some seeds, such as onions, the window for harvesting was a short one, so all hands, including male children, were employed when the time (and the plants) were ripe.

In the barns, the seeds were separated from the harvested flowers, sorted, washed, and thoroughly dried. The drying phase was critical for insuring that seeds would not mildew when packaged: otherwise they would not germinate when planted. While all of this was being done, the press in the Shakers' print shop was busy running off tens of thousands of printed paper envelopes. In the peak

Fig. 3-2. This rare two-color advertising poster dates to just before New Lebanon changed its name to Mount Lebanon, in the fall of 1861. The sophisticated style of border and the large overall size suggest that it was printed outside of the community, a practice that became common in the 1870s as the Shakers faced increased competition from the World.

Fig. 3-3. The two seed envelopes at the right date to the final years of the industry at Mount Lebanon and were commercially printed by color lithography. The business was reorganized in 1884 as the Shaker Seed Company, but it folded in 1888, as the community no longer had the resources to compete successfully in the now-crowded marketplace.

Fig. 3-4. New Lebanon issued its first garden seed catalogue, *The Gardener's Manual* (sic), in 1835, followed by increasingly more elaborate catalogues up to 1888. These pamphlets were filled with advice about cultivation and food preparation, in addition to listing the varieties available. Later versions also contained many line-cut illustrations of the varieties offered.

year of 1860, nearly a quarter of a million envelopes were produced. At the same time, brethren and sisters printed most of the other paper supplies needed to support the industry— seed lists, catalogues, invoices, billheads, letter-heads, receipts, and box labels. An enormous number and variety of paper supplies were required for this enterprise to function efficiently. This type of printed paper intended for one-time or short-term use is known collectively as ephemera (figs. 3-3, 3-4). Eventually, box labels produced by multi-color letterpress and later by color lithography would be bought from commercial printing firms in the World, along with catalogues and seed envelopes.

In other workshops, brethren fashioned seed boxes from boards of clear pine. These were simply nailed together until later in the nineteenth century, when machine-cut dovetails were used. The lids were fastened with leather or wire hinges, and a protective coat of red paint was applied to the boxes; although at first the boxes had no finishing coat. Whenever possible, boxes from the previous selling season were cleaned and fresh labels applied inside and out, for recycling saved the Shakers time, material, and money. Thrift has long been an under-appreciated facet of Shaker life, as it was for most people who earned their living from the soil.

In the seed shop, sisters trimmed, folded, pasted, and filled the seed envelopes, which were packed in wooden boxes, whose contents were marked on the inside labels. The entire process of preparing, packaging, and boxing seeds took place from early fall through mid-winter. Toward the end of winter, the Shakers engaged the World, as brethren loaded sleds or wagons (railcars later in the century for bulk shipments) for delivery along well-established seed routes. These routes and the territories they served were a potential (or some-times real) source of conflict between communities and were sometimes the subject of spirited negoti-ations. At New Lebanon, the "western load," which followed the east-west course of the Erie Canal, was its most profitable. This was before the area

around Rochester, New York, became a major seed-producing region in its own right.

Shaker brothers would leave full seed boxes at country stores on a consignment basis. The merchants agreed to a fixed commission rate—generally 33 ⅓ percent—and when the boxes were retrieved at the end of summer, all the Shaker brother had to do was account for the number of missing envelopes in order to calculate what had been sold and what was owed him. All seeds that were packaged in the "standard" format, envelopes measuring 2 ½ by 4 inches, were sold for the same price, six cents, so the process of settling accounts was quite simple (fig. 3-5).

The basics of the seed business, so far as we can tell, were similar at the other Shaker villages. What changed over the course of nearly a century of activity were the printed materials and the competition. The Shakers have always been a progressive society, embracing new technologies as they became available. They were often the first in their area to have telephones, electricity, and automobiles. When water was the only available source of power, they designed a more efficient turbine. When steam power became available, they switched to this source of energy. Today the Shakers at

Sabbathday Lake conduct an international business in culinary herbs over the Internet.

For the garden seed industry the Shakers used up-to-date printing technologies as they evolved, even though it meant having the printing done for them rather than by them. The Civil War and its aftermath had an impact on every facet of American society, and the Shakers were not insulated from some of these changes. After the war, competition in the World to sell garden seeds on a retail basis increased markedly. The huge seed business in Enfield, Connecticut, which was almost totally dependent on Southern markets, folded as a result of the wartime embargo on Northern goods. On the other hand, business in South Union, Kentucky, thrived because so much commercial seed stock in the South had been destroyed during the war.[14] This was the time when Mount Lebanon (renamed in 1861) began using commercially printed papers with the saturated colors of lithography as a competitive necessity. This change was accepted as a natural transition in a group already known for being forward-thinking in the business world.

Each of the eighteen communities that lasted for at least seventy years had a seed business at

Fig. 3-5. This colorful label was pasted under the lid of a wooden box that was filled with seed envelopes. It was designed to attract the eye of a would-be buyer when the lid was left open on a merchant's countertop. At the right is a list of the contents of the boxes, with root vegetables (beets, turnips, and radishes) being the most numerous offerings. The label dates to the last few years of the enterprise.

Fig. 3-6. The pail on the left is a typical form for one made at Canterbury, New Hampshire, in the second half of the nineteenth century. Most of the cooperage from this community came with lids, though this is an unusually elaborate one. The exterior has a machine-made appearance, having been finished on a lathe, after the staves were assembled and bound.

The two New Hampshire communities, Canterbury and Enfield, were the only Shaker centers for the manufacture of tubs and pails for sale. The large tub on the right, measuring 20 inches across the top, has brass bands to hold the staves in place, a feature found only on Enfield-made cooperage. Probably made in the 1880s, it too has a polished, lathe-turned surface.

some time in their history, with the possible exception of Watervliet, Ohio (not to be confused with Watervliet, New York), from which no evidence of this survives. For some—Enfield, Connecticut; Hancock, Massachusetts; and South Union, Kentucky—seeds were a major source of revenue throughout most of the nineteenth century. Nowhere, however, did it reach the scale that it did at New Lebanon. For example, as early as 1805, this community sold seven tons of seed, realizing a net profit of $1,240,[15] entirely from packages that sold for only six cents apiece! For eight years between 1840 and 1847, this community valued their stock of seeds, envelopes, and boxes at $79, 880,[16] the approximate equivalent of $2 million in 2006. Nonetheless, the temporary disruption of lucrative sales in the Southern states during the Civil War, the intense competition from large seed houses in the World after the war, the loss of many able-bodied male members in the 1870s and 1880s, and the high cost of hired labor all conspired against this industry. In 1888, the last of the Shaker communal seed industries came to an end at Mount Lebanon.

One final consideration about the seed industry at New Lebanon is the matter of pride. Shakers,

from the earliest times, were discouraged from demonstrating individual pride in their work, so few pieces of furniture made before 1830 were signed by their makers. Group pride, by contrast, was ever-present. Thus the seeds put up at New Lebanon by the North, East, and Second Families were marked on their packages, respectively, N.F., E.F., and S.F. Furthermore, the community of origin for nearly all Shaker products was identified throughout most of their history. Even today, the herbs and wool sold by the Shakers at Sabbathday Lake proudly display their community's name.

EARLY CRAFT INDUSTRIES

Alongside the spectacular success of the garden seed industry—a phenomenon characterized by invention and innovation—was the income provided by the more conventional trades of blacksmithing and hide tanning. From the former came such finished goods as nails, horseshoes, door latches, and hinges, as well as a variety of farm tools, such as hoes and plows. From hides came harnesses, saddles, shoes, boots, and whips. Unfortunately, there are no identifiable remnants and no reliable sales records from either of these apparently modest enterprises. At about this time, however, just before 1800, the Shakers, at least those at New Lebanon, began crafting wooden wares for sale. These endeavors, which would ultimately bring enduring fame to the sect and would survive in some form (such as oval box making) into the twenty-first century, began with the manufacture of dippers, cooperage (tubs, pails, churns, barrels, and firkins), and oval boxes. Each of these was an industry whose output was intended for sale in the World; much more was crafted for use within the community but falls outside of the subject at hand. Fortunately, there are identifiable surviving examples of each of these commercial crafts, most of them made before about 1840.

New Lebanon was the first community where the large-scale manufacture of staved and bound wooden vessels, or cooper ware, is documented. This took place between about 1790 and 1830.

Although many Shaker villages made cooperage for their own use, it was made for sale at only two others, Canterbury and Enfield, New Hampshire.[17] A brief look at some examples of their cooper ware is instructive in showing how a Shaker-made pail was different from one made in the World.

All wooden wares made by Shakers reveal a thorough understanding of the inherent qualities of wood—its strengths, weaknesses, and physical characteristics—and the methods for using it. While it is true that skilled craftsmen in the World had abilities equal to those of skilled Shaker brothers, the latter had something that their counterparts did not—the "luxury" of time. In spite of the need to help support their communities with their craft output and the ever-present profit motive, the Shakers never seemed to hurry in their jobs. A crucial aspect of their work ethic is contained in the following quote from Mother Ann Lee (recounted by Mother Lucy Wright): "Do all your work as though you had a thousand years to live, and as though you would if you knew you must die tomorrow."[18] In other words, do your very best work so that it will endure, no matter how much time is required; yet do not tarry. The results were usually products of a higher quality than those produced in the World.

For the construction of a pail, for example, the Shakers chose clear, straight-grained white or yellow pine, a relatively soft wood that expands across the grain when it comes in contact with moisture, making the staves watertight, a necessity in all pail construction. Carefully chosen wood with no knots or defects will allow a tighter fit over a longer period of time with less chance of warping. All the pails made at New Lebanon have staves that meet as flat butt joints, a standard practice for cooperage in this period. Later in the century, Canterbury and Enfield used staving machines to form the edges of staves into V and U shapes, respectively (fig. 3-6). These configurations increased the surface area of contact and insured an even snugger fit with less distortion.

Shaker craftsmen beveled the top and bottom edges of staves and the ends of the wood handles,

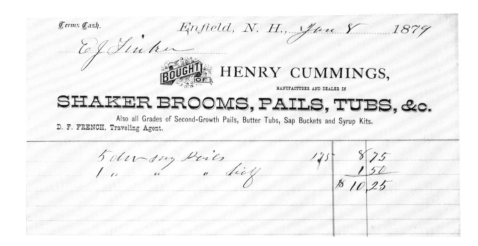

knowing that the end grain was susceptible to splitting. When metal bands were used to secure the staves, they were of a higher gauge than Worldly examples (as were their diamond-shaped bail plates) and were trimmed to a V or U shape to keep them from cutting, snagging, or pulling away. Bands on non-Shaker pails are of thinner stock and cut straight across on a diagonal line. The Shakers generally finished their pails with a protective coat of paint inside and out. The net result of such attention to every detail of construction was a product that functioned better and lasted longer. Many of the pails that were made 100 to 150 years ago still look almost new. Not surprisingly, it did not take long for Shaker products to be sought out because of their quality.

Yet it was not always sufficient for the Believers to have high-quality products available, because from the beginning they had purposefully separated themselves from the very people whom they now needed to do business with. Although they were separated from the World, the Shakers could not afford to remain isolated. Therefore, they had to develop strategies to market their products, and in the early nineteenth century there were few marketing models for them to follow. This is where their innovative problem-solving came to the fore. Their answer would today be called "branding."

One approach that the Shakers used early on has already been discussed with reference to the

Fig. 3-7. Ephemera, a wide variety of paper material, intended for one time or short-term use, was needed to support all of the Shaker industries. This 1879 billhead was printed for the Enfield, New Hampshire, community, to record the sale of their cooperage. Henry Cumming was a trustee there, a Shaker who was designated to conduct business with the World.

Fig. 3-8. Wooden dippers, made for handling dry material such as grain, were an early industry at New Lebanon. The straight seams were secured with a virtual "ribbon" of tacks to prevent warping or separating. The dipper at the left has the initials of Trustee David Meacham Sr.—D.M.—stamped on the underside.

Fig. 3-9. A craftsman at Mount Lebanon, New York, made this nest of oval boxes. Dome-headed tacks indicate that they were probably made after the mid-1870s. The broadside advertises oval boxes at wholesale prices. "One full nest" (eleven graduated sizes) is advertised as costing $5.00 ($89.00 in today's dollars).

seed industry at New Lebanon: they printed the initials of a highly regarded trustee, David Meacham Sr., on paper seed envelopes. This was intended to be an implied guarantee of quality. In the same way, Canterbury and Enfield, New Hampshire, and Hancock and Tyringham, Massachusetts, used, respectively, F.W. (Francis Winkley); N.D. (Nathaniel Draper); D.G. (Daniel Goodrich); and F.S. (Freeman Stanley)—each an early and beloved trustee at his community. Later

in the nineteenth century, the full names of various trustees were often used for the same purpose: Robert Wagan for chairs and D. C. Brainard for foods and medicines at Mount Lebanon; Thomas Corbett for preparations and medicines at Canterbury; and William Dumont for medicines at Sabbathday Lake, Maine. The net effect of these tactics was a century or more of reasonably successful sales. This use of trustee's initials and names, incidentally, was seldom if ever employed by the Shakers in the West. Most of their sales were conducted through Worldly wholesalers who simply used the Shaker name—Shaker Sarsaparilla, Shaker Cough Syrup, Shaker Nervine.

Another example of the "branding" of Shaker products, from New/Mount Lebanon in particular, was the use of the word *genuine*. We find Genuine Vegetable & Flower Seeds, Genuine Hand-Made Shaker Cloaks, Genuine Shaker Apple Sauce, and Genuine Shaker Chairs, among other examples. The seemingly simple yet sophisticated marketing strategy was surely meant to connect the notion of quality with their products. And throughout the nineteenth century at least, the strategy worked!

Two other important categories of woodcraft that the Shakers began to make before 1800 were dippers and oval boxes. The former were made only at New Lebanon and were to be used for scooping and measuring dry material such as grain (fig. 3-8).[19] Dippers were constructed from thinly planed and steam-bent strips of maple wood. A cylinder was formed around a solid wood mold that was usually 3 to 4 inches high. The straight vertical seam was secured with many copper tacks (to prevent warping) and attached, with wooden pegs or copper points, to a round pine disk that formed the bottom. The diameters varied from 4 ½ to 6 inches. A turned maple wood handle was fixed to one side with an iron rivet, and an iron nail was added to keep the handle from rotating. These dippers were made until at least 1835, with standardized sizes first recorded in 1830.

Oval boxes, by comparison, were made and sold by many communities (fig. 3-9). Yet even with this most ubiquitous of Shaker forms, only at New

Fancy Oval Covered Wooden Boxes.

ONE FULL NEST, ... $5.00

Lebanon was there an effort made to standardize their sizes, a significant hallmark of any industry. The construction of the oval boxes was similar to that used for dippers. The sides were almost always of maple, with tops and bottoms of clear pine. The joints for these, however, were formed by a series of "fingers," or "swallowtails." When these boxes are viewed with the fingers perpendicular to the ground, they display a series of Gothic arches, with their edges finely beveled and their tips in intimate contact with the box.[20]

The purpose of shaping the joint in this manner was to allow for a slight expansion or contraction across the grain of the wood without allowing the joint to buckle. This problem is seldom seen on dippers because they are generally smaller and use many tacks to secure the joint. Although there is no written evidence of the fact, it seems likely that finger joints would also have been more appealing to the eyes of "city folk," the primary sales target of these storage boxes. Urbanites had little need for dippers or grain measures, so the Shakers did not spend the extra time making fingers that would presumably attract greater sales.

In order to standardize their sizes, as with the dippers, Shaker box makers used a series of solid wooden molds, this time oval in shape, around which planed and steamed maple sides were bent. A metal plate on one side of the mold forced the tips of tacks that were driven through the joints to bend, or "deaden," thus insuring that they would not loosen and pull out over time. By the 1870s, when a rare illustrated advertisement for them was published, "Fancy Oval Covered Wooden Boxes," they were offered in eleven sizes—the largest being 15 inches across—and sold for between $3 and $9 per dozen. Clearly these boxes were intended for the wholesale market. Without either production or sales figures, we can reasonably estimate that perhaps twenty to forty thousand oval boxes were made and sold by New/Mount Lebanon alone over a period of about eighty years. Many more were made at Alfred, Canterbury, Sabbathday Lake, and Union Village, among other communities.

MEDICINAL HERBS AND PREPARATIONS

As the size of their villages continued to grow during the first decades of the nineteenth century, the Shakers faced a daunting new challenge: how to provide additional income as their needs began to exceed their industrial output. Since their local markets were not expanding at the same rate, producing more seeds or more wood, metal, and leather goods was not the answer. In the 1820s, distant markets were growing, especially to the south and west, but without a well-developed network of rail transport—the Erie Canal did not open until 1825—the Shakers' means of bringing their goods to these markets was limited. Fortuitously, at about this time, a groundswell of interest in nontraditional medical practice was becoming far more widespread, albeit less intense, than the religious fever that had gripped parts of the Northeast a generation or two earlier. Once again the Shakers responded to this need with great energy and in novel ways. They developed an industry of medicinal herbs and herbal medicines that by mid-century overtook garden seeds—at least in the villages of Canterbury, Harvard, New Lebanon, and Union Village—and became the greatest source of their revenue.[21]

From the time their relatively self-sustaining communities were founded, the Shakers approached matters of health in a holistic way. They believed that "living the [Shaker] life" conferred certain advantages on them that many in the World did not enjoy. These included a regulated life, in which work, rest, and worship were carefully balanced. Appetites were fully nourished by a healthful, varied diet based on the freshest possible ingredients. Some pipe smoking and the modest consumption of alcoholic beverages (for "good digestion") were tolerated, if not overtly encouraged. In addition, Believers' rooms were well ventilated; periodic bathing was provided for and personal hygiene encouraged; clothing and bed linens were laundered regularly; work assignments were rotated to prevent stress, boredom, or carelessness; and safe working environments were a priority.

BAYBERRY BARK,
Myrica Cerifera.
D. M. & Co.,
WATERVLIET, N. Y.

Balmony or Snakehead,
Chelone Glabra.
D. M. & CO.,
WATERVLIET, N. Y.

Prickey Ash Bark.
Xanthoxylum aMericanum.
D. M. & Co.
Watervliet, N. Y.

Yellow Dock Root.
Rumex crispus.
M. & Co.,
WATERVLIET, N. Y.

Pennyroyal.
D. M. & Co.
Watervliet, N. Y.

BONESET.
Eupatorium perfoliatum.
D. M. & Co.
Watervliet, N. Y.

BITTERSWEET,
S Janum dulcamara.
D. M. & Co.
WATERVLIET, N. Y.

GOLD THREAD,
Coptris trifolia.
D. M. & Co.,
WATERVLIET, N. Y.

Burdock Root,
Lappa major radix.
D. M. & Co,
Watervliet, N. Y.

LOBELIA
Inflata.
D. M. & Co.
Watervliet, N. Y.

HEMLOCK BARK, FINE,
Pinus canadensis.
D. M. & Co.
WATERVLIET.

Mayweed.
D. M. & Co.
Watervliet, N. Y.

MULLEIN,
Verbascum thapsus.
D. M. & CO,
Watervliet, N. Y.

HOREHOUND
Narrubium vulgare.
D. M. & Co.
Watervliet, N. Y.

Fig. 3-10. These 14 herb labels were used to identify one-pound "bricks" of medicinal herbs put up at Watervliet, New York. Each brick was in turn made up of 16 individual one-ounce "cakes," which were more convenient to use. All of these herbs, and fifty others, were on Samuel Thomson's list of recommended "botanic" herbs, which were to be consumed as infusions (or teas).

By the 1820s, some members of the first generation of converts from the 1780s were approaching the age of seventy or eighty, and even though Shakers have historically led long and productive lives, illness and infirmity were becoming an increasing burden, especially in the eastern communities. The Believers took two approaches to matters of health care for the sick among them—traditional and nontraditional medicine. This was a curious bifurcation of philosophies and once again exposes the fallacy that Shakers were and are a monolithic sect.

On the one hand, the traditional approach relied on methods favored by most "regular" physicians in the World. Organized medicine before and during the first half of the nineteenth century was both empirical (trial and error) and "heroic." The latter relied on removing what was believed to be the offending agent or the affected part. This generally meant purging, bleeding, surgical excision (including amputation), and the ingestion of chemical substances such as calomel. Since germ theory was not enunciated until 1857–58 by Louis Pasteur, treating the symptoms of illnesses rather than their causes was the standard of care. Medicine was

closer at that time to what surgical practice is today. To make matters even worse, most of these drastic approaches were dangerous, unpredictable, expensive, and often unavailable, especially to people living in rural areas.[22]

Nevertheless, starting at New Lebanon in 1821, an Order of Physicians and Nurses was established.[23] In reality, women and men had been functioning as nurses and physicians for some years before this, but the codification of this Order in the Millennial Laws of that year demonstrates their importance to the physical well-being of the communities. Also, at about this time, the Shakers began sending young brethren who showed promise to study with trained physicians in the World. All returned after a year or two to serve their respective communities. One of these, Thomas Corbett, will be considered in some detail below.

Nontraditional medicine, on the other hand, held a powerful attraction for many Believers. It should come as no surprise to learn that a group like the Shakers, who lived lives so radically apart from the mainstream in nearly every way, would also look for an alternate path to health care. From their beginnings in America, the Shakers have both elicited suspicion from the World's people and been suspicious of them. Many Shakers were mistrustful of the Worldly rules and institutions, whether they governed political, social, economic, or, in this case, medical policies. In this last instance, it turned out that many other Americans felt the same way.

Those Shakers who, for whatever reasons, eschewed traditional medicine turned to a variety of what we now call folk remedies to treat their ailments. It is likely that much if not most of this lore came from local Native Americans, and some Shakers apparently accepted it early on. There is anecdotal evidence that long before the sale of herbs and herbal products became an industry, a few Shakers gathered wild herbs for their purported medicinal properties in self-administered remedies. It is impossible now to know, let alone understand, the rationale for all of the modalities used—how much of which plant and in what combinations—but we do know that if a Believer returned to health, it could have been because of these remedies, or in spite of them. (One must not, of course, discount the potential benefits of the placebo effect or "tincture of time.")

One individual in the first decades of the nineteenth century truly revolutionized nontraditional medicine: Samuel Thomson (1769–1843).[24] The acknowledged "father" of herbal medicine in this country, Thomson was a self-taught, New Hampshire-born "physician," whose experiences with the healing properties of a single herb in his youth—*Lobelia inflata* (a potent emetic)—convinced him that the true path to overcoming sickness was with natural plant materials. He termed this approach "botanic medicine," and it stood in direct opposition to the use of "mineral" or chemical substances that regular physicians often promoted.

In 1822 Thomson published *A New Guide to Health; or, Botanic Family Physician*, an extremely influential book that was issued in several editions. Thomson's basic premise was that cold obstructed bodily functions and was the underlying cause of all disorders and diseases in humans. The cure was simply to use heat, which could be applied externally (by such means as steam baths) or internally (by consuming *Capsicum annum*, a hot cayenne pepper, in pulverized form). Either would promote excretions and secretions, thus restoring the body to health. *The Thomsonian Materia Medica or Botanic Family Physician*, published in 1812, listed sixty-eight herbs that were capable of moving "waste matter" out of the body by promoting catharsis, emesis, or an increase in urination, perspiration, or menstrual flow. Although we may scoff at Thomson's simplistic approach today, it should be understood that he was at least attempting to come to terms with the causes rather than simply the manifestations of illness, a still radical notion at the time. Some Shakers certainly bought into Thomsonian medicine for themselves, whereas many others became involved in the production of at least sixty of his sixty-eight recommended herbs for sale to the World. The net result was over-

whelming financial success for a number of communities and perhaps even a measure of better health to the nation as a whole.

In 1820 or 1821, the first Shaker herb industries began at Harvard, Massachusetts, and New Lebanon, and it is no coincidence that their success came soon after the publication of Samuel Thomson's *Guide* in 1822. He helped to create a demand; they helped to provide a supply. Canterbury; Union Village, Ohio; and Watervliet, New York, soon followed suit with important herb businesses of their own (fig. 3-10).

The Shakers have always been a practical people when it comes to nonspiritual matters, so they were not averse to combining traditional with nontraditional medicine in an effort to get the best of both. In 1813 the Canterbury community directed thirty-three-year-old Brother Thomas Corbett to become trained as a physician by apprenticing with a Worldly doctor as well as taking classes at one or two medical colleges.[25] Once there, he came under the influence of doctors who both accepted and rejected Thomsonian practice, and Corbett was influenced by both persuasions, as evidenced by his many fruitful years back in the community. After he returned to Canterbury in 1816, he established a small "physic garden" and cultivated medicinal herbs for the community's own use. By the mid-1820s, they were selling excess herbal material to the New Lebanon Shakers, and in the early 1830s, the business was netting more than $1,400 annually in much-needed cash for the community. Canterbury issued its first bound herb catalogue in 1835.

In spite of a thorough grounding in Thomsonian practice, Dr. Corbett (as he was known, although he had no medical degree) and a physician from Dartmouth College, Dr. Dixi Crosby, modified, in the early 1840s, a formula that was first supplied by New Lebanon. The result was marketed as Corbett's Shakers' Compound Syrup of Sarsaparilla. The main

Fig. 3-11. This "Price List" from 1874—the heyday of prepared medicines at Mount Lebanon—contains about 400 items. In spite of the fact that "Medicinal Preparations" appears in the title, most offerings were "simples," that is, herbs, roots, and barks in various forms. Concentrated liquid extracts were put up in bottles such as these and placed inside green cardboard cylinders for sale. The "Indian Hemp" bottle and box are a rare if not unique surviving set.

Fig. 3-12. For most of the 19th century, Harvard's main industry was raising and selling medicinal herbs. These six catalogues, printed in the format of either broadsides or bound pamphlets, range from the earliest (top, center), issued about 1830, to the latest (right, center). This last one was published in the early 1890s; the term *reduced* here refers to prices, not to the number of the offerings (which remained fairly constant over the decades).

Fig. 3-13. The community at Harvard, Massachusetts, like those at Watervliet and New Lebanon, New York, sold their herbs in a compressed form, both as one-ounce cakes (right) and as one-pound bricks. For a short time, in the 1870s or 1880s, they were also packaged in small cardboard boxes. This is one of the few remaining examples of the powdered product, which was put up in bottles. Goldenseal was used as a mild laxative.

ingredient, sarsaparilla (*Aralia nudicaulis*), was not listed in Thomson's *Materia Medica*, and other ingredients, such as Epsom salts and alcohol (10 percent), were mineral rather than vegetable. This demonstrates that the Shakers could be flexible when there was a demand to be met and a profit to be realized. This product was manufactured at Canterbury for almost seventy years and, along with financial and popular success, was rewarded with a United States patent in 1886.[26]

The Harvard community, by way of contrast, never made finished medicines. Instead, from 1820 to about 1910, they furnished the market with large quantities of dried herbs in a variety of forms— roots, barks, berries, leaves, seeds, or extracts (fig. 3-12). Except for the latter, the dry product was generally compressed by large steam presses into one-ounce "cakes" or one-pound "bricks" (fig. 3-13). These packages were wrapped with blue or gray paper, and an identifying label was affixed to one end. In some instances, the dry product was packaged in a small one-ounce cardboard box, but this form was relatively uncommon. Pulverized herbs, also uncommon, were put up in bottles with tin screw tops. The customary four culinary herbs—marjoram, sage, savory, and thyme—were sold in tin cylinders that were either 2 or 3 ¾ inches tall. In addition, a variety of mint plants that are used in the kitchen today were raised and sold

for teas that were used for medicinal purposes.

Harvard issued its first printed list of offerings in about 1830, its last in the 1890s. In between they published a series of bound catalogues along with other single-sided broadside lists. It is remarkable how consistent the number of offerings was over the sixty-plus years of this industry, between 140 and 172 varieties. The herb industry was similar to the garden seed industry in many ways: vast acreage was put under cultivation; specialized structures had to be built to dry, process, and package the material; an array of ephemera was required to label, advertise, and record sales of the product, and then it had to be sent it to market. (Unlike some Shaker products, virtually all sales of seeds or herbs took place outside of the community.) All of these procedures naturally required much coordinated labor. An enormous Herb House was constructed at Harvard in 1848–49 and within five years, the Shakers there were processing eighteen tons of products. (Even the huge medicinal herb industry at New Lebanon, with fifty acres set aside for herb gardening, did not match this.)

SPECIALIZED WOODEN WARES

By the middle of the nineteenth century, when herbs and medicinal preparations began to overtake garden seeds in importance, several Shaker communities

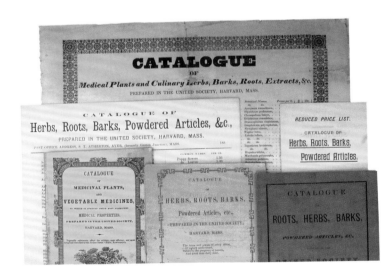

returned to the manufacture of rather specialized wooden wares as commercial ventures. This activity took place mainly at communities whose income was not dependent upon a seed or medicinal herb business, and in most instances, a particular brother was responsible for innovating these ventures. At Hancock in the late 1840s, Elder Thomas Damon started the business of making folding table-mounted yarn winders, or swifts (fig. 3-14). Their slats were designed to expand to accommodate a skein of wool that could then be unwound to form a ball, which was held by a cup mounted on top of the shaft of the swift. These devices, available in five sizes, required several pieces of machinery and "jigs" dedicated to cutting and shaping all of their standardized parts: shaft, cup, two clamps with thumb screws, and twenty-four slats. Elder Thomas designed and built all this machinery himself. Nearly one thousand swifts were sold every year for several decades, mainly to the wholesale market. Made well and used carefully, many of these objects survive today in excellent condition.

At Sabbathday Lake, Brother Granville Merrill was the moving force behind a business of making wooden dry (i.e., grain) measures in the 1870s (fig. 3-15).[27] This was a common form, at least throughout New England; the Shaker innovation here was to make these in metric sizes, additional evidence for the progressive nature of the Shakers. The United States government had formally authorized the use of metric measurements on several occasions, but, as is evident even in our own time, the public has not accepted the use of this system. Nevertheless, these measures were made in limited numbers at this community for more than half a century.

What did take hold to become perhaps the icon of all Shaker crafted work were the chairs that were made exclusively for sale. These were different from the chairs that were made for use within the communities, chiefly because the chairs made for the World were standardized, an industry hallmark. "Communal" chairs often display some characteristic details of design and construction that allow us to identify their community of origin, but there was little effort to achieve any degree of uniformity. At

Fig. 3-14. Folding, or "umbrella," yarn winders—called swifts— were the only large-scale crafted items made at Hancock, New Hampshire. Constituting a true industry, swifts were made in five standardized sizes, each size having all interchangeable parts. They were designed to fold up when not in use to conserve space. Most swifts were covered with a protective layer of bright yellow paint.

Fig. 3-15. The water-powered mills at Sabbathday Lake, Maine, were employed late in the 19th century to make dry measures in 10 sizes. These were graduated from the size of one-tenth of a liter to 20 liters (or "2 Deka," as shown here in the center). The forward-thinking Shakers apparently believed that the more progressive metric system would eventually prevail in this country; clearly, they were mistaken.

Mount Lebanon in the middle 1860s, however, all of that changed.

It is difficult to identify a single innovator, since the design that was used for sales chairs derived from vernacular styles common in the World and since New Lebanon was already selling some type of chair before 1800, although we don't know what these looked like. Nevertheless, as the chair business developed into an industry, an elder named Robert M. Wagan (1833–1883) may rightfully be regarded as its prime mover and chief innovator. As with the initials D.M. (David Meacham), Wagan's name was used as a tacit guarantee of quality by Mount Lebanon until the industry closed completely in the late 1930s, more than fifty years after Wagan's death.

Elder Wagan was responsible for building a large structure at the South Family of Mount Lebanon that was dedicated to the manufacture of chairs and stools in 1872 (fig. 3-16). Inside was machinery that turned out many thousands of interchangeable parts for the eight standardized sizes that were put together in assembly-line fashion. There were two basic forms required for all chairs: turned posts and dowels for the vertical and horizontal components, respectively, and flat-planed strips required for back slats and rockers. All of the wood was maple.

Beginning about 1870, chair sizes ranged from the smallest, #0, to the largest, #7. Each size was offered in a number of versions: with or without arms; with slatted or taped backs; with or without rockers; and with or without a doweled bar across the top of the back from which a cushion could be suspended (figs. 3-17, 3-18). As if these were not enough choices, several different wood finishes and

Fig. 3-16. This rare and possibly unique surviving broadside is the earliest-known illustrated rendering of the nascent chair industry at Mount Lebanon, New York. Printed in 1867, at about the time the industry was being organized, it shows seven sizes, #1 (for the smallest) to #7. In the 1870s, a doll-sized #0 was added to the line. All eight sizes were made through the 1930s.

Fig. 3-17. This is an intermediate-size "straight" (non-rocking) chair, designated #5. Instead of acorn-shape finials on the rear posts, this chair has a curved dowel from which a back cushion could be suspended. The #5 size sometimes came with four back slats, as did its larger siblings, the #6 and #7. The wood here is figured maple and the finish is a nut-brown stain.

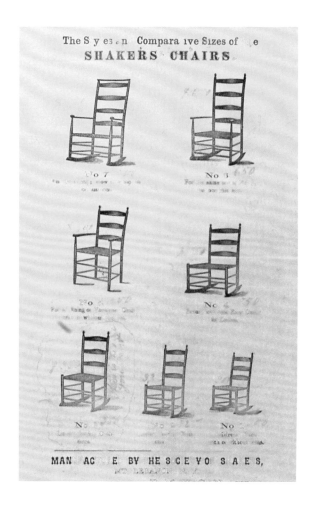

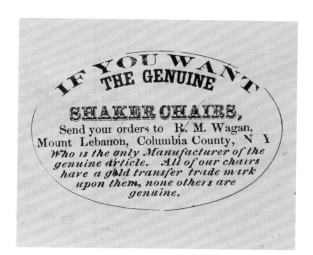

many colored wool seat tapes were also offered. Footstools of two designs were also made—one with a low, canted plank top, the other taller, with a flat, taped top. The South Family continued to be the site of production until the business relocated to the Second Family about 1910. After this time, the South Family was mainly involved with the repair and retaping of older production chairs, as well as selling chairs made at the Second Family factory (figs. 3-19, 3-20).

It goes without saying that the chair industry provided a major boost to Mount Lebanon's economy as the century progressed. Shaker production chairs were honored with a Certificate of Award at the 1876 Philadelphia Centennial Exhibition; in the 1880s they found themselves having to buy parts from outside sources to meet increasing demand. Most of the chairs that the community manufactured were sold wholesale to large furniture and department stores, rather than being sold retail to the carriage trade, a sales strategy that we see repeated over and over until late in the nineteenth century, when the communities that had objects to sell happily opened their doors to the World's people. Within a few years of Mount Lebanon's closing in 1947, chairs were still being repaired and seats retaped there. The ultimate tribute to the popularity and sturdiness of these chairs, as well as the special place that they held in people's homes and

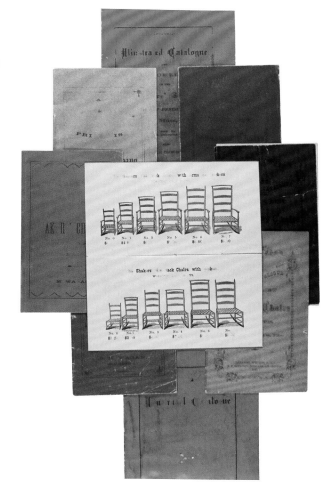

Fig. 3-18. By the time of the 1876 Centennial Exposition in Philadelphia, a number of companies were imitating the already-celebrated Shaker chair. Mount Lebanon countered by branding theirs "The Genuine Shaker Chairs," and they added a trademarked, gold-colored transfer decal to every chair and stool made. Thereafter, genuine Shaker Chair(s) appeared in all advertising copy for these products.

Fig. 3-19. By 1920, half a century after its founding, the once-busy chair industry was showing signs of decline. Sister Lillian Barlow and Brother William Perkins, however, injected new life into the business, and when this billhead was printed in the 1920s, the industry was quite active again. As seen here, Mount Lebanon often sent out samples of chair tapes to help customers choose their colors.

Fig. 3-20. In the years between 1874 and 1880, Mount Lebanon issued a series of illustrated chair catalogues, all with colorful covers, line cuts of chair styles available, and directions for ordering. The Shakers' response to the threat of competition from 1875 on was also evident: "Look for our trademark before purchasing—no chair is genuine without it. Our trade-mark is a gold transfer."

hearts, may be the large number that survive to the present day. Even President Lincoln had one in the White House.[28]

FINISHED MEDICINES

In 1880, when the Shaker chairs were achieving great financial success, Mount Lebanon still had 340 members. The next largest of the eleven eastern communities then was Canterbury, with fewer than half that number.[29] This strength enabled Mount Lebanon to lead the way in the area of compounded or finished medicines. (These were in addition to other herb-based products designed strictly for external use.) Among this group were Imperial Rose Balm, a lotion whose recommended uses were as a "cosmetic, dentifrice, perfume"; Shaker Hair Restorer (fig. 3-21); The Shaker Asthma Cure; and Shaker Toothache Pellets.[30]

The last of these was in some ways the most interesting, for it was developed by a former prominent member from Mount Lebanon, James V. Calver. He left the community in 1871, and in 1880, at the age of forty-one, he enrolled in dental school in Baltimore. Following graduation (and marriage), he established a private practice in Washington, D.C. Over the years, he maintained contact with his for-

mer home, and in 1888 he brought a formula to them that he had developed for the palliative treatment of toothaches (fig. 3-22). The formula contained three active ingredients: pure wood creosote, oil of eucalyptus, and oil of cloves. It should be noted that his wife was also a trained chemist and that she carried on the business after his death in 1913, relocating to Los Angeles in the 1920s.

An entrepreneurial trustee at Mount Lebanon, Benjamin Gates, agreed to manufacture, package, and sell the medicine—in the form of saturated pellets of wool, housed in small glass vials—returning a share of the profits to Calver. We do not have sales figures for the product, but we know it was marketed from 1890 until the 1920s. Calver assumed full control of manufacturing and sales in 1897, probably because total membership (including children) at the community had dropped from 340 in 1880 to just 116 in 1900. This chain of events foreshadowed the next major challenge facing the Shakers.

By the 1880s, the cumulative weaknesses that had been plaguing most Shaker communities for years were becoming painfully evident. The number of recruits at many villages, but not all, had been steadily diminishing since the 1860s, while the number of children who chose to remain after

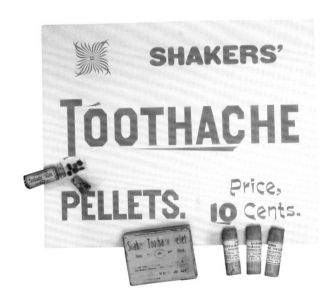

their teen years also continued to drop.[31] Longtime members were aging, becoming less productive, and requiring more care, and effective leaders—especially among the men—were becoming increasingly difficult to find. Poor money management, even occasional malfeasance, caused some societies to go into debt. If this litany of woes was not enough, competition from the World was largely responsible for the collapse of their two largest industries, garden seeds and medicinal herbs. In 1875 the first of the eighteen long-lived villages (Tyringham, Massachusetts) closed, and North Union, Ohio, and Groveland, New York, would follow suit before the end of the century.

At this point, one might expect a group whose entire history in America was marked by the need to respond to challenges from both without and within to resign themselves to their "fate"—their continued diminishment toward an inevitable vanishing point. Yet this did not happen. In 1900 the Eastern communities, with a quarter of the membership they had had only forty years earlier, were still managing to hold on. (In the West, the last of the six communities closed by 1922.) All in all, it was a discouraging picture, but against all odds the movement soldiered on.

LATE TEXTILES AND HAND CRAFTS

In the last two decades of the 1800s, it was mainly Shaker sisters who met the challenge of keeping their movement alive and who rose to the occasion, all by dint of their hands. In particular it was the women at Alfred, Maine (who later transferred their energies to Sabbathday Lake, after Alfred closed), Canterbury, Enfield (New Hampshire), and Mount Lebanon—supported by a few strong men, such as Brother Delmer Wilson at Sabbathday Lake—who brought their communities into or through the twentieth century. They developed an economy that largely turned its back on the land as the primary source of income and developed two industries that were new to them—commercial textiles and fancy goods.

Fig. 3-23. In 1940, Sister Aida Elam of Canterbury visited with Charles Adams, director of the New York State Museum in Albany. Adams's daughter, Harriet, subsequently ordered a cloak from Sister Aida. This group of ephemera includes a note to Harriet, an order form (showing views with the hood up and down), and samples of wool broadcloths and lining silks.

Although it is true that in the twentieth century Shaker farms continued to produce foodstuffs for communal use and to a small extent for commerce, they now played a minor role in their communities' economies. It is also true that whereas Believers produced flax (for linen), wool, and leather from their earliest days and fabricated their own clothing, by 1890 they had been buying most of these goods from the World for half a century.

Now, however, they began making textile goods for the World. The earliest of the mass-produced items of clothing in standardized sizes, shapes, colors, and options (such as with or without hoods or pockets), were cloaks and capes, the latter a two-thirds-length version of the former. It is believed that Eldress Dorothy Durgin, a sister at Canterbury, made the first of these, supposedly patterning the first one on the design of her own raincoat,[32] hence the trademark-protected name "The Dorothy." Enfield (New Hampshire), Mount Lebanon, and Sabbathday Lake also developed cloak industries, but the number of surviving examples indicates that Canterbury seems to have been the largest.

The Shakers used finely woven wool broadcloth imported from France to make the cloaks, and when they were lined, satin-woven or brocaded silk was used. Some of the success of the industry may

Fig. 3-24. A postcard image of the gift store at Sabbathday Lake in about 1909. Located on a public road in each village, these stores served as an "interface" between the Shakers and the World. Collection of Canterbury Shaker Village, 46-P194.

Fig. 3-25. In the first quarter of the 20th century, Canterbury also made sweaters for sale. This V-neck example uses a heavy-gauge "Harvard Crimson" red wool and weighs more than a pound. Shaker-knit sweaters were available in many other styles, including cardigans and turtlenecks, and in other Ivy League colors. Sweaters were packaged in the type of cardboard box seen in the background.

be attributable to the large number of options available to the women who ordered them. Most orders were made by mail. Customers would receive an order blank that contained instructions on what measurements were necessary (back and front lengths, across chest, and around neck) and what options were available. The top of the line was fully lined and included a pleated hood and pockets. All cloaks and capes came with the following assurance: "Quality of material and workmanship guaranteed to give satisfaction."

Another textile industry, this one unique to Canterbury, was the manufacture of Shaker-knit sweaters (fig. 3-25).[33] The community began making these sweaters on site using commercially made knitting machines purchased from the World in 1886, and they continued doing so until 1923. These, too, were offered with a number of options, including several styles (V-neck, cardigan, shawl collar, and turtleneck collar), weights (light, medium, heavy, and extra heavy), and colors. The Ivy League provided a steady source of customers, and among the colors offered were "Dartmouth Green" and "Harvard Crimson." The heaviest gauge examples sold for $6 in 1910, and 1,489 sweaters were made that year.

The modest success of Shaker textiles was altogether overshadowed, however, by the development of their fancy goods (or fancywork) industry. It is fair to say that this was the late-nineteenth- and early-twentieth-century equivalent of the garden seed industry some seventy-five or so years earlier. In other words, it was not only a large enterprise, relatively speaking, but it was also hugely important in the economies of the communities that survived past 1920. Alfred, Canterbury, Mount Lebanon, and Sabbathday Lake depended on the manufacture and sale of fancy goods for their very survival, while at Enfield and Hancock, these were more of a sideline. There were three general types of goods produced and sold: poplar ware, outfitted sewing carriers, and a miscellaneous group of "others."

There is every reason to believe that woven poplar-covered boxes (fig. 3-26) were wholly a Shaker innovation, for we know of no corresponding form in the World. The specifics of the early development of this process are somewhat obscure, but it first emerged as a distinct craft about the time of the Civil War, probably at Mount Lebanon.[34] A closer look at this industry reveals another aspect of the Shakers' perennial genius for overcoming adversity, in this instance by "spinning dross into gold."

In the 1860s, the Shakers clearly needed a product to sell that could compete successfully in the World. At that time, only Mount Lebanon had a dependable income from the sale of garden seeds and, along with Harvard, still had a large medicinal herb business. Several communities had large supplies of poplar trees available, the wood of which served primarily as a secondary wood for Worldly cabinetmakers. Mount Lebanon was one village that had a number of looms no longer being used

Fig. 3-26. Poplarware boxes were made in several communities, in an assortment of shapes and sizes. Top row (left to right): Canterbury, Sabbathday Lake, Canterbury. Bottom row (left to right): Canterbury, Sabbathday Lake, Alfred. These were immensely popular sales items, from the 1890s into the 1940s, and examples abound to the present day.

Fig. 3-27. This spool stand (center) was probably made at Canterbury, early in the 20th century, although several communities made similar-looking ones. The pincushion (right), also from Canterbury, is trimmed in "rickrack," a form of poplar weaving supposedly learned from local Indians. The scallop shell pincushion was made at Sabbathday Lake, around 1880.

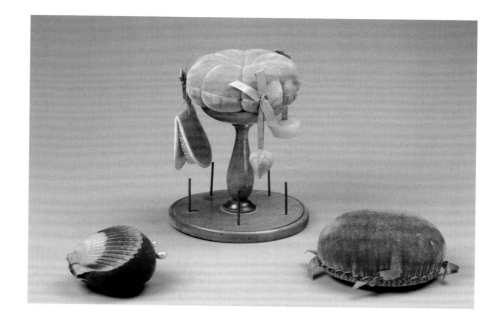

much for weaving. There were also many (women's) hands available that could be spared from the soil-based industries, which were in slight decline and certainly less active in the winter. Most importantly, however, the Shakers had vision and were able to devise a plan to turn an almost worthless tree into a craft industry. Looking back from nearly 150 years later, we find it difficult to believe the extent of their insight or to foresee the eventual success of this undertaking. Yet they pushed on, and in the twentieth century, more poplar ware was made and sold than any other type of Shaker crafted goods. Brethren first cut down poplar trees and reduced them to manageable lengths at their sawmills, which were otherwise idle during the winter.

This was also a time when other farm chores demanded less time and when poplar wood could be readily split, shaved into pliable strips, and dried on the racks in the laundry building. At this point, the sisters took over, further processing the shavings into very thin, narrow strips of wood. These were taken to cotton-warped looms and woven into a poplar "cloth." It is said that the young girls at Canterbury would spend time weaving every morning before their school day began.

Sisters backed the cloth with paper for addi-

tional strength, and then trimmed and fashioned it into a wide variety of box shapes around solid bases of poplar or pine wood. The interiors of the boxes were lined with satin-woven silk, and the edges of the poplar cloth were trimmed with white kid leather. In the final step, matching colored ribbons were added to the boxes to hold sewing implements and to secure the lids.

The process of producing poplarware was labor-intensive in the extreme, which is probably why nobody in the World seems to have shown an interest in competing with Shaker production. The Shakers' long tradition of excellent hand work, however, was the ideal answer to the World's growing interest in fancy objects that characterized late Victorian taste (figs. 3-27, 3-28).

Sales of these goods (and other fancy products as well) occurred in one of three ways: at gift stores inside the trustees' offices of Shaker villages that straddled well-traveled roads, where the public was always welcomed; by mail order, through illustrated catalogues; or by direct contact between Shakers and customers at sites outside the communities. To accomplish this last, Believers made sales trips, first in horse and wagon and later by automobile, to resorts throughout New England (and beyond), and they also set up booths at local and regional fairs. The poplarware industry was a vital enterprise for the economic well-being of Alfred, where it lasted into the 1930s, and at Sabbathday Lake and Canterbury, where it continued into the 1950s.

Another late craft industry that developed from an available Shaker resource and that met with an interested buying public was the manufacture of outfitted sewing carriers. Fortunately, we can identify a specific time, place, and individual to whom credit for this enterprise can be given. The resource here was mainly wood, and the technique derived from a long tradition of making oval boxes. In 1894 Brother Delmer Wilson of Sabbathday Lake was shown several oval boxes that had been made at Mount Lebanon and then fitted out with handles. Several sisters at Sabbathday Lake decided to line these carriers (which were almost always oval-shaped boxes with either a fixed or a pivoting

Fig. 3-28. In the first two decades of the 20th century, Alfred (lower left, 1908), Mount Lebanon (lower right, 1910), and Sabbathday Lake (top left, 1910, top right, ca. 1920) issued catalogues with illustrations of their fancy goods. The two Maine societies used photo-engravings to display their goods whereas Mount Lebanon resorted to simple line drawings.

"swing" handle) and to add sewing implements. They brought the sewing carriers to a large resort hotel located in Poland Spring, only a few miles north of the community, and, as Brother Delmer reported, "It started a craze."[35]

In 1896 Brother Delmer began to make his own carriers, which the sisters outfitted with silk linings and four sewing accoutrements: a piece of beeswax to strengthen thread, a strawberry-shape emery to sharpen needles, a pincushion, and a needle case made from several leaves of felt with poplar-ware covers. Each object was attached to the inside of the carrier with a silk ribbon. Only thirty of the boxes were made during the first year of production, all of cherry wood and all round in shape (fig. 3-29).

After this, all of the sewing carriers made by Sabbathday Lake and Alfred were oval in shape and had swing handles, but none had lids, unlike those produced by the sewing carrier industry that developed at Mount Lebanon in the 1920s, where all the carriers were lidded. The sides were often made from locally available apple wood (there was a large orchard on the property), but maple and quarter-sawn oak were occasionally used as well. Sewing carriers were available in four lengths, from 7 to 11 inches. Many thousands of these were made over the next fifty years or so, more than one thousand in Brother Delmer's peak production year of 1923. The Poland Spring Hotel remained a major point of sales for the Sabbathday Lake Shakers well into the twentieth century (fig. 3-30).[36]

In the early years of the twentieth century, many other hand-made goods were added to the few we have considered, most of them intended for household tasks (fig. 3-31). Indeed, nearly all of the objects were made by Shaker sisters to be sold to women for their personal use. Although none of these achieved anything like the success of poplar-ware or sewing carriers, because they were made one by one on a relatively small scale, they nonetheless show how the communities of Alfred, Canterbury, Mount Lebanon, and Sabbathday Lake—all dominated by women—met the challenges of a new century in the near absence of Shaker brothers.

Fig. 3-29. This simple round sewing carrier, made at Sabbathday Lake in 1896, was the progenitor of a rather large-scale industry, later carried on at Alfred and Mount Lebanon as well. After the first few were made, all of the rest (made into the 1950s) were oval-shaped. Typically they were outfitted with a pincushion, needle case, emery bag (to sharpen needles), and wax (to add strength to thread). Most carriers were lined with satin-woven silk.

Fig. 3-30. These three sewing carriers were also made at Sabbathday Lake, at some point in the first half of the 20th century. Precise dates cannot be assigned, since no changes were made until felt-covered needle cases replaced woven-poplar ones about 1950. Brother Delmer Wilson made these in four sizes, from 7 to 11 inches long, using cherry, maple, ash, and apple woods. Sisters at the community lined and outfitted them.

Fig. 3-31. Many Shaker villages made brooms, brushes, and mops for sale. The two horse-hair brushes in the center, 8 ½ and 10 inches long, were made at Sabbathday Lake, probably in the 1920s. The two longer pieces, made with wool, are referred to in catalogues as both dusters and dish mops, and perhaps they could have been used for either. Most of these came from Canterbury and Mount Lebanon and were made for many years.

The list of items in this category includes fans made of palm leaf, paper, turkey feathers, and poplar; small hat or clothing brushes; pincushions in a wide variety of forms and sometimes encased in such novel materials as scallop shells and poplar-ware bases; roll-up sewing cases; knit and fur gloves; eyeglass wipes; pen wipes; pot holders; and doll's clothing. Some of these goods were first made toward the end of the nineteenth century, but their crafting continued for at least the first decades of the twentieth.

FOOD PRODUCTION

In addition to these hand-made items must be added panoplies of comestibles, such as jams, jellies, syrups, candies, pickled and canned fruits, and above all else, fresh and preserved fruits and vegetables. Each of these products was available at one or another of the communities, nearly all of which had acreage set aside in fields and orchards through most of the nineteenth century for commercial food production. Fresh, whole fruits and vegetables required little hand labor once they were planted and harvested, but processed foods were a different story (figs. 3-32, 3-33).

Few financial records were kept or have survived for this type of industry, but it must have been sufficiently profitable to justify the time and effort or the specialized machinery (such as corn-shelling and drying devices), additional ingredients (such as sugar and vinegar), and packaging materials (firkins, barrels, and glassware) necessary to carry it out successfully.

The list of processed foods that were important sources of revenue included apples for cider in barrels and sauce in jars; string, lima, and butter beans, which were boiled and canned; dried sweet green corn in cardboard boxes and formed wooden containers; honey, gathered and put up in jars; tomatoes made into catsup; pickled cucumbers; and sugared nuts. The list goes on and on. Although no single product constituted a major industry in itself, cumulatively they were steady sources of communal income into the first decades

of the twentieth century (fig. 3-34). These were not industries characterized by a great degree of standardization, and this may explain the dearth of sales records. What we do have are many anecdotal recordings scattered in private dairies and shop journals.

THE LATER YEARS

Sabbathday Lake, the last active community, reached a precarious state at several points during the twentieth century. It was physically isolated from the rest of the movement and also suffered from the ailments common to its sister communities, especially the lack of young, spiritually strong members. In 1931 it took in a group of mostly younger and enthusiastic sisters from nearby Alfred when that village closed. These women (there were only two elderly men left at Alfred) infused their new home with a spiritual vigor that altered the trajectory of traditional Shakerism for at least another forty years.

The death of Brother Delmer Wilson in 1961, the establishment of the Shaker Trust Fund, and the lack of attention paid to several new applications for membership in the society all contributed to rumors that the Shaker covenant was "closed." However, this was never the case. In fact, when Brother Theodore Johnson (1931–1986) joined the community at about this time, the second renewal in the century of the Shaker spirit took place. Brother Ted, as he was called, helped revive certain religious practices, as well as the latent industry of raising and selling dried and packaged culinary herbs and herbal teas. By the 1970s, dozens of varieties were offered in small tins, either through outlets (often museum gift shops) or by mail order. This business is still active, with most sales now made through the Internet. Sabbathday Lake also has a hugely popular annual Christmas Fair, where hand-made goods and homemade sweets are sold. Nevertheless, culinary herbs and teas, along with wool from the village's sheep, remain the steadiest source of income for Shakers in the twenty-first century (fig. 3-35).

* * *

The influence of the Shakers in many areas of American culture has always been disproportionate to their small numbers. Whereas it is the aesthetic of spare furniture design that is uppermost in the contemporary consciousness, it is their legacy of effective commerce that has arguably been their most profound contribution. It is certain that without a solid economic base for communal living, the Shakers could not have lasted very far beyond their founding. When they reached their peak population of almost 5,000 members in the late 1840s, the population of the rest of the United States was approximately 23 million. Thus, they accounted for a mere .0002 percent of the total. Yet, as we have seen, their impact in two broad areas of commerce—garden seeds and medicinal herbs—was enormous.

By developing a seed industry that catered to the retail market, the Shakers were the first to address the needs of consumers who wanted to plant small gardens. Soon afterward, they met the nascent but growing demand for medicinal herbs by those individuals who sought help outside standard medical practices. In fact, by 1850 herb production exceeded garden seeds as the largest source of revenues in the movement. Although we

have considered only the preparation of medicinal herbs for the retail market, many more tons were also sold wholesale to large commercial houses that marketed non-Shaker "patent medicines." And, while these two ventures accounted for most of the income at nearly all, if not all, Shaker villages, the crafting of woodenwares and processing of food-stuffs remained reliable moneymakers as well.

From 1850 to the present, the numbers of Shakers steadily declined as those for the general population grew dramatically. Today there are only a small handful of Believers remaining at the single active community of Sabbathday Lake, Maine, while the population of the United States has soared past 300 million. There were many factors that contributed to this decline apart from the matter of the Shakers' core belief in celibacy: a failure to recruit new members can partially be attributed to complacency—a falling away from the fervor of the first generations; a lack of effective leadership, especially among the ranks of the brethren; and the disruptive presence of a disproportionately large number of children in many communities—children who, after a huge investment of the societies' resources, seldom remained in the faith when they reached the age of majority.

Yet even the raw numbers do not tell the whole story. Another overwhelming factor over that span

Fig. 3-32. Most Shaker villages had fruit orchards, among which were many acres of apple trees. This versatile fruit was processed into sauce, cider, and butter, as well as being baked or eaten whole. Applesauce was sold in jars, firkins, and even barrels. These two labels, measuring about 10 inches across, were intended to be pasted on barrelheads and differ only in the trustees named: R [obert] Valentine (of the Church Family) and G. H [enry] Cantrell (of the North Family), Mount Lebanon. They date to about 1890.

Fig. 3-33. New Lebanon was the first Shaker village, in 1828, to develop the equipment needed to successfully dry sweet corn for commerce. Enfield, Connecticut, and Hancock, Massachusetts, later followed suit. The Hancock Shakers put up this container, made of bentwood, late in the 19th century. Instructions for use were printed on the label and included "soak for two hours previous to cooking."

of time was the demographic shift that took place in this country. In 1850 only 15.4 percent of people counted in the U.S. Census was classified as "urban." In the most recent census of 2000, 81 percent of the population was designated "urban." At the start of this essay, Shaker communal villages were likened to large farming collectives. The simple fact is that over the past 150 years, a great many people have chosen to abandon the farming life and this has had no small impact on the number of individuals who have chosen to live the Shaker life.

If one were to ask the present-day Shakers about their prospects for the future, their response would likely be that it is in God's hands. For them, the small number of members is not a meaningful measure of their lives. They simply go about doing their work as they live out their vision of the Christlife in the here and now, each and every day. Furthermore—and this is essential to our understanding of Shakerism in our time—they remain secure in their belief that if the first founders of the sect were to reappear at Sabbathday Lake today, they would fully recognize and be "in union" with the Believers there.

On the other hand, for so many of us who live in the World, a curiosity about these people that began well over two hundred years ago continues unabated. As this exhibition and this publication should make abundantly clear, the Shakers—past and present—still matter.

Fig. 3-34. In the 1870s and 1880s, Sabbathday Lake shipped barrels of pickles, horseradish, and catsup to a merchant in Portland, Maine, named E. D. Pettingill. He put these up in bottles (and some catsup in large, ceramic jugs) to sell in the World. Following his death, Pettingill's widow filed papers with the state that allowed her to carry on the business using the "Shaker brand" trademark.

Fig. 3-35. The most important business at Sabbathday Lake—the last active community—is the raising of herbs for culinary use, including many herbal teas. Ever since this industry was revived in the 1970s, these products have been packaged in small round tins, with labels that are still printed at the community. The always-progressive Shakers now make most of their sales through the Internet.

All objects illustrated in this chapter are from the collection of M. Stephen and Miriam Miller." Figs. 3-6, 3-14, 3-15, 3-17, 3-27, 3-30, 3-33, 3-34, 3-35, photographed by Bruce White. Fig. 3-24 photographed by Canterbury Shaker Village. All other photographs by M. Stephen Miller.

The author wishes to express his profound gratitude to Magda Gabor-Hotchkiss and Stephen Paterwic for their careful readings of this manuscript, followed by insightful commentary and suggestions. The world of Shaker scholarship is well served by their integrity, intelligence, and energy. Many other sources were drawn upon in preparing this essay: those not specifically cited in footnotes may be found in *From Shaker Lands and Shaker Hands: A Survey of the Industries* (2007) by this author.

1.   This distinction of the two names will be observed for pre- and post-1861 throughout this essay.

2.   New Lebanon and Union Village each had more than 600 members in the mid-nineteenth century.

3.   M. Stephen Miller, *From Shaker Lands and Shaker Hands: A Survey of the Industries* (Hanover, N.H., and London: University Press of New England, 2007) The specifics of all of the Shaker industries that are addressed in this essay, and much more, are covered in this book.

4.   The Shakers produced many foods, such as milk, cream, butter, cheese, eggs, wheat, oats, rye, barley, corn; beef, lamb, pork, poultry; fruits and vegetables (either fresh, prepared, or preserved); maple syrup, honey, and a few culinary herbs.

5.   Indeed, many Shakers partook of some spirits—in moderation—at some communities and at some periods in their long history. In the 18th and 19th centuries at least, these were believed to be aids to digestion. Hard cider was almost always available with meals and was made from apples from their own orchards. New Lebanon produced at least 17 varieties of wine—for "medicinal purposes"—by the mid-1800s. In the second half of the 19th century, a good deal of effort went into grape culture for wine production, at New Lebanon and especially at Union Village, Ohio.

6.   Single women, in New England at least—spinsters, widows, divorcees, and abandoned wives—were often extended additional rights that allowed them to earn a living for themselves and the children living with them. Glendyne Wergland: Personal communication. Ms. Wergland's full-length study of the role of women in Shaker communities, *Sisters in the Faith: Shaker Women, 1780–1900* is in the process of being published.

7.   Margaret Frisbee Somer, *The Shaker Garden Seed Industry* (Orono: University of Maine, 1966): 10, n. 1. Somer documents the existence of a wholesale seed house in Philadelphia, David Landreth & Son, which opened in 1784.

8.   Edward Deming Andrews, *The Community Industries of the Shakers* (Albany: University of the State of New York, 1933): 66–82. I am heavily indebted to Dr.

Andrews and this book, the first in-depth study of the multifarious Shaker industries, and its importance, even 75 years later, cannot be overstated.

9.   In reality, however, the greater the distance another community was from this "parent," the less likely they were to be in step with it. This was most apparent in Maine and in the Shaker West.

10.   Cheryl Bauer and Rob Portman, *Wisdom's Paradise: The Forgotten Shakers of Union Village* (Wilmington, Ohio: Orange Frazer Press, 2004): 268–69; and Priscilla J. Brewer, *Shaker Communities, Shaker Lives* (Hanover, N.H., and London: University Press of New England, 1986): 215–16. Union Village's population peaked at 634 in 1818 and declined in the ensuing decades; New Lebanon reached its maximum of about 550 in 1860. At one time, Union Village had at least nine families but in 1860 it had only 372 members.

11.   Stephen Bowe and Peter Richmond, *Selling Shaker: The Commodification of Shaker Design in the Twentieth Century* (Liverpool: Liverpool University Press, 2007). The bibliography (pp. 246–49), lists 41 references for the Andrewses. Also see Christian Goodwillie and Mario DePillis, *Gather Up the Fragments: The Andrews Shaker Collection* (New Haven: Yale University Press, in press).

12.   Edward Deming Andrews Memorial Collection, Winterthur, Del., # SA 1452.

13.   Rita Buchanan, *The Shaker Herb and Garden Book* (Boston and New York: Houghton Mifflin Company, 1996): 64. This book contains a wealth of information on the Shaker garden seed and medicinal herb industries.

14.   This prosperity ended when Northern companies once again penetrated Southern markets, and by 1880 South Union, too, was out of business.

15.   Andrews, *Community Industries* (1933): 67.

16.   Ibid., 73.

17.   These communities made mainly pails and then only in the second half of the 19th century. In fact, only the sap pails made at Enfield can be considered a true industry, for these alone used standardized sizes with uniform construction.

18.   Rufus Bishop and Seth Y. Wells, *Testimonies of the Life, Character, Revelations and Doctrines of Our Ever Blessed Mother Ann Lee. . .* (Hancock, Mass., 1816): 309.

19.   Tin dippers were also made and sold by New Lebanon for use with liquids. It is nearly impossible now to distinguish any Shaker–made tinware from Worldly examples. Although there are documented examples of tin wares used at and acquired from some of the communities, no one can be certain that they were actually made by Shakers. The one exception is dust pails, which were made in a distinctive—perhaps unique—manner that incorporated a round wire around their rims. They were generally made from tin-plated sheet iron; the iron gave them rigidity and the plating prevented rusting.

20.   Reproduction boxes, by contrast, are rarely able to achieve the intimate contact between fingers and

body that well-made 150-year-old Shaker examples consistently did.

21. The following books are invaluable sources of information on the Shaker medicine industry: Galen Beale and Mary Boswell, *The Earth Shall Blossom: Shaker Herbs and Gardening* (Woodstock, Vt.: The Countryman Press, 1991); Amy Bess Miller, *Shaker Medicinal Herbs: A Compendium of History, Lore, and Uses* (Pownal, Vt.: Storey Books, 1998); and Buchanan, *Shaker Herb and Garden Book* (1996). In addition, this essay is indebted to my late friend Professor Emeritus J. Worth Estes of the Department of Pharmacology and Experimental Medicine, Boston University of Medicine. Dr. Estes published several articles late in his career about Shaker medicines. These include "The Shakers and their Proprietary Medicines," *Bulletin of Historical Medicine* 65 (1991): 162–84, and "Shaker-Made Remedies," *Pharmacy in History* 34 (1992): 63–73. "The Pharmacology of Nineteenth-Century Patent Medicines," *Pharmacy in History* 30 (1988): 3–18 is useful in providing a context for Shaker remedies.

22. The U.S. census of 1820 did not distinguish between rural and urban populations, but the dominance of the former may be inferred from the fact that six times as many people were listed as engaged in agriculture as in manufacturing.

23. Beale and Boswell, *The Earth Shall Blossom* (1991): 103.

24. There were, in fact, several other individuals who, along with their published works, had a profound influence on the practice of nontraditional medicine just before Thomson. These included William Buchan, M.D., and his *Every man his own doctor . . .* , Amos Eaton's *Manual of Botany . . .* , and Constantine S. Rafinesque's *Medical Flora. . . .* Each of these is cited in Rita Buchanan, *The Shaker Herb and Garden Book* (1996): 100–101.

25. Beale and Boswell, *The Earth Shall Blossom* (1991): 32–34, 118–20.

26. Another myth is exposed here: the Shakers received patents for many of their products and inventions, their legendary altruism notwithstanding. It should be understood, however, what a patent meant: far from being secret, the ingredients in a product were named. The patent simply guaranteed that their manufacturer was granted exclusivity for a specified period of time. A proprietary, by contrast, was a drug with an unpublished formula.

27. Gerard C. Wertkin, *The Four Seasons of Shaker Life* (New York: Simon & Schuster, 1986): 81, 90.

28. Charles R. Muller and Timothy D. Rieman, *The Shaker Chair* (Winchester, Ohio: The Canal Press, 1984): 174 reproduces the letter sent from the Executive Mansion to New Lebanon, dated 1864. This book is also an excellent source of information about the entire chair industry.

29. Brewer, *Shaker Communities* (1986). This is an invaluable resource for information about the forces that shaped Shaker communities and their members, including statistical data for the Eastern communities.

30. Miller, *From Shaker Lands and Shaker Hands* (2007): 66–72. More information about each of these products (and several others intended for external use) will be found here.

31. Ibid., 7–19. Contributing scholar Stephen Paterwic devotes much of his essay "Who Were the Shakers?" to the matter of the decline of Shaker communities in the 19th century.

32. Scott T. Swank, *Shaker Art, Life, and Architecture* (New York: Abbeville Press, 1999): 195–96.

33. Ibid., 195.

34. Gerrie Kennedy, Galen Beale, and Jim Johnson, *Shaker Baskets & Poplarware* (Stockbridge, Mass.: Berkshire House Publishers, 1992): 86–135. This is the best source for information about this industry.

35. *The Shaker Quarterly* 15, no. 4 (1987), and 16, no. 1 (1988).

36. David L. Richards, *Poland Spring: A Tale of the Gilded Age, 1860–1900* (Durham: University of New Hampshire Press, 2005). This book discusses the early, warm relations that developed between the community and the resort.

The Spiritual World

4   The Problem of Female Leadership in Early Shakerism

JEAN M. HUMEZ

Most students of early Shaker history are familiar with the story of how the founding visionary leader, the English-born Ann Lee (1736–1784), established her right, as a woman, to head the new church she and her closest religious associates founded in America. According to Jethro Turner, one of her early male American followers, she was specifically asked by potential converts Joseph Meacham and Calvin Harlow about the apparent contradiction between her leadership role and her gender. She answered with an illuminating metaphor, comparing the governance of the church of Christ to the governance of the family.[1]

> Mother answered, "The order of man, in the natural creation, is a figure of the order of God in the spiritual creation. . . . Where they both stand in their proper order, the man is the first, and the woman the second in the government of the family. . . . All the children, both male and female, must be subject to their parents; and the woman, being second, must be subject to her husband, who is the first; but when the man is gone, the right of government belongs to the woman: So is the family of Christ."

Joseph Meacham acknowledged Ann Lee's spiritual authority as a result, we are told.

> He saw Jesus Christ to be the Father of the spiritual creation, who was now absent; and he saw Ann Lee to be the Mother of all who were now begotten in the regeneration, and she being present in the body, the power and authority of Christ on earth, was committed to her; and to her appertained the right of leading, directing and governing all her spiritual children.

The feminist theologian and Shaker scholar Marjorie Procter-Smith wryly characterizes this as Lee's "absent husband theory of female leadership." As Procter-Smith has pointed out, Lee's answer to Joseph Meacham in this text, "while not denying Lee's leadership over the group, still legitimates patriarchal authority structures."[2] Indeed, Ann Lee's accommodationist strategy for claiming female authority in family and church only in the metaphoric "absence of the male" seriously undermined the claim to authority of future female Shaker leaders.

A dramatic ambivalence about the legitimacy of women leaders who were not clearly "under obedience" to males is amply documented in the first half century of Shakerism, after what had been a millenarianistic religious movement became institutionalized as a growing communal religious society, dependent upon new conversions for its growth and ultimately embodied in eleven distinct communities in New York and New England and another seven thriving villages in Kentucky and Ohio.[3] In a significant number of instances, the resistance of some Shaker males to church government headed by a woman was a key component in political turmoil within and between Shaker communities. Even when other governance problems were probably more important sources of the conflict, the accusation of "petticoat government" could be and was used by rebellious or dissenting Shaker males to put the established leadership on the defensive. Several cases of this kind of conflict highlight a dynamic tension between the sexes over female political power, stemming from Shakerism's original uneasy marriage of conservative and radical strains of gender ideology.

Fig. 4-1. Grave of Ann Lee, Watervliet, New York. Photo: Jean Burks.

THE LEGACY OF SACRED ANN LEE IMAGERY IN EARLY SHAKERISM

Ann Lee was arguably one of the most influential female religious leaders in Anglo-American history, yet because she was illiterate, all of our knowledge of her thought and achievements is indirect, refracted through the imaginations and writing of her followers. One of the earliest collections of Shaker testimonial literature, the 1816 *Testimonies*, contains dramatically contradictory images of Ann Lee based on the memories of her early followers, collected from twenty to thirty years after her death.

Stories about the doings and sayings of Ann Lee circulated in oral form for two or three decades before they were ultimately fixed in writing and published. The collectors and editors of these memories faced the challenging task of creating a permanent "gospel story" to guide future Shakers who would have no first-hand experience of the leader herself.[4] This task was undertaken during a period when Shakerism was still very much under attack—the first quarter of the nineteenth century. Much of the public criticism of the United Society by seceders and other anti-Shaker writers focused on a hostile representation of the figure of Ann Lee herself—as a "woman in authority over men," a pretended "second Christ," a fortune-teller, a drunkard, a false prophet, or miracle worker.[5] Thus the image of her that emerges from early Shaker literature, whether public or private, is shaped by three needs: to comfort and inspire Believers, to educate and impress would-be converts, and to repel and chastise enemies.

The massive *Testimonies* of 1816 was designed as an internal community document, created in much the same spirit as oral history in the modern age—in an effort to preserve as much accurate detail about the past as possible for the instruction of future generations.[6] It is generally recognized as providing both the earliest and the fullest evidence of any Shaker publication of the impression Ann Lee made on her American followers,[7] but it is less often understood as a major source of the widely different and at times conflicting images of Ann Lee

as a female religious leader, with which later Shaker women in authority would have to contend.[8] Certainly any public figure—perhaps especially the religious or political leader—enters "history" at least in part through the medium of the imaginations and memories of her or his followers. In the case of the female religious leader—already an anomaly by virtue of her unusual authority over men—the story of how her historical image is created and affects subsequent generations is necessarily even more complex.

The tension among contrasting characterizations of Lee in the 1816 *Testimonies* reflects a real tension within Shakerism from the outset over the meaning of her ministry.[9] A series of personal-experience narratives recalling the earliest days of her charismatic ministry provides rich evidence of the ambivalence she aroused as a powerful woman in authority over her followers. On the one hand, she evidently inspired many individuals and families in rural settings in New England and New York to leave their familiar worlds behind and join the United Society of Believers in Christ's Second Appearing—the fledgling Shaker church. On the other hand, memories of her as a frightening power help explain some of the strong and continuing resistance, of male Shakers in particular, to female leaders after Ann Lee's early death.

In the first kind of narrative, the personal-experience stories of her followers, we see Ann Lee primarily from the outside and, as it were, from a very much lower level. The tellers of these stories were generally both considerably younger than she was when they knew her, and they were often recent converts at the time of the events they describe. In these stories, she frequently emerges as a towering figure—awe-inspiring and sometimes terrifying—with two central aspects, the Seer[10] and the Strict Mother.

ANN LEE AS THE SEER

In most of the conversion stories included in the 1816 *Testimonies*, the seeker is convinced of the truth of Mother Ann's gospel through a direct experience of supernatural or divine power, which often occurred through her agency and had the effect of overcoming the seeker's original skepticism or doubt. Although she is not the only one among the elders who is remembered as reading minds, this was certainly among her powers.[11] For example, John Farrington tells a story about how he attempted to leave without confessing his sins, but "she told him many secret things that he had done, which he knew that she could not have known otherwise than by the revelation of God" (p. 26).

The Believers also remember falling into states of physical or psychological paralysis, apparently as a result of being in Lee's presence, if they tried to resist belief. For example, Hannah Knapp remembered being brought as a young girl to see Ann Lee and the elders by her own mother. Initially repelled by the physical "operations" for which the Shakers received their name, she said Mother Ann "acted like a drunken squaw." Immediately she "fell under . . . judgment" and was not "released" until Mother Ann "took her into her arms" and forgave her—at which moment the "judgement was taken away" (pp. 33–34).[12]

Not all of the conversion stories turn on the fear of punishment for skepticism, of course. Some clearly show the converts' confidence in Ann Lee's promise of spiritual and temporal rewards—such as the ability to convert their families, the recovery from worldly debt or illness, and, in the case of male converts especially, a future role as preacher or church leader.[13] Moreover, Believers sometimes had visionary experiences themselves, which were later explained by Lee and often confirmed with a visionary experience of her own. For example, Ebenezer Cooley had a predictive vision of a woman with a face as "bright as the sun" before he saw Ann Lee, and he recognized her as this woman at first sight. She, in turn, confirmed this by saying she had also seen him in vision and sending him to "go forth and preach the gospel" (pp. 26–27).[14]

Many of her followers told stories of the physically manifested "great sufferings," or "laboring under the power of God," which preceded and clearly indicated the onset of her special visionary states or prophetic utterances. In one vividly remembered example,

> One day, as Mother was walking the floor, and singing the melodious songs of the New Jerusalem, she turned to the people and said, "I feel a special gift of God; I feel the power of God running all over me." And stretching forth her hand toward the south west, she said, "The next opening of the gospel will be in the southwest; it will be at a great distance, and there will be a great work of God." And looking upon Elphalet Slosson, she said, "You may live to see it; but I shall not." (p. 222)

In several stories of Mother Ann's healing gifts, the touch of her hand or finger is vividly remembered.[15] In the most "miraculous" case, she strokes the sides of a little girl whose hip is put out, and this brings about a cure (p. 259). In general, however, her touch is represented more simply as immediately relieving exhaustion or anxiety. For example, John Bishop arrived at Ashfield to visit Mother after two days of traveling on foot. He was initially too tired to stand, but after Mother Ann took his hand, in the narrators' words: "The effect was like the sudden operation of an electric shock; he was instantly released from all weariness. John then felt as though he could willingly have danced all night" (p. 261).

Without question, the most impressive of Ann Lee's supernatural powers, as recorded in her followers' personal-experience narratives, is her ability to witness, report on, and perhaps even influence events in the world beyond death. There are many stories, particularly remembered by the women, of her visions of angels. Lucy Prescott remembered an occasion when Lee said in meeting, "The room over your heads is full of the angels of God. I see them and you could see them too, if you were redeemed from the nature of the flesh" (p. 230). She is also remembered as able to see "evil spirits" surrounding a Believer who was harboring secrets.[16] Frequently her reports on the movements of angels and evil spirits seem clearly aimed at influencing individual Believers' behavior, at bringing them to confess and forsake all sin. For example, Mary Spencer remembered Lee speaking directly to a convert about the presence of such invisible influences: "When you was speaking, I saw two souls standing by you, one at your right hand, and the other at your left. The one that stood at your right hand, was a bright, active, glorious soul; but the one on your left was a black, dark, dismal soul; and he laid his head on your shoulder" (p. 301).[17]

Lee's followers vividly remembered her ability to visit both the heavens and the "prisons of hell" in vision, and to report back in detail on the states of individual named spirits there. Frequently she spoke of witnessing the passage into the resurrection of the souls of the dead relatives of living Believers.[18] She would also report seeing the souls of recently deceased Believers in the spirit world, as when Jane Kendall died, and Lee told Jane's sister Sarah that she saw "Jane in the world of spirits . . . praising God in the dance" (p. 239). This was a highly comforting kind of vision to hear about, of course—one that was commonplace in the later Shaker spiritualism of mid-century, and one that helps explain the depth of the emotional appeal Shakerism had for many of the early Believers.

However, there was an unsettling side to this aspect of Ann Lee's power—an ability to see the unredeemed dead in their "lost state." She is remembered by Lydia Mathewson as having described exactly what it was like to begin the visionary journey into the underworld beyond death: "I felt the power of God come upon me, which moved my hand up and down like the motion of wings; and soon I felt as if I had wings on both hands; and I saw them, and they appeared as bright as gold. And I let my hands go as the power directed, and these wings parted the darkness to where souls lay, in the ditch of hell; & I saw their lost state" (p. 212).[19]

She is remembered as having taught that the unredeemed dead would visit their living Shaker relatives, in order to get help in starting toward redemption. Symptoms of bodily or psychological disturbance on the part of the Believer would often be read as signaling the presence of the dead, as when David Slosson visited Mother Ann at Ashfield and "felt himself as in the presence of God, and under great weight of body and spirit; but knew not the cause. Mother looked him full in the face, and then turned and looked on the elders, without speaking. After a short pause, she said, `David, you know not what you feel. I see the dead around you, whose visages are ghastly and very awful. Their faces almost touch thine. . . . Be of good comfort, and be not cast down; for the dead gather to thee for the gospel, which thou hast received'"(p. 240).[20]

The early Believers were frequently told of their own responsibility to help "bear for" the spirits of their dead relatives. This meant they had to suffer vicariously for the sins of those who had died without hearing the completion of the gospel, Ann Lee's testimony against all sin.[21] Even more fearsome, perhaps, was the doctrine that Believers had to participate in the salvation of their dead relatives, in order to find salvation themselves. Abijah Worster tells a story of having felt "peculiar operations" when kneeling by William Lee's bed. Mother Ann interpreted these for him: "You are not going into the kingdom without the progeny from which you sprung"(pp. 240–41).

Such stories allow modern students of Shakerism to see something of Ann Lee's skills as a religious leader who relied very largely on her own spiritualistic and visionary experiences to attract, convert, and teach others about the only path into the resurrection. However, reading about how Ann Lee's spiritualistic beliefs and enactments were seen through the eyes of her followers, it is also easy to see how she earned her persistent reputation as a sorceress or witch among nonbelievers.[22] She was clearly respected, if not feared, as a female prophet and clairvoyant—a woman with special powers that enabled her to search out and reveal what was hidden, whether within a person's mind, in heaven, or in hell. To confess one's sins at her bidding and promise to forsake them and start a new life would not only be a great psychological relief, for some converts, but perhaps their only course of safety as well.

THE STRICT MOTHER

The second major aspect of Lee's characterization in her followers' personal-experience narratives is what I would call "the strict mother"—and it is particularly strong in the chapters on her public and private speeches (chaps. 30–37). She is still very powerful and in some situations dangerous, though no longer supernaturally so. One can certainly point to mitigating stories, in which she is remembered as warm and emotionally expressive toward her followers. For example, we catch a glimpse of her kissing and blessing the child of Nathan Farrington (p. 276); or at another time she greets Sarah Hannum, "The king's daughter is all glorious within!" (p. 319). Yet the overall emphasis is on her role as strict disciplinarian as she instructs her spiritual children in how to live the new life.[23]

There are some stories in which Mother Ann's punishment of Believers for relatively minor offenses seems to border, for modern sensibilities, on the sadistic. For example, Mother Ann is remembered as making one Believer, who cut her nails on the Sabbath, kneel and walk on her knees to Elder James to be taught to pray (p. 314). Such stories are reminders that these were Shakerism's highly ascetic days, when bodily mortification exercises were practiced as necessary techniques for gaining access to the desired state of earthly sinlessness.[24]

In the memories of her followers, Ann Lee's references to hell and the threat of damnation are frequent. To a modern sensibility, they sometimes seem quite out of proportion to the situation that apparently called them forth. One example is an anecdote from Rebeccca Slosson, about a time when Mother reproved some Watervliet sisters for their wastefulness while washing: "It is a sin to waste soap, or any thing else that God has given you. If you knew the torments of hell, you would fear God in all you do and say" (p. 288). Hell and damnation are repeatedly pictured as the consequence of indulgence of "lusts," especially in the sexual sense. Mehetabel Farrington remembered her saying that souls that gratified their lusts in life "will be bound and tormented in the same parts

where they have taken their carnal pleasure" (p. 304).[25]

Even when her message was love, Ann Lee's strategy was frequently to threaten with damnation. For example, on one occasion, she is remembered as speaking authoritatively in front of a large group of Believers: "Hear ye my words, you that have hard feelings one against another, and yet think to keep the way of God! You are awfully mistaken; you cannot prosper. Though you may hang on for a while; yet you will certainly fall off, like withered branches; and when you drop into hell, these hard feelings will be like devouring worms, to torment you. Remember my words! You can never enter the Kingdom of God with hardness against any one: for God is love; and if you love God, you will love one another" (p. 281).[26]

A whole chapter of the 1816 *Testimonies* is devoted by the editors to Lee's "Reproof and Instruction" (chap. 22). The editors introduce the section with the comment that Mother's "power" in reproving and condemning sin "was beyond description . . . when she felt a gift of God to reprove . . . wickedness, the power of her spirit seemed like flames of fire, and the words of her mouth" were "more dreadful than peals of thunder; so that the most stubborn and stouthearted would shake and tremble in her presence, like a leaf shaken with a mighty wind" (p. 280).

There are several possible explanations for the prominence of the stern or harsh mother image in the 1816 *Testimonies*. One is simply that there was probably some historical reality here—the more sentimental Victorian ideal of the mother with which we moderns are so familiar had simply not yet been invented. As a pious working-class Englishwomen of her day, Lee would have very probably had what to modern minds would seem a rather severe, straitlaced attitude toward children. We can glimpse this through her remembered injunction against toys for children—they are not to have playthings to distract them from "the work of God in their creation" (p. 278); her advice that they should be "made to lie strait, to prevent them from growing crooked" (p. 277); and her belief that they must not be allowed to be idle, lest "they . . . grow up just like the world's children" (p. 277). She is quoted as saying that "a child four years old, indulged in sin, will bring the judgement of God upon a family" (p. 278). With this belief about the parent's responsibility for the spiritual condition of the child in the natural family, it is to be expected that her own behavior to her spiritual children would be modeled on this view. As she put it to one Believer she had severely chastised: "the reproof of a friend is better than the kiss of an enemy."[27]

Secondly, the way in which memories were collected and edited may have contributed to an overemphasis on the fierceness of Lee's behavior as a spiritual "mother." Collecting memories so long after the events probably disproportionately favored the most emotionally charged—those less laden with feeling having been more likely to be lost through the passage of time. The narrative point of view may also contribute to the emotional distance communicated in the portrait; the stories are generally collected from those who were quite young and by no means her equals in age, experience, or status in the Shaker communities. Their sense of their own weakness and powerlessness in relation to "the Mother" comes through in many of the stories they tell. In addition, the editorial decision to cluster the "reproof" stories together with an introduction emphasizing her voice "like thunder" undoubtedly plays its part. Although one can only speculate about this, editor Calvin Wells may have felt decided to portray Lee whenever possible as strong, authoritative, and even intimidating—perhaps as a counterbalance to the essentially weak image created in the narrative history of the mission to New England, which features her persecution and vulnerability as a "weak woman."[28]

THE WOMAN ABUSED: THE COMPOSITE NARRATIVE OF PERSECUTION IN NEW ENGLAND

In the center of the *Testimonies* we encounter a long series of chapters devoted to a narrative history of the persecution of the Believers during a

missionary trip through New England taken by Mother and the elders in 1781–83. The writer, apparently Calvin Green, is evidently concerned that divine guidance and protection can be seen in these events, despite many occasions when Mother Ann was insulted and assaulted and the pacifist Shakers were physically injured and driven off by mobs. Thus, stories are included of the "miraculous feeding" of the Shaker multitudes, seemingly patterned on the "loaves and fishes" story from the New Testament (e.g., p. 138); of the spontaneous healing of wounds caused by the mobs; of the way the trampled fields of grass miraculously sprang back after the Shakers had danced, so that their enemies could not say that they had caused their farmer friends any financial loss (pp. 169–70, 180).

At the end of the volume, two chapters on "Remarkable instances of the judgements of God upon reprobates and persecutors" act as a kind of epilogue to this history of persecution, showing how Shaker enemies were providentially punished by later illness, penury, and unpleasant modes of death. This reminds us again of the context in which the book was assembled—a time of continuing anti-Shaker activity, when Shaker leadership felt under attack by the wicked in the outside world. The fact that this book was intended for Shaker eyes only helps explain why it can afford to present the non-Shaker "world" in such a consistently hostile way.

The historical narrative of persecution contains a quite contradictory portrayal of Ann Lee as a leader of her community in time of trouble. A tension apparently exists between the narrator's ideal for a leader of an embattled community and his view of her as a woman. Therefore, on some occasions she is seen as heroic, defending her community against attack; but even more frequently, great emphasis is placed on her victimization—and particularly on the way her sex makes her vulnerable to victimization. An excellent example of her heroic aspect occurs in one story about a potential mob attack, when the narrator presents Mother Ann's reproof as almost supernaturally efficacious against Shaker enemies:[29]

One evening, while Mother and the elders were at Nathan Goodrich's, and a large collection of Believers assembled in the worship of God, there came a company of unruly men, rushing up to the door on horse-back. Mother, on hearing their noise, went to the door and spoke to them, and bid them, "Draw back." But the men refusing to obey, she raised her hand, and with great power and authority, cried aloud, "Draw back, I say, or I'll smite the horse and his rider." On uttering these words, all the power of resistance seemed instantly to be taken from the men, and their horses immediately ran backwards, from the house down to the road, . . . nor did it seem, to those who saw it, to be in the power of their riders to govern them, till they got quite into the road; and then they peaceably turned their horses and departed (p. 170).

On the other hand, there are repeated examples of her acting overwhelmed by her past sufferings—at the end of her courage and physical strength, seeking nothing but a place to hide. On one occasion, after a mob attack, she shows her bruises and weeps, saying, "So it has been with me, almost continually, ever since I left Neskeyuna; day and night—day and night, I have been like a dying creature." When the mob gathers again that evening at Nathan Farrington's and demands to see "that old woman," also calling her "an old witch," she is frankly presented as frightened: "On hearing the tumult, and perceiving that a mob had gathered, Mother wept and said, 'This comes sudden upon me; what shall I do? I do not feel as though I could endure any more'"(pp. 196–97).

On more than one occasion, she is seen as using her sex to shame her enemies into leaving her alone. In talking with mob leaders, she says, "What do you want of me? . . . I am a poor weak woman—I do not hurt any body."[30] Another time, when Lee is suspected of being a male British spy in women's clothes, the narrator presents her as "prudently" allowing herself to be examined by a female jury. Afterwards, she reproves the colonel that had ordered the investigation, charging him

with behavior unbecoming in a "gentleman" toward a "poor weak woman." The narrator assures us that "Abashed at this reply, the Colonel attempted no further opposition" (pp. 143–44).

One wonders about the repetitions of her self-proclaimed weakness as a woman and about the narrator's indignant emphasis on exposures of her body during mob actions: the physical examination to determine whether she was a woman, such as the time when she was dragged out of hiding in a bedroom "feet foremost," and the anecdote of her kidnapping, which lays stress on the violation of her modesty: "In the struggle with these inhuman wretches, she lost her cap and handkerchief, and otherwise had her clothes torn in a shameful manner. Their pretence was to find out, whether she was a woman or not."

It seems likely that the heavy, almost melodramatic emphasis laid by the narrator on Ann Lee's vulnerability as a woman is a result of a more or less conscious effort on the part of the brethren who were assembling the book to arouse a partly chivalrous, partly filial sympathy for the Mother, felt by young male Believers in particular, and corresponding anger at her "inhuman" persecutors. Whatever the motive, the portrait of her as an abused woman is at odds with the effort to portray her elsewhere in the narrative as a heroic leader and suggests the continuing unresolved tension for her male followers between her headship of the church and her womanhood.[31]

THE QUESTION OF FEMALE FIRST ELDERSHIP AFTER LEE'S DEATH[32]

According to the best surviving evidence, Ann Lee herself did not provide for future participation of women in the governance of the Shaker church—let alone for a situation like her own, in which a woman was acknowledged to have the highest authority in the sect. Lee's followers later attempted to read into some of her remembered utterances a prophetic knowledge of the leaders to follow her. But no specific instructions relating to future female leaders are attributed to Lee in the

1816 *Testimonies*, where such sayings would certainly be found if she had made them.[33]

After her death in 1784, Lee was succeeded by James Whittaker, the English follower who had emerged during the latter years of her life as the chief public preacher of the growing band of Shakers. Procter-Smith argues that the shift from female to male public leadership, which characterized the period after Lee's death, may have begun during her lifetime as a matter of "competition with other religious groups" and the consequent need of the sect to consider its "appearance before the world."[34]

After the initial precedent set by James Whittaker's succession, male dominance of the future governance of the sect would have been the expected norm. Yet the next male first elder, Joseph Meacham—the former Baptist minister from Connecticut who questioned Lee about a woman's right to head a church—acted unexpectedly to create Shakerism's dual-gender and hierarchical formal governance system. According to one early seceder, Meacham was responsible for replacing an earlier, looser "system of fathers & mothers" initiated by James Whittaker (whereby all the elderly Shakers had courtesy parental titles), with one in which he was the exclusive "father" and Lucy Wright the exclusive "mother."[35] Another seceder euphemistically described the resistance of some early Shakers to Meacham's "mother gift" in 1788: "as to a mother, it was such a new thing and so unexpected that there was something of a labor before the matter was finished."[36]

Later Shaker historians would claim that both Meacham's creation of the "joint parentage" and his selection of Lucy Wright as First Mother of the Church were based on divine revelation. Calvin Green wrote about a series of divine revelations or "gifts" by which Joseph Meacham was guided, first in bringing the scattered Believers into communal living at New Lebanon in December 1787 and then in establishing church's parallel male and female governance hierarchy early in 1788. Meacham had received a recommendation of Lucy Wright "as the one most proper for the sisters to pattern after" directly from Ann Lee, according to Green. In addi-

tion, Meacham confirmed this by putting "numbers of the people to labor for a gift to know who their visible Mother was in the spiritual order of the Church. And soon manifestly, by the moving of the spirit they spontaneously felt & declared that it was Lucy Wright."[37] (The second story has the interesting effect of claiming both divine inspiration for the choice and also democratic consultation of the other Believers.) As late as 1904, Shaker eldresses Anna White and Leila Taylor of New Lebanon recorded an oral tradition that both Childs Hamlin and Joseph Meacham independently received divinely inspired knowledge that Lucy Wright was to be chosen as the First Mother of the Church.[38]

Meacham's elevation of Lucy Wright to a position parallel to his in the emerging church governance was of tremendous importance for later Shaker history, of course. However, the appointment of female leaders to supervise the affairs of the Sisterhood was in some sense required by a system in which the separation of the sexes was to be maintained in a dual-gender celibate social organization.[39] Meacham's more genuinely radical decision was to appoint a woman first in the line of succession after his death, thus establishing a precedent of female first eldership of the entire society.

It should be remembered that this appointment might easily have been bestowed on his highly respected male assistant in the ministry, Elder Henry Clough.[40] The principle of gender-based succession—that male leaders are appointed to replace males and females to replace females—might have been clearly established at this point, as it was to be later. But in a letter written to Lucy Wright shortly before his death, Meacham addressed her as "one whom I esteem my equal in order and lot, according to thy sex" and stated clearly her right to succeed him as first elder of the entire society:

> Christ Jesus our Lord & Mother are the two Chief anointed ones that stand before God in relation to the salvation of all souls. . . . No soul can find Salvation in this latter day without faith in the latter as well as in the former. . . . Inasmuch therefore as both the man & the

woman have Equal Rights in order & lots, & in the Lord, & Governance of the Church according to their sex in this Latter day, & as thee, tho' of the weaker sex in man, will be the Elder or first born after my departure, I believe the greatest measure of the wisdom & knowledge of God for the protection of souls will be given unto thee, especially in counsel.[41]

Meacham's confidence at the end of his life that Lucy Wright would receive the gifts of "wisdom & knowledge" that she would need to perform the work of first elder successfully, despite the disadvantage of being of "the weaker sex in man," probably reflects his positive experience as a follower of Ann Lee for four years, and then with Lucy Wright as his administrative partner for seven more. Perhaps remembering his own initial doubts about a sect headed by a woman, Meacham felt the need as he wrote this letter to make Lucy Wright's authority absolutely unquestionable—particularly since in this last year of his life a rebellion among the youth and young men at New Lebanon and Hancock had already begun.[42]

The whole question of female first eldership at this time was probably complicated by the policy of the sect, under Meacham and Wright, of maintaining public silence about Ann Lee. Her name, role as church founder, and relationship to Christ are not mentioned in the first Shaker publication, apparently authored by Meacham, a concise statement of the only true church (1790).[43] Meacham seems to have deemed it politically inexpedient to inflame enmity against Shakerism during its early years of community building, by emphasizing the controversial nature of the sect—especially its founder's gender and the theological implications her followers drew from this fact. This is suggested by Calvin Green's assertion that Meacham "had an inspired view of the order of Father & Mother in the nature of God . . . but thro' motives of wisdom did not manifest it publicly."[44]

Not all early Shaker males shared Meacham's confidence in Wright in the late 1790s, and at least some publicly doubted then and afterwards whether a sect headed by a woman could prosper.

Perhaps Meacham's appointment of Wright as his successor raised for many younger Shaker males the specter of a permanent matriarchy evolving after a brief but formative period of male headship. Lucy Wright's authority as female first elder, at any rate, was questioned repeatedly during her twenty-five-year administration.

LUCY WRIGHT AND THE THREAT OF A SHAKER MATRIARCHY

Beginning in the year preceding Joseph Meacham's death, the New Lebanon and Hancock Shaker communities experienced a five-year period of dissent and rebellion, which culminated in a jarring loss of at least twenty boys and young men, including the head of the youth order at New Lebanon. Discontent with Lucy Wright's headship was one source of the young males' rebellion, as we can clearly see in the manuscript letters of the apostate Angell Matthewson to his brother.[45]

Angell Matthewson was a boy of twelve when he first visited the Shakers with his family during Ann Lee's visit to Ashfield, Massachusetts; and he was a disillusioned man of thirty in 1799, when he was finally ejected from the New Lebanon community as disorderly and disobedient. His manuscript letters to his brother Jeffrey show that the process of creating a hierarchical community organization both at New Lebanon and throughout the Shaker communities caused considerable resentment among some who were not part of the governing elite. Matthewson expressed many grievances against the New Lebanon leadership and its policies. As a member of the second order, he was personally angry at being excluded from the Church's sabbath meeting. He protested the restrictions on freedom of movement on "mechanics" and farmers and the failure of the society to provide minimal literacy or direct access to the scriptures to its younger members.

Matthewson also gave an acid account of the administration headed by Wright (called by the name James Whittaker had given her, "Lucy Faith"). As "supreme head of eleven churches," she had neither domestic labors nor onerous spiritual labors to perform: "In fact she has nothing to do except to consult the oracles & give out orders of God, eat & drink & ride to Watervliet & back again in a curious pleasure wagon drawn by a complete span of horses & a driver to wait on her. . . . I have no historical knowledge of ever any goddess on earth faring so sumptuously and being so well obeyed as Lucy Faith."[46]

Matthewson sarcastically claimed that Elder Abiathar Babbitt was appointed by the "goddess" as the first male in the ministry because "she wanted a man to live in the meetinghouse with her to carry orders of God from her to the elders of distant churches." Matthewson also implied that because of Lucy Wright's elevated position, her former husband, the educated and able Elizur Goodrich, was "overlooked" for the ministry after Meacham and Clough died. Instead, the inferior Abiathar Babbitt, "a portly man of but few words & never acts as Elder," was selected instead—presumably because he represented no threat to her exercise of absolute power.

Matthewson's personal discontent with the evolution of Shakerism under Lucy Wright came to a boil when he was censured by his Second Order elder, Adonijah Jacobs, for a violation of the rules for separation of the sexes—speaking with a Shaker sister without two other Shakers present. When the elder argued that "we enjoy the privileges of conversing in public with the sisters every evening & we are a free people, & what can we ask more?" Matthewson responded:

> "That is enough," said I. "As we have a woman for the head of the church and are entirely ruled by women & you mention freedom. How can you call our church government freedom?"
>
> Three days after this conversation with the elder, he was visited in his shop by a group of eldresses, and was "scolded" while keeping an angry silence. What particular branch of wisdom they intended to learn me I know not, except to know that women are fools & that men that are willing to have a woman to rule over them are fools also.

In characterizing his decision to leave the society, Matthewson obviously hoped to shame and humiliate the male leadership by implying that those who submit to female rule are themselves "no better than women." In contrast, he represented himself as too large-minded to "follow every odd whim conjured up by women or elders ruled by women." Thus, though his essential conflict seems to have been primarily with his male elders and deacons, with whom he struggled over the increasingly hierarchical structure of the church, his strategy in describing his experience of expulsion is clearly to associate female rule with an intolerable loss of "freedom" as a male.[47]

Matthewson was not the only Shaker male to rebel against the administration of Lucy Wright by using her headship as a symbol of a central ministerial authority gone fundamentally astray. Near the end of her administration, a major critical attack was launched by John Barns, one of the ministry elders appointed by Meacham and Wright in 1793 to gather in and head the Shaker communities in Maine.[48] Barns was asked to resign his post in 1814 while visiting the New Lebanon lead ministry, for reasons not fully clear in the remaining documents, but apparently relating to doctrinal disagreements. He did agree to resign initially and was recalled to New Lebanon in 1815.[49] He changed his mind after only a few months and returned to live in Maine, where he continued as an embittered common member to foment rebellion against the New Lebanon lead ministry. The Maine ministry wrote to New Lebanon about Barns's "disorderly" behavior, which included accusing some New Lebanon elders of drunkenness, and "preaching" that "the male prophecy has ceased, and [that] the lead being in the female brings great distress upon the body, so the famine spoken of by Father James is fulfilled."[50]

Barns furthermore denied the right of the New Lebanon ministry under Wright to remove him from office. He claimed that "he was planted here by M Ann & F Jos and no one on earth has a right to remove him"; and "he was established by the finger of Almighty God to be a Bishop to all the believers in the Province of Maine, and let him do what he may, no one has a right to remove him."[51]

In July 1816, a letter signed by twenty influential New Lebanon male leaders was dispatched to the ministry, elders, deacons, brethren, and sisters at Alfred. The objective was to show the falsehood of a list of ten accusatory rumors reported as being circulated in Maine by the enraged Barns. One was the assertion that the New Lebanon brethren had "become weary of petticoat-government":

> Answer. We have for many years been satisfied that, petticoat-government, and breeches-government both belonged to the flesh, and have no part in the government of Christ; and we would to God that all Believers, both male and female, might be so sick of it, as to be willing to be made free from it by the law and government of Christ, which is neither male nor female separably, but the union of the spirit between them both. Therefore, it is not man, nor woman, that is to govern the Church, but it is Christ: and whether Christ governs us through the medium of man, or woman, it is the same unction from the Holy One, and we are equally satisfied. And as it respects our precious Mother, who is the first visible pillar of the Church of Christ on earth; we feel an unshaken faith & full confidence in her gift, and as well satisfied with her administration, as with any that have preceded it.[52]

Barns's anger about petticoat government can only have been increased by his feeling that his longtime and original female partner in the ministry, Sarah Kendall, had betrayed him at the time of his forced resignation. One of the other charges he is alleged to have made when he returned to Maine was "That a number in the [New Lebanon] Church told him that there was not another woman on earth that would have gone off and left a man, as Sarah went off and left him, and that, there is a womans church at Alfred that has got no head."[53]

Barns continued his agitation for another decade and, as a result, contributed substantially to unstable relations between leadership and community members in Maine. But for the time being,

this closing of ranks by the New Lebanon leading males effectively supported a woman's right to be first elder among Believers. Lucy Wright's death in 1821 brought a "natural" end to female headship of the entire United Society, and thus finally undercut Barns's claim that her headship was a major source of the society's problems.

THE OVERTHROW OF MOTHER LUCY IN THE WEST

Just a decade after Lucy Wright successfully weathered the Barns challenge, another "Mother Lucy," Lucy Smith of the Pleasant Hill, Kentucky, Shaker community lost her office in a political crisis in which the charge of petticoat government again played an important role. As is clear from the leadership correspondence from this period, the difficult repercussions of the earlier rebellions against female rule greatly influenced the way New Lebanon leadership reacted to the new challenge in the west.

The Pleasant Hill community suffered a long and complex leadership crisis beginning in 1818, when Father John Meacham (one of Joseph Meacham's sons) "lost his gift"" and was recalled to New Lebanon.[54] The New Lebanon lead ministry then wrote to the remaining Pleasant Hill ministry, including Meacham's partner, Mother Lucy Smith, and his assistant, Elder Samuel Turner, rebuking them for spiritual disobedience and spelling out necessary changes. They must "purge out" the wearing of silver and gold, work with their hands as common members did, and instate the practice of yearly confession of sins, as was standard in the eastern communities.[55]

In a private letter written at this time to the Union Village ministry, New Lebanon expressed doubt that two remaining male leaders, including Samuel Turner, would be able to "subject" themselves to Mother Lucy Smith, as they "ought."[56] Samuel Turner was retained as the first male in the ministry at Pleasant Hill. However, he was pointedly not given the formal title of Father (which would have indicated at least equivalent authority to Mother Lucy Smith's). Thus the same situation that had fueled John Barns's accusations against the Lucy Wright administration was replicated just two years later in the west. A female leader remained first in authority in the absence of her original male partner. With hindsight, we can see that the Pleasant Hill community was ripe for the petticoat government charge.

Why did the New Lebanon lead ministry, still under Lucy Wright's headship at this time, fail to create an evenly balanced male-female leadership structure at Pleasant Hill? At least part of the answer lies in New Lebanon's effort to create a clear hierarchical order among the communities in the west, which would replicate that of the eastern Shaker organization.

New Lebanon had been trying to persuade the ministries of the other western communities to acknowledge the Union Village ministry as their spiritual "parents," just as the New Lebanon ministry was acknowledged in the east as the source of central policy for all communities of Believers. There was some recognition by Lucy Wright and her companions in the lead ministry at New Lebanon that administration of the west by infrequent letters from the east was proving awkward and ineffective. In addition, reducing the number of leaders who could use parental titles was probably intended to protect the prestige and authority of Shaker leadership in the eyes of the society's members from further erosion, in the wake of the Barns rebellion.

The removal in 1815–16 of the rebellious but "anointed" Father John Barns had reverberated widely through the Shaker communities, including Pleasant Hill, and encouraged a jaundiced view of the claim that each community's ministry were "oracles of God." Elder Samuel Turner of Pleasant Hill received an incendiary letter from one of the Alfred, Maine, rebels at about the time of Lucy Wright's death, accusing her among other things of setting up as Shaker government "those agents who had changed the oracle of God into a lie."[57] Alluding to the removal of John Barns (and two years later Barns's partner Sarah Kendall), Canterbury ministry eldress Mother Hannah

Kendall was reported to have said: "it sounds more awful to hear of Parents loosing their gift, than it does to hear of Elders loosing theirs."[58]

New Lebanon's efforts to cut back on the number of leaders using parental titles may also have been in anticipation of the political difficulties to be expected to occur at Lucy Wright's death. There were no clear instructions from Ann Lee, James Whittaker, Joseph Meacham, and perhaps even Lucy Wright herself, about how to select a new first elder of the eighteen Shaker societies. Clearly those who were already serving as "fathers" and "mothers" could be seen as having more of the authority derived from Ann Lee than anyone else. When Lucy Wright died in February 1821, the New Lebanon church leaders offered the headship of the society to Father Job Bishop of the Canterbury, New Hampshire, ministry, on the ground that he was the last surviving "Parent" in the eastern communities.[59] Only when he refused, apparently, could an entirely new New Lebanon lead ministry group, a carefully gender-balanced quartet, be formed.[60]

New Lebanon's effort to contain the proliferation of parental titles in the west had encountered some resistance at Pleasant Hill and South Union. In an 1814 letter to a New Lebanon Church Family eldress, Lucy Smith resisted New Lebanon's move to impose the parental authority of the Union Village ministry over all the other western leaders. She acknowledged that she had "good & Kind Elders in this country" but added that "experience has taught me that it is impossible for Elders to feel the same degree of charity, tenderness & care for youngsters, that Parents can feel for children—it cannot be." In writing to Lucy Wright at New Lebanon in 1814, Samuel Turner referred to the fact that Elder John is now called "Father" at Pleasant Hill, and he then went on to refer to "Mother Lucy" and "Father John" himself, despite his also calling Lucy Wright "the only Parent that we have left us in this world."[61]

One community's ministry, that at South Union, which was headed by Benjamin Youngs and Molly Goodrich, acceded to the newly enunciated rule. However, when John Meacham was recalled to New

Lebanon and removed from office in 1816, the New Lebanon lead ministry inconsistently allowed Mother Lucy Smith to retain her title. They told the disgruntled Benjamin Youngs that they did this on the advice of the Union Village ministry, who believed that to remove the "beloved" Mother Lucy Smith's title would cause hard feelings among her people.[62]

In 1820, during a tense time at Pleasant Hill caused by a financial crisis in Kentucky, the Pleasant Hill Believers began to "jerk" under the "power of God," and Mother Lucy Smith encouraged the outbreak of vision and other ecstatic behavior.[63] By the next year, Samuel Turner reported to New Lebanon that a visionist had predicted that the exiled and demoted former Father John Meacham would return to the west. Turner assured the New Lebanon leaders that "we hope never to see his face in this world."[64]

Pleasant Hill's instability gradually ripened into a full-scale "rebellion." A movement to allow for the election of leaders by the membership was well under way by 1827.[65] The issues undermining inter-community harmony were quite complex, as in the Matthewson and Barns situations. And again the problems were clearly exacerbated by tension over female governance—in this case by the evident power imbalance between Mother Lucy Smith and her subordinate partner Elder Samuel Turner.[66] "How can the people get united while their head is divided?" New Lebanon asked rhetorically when the extent of the disunity between Mother Lucy Smith and Elder Samuel Turner was reported to them.

New Lebanon showed considerable understanding of how female and male leaders might be played off against each other by factions of discontented Believers at Pleasant Hill, just as parents might be in a secular family by their children:

> The people there being somewhat divided, have a powerful effect in separating the feelings of Mother Lucy and Elder Samuel still further from each other. For doubtless such brethren as have but little faith in Elder Samuel will go to Mother Lucy, one side of El. Saml, for union and counsel, and even in matters which they know she can have but little understand-

ing about. This you know will have a tendency to shut br Samuel's feelings farther off from Mother Lucy, and from such brethren, and weaken his confidence in her.[67]

This time, perhaps because they remembered John Barns, or perhaps because they were no longer headed by a female first elder themselves, the New Lebanon ministry responded warily to the suggestion by Union Village that the male leader, Samuel Turner, be recalled to the east. "We fear the consequence," they wrote,

> For the people there may have in a great degree lost their confidence in him, yet he has doubtless some friends . . . who in their rebellious sense will think and speak something according to the following language, namely: "Now we shall be ruled by petticoat government with a witness; for these three women have purged out our Father and the two Elder brethren, and we don't know what they will undertake next; it is evident that no brethren can live with them, unless they yield perfect submission and subjection to them."

New Lebanon hoped that Elder Samuel Turner could be persuaded to resign, which "would make the case much easier than if he were sent for and then detained with a load of hardness against the Ministry there for misrepresenting him, and us for believing them." They pointed to the difficulties they had already encountered "from those who have already returned from the West," obviously thinking especially of former Father John Meacham, to justify their caution.[68] Some Pleasant Hill brethren, indeed, were also thinking of John Meacham. There were those who were writing to New Lebanon by this time urging the dismissal of the Pleasant Hill Ministry and the return of their former "Father" from the east.

The New Lebanon ministry handed the hot potato over to Union Village. Since the Union Village ministry had originally appointed the ministries for the other western communities, "it justly belongs to you to be the actors in this case," New Lebanon wrote. But Union Village should act decisively before the Pleasant Hill people were "driven to the necessity of dismissing their own leaders" for that would be "contrary to the order of God."[69]

Ultimately Samuel Turner survived the crisis, while Lucy Smith "fled" to temporary exile in Union Village.[70] Reporting on what he found at Pleasant Hill when he arrived to help bring the community back under central leadership control, Solomon King of Union Village offered the opinion that "Mother [Lucy] will never be able to profit this people anymore in consequence of her decline of life and her debilitated state of mind."[71] At the same time, he warned New Lebanon that it would be "trying . . . particularly to the Sisters," if Lucy Smith were to be recalled to New Lebanon.[72]

Benjamin Youngs of South Union, who also wrote a confidential account at this time of the Pleasant Hill disorder and the overthrow of Mother Lucy, condemned the Pleasant Hill community of the past decade as "very selfish."[73] They had "considered themselves superior in gifts and talents; in order and arrangements to any order of believers in the Western country, if not to any order of believers anywhere. This idea no doubt commenced at the head and pervaded the body." His critique of leadership pride seems especially to apply to Mother Lucy Smith, although he also sympathized with her in an exile he considered a "cruel banishment." In his account, Samuel Turner and his supporters increasingly and naturally resented Lucy Smith's control of whole arenas of business activity that should properly have been in male hands.

> All applauded their Mother, as a being superior to all others on Earth. All the concerns spiritual and temporal, were almost solely in her hands, and under her personal counsel and direction. Such a state of things could not exist very many years. Elder Samuel was the first man. It was not supposed by every one that Mother knew as much about some particular kinds of business as Elder S. or even as much as any of the rest had got to know—counsels of course, became clashing, and by & by discoverable.[74]

After Lucy Smith had been in exile in Union Village for over a year, the New Lebanon ministry gave her the option of returning to New Lebanon, but only if she would resign her office and relinquish her claim to the parental title Mother. Under this kind of pressure, Lucy Smith did decide to resign and return to New Lebanon, leaving Samuel Turner the clear survivor (at least for a few years) in the reorganized Pleasant Hill leadership.[75]

Thus, the leadership correspondence strongly suggests that one reason for the choice of Elder Samuel Turner over Mother Lucy Smith was New Lebanon's feeling that the United Society could not afford to fight yet another petticoat government charge. This was at least the third occasion of rebellion by Shaker brethren against the headship of a woman since the original decision by Joseph Meacham to pass the first eldership of the society to Lucy Wright. The practice of allowing communities to have female first elders had been one important factor in creating major turmoil in the already unstable, anti-authoritarian western communities. Knowing of Lucy Smith's strong factional support, particularly among the Pleasant Hill sisters, the New Lebanon leadership clearly dreaded removing her and thus potentially producing another martyr in the minds of the many critics of centralized Shaker authority. Yet it was politically less difficult to sacrifice a Mother who seemed to some of her male subordinates to have too much power than to risk allowing a fundamental challenge to the hierarchical system of Shaker government to succeed. The removal of Lucy Smith may also have seemed an opportune way to end once and for all the use of parental titles in Pleasant Hill.

PHILEMON STEWART AND THE SCAPEGOAT OF FEMALE RULE

For many years after the death of Lucy Wright, the New Lebanon lead ministry was very wary about the appearance of "petticoat government" (or indeed "breeches government") in the eastern societies—especially at New Lebanon. When lots in the ministry became vacant through illness or death, the person was speedily replaced, generally through the promotion of the assistant, or through nominating a prominent church family leader of the same sex. Parental titles ceased to be a divisive issue once all those in the east who had once held them had died, and the new policy of reserving the titles only for the lead ministry took hold.[76]

In the interest of maintaining stability and order, the New Lebanon central leadership tried to keep an even balance of competent and obedient brethren and sisters in governance positions, and the official line was that harmony between male and female in the leadership partnerships was necessary as an example for the harmonious relationship of the brotherhood and sisterhood in the ranks. As the New Lebanon ministry were reported to have said on the occasion of a new outbreak of rebellion at Alfred in the early 1830s (which seems to have pitted a group of women against both Maine and New Lebanon leadership), if the ministry "were united male and female, in the gift & spirit of the Gospel, & put their mites together, and worked in union . . . they could work wonders."[77]

The selection of new leaders was never a fully democratic process, but it came to be much more a matter of negotiation, bargaining, and backroom politics than formerly, as Shaker communities passed through the turbulent mid-century spiritualistic revival, which had brought internal conflict, disillusion, and apostasy, as well as spiritual renewal. Beginning perhaps in the late 1840s, and accelerating through the 1850s and '60s, as Priscilla Brewer has documented, a shrinking and aging leadership pool began to become a serious problem for many Shaker communities.[78]

Among other issues that began to be matters of negotiation between newly nominated subordinate male leaders and higher ranking leaders was the selection of their female partners in office. Several cases appear in the correspondence and journals of the New Lebanon leadership of male leaders who attempted to control the selection of their female partners. A particularly interesting one involves Elder Otis Sawyer, who, as one of his reasons for refusing to serve as a trustee in Sabbathday Lake, Maine, in 1851, objected to "going in with the present Elder Sisters." In this case, the New Hampshire ministry had been willing to give in: "This was taken out of the way; for it was expected when a change was effected on the brethren's part, one would be made on the Sisters: Still no effect."[79]

One of the most spectacular examples of a Shaker brother who attempted to control the selection of the sisters with whom he would share authority and work is Philemon Stewart, the New Lebanon spirit medium who produced *The Sacred Holy Roll and Book*.[80] His behavior as a would-be leader who had great difficulty sharing power with anyone and his attitudes toward women in office within Shaker communities are fully documented in his own surviving writings and in the private correspondence and journals of the New Lebanon ministry. Although he is by no means advanced here as an example of a "typical" Shaker brother of his community and era, he nonetheless allows us to see in a particularly striking way how convenient the petticoat government issue could be for salving the wounded pride of an ambitious would-be male leader.

Stewart lived nearly his whole life as a Shaker, from age seven, when he joined the Second Family at New Lebanon, until his death there in 1875, but he never held a position in the ministry there, unlike his elder brother, Amos. During the spirit-inspiration period of the 1830s and 1840s, Philemon Stewart emerged as one of the few but very influential male spirit mediums, having been given official sanction as an instrument of prophetic messages from the spirits through Elder Rufus Bishop. Stewart continued to have occasional spirit visitations even in the 1850s and 1860s, when much of the earlier work of spirit inspiration had been discredited by skepticism and waves of apostasy, but these messages were largely ignored by the next generation of New Lebanon leaders.[81]

Stewart had very strong ideas about what policies Shaker leaders should be pursuing in many areas of spiritual and temporal affairs, including diet, health care reform, farm management, child care, and the relationship of spiritual and temporal governance.[82] When his gift as a medium for the spirits was supported by the leadership, he communicated these ideas primarily in the form of long prophetic messages, both oral and written.[83] After this gift began to be discounted, he turned to writing direct critical treatises on such issues to leaders he increasingly felt were ignoring him. These "manifestos" to the ministry are full of frank and even bitter criticism directed against most of the current male leaders.[84] In them he emerges as an exceptionally combative, opinionated, and hardworking (even "driven") personality, completely dedicated to his view of Shaker truth and utterly sure of the rightness of his views. We also get an unusually full expression of an ambivalent attitude toward female leaders, which may have been exacerbated by his own disappointments as he ventured into leadership positions.[85]

Because of Stewart's behavior as a pugnacious ideologue, his record was predictably disastrous when he himself took on leadership roles. He acted as a family elder three times, the first appointment being less than a year's duration, in the New Lebanon Church Family, during the height of his prominence as a spirit instrument.[86] In his other two experiences in the eldership, in addition to a host of other problems, he ran into difficulties with women in authority, and he has left us an unusually full account of these difficulties and his ideas and feelings about them.

Stewart was spent just under four years as first elder at the Second Family, New Lebanon.[87] The correspondence reveals that he was involved in a series of controversies during this time, in which the lead ministry had to intervene.[88] Finally, on the occasion of his release from this responsibility, his older brother, the New Lebanon lead ministry Elder Amos Stewart noted in the ministry journal: "For a year or more past Elder Br Philemon has repeatedly urged the necessity of quite a change or removal of the Female leaders in that family—(especially the elder sisters,) and others chosen to fill their place that would better harmonize with his peculiar views of progressive reform, or gospel increase as he would term it. This the Ministry could not accede to, not finding sufficient cause to do so."[89]

Philemon Stewart did not retire gracefully, it appears, but insisted on "some further conversation about business affairs." He proposed remaining at the Second Family as manager of the grape business and the factory and chair business and to act as "a sort of third deacon at the office." When the ministry refused, "this was considered by him as entirely unjust and oppressive in the extreme, called forth quite unpleasant conversation not respectful to the order of Ministry." Stewart was placed in his retirement in the Second Order, rather than the First, and this became a grievance he vented repeatedly in his later manifestos.

Less than two years later, in May 1860, Philemon Stewart was sent to act as assistant to Elder John Kaime in the eldership in the Poland, Maine, community, in a time of unusual financial difficulties for Maine.[90] Again the New Lebanon ministry's correspondence and journals tell a story of a turbulent tenure. He made several visits to New Lebanon "in some little fuss & trouble" and "in trouble, in consequence of his own will," as Daniel Boler put it.[91] Less than a year after he arrived, Daniel Boler was writing to Philemon to explain why no more New Lebanon brethren could be sent to assist at this time and advising him not to try "coercive" measures with the Poland trustee Isaiah Wentworth. New Lebanon was already coaxing him to remain in Maine, where his "labors and exertions for the good of the family are greatly appreciated by all the faithful brethren & Sisters on Poland Hill." Yet New Lebanon had just received a letter from Elder Otis and the ministry in Maine, informing them

> that Br Philemon had refused to take any further responsibilities in the family if Hannah Davis was appointed Elderess, and unless some suitable person from some other quarter, (prefering one from New Lebanon,) could be furnished to fill the place, he would not remain in the family, etc.—that the Elders had virtually refused to support the appointment if made, both declaring that Sister Hannah was unfit for the place, & were unwilling to accept her.[92]

Stewart also had difficulties getting along with his male colleagues in the eldership and with the Maine ministry,[93] but the final issue that caused his ignominious expulsion from Maine was apparently his relationship with an "adopted" Shaker Sister there.[94] In April 1863, the Maine ministry wrote to New Lebanon requesting that Philemon Stewart be recalled "on account of his associate conditions in that Society," as the New Lebanon Ministry Journal puts it; and Boler wrote to "rebuke" him and recall him on April 16.[95]

Philemon Stewart's own account of the event can be pieced together from several of his later writings. In one of his manifestos, a pamphlet detailing both personal and political grievances, begun shortly after his return to New Lebanon in 1863,[96] he refers to his stay in Maine being rendered "unendurable" by "Judases," and later on he complains about the high-handedness of the leadership in refusing to allow him to bring back from Maine with him a child whom he legally adopted there "in order to save" it "from being carried off by its Mother who was about to leave Believers."[97] Because he was not "a favorite of some leading females (as it was understood the Brethren had no objection to the agreement being carried out, and the child removed)," the child was left "in conditions" Stewart considered unsuitable "for a child of that age"—and all this was done through "falsifying his most solemn articles of agreement."[98]

Finally, in a letter to the ministry written as he returned from a missionary journey in 1867, the details of the scandal become fully clear. Stewart tells of meeting Anna Guerney, a young ex-Shaker sister who had been expelled from Poland, Maine, in Jordan Marsh, a Boston department store, where she was working as an overseer in the dressmaking department in 1867. In his narrative, she bursts into tears, calls him her "kind Father," and tells him her difficulties in supporting herself and resisting the improper advances of suitors. He assures her of his continuing "fatherly" feelings for her and urges her to continue to live the Shaker life even in exile.

She said she had lately been to Poland and made a short Visit. They as a general thing wished her well. But things did not look prospering. Isaiah managed his out farms to line his own pockets. She furthermore said, that some of them asked her, seriously, if she did not expect to win my feelings so when I was there, that I would consent finally to go off, and marry her. Nay, she told them, it never even entered her heart. She never had any such feeling in the least towards me, but her love, and attachment to me, was of a very different nature, it was for my Fatherly, kind, noble and generous treatment of Her. . . . I told her I was perfectly aware of those feelings and false judgings, before I left, and from whence they sprang. . . . As God is true, some who have had the decision of matters, respecting that poor Girl, as well as some other souls that I knew of while at Poland, will have something serious to meet in Eternity, on their account, or justice has ceased to have its perfect work.[99]

Stewart clearly blamed the expulsion of Guerney and himself on the influence of the female leaders in Maine. This, together with his expulsion from the Second Family at New Lebanon in the late 1850s, leads him to a broadside attack on petticoat government: "And again, I have no faith to believe that the blessing of God will ever rest in peace and prosperity, in this day, where the Female take the rule, even as much as they have, in some places where I have been. I am not sensible but what I have been and still am as ready to give Sisters their proper place, and treat them as kind and tenderly, as any one when they were willing to keep their place."[100]

He goes on to reminiscence about the problems he has seen himself, when a woman is allowed to "bear the first sway." When he was at the Second Family, New Lebanon, he intervened in a situation in which James Farnham was in some way victimized by "Female dickerings"—possibly a sister's accusations about his having improper relations with the opposite sex.[101] Stewart attributes the damage done by women not restrained by males to an innate female character, which is apparently not often ameliorated by life as a Shaker sister.

For I find, as by experience I had to study the Female trait a little, as a general thing they are apt to be all fondness, or all predjudice and hatred, and when they get a going they seem to know no bounds, but few Females are rightly balanced to take the medium course. Eldress Ruth was an exception, one in a Thousand. Her judgement and candour, with nobleness of action and decision, was far superior to the most of Men, I never discovered in her anything but Womanly nobleness in all her decision, nothing tinctured with prejudice, or meanness—.

In recounting his disappointment at being retired to the Second Order, he describes the ministry's decision as feeling to him "unmanly & unfair, and like falsifying their own agreement, and quite too much like Quibbling in high places. And I have always believed that alteration came, thro the influence of some certain Females" (p. 122). Perhaps most revealing of his personal gendered anger at women in authority is his retelling of an anecdote told to him by Adonijah Jacobs, a contemporary of Lucy Wright and Joseph Meacham, who was sent to Watervliet to help and who encountered a family in which "a certain high sens'd Female, then standing as one of the Leading Sisters with Aaron Hood, took pretty much the whole lead both in Meeting and out, which made it very hard for Adonijah . . . both about getting anything to eat, if he happened to get behind (as he was drawing coal), or even getting his washing done, if he happened to be a few minutes behind with his cloths." When Jacobs reported the situation to Joseph Meacham,

> The Elder at that time made few if any remarks, but a few evening afterwards, he came into Meeting, and walking up and down the Alley between the Brethren and Sisters, he spoke with a loud and stern voice, and said, "Is it Peace! I say, is it Peace! What have I to do with peace, as long as your Mother Jezebel Rules." Repeating the sentence twice over. After that Meeting Adonijah said, the remainder of the time he staid at Watervliet, he was treated decently.

Stewart is not hostile to Shaker sisters who agree with him, even when they exercise some leadership, and he uses the term "womanly" in an honorific sense on several occasions. For example, he praises Elizabeth Sears, who sympathizes with his position on diet and health reform and has worked hard in the Second Order with him on this issue, by saying she "had acted womanly" in sticking to the progressive Graham diet reform against increasing opposition.[102] He is saddened at the death of Miranda Barber and refers to her role as "Holy Mother's Instrument" during "Mother's Manifestation. . . . She was a great comfort to my soul, through that Manifestion."[103] But he insists on women, even Shaker sisters, knowing their "place" and their limitations. Of his friend Elizabeth Sears, who was inexplicably ill in 1874 despite her adherence to the hydropathic health system that Stewart supported, he wrote: "she has distroyed her health by overdoing, and doing that kind of work, and more of it than any Female, ever ought to do."[104]

THE PARADOXES OF FEMALE LEADERSHIP

Female first eldership was always a problem in Shaker history, although it was a problem solved differently in different eras. Ann Lee had said: "when the man is gone, the right of government belongs to the woman," and Joseph Meacham had acted on that principle in appointing Lucy Wright his successor. In so doing, he established the radical precedent of first eldership by seniority, regardless of gender, rather than the gender-based succession that came to characterize Shaker governance after Lucy Wright's death.

In several petticoat government conflicts during the Shakers' first half century, male resentment of female headship can clearly be seen as a weapon waiting to be used when other political issues were not resolved satisfactorily by family, community, or society leadership. Frequently, "female rule" seems to have symbolized the arbitrary and unresponsive use of authority by leaders who were seen as departing from the first principles of Shakerism.

Thus, although Joseph Meacham was in fact responsible for creating the hierarchical (and to some eyes elitist) system against which Angell Matthewson chafed, it was the "goddess" Lucy Wright whom he blamed for making Shakerism intolerable for freedom-loving young males.

By the late 1820s, the central ministry had had enough experience with the explosive potential of rebellion against "female rule" to retreat from the gender-blind succession system established by Joseph Meacham. Still smarting from the John Barns rebellion of 1815–16, in which the female head of the entire United Society was challenged, the New Lebanon ministry approached the Pleasant Hill conflicts ten years later in an anxious mood. Lucy Smith was acknowledged as "much beloved," and New Lebanon hesitated to remove yet another anointed "parent." But at last her removal was authorized, and thereafter, while there were any males competent to be appointed, the New Lebanon ministry carefully hewed to the more conservative approach to dual-gender government also authorized by Lee's original saying: "where they both stand in their proper order, the man is the first, and the woman the second in the government of the family."

In situations of conflict among male leaders, in times of financial difficulty, and perhaps especially as the male population began to decrease dramatically in proportion to the female population, the concept of petticoat government was always available to hand. Neither Ann Lee's "absent husband"

theory of female governance, nor even Joseph Meacham's elevation of Lucy Wright to an unprecedented equality in "lot" and first position in the succession, had served to undermine many Shaker brethren's acceptance of the traditional patriarchal view of the "unnatural" and emasculating rule of women. Philemon Stewart's feelings about the dangers of female rule may represent a final "flowering" of Shaker male resentment against living in a society that was increasingly disproportionately populated by women, in which many traditional Shaker values seemed in decline, and in which his own personal efforts to effect the changes he saw as needful were frustrated at every turn. Looking for scapegoats, Stewart found many, of course, and powerful women were among the easiest targets.

The tendency of the more ambitious brethren in particular to hold "female rule" responsible for many of the Shakers' ills had been there all along, expressed even in the ambivalent memories of the often frightening seer and strict mother Ann Lee, but held in tenuous check by reverence for Lee and her spiritual companions and by acceptance of the parallel male-female governance system that was required and justified by Shaker celibacy and theological dualism. Early Shaker history is a fascinating saga, in part, of the struggles of the Believers with the paradoxical legacy of a charismatic female spiritual leader who only claimed her right to head the church in the absence of Christ, her metaphorical husband.

A Note on Shaker Community Leadership Organization

By the late 1820s, when the full complement of major Shaker communities had been established, a strictly hierarchical governance system was in place, with its authority ultimately deriving from appointments said to have been made by Ann Lee and the early elders. Two male and two female central or lead ministry elders had acknowledged spiritual authority over the entire society, and it was they who decided upon their own replacements, as well as the appointments of elders for the other communities. Each communal family within an individual community also had four spiritual elders who reported to the community's elders. At each level, one elder and one eldress were considered senior and the other two junior or "assistant"—though the four represented themselves as harmoniously operating as a decision-making unit. According to an ideal established in New Lebanon (as the earliest and largest organized community in the east, New Lebanon was regarded as the model that other communities should strive to follow), one communal family, designated the church family, was regarded as most spiritually advanced, with others ranked lower according to their lesser level of spiritual travel. Believers who ultimately became leaders would generally be selected for gradual promotion to higher levels of authority within their family or community by their elders and the ministry. Family or even community leaders could be removed from office if in the judgment of the lead ministry "their gift was out"—the Shaker euphemism for loss of effectiveness.

This governance structure was mirrored at the regional level, east and west.[105] Clusters of two or more neighboring communities, called bishoprics, had four designated ministry elders who would split their time between the communities and make decisions about appointments to leadership positions, in consultation with the lead ministry at New Lebanon or, in the west, at South Union.

1. [Rufus Bishop, ed.], *Testimonies of the Life, Character, Revelations and Doctrines of Our Ever Blessed Mother Ann Lee, and the Elders with Her. . .* (Hancock, Mass.: J. Talbott & J. Deming, Jrs., 1816): 21–22. This story about Joseph Meacham is attributed to Jethro Turner.

2. Marjorie Procter-Smith, *Women in Shaker Community and Worship: A Feminist Analysis of the Uses of Religious Symbolism* (Lewiston: Edwin Mellon Press, 1985): 15.

3. In order of founding, the principal Shaker communities were: Watervliet, New York; New Lebanon, New York; Hancock, Massachusetts; Enfield, Connecticut; Canterbury, New Hampshire; Tyringham, Massachusetts; Alfred, Maine; Enfield, New Hampshire; Harvard, Massachusetts; Shirley, Massachusetts; New Gloucester (Sabbathday Lake), Maine; Union Village, Ohio; Watervliet, Ohio; Pleasant Hill, Kentucky; South Union, Kentucky; West Union, Indiana; North Union, Ohio; Whitewater, Ohio; and Sodus Bay and Groveland, New York (See William Deming Andrews, "Statistical View of Shaker Communities," Appendix to *The People Called Shakers*, 3rd ed. [New York: Dover, 1963]: 290–92). See the Note on Shaker Community Leadership Organization at the end of this essay.

4. As Seth Y. Wells writes in the preface to the 1816 *Testimonies*: "Having been eye and ear witnesses of all that our blessed Mother and the first Elders have done and taught among us, from the time that they first opened the gospel in America, till they left this world, it seemed good unto us, in answer to the request of our beloved brethren and sisters, who have never seen those blessed Ministers of Christ in the body, to make a faithful record of those precepts and examples and other contemporary events which most evidently manifest their real characters" (*Testimonies* [1816]: iii).

5. For an assortment of the most defamatory of the seceders' accounts, see Mary Marshall [Dyer], *A Portraiture of Shakerism* (1822; repr. New York: AMS Press, 1972). Andrews, in *The People Called Shakers* (1963), also reviews the major attacks on Lee found in early apostate literature. See also Clarke Garrett, *Spirit Possession and Popular Religion: From the Camisards to the Shakers* (Baltimore: Johns Hopkins University Press, 1987), for a judicious and ultimately convincing discussion of the two primary scandalous accusations made in a number of early Shaker seceders' accounts. He concludes that both naked dancing (as a self-mortifying religious practice) and the alcohol addiction of Ann Lee and her brother William during the very last two years of life probably had some basis in reality. He suggests the possibility, following the seceder William Haskett, that "the practice of using alcohol as a means of generating visions and gifts" may have "developed only gradually" and "become a serious problem only after the leader's return to the Berkshires in 1783 (pp. 202–12).

6. The editors go on to state that it is not for "the wicked" that "we record these things; . . . but for the benefit of those who have honestly confessed and forsaken their sins, and have set out, once for all, to follow Christ in the regeneration" (*Testimonies* [1816]: iv).

7. See the discussion of its value as a source by Procter-Smith, in *Women in Shaker Community and Worship* (1985): xiv. Other scholars of Shaker religion have profitably drawn on the 1816 *Testimonies* more recently, including Garrett, *Spirit Possession and Popular Religion* (1987), and Stephen J. Stein, *The Shaker Experience in America* (New Haven: Yale University Press, 1992).

8. See Procter-Smith (*Women in Shaker Community and Worship* [1985]) for invaluable analyses of the stories in the *Testimonies*, as sources of information about the role and function of Ann Lee and as a location for images of women important to later Shaker religious thought and practice.

9. For a more fully developed argument about the impact of the different types of stories on the reader's understanding of Lee, see Jean M. Humez, "Ye Are My Epistles: The Construction of Ann Lee Imagery in Early Shaker Sacred Literature," *Journal of Feminist Studies in Religion* 8, no. 1 (Spring 1992): 83–103. (The present essay relies upon some sections of this article.)

10. The highly impressive impact of her external behavior as seer and prophet is a dominant theme in both the section on Believers' first meetings with Ann Lee and the elders (*Testimonies* [1816]: chaps. 3–6); and in a subsequent set of chapters on Ann Lee's visionary and spiritualistic powers (chaps. 23–29).

11. Other early Shaker associates of Ann Lee were credited with various prophetic, visionary, and spiritualistic powers, of course, and this included mind reading. As one example, Hannah Goodrich tells a story in the *Testimonies* of having "one of the Elders" reveal her thoughts (*Testimonies* [1816]: 32).

12. Another example of this is Hezekiah Hammond, who, according to Prudence Hammond's account, was not originally persuaded to confess his sins by William Lee and was attempting to distract himself from William's words by concentrating on the horse whip in his hand. "Mother soon came into the room, and perceiving Hezekiah's feelings, she spoke and said, 'Put down that whip and hear the word of God, you idle old man! It is the Devil that makes you do that, to shut out the word of God.'" Hezekiah gives attention to Father William, and "soon the power of God fell mightily upon Hezekiah; his arms were instantly brought back up to his sides, and fixed, like a criminal pinioned for execution; his head was braced back, and his whole body bound, in such a manner, that he could neither move nor speak." When Ann gave him permission to confess, he did so and only then "was released" (*Testimonies* [1816]: 26).

13. David Meacham, Ebenezer Cooley, and Israel Chauncey are examples of the male believers promised a role as preachers; Abel Allen was promised the conversion of his whole family.

14. Similarly, Elizabeth Chauncey had a vision of her hus-

band, then visiting the church, "in great distress of soul and body, and his flesh was turned to a purple color." In her vision, when Mother Ann forgave the husband's sins, his flesh turned back to its natural color. Later, when Elizabeth was visiting the church with her husband, Mother Ann told them that during the husband's former visit, when his flesh had turned purple, Ann had seen his dead mother "come into the resurrection" at the moment his flesh was restored to its "natural color" (*Testimonies* [1816]: 31). Thus she confirmed and further elaborated upon Elizabeth's vision—adding an element of reward, the assurance of the salvation of the husband's mother.

15. This tends to confirm the impression given in the healing testimonials in another early Shaker publication, [Benjamin Youngs'] *The Testimony of Christ's Second Appearing. . .* (Lebanon, Ohio: John McClean, 1808), that she did not particularly have a reputation as a miraculous healer with her followers. Of the dozen or so healing gifts in the 1808 volume, only one actually involves Ann Lee directly—the rest come through her associates, or spontaneously. It would seem that her general pattern was to rely on other members of her core group, such as John Hocknell, to perform miraculous healings, just as she generally deferred to Elder William or Elder James as preachers. Phebe Spencer remembered Ann as having called upon John Hocknell for a gift to "cast out evil spirits" (*Testimonies* [1816]: 259).

16. For example: "At Watervliet, in the presence of Cornelius Thayer, William Scales and others, Mother said, 'I saw William Scales in vision, writing that which was not according to the simplicity of the gospel; and the evil spirits hovered round him, and administered evil to him. They looked like crows.' And Mother reproved William sharply" (*Testimonies* [1816]: 231).

17. Mary Spencer recalled that this occurred after Mother Ann had expounded her theory of spirits: "Every soul is accompanied by good or evil spirits; and the good or evil spirits, gather mostly, to that part of the body which contains the most sensations and faculties. The head is the ruling and governing part of the whole body; therefore it will contain the most good or evil of any part of the body. . . . The head of a wicked man will suck in evil spirits until it is full of them . . . so likewise the faithful, who are laboring to resist every temptation, . . . will be filled with good spirits, and will be guarded by the angels of God, who will protect them, day by day" (p. 301).

18. According to Hezekiah Morey's story, "When Mother was at William and Hezekiah Morey's, in Norton, she spoke to them and said, 'I saw your father, about a week ago, in blackness and darkness, and before we left the house, he desired the prayers of the Church; and I saw your natural mother, with her mouth wide open in prayer to god for him. Since that time, he has appeared to me again, and has risen from the dead, and come into the first heavens; and is traveling on to the second and third heavens'" (*Testimonies* [1816]: 241).

19. Two other stories included in the *Testimonies* have her describe a "vision" in which she had wings given to her to go into the realm of death. In the first she is remembered as saying "I have seen a vision: I saw myself flying up a great gulf—I had great wings; and with the ends of my wings, I uncovered the dead, who lay on the banks of the gulf" (*Testimonies* [1816]: 238). And in the second, she elaborated: "I saw a great gulf, fixed between God and the world of mankind; and I had two great wings given to me; and my work was to go up that gulf and fan it away. . . . I did go up the gulf, with my two great wings, and did fan it away—I did fan it away with my two great wings, so that poor lost souls could come to God" (*Testimonies* [1816]: 234).

20. Similarly, Hannah Kendal remembered when she was "unwell" being told by Mother, "I do not wonder that you feel as you do; for you have been bearing for the dead. I see a tall soul behind you right now" (*Testimonies* [1816]: 241).

21. One interesting example of this is Lydia Mathewson's story of the burden of her father-in-law's soul, falling on Philip Mathewson. Lydia Mathewson remembered having told Mother Ann of her anxieties about her deceased father-in-law, Thomas, who "was a very senseless man, as to the things of God." Mother Ann told her shortly afterward of having "labored" for Thomas, and visited "the ditch of hell" in a vision. She was able to see the dead father's soul rise and come stand near the living son Philip Mathewson, who was prostrate on the meetinghouse floor. When the father was seen as coming into the resurrection, the son was released from his trance. "I saw a number of the dead, who were willing to hear; and they arose at the sound of the trumpet of the gospel, through the preaching of Elder James. And Thomas Mathewson arose, and went into the meeting house. After this, I felt a gift to go into the meeting house, without any knowledge of what I was going for; but being led by the power of God; I went through the assembly, and found Philip Mathewson lying on the floor, apparently like a dying man. His father's state had fallen upon him. I took him by the hand, and told him to rise up, and he obeyed; but it was some time before he was fully released from that state which had fallen upon him. But his father united with the testimony of the gospel" (*Testimonies* [1816]: 242). In another version of the story, Elizabeth Davis remembers Mother Ann looking at the distressed Philip Mathewson in the meeting house, and announcing: "'He is bearing the last pains of death and hell for his father, who has been hanging about me these two weeks. He is now released'" (*Testimonies* [1816]: 243).

22. Procter-Smith believes that "the charge of witchcraft was partly founded in Lee's power and apparently mysterious charismatic personality and the hypnotic quality of the ecstatic worship practiced by the Believers. It was also a conventional response to a woman who claimed and exercised such considerable and unconventional power" (*Women in Shaker*

Community and Worship [1985]: 19). I would agree, and also add that the spiritualistic practices—especially apparent contact with the dead—may also have entered into it.

23. Procter-Smith identifies two aspects of Lee's image here—the nurturing mother and the severe judge, the "mother in Israel" (ibid., 12–16.). I see these as largely fused in this section of the *Testimonies*, as the judging or judgmental mother.

24. The Shakers were accused by several apostate accounts of specifically sexual humiliation practices, as part of their ecstatic asceticism. For a particularly nasty set of stories, see the affidavit collected by Mary Dyer Marshall from Asa Patee. For a good discussion of the problems of determining the truth of apostate accusations of Shaker sexual sadism during the early days, see Lawrence Foster, *Religion and Sexuality: Three American Communal Experiments of the Nineteenth Century* (New York: Oxford University Press, 1981): 41–43.

25. Foster has commented with considerable astuteness on this passage, as an indication of how deeply Ann Lee personally may have felt tormented by her own past sexual history (ibid., 269, n. 26). The apostate Daniel Rathbun also accused Ann Lee and the elders of threatening those who disobey them with damnation.

26. There is a second story of reproof, with a similar "plot"—Ann Lee chastises two quarreling women, calling them "wicked" and telling them they can't be "saved" unless they "love one another." The effectiveness of this kind of threat is shown in the women's reaction. They are "amazed" and immediately fall to their knees and make mutual confession (*Testimonies* [1816]: 283). An interesting story told by Phebe Spencer allows us to glimpse Mother Ann's apparent belief that a reproof, like a medical treatment, must be allowed sufficient time to do its work—it must not be "taken off" too soon. She had been chastising the Spencer family "for their idleness, nastiness, covetousness, and pride," and when an unexpected visit from Elder Hocknell elicited an invitation from Phebe Spencer to stay overnight, Mother Ann refused to give her permission, telling Phebe "You want him to stay to take off the reproof." Two weeks later, when Phebe visited her, Mother Ann said, "I am glad to see you. I have been thinking about you; why it was that you staid away so long. You may always remember that the reproof of a friend, is better than the kiss of an enemy" (*Testimonies* [1816]: 281–82).

27. One of the brethren remembered a very sharp "motherly" reproof from Mother Ann when he first saw her. Again, she uses an occasion that seems minimally sinful to deliver a strong warning about sin: "Jonathan, with his back to the fire and the skirts of his coat drawn forward, asked, 'How does Mother do?' To which she replied, 'If I am your Mother, young man, I'll teach you to turn your face to the fire, not your back: for heating your backside by the fire enrages lust. It shows ill breeding, and bad behav-

ior, for people to stand heating their backsides by the fire'" (*Testimonies* [1816]: 284).

28. For a more developed discussion of the composite narrative of Mother Ann's persecution during her New England missionary travels in 1781–83, see Humez, "Ye Are My Epistles" (1992).

29. Another instance of her boldness is the story of the mob attack on the New Lebanon Believers in 1783, when Ann and some of her followers are brought up on charges before Eleazar Grant, the hypocritical judge who is actually (in Shaker eyes) in league against them. She is remembered as reproving him "for sitting as a magistrate, and suffering such riotous mobs to abuse innocent people contrary to the law, without attempting to suppress them." In a revealing footnote, the Shaker editors quote her as telling him in much plainer language: "It is your day now; but it will be mine by and by Eleazar Grant; I'll put you in a cockle-shell yet!" (*Testimonies* [1816]: 191).

30. The editors conclude righteously, "The guilty wretches had not confidence to speak to her, nor to look her in the face; but hung down their heads, and began to sheer off" (*Testimonies* [1816]: 198–99). In another extended persecution story, when a mob is forming against the Shakers at Ashfield, a town committee came to visit the Shakers, in an effort to forestall violence, Mother Ann again is seen as emphasizing her need for male protection and getting a chivalrous response: "The committee, consisting of Thomas Stocking, a captain of militia, and two other respectable men, came to Asa Bacon's and desired to see Mother. She went to the door to see them, and said, 'I am a poor weak woman, and I have suffered so much by mobs, that it seems to me as though I could not endure any more.' Stocking replied, 'You need not be afraid, Ma'am; we have not come to hurt you; but to defend you'" (p. 140). There are also several stories given without named sources in the introductory narrative by Wells, however—including those that involve Abraham Stanley's departure in New York.

31. The portrait is also at odds with Lee's autobiographical portrait, as embedded in the memories of the stories she told about her own earlier life. See Humez, "Ye Are My Epistles" (1992) for a fuller discussion of this third set of Lee images in the 1816 *Testimonies*.

32. This section of the essay draws upon my published article, "'Weary of Petticoat Government': The Specter of Female Rule in Early Nineteenth-century Shaker Politics," *Communal Societies* (1992): 1–17.

33. The 1816 *Testimonies* contains two brief stories referred to in the index as "Mother's [Ann Lee's] vision and prophecy regarding her [Lucy Wright]" (pp. 223, 234). Neither clearly refers to Wright's future leadership.

34. Procter-Smith, *Women in Shaker Community and Worship* (1985): 30–31.

35. Angell Matthewson, "Reminiscences in the Form of a Series of Thirty-nine Letters to His Brother Jeffrey,"

New York Public Library Shaker Manuscripts, Item 119, Letters VIII and XI; Calvin Green, "Biographical Account of the Life, Character, & Ministry of Father Joseph Meacham" (1827, repr. in *Shaker Quarterly* 10, 1 [Spring 1970]: 21–102).

36. Reuben Rathbun, *Reasons Offered for Leaving the Shakers* (Pittsfield, Mass: Chester Smith, 1800): 9.

37. Calvin Green, "Biographic Memoir of Father Joseph Meacham," (1970): 30–31. For a published version, see Calvin Green, "Biographical Account of the Life, Character, and Ministry of Father Joseph Meacham," edited by Theodore E. Johnson, *Shaker Quarterly* 10 (1979).

38. See Anna White and Leila Taylor, *Shakerism: Its Meaning and Message* (Columbus, Ohio: Fred J. Heer, 1904): 74.

39. Louis Kern was among the first to make this point, in *An Ordered Love: Sex Roles and Sexuality in Victorian American Communes* (Chapel Hill: University of North Carolina Press, 1981).

40. Reuben Rathbun says Clough "was not first in the ministry, but was subject unto her whom he called his mother, which was the partner of Elder Joseph" (*Reasons Offered* [1800]: 11).

41. Joseph Meacham to Lucy Wright, 1796, Western Reserve Manuscript Collection (hereafter WR), New Lebanon Correspondence IV-A:30.

42. This rebellion is discussed below.

43. Clarke Garrett believes that Ann Lee's role as founder and spiritual leader was de-emphasized during the Meacham years, even to the point of denial of her role as founder of the sect. He makes an interesting speculative case for this denial as part of a revisionist understanding of the "regeneration" or "new birth," which de-sacralized Lee (*Spirit Possession and Popular Religion* [1987]: 231–32).

44. Green, "Biographic Memoir of Joseph Meacham" (1970): 59.

45. Priscilla J. Brewer counts twenty apostates out of 180 New Lebanon Church Family members in 1795–96, in *Shaker Communities, Shaker Lives* (Hanover: University Press of New England, 1986): 28. Clarke Garrett, whose study of this period originally drew my attention to the Matthewson letters, notes that Matthewson resented government by a woman but oddly goes on to assert, citing no specific evidence, that "it is doubtful that very many believers shared Matthewson's objections" (*Spirit Possession and Popular Religion* [1987]: 237). It seems to me much more in line with what we know about dissension caused by female leadership in other churches at this period, as well as with other manuscript evidence I will be citing in this paper, to assume the contrary. Lawrence Foster also suggested that the apostasy of 1795–99 was in part in reaction to Lucy Wright's leadership (*Religion and Sexuality* [1981]: p. 37, p. 271n).

46. Matthewson, "Reminiscences," Letter XXII to 1798, 2 December (New York Public Library).

47. Matthewson, "Reminiscences," Letter XXIIII to 1799

48. John Barns of Gorham, Maine, and Sarah Kendall of Harvard, Massachusetts, were appointed "Father" and "Mother" of the Maine ministry in 1793, the year in which the Maine communities were gathered (Otis Sawyer, "History of Alfred, Maine," MS in Shaker Library, Sabbathday Lake, Maine).

49. See WR Correspondence (hereafter WR Corr) Alfred IV-A:1, 21 June 1815; 20 November 1815 Alfred to Harvard; NL IV-A:33, 2 December 1815, Abiathar Babbitt (and Lucy Wright?) to Alfred ministry and elders; Alfred IV-A:1, 12 February 1816; 26 March 1816, to Seth Babbitt, Harvard; and 4 May 1816, Alfred ministry to Seth Babbitt. According to Otis Sawyer's "History of Alfred, Maine," Barns was told in May 1814, when visiting New Lebanon, that they wished him to resign; a copy of his letter of resignation, dated 1 July 1815, and pleading "age and infirmity" as the reasons, is included in Elder Otis's manuscript.

50. WR Corr Alfred IV-A:1, Alfred ministry to Seth Babbit, 4 May 1816.

51. WR Corr NL IV-A:33, 30 July 1816.

52. Ibid. Green notes that "Mother manifested a gift for Believers to labor in a further work of purification than they had ever done before" at Christmas in 1816—perhaps this was in response to the Alfred rebellion, the most serious direct challenge to her authority yet.

53. Ibid. New Lebanon ministry and church brethren to Alfred. Thomas Cushman, the assistant ministry elder who succeeded Barns, died suddenly of bilious colic in October of the same year, leaving Sarah Kendall and Lucy Prescott alone in the Maine ministry for a short period; Sarah Kendall lost her gift in 1818 and was removed.

54. Like Barns, Meacham was invited to visit Mother Lucy, only to be told when he arrived there that he would not be allowed to return to the west (WR Corr, NL, IV-A:33, 13 February 1818). For a fuller discussion of the other internal political issues at Pleasant Hill, see F. Gerald Ham, "Shakerism in the old West," Ph.D. dissertation, (University of Kentucky, 1962): 181–87.

55. WR Corr NL, IV-A:33, 10 June 1818. New Lebanon based this knowledge on private information obtained in letters from David Darrow and Ruth Farrington from Union Village and in person from the visiting South Union leaders Benjamin S. Youngs and Comstock Betts.

56. WR Corr NL IV: A-33, 9 December 1818 to ministry at

Union Village.

57. The James Anderson letter was dated 16 January, according to Samuel Turner. WR Corr Pleasant Hill (PH), IV-A:52, 24 April 1821, Pleasant Hill ministry to New Lebanon.

58. Shortly before her death, Lucy Wright reportedly secured the agreement of the Canterbury ministry to shed their parental titles. On this occasion Mother Hannah Kendall of Canterbury was said to have thought it would have been better if the ministries in Maine and New Hampshire had never taken such titles. WR Corr NL, IV-A:33, 19 May 1821, to Elder Benjamin S. Youngs.

59. "We believe it to be your right to come first, if it is your choice," they wrote (WR Corr NL, IV-A:33, 22 March 1821, ministry and elders at New Lebanon to ministry at Canterbury).

60. Significantly suggestive of his political weakness is the fact that Elder Abiathar Babbitt, though Mother Lucy's subordinate elder, was not even retained as one of the assistant ministry elders in the new group, which was headed by Elder Ebenezer Bishop and Eldress Ruth Landon.

61. In the letter to New Lebanon Church Family Eldress Rachel Spencer, Lucy Smith seems to parry a suggestion from New Lebanon that she communicate through the Union Village Ministry, rather than directly to Lucy Wright (WR Corr PH IV-A:52, 21 May 1814; 19 August 1814, Samuel Turner to Lucy Wright).

62. WR Corr NL, IV-A:33, 6 September 1819, to Benjamin S. Youngs, South Union.

63. She wrote on 25 June 1820 to the elder sister at the New Lebanon church of her own visionary "gift" to visit New Lebanon; and after the death of Lucy Wright, she wrote of troubling dreams that had preceded hearing the news. See WR Corr PH, IV-A:52-3, 23 February 1820; 25 June 1820; and 1 April 1821.

64. WR Corr PH IV-A:53, 24 April 1821. Turner's letter also reported on a disturbing letter received at Pleasant Hill from James Anderson of Alfred, Maine, accusing Lucy Wright of putting down learning and setting up as leaders "those agents who had changed the oracle of God into a lie."

65. Gerald Ham's section on the Pleasant Hill rebellion focuses on the complaints of John Whitbey, a seceder who took an interest in the ideas of Jeremy Bentham and Robert Owen, and who ultimately joined the New Harmony Society in 1825 when his ideas for changing Shakerism were rejected. He "returned in 1827 from the Owenite failure at New Harmony" and joined other Pleasant Hill dissenters and seceders in trying to dissolve the Covenant. By 1827 the three church families at Pleasant Hill were all "autonomous" and had elected their own elders (Ham, "Shakerism in the old West" ([1962]: 185–86).

66. Confidential letter from Benjamin S. Youngs to New Lebanon Ministry, 8 September 1828, reprinted in Stephen J. Stein, *Letters from a Young Shaker* (Lexington: University of Kentucky, 1985): 120–24; and Solomon King to Ebenezer Bishop, WR Corr PH,

IV-A:53, 14 February 1828.

67. WR Corr NL IV-B:7, 18 August 1827.

68. WR Corr NL IV-B:7, 23 June 1827.

69. WR Corr NL IV-B:7, 18 August 1827.

70. Samuel Turner, writing to New Lebanon retrospectively about the rebellion after it was contained, was not overtly critical of his former spiritual Parent, Lucy Smith. WR Corr PH, IV-A:53, June 1828.

71. WR Corr PH IV-A:52, 14 February 1828.

72. King also felt that the people in general were now relatively "united" with their Ministry, and indeed that many would leave if the ministry were removed.

73. Youngs was far from impartial in his judgment, of course. He had been complaining to New Lebanon for years about the inequity of Pleasant Hill's ministry retaining their parental titles, while he and Molly Goodrich at South Union refrained from adopting such titles.

74. Stein, *Letters from a Young Shaker* (1985): 120.

75. She is also warned that she will be carefully watched by members of her community, as are other leaders who have lost their appointments, "to see if they live up to what they have taught others" (WR Corr NL IV-B:7, 13 April 1829). Samuel Turner was also ultimately recalled under a cloud seven years later, in 1836.

76. New Lebanon lead ministry members after the death of Mother Lucy were only occasionally referred to as Father or Mother, and generally not as a formal title.

77. WR Corr Alfred IV-A:2, 4 May 1831.

78. Brewer, *Shaker Communities, Shaker Lives* (1986): 143–45. Brewer also notes that the scarcity of potential leaders led to changing strategies for maintaining order and obedience (p. 145).

79. WR Corr NL IV-A:6, 23 April 1851.

80. This section is based on my more extensive published essay, "I Had to Study the Female Trait: Philemon Stewart, 'Petticoat Government' Issues and Later 19th century Shakerism," *The Shaker Quarterly* 22, no. 4 (Winter 1994): 122–52.

81. He claimed in one of his later writings that he had been told directly by Giles Avery that the authenticity of his own earlier gift was in doubt.

82. Stewart was one of the New Lebanon Shakers who became very interested in diet reform and related health issues. He experimented with a Graham diet as early as the 1830s and he acted as the medium for a lengthy spirit message on ending the use of pork in Shaker communities, which later became a source of much internal political conflict. He was also deeply involved in the hydropathy, or "water cure" movement, writing in a lengthy journal in the 1870s about his struggles to observe the practices of this movement while living in a family that subscribed to a different medical and dietary system.

83. Philemon Stewart's Journal, "Poland Book No. 1," 1870–74, Winterthur Museum (Andrews Collection SA 776).

84. Personal complaints characterize his journalizing from the 1830s through the 1870s, although the increase in numbers of grievances and bitterness is remarkable

over this time. Stewart felt aggrieved by the apparent mismanagement and neglect of those in authority over him, it would seem, for much of his life. He ran into conflicts with most of those with whom he had dealings, including the major male figures in the Shaker leadership at New Lebanon: Amos Stewart (Philemon's own older brother), Daniel Boler, Giles Avery, and Calvin Green. He expresses strongly affectionate feelings for only one male leader, Rufus Bishop (who had had confidence in his spiritual mediumship), and he praises one ministry eldress, Ruth Landon.

85. Just as clearly in the New Lebanon leadership records from the 1850s through the 1870s, kept by Amos Stewart, Daniel Boler, and then Giles Avery, a high level of irritation toward Stewart is manifest. Interestingly enough, he does not seem to have been regarded as "deranged" by the leadership, as quite a few other individuals described in these records were, and he managed to survive several quite scandalous events without being pushed into a state of "disunion" that would lead to a final break with the society. Perhaps the very high esteem in which he had once been held for his role of spirit instrument by Rufus Bishop during the Era of Manifestations made it politically impossible for later ministry brethren to pressure him to leave the community.

86. He noted in a private journal kept at that time that he was glad to retire in 1842: "I am truly thankful (if that should be my happy lot) to enjoy the peaceful & quiet breezes, which waft upon, a truly Justified soul when placed in such a lot & station, in life, as no other one covets. . . ." WR Journals V-B:136, entry for 25 November 1842.

87. He was appointed in December 1854, because he was "blest with a good spiritual administration, which every good believer will prize," according to a letter from Amos Stewart to the Harvard ministry. Besides, "We think his help is needed more there than in the Church at present." WR Corr NL IV-B:10, NL to Harvard, 17 December 1854.

88. Letters from the central ministry to and about Stewart during this period are revealing. For example, Amos Stewart wrote to give Philemon advice on how to run the public meeting better, 29 April 1855; on 9 May 1858, Amos Stewart declined to intervene in some issue related to moving the Lyall boy from the Second Family. (IV-B:10); on 21 February 1858, Daniel Boler responded to a complaint by Philemon that the Ministry gave more support to "Benjamin and Alonzo" than they should; and on 23 February 1858, Daniel Boler wrote to Daniel Crossman, telling him about a "tempest" in which Philemon was involved, and warning him that Philemon might seek his help (IV-B:11).

89. NYPL #3, "A Journal or Register of Passing Events, Continued from Former Volumes, Kept by Rufus Bishop. January Eighteen Hundred Fifty." Entry for 5 December 1854. We also hear that "Elder Br Philemon has been laboring for the good of the

Second Family for about 4 years; and we believe he has labored earnestly and faithfully according to the best of his understanding to benefit that order and family—But for some time past has felt as though his gift was about out in the Order unless there could be a great change made in the leaders standing nearly connected with him, and others chosen to fill the place that would better harmonize with his peculiar views and ideas of progressive reform, or gospel increase as he would term it.—Short of this, he did not feel able in body or mind to remain as Elder in the family, and has repeatedly tendered his resignation in pretty strong terms both verbal and written" (WR Corr IV-B:11, NL Min to Several Orders of Ministry, 31 October 1858).

90. NYPL #4, entries for 12, 14, 15 May 1860.

91. NYPL #4, entries for 26, 28 September 1860; 31 January 1861; 6–9 June 1862.

92. WR New Lebanon Corr IV-B:11, 25 March 1861, to Br Philemon Stewart, Poland, Maine.

93. In May the following year, New Lebanon responded to a "dictatorial sheet" from Stewart, telling him: "we discover that your own declaration is conclusive evidence of your opposition to Elder Otis & Elder John, which certainly was manifested in spirit and feeling, if not in action." They urge him, nevertheless, not to resign but to stay on at least through September, when they will return from a western tour (WR NL Corr IV-B:11, 31 May 1862).

94. Elsewhere we hear that he had "adopted" a child, and that the ministry refused to allow him to bring the child with him when he returned to New Lebanon ("One of Philemon Stewart's Manifestos to the Ministry," 1863, VII-B:124, pp. 81, 83–85).

95. NYPL #4, entries for 8, 16 April 1863.

96. The first of his several long manuscript booklets of grievances, claiming that he had to write because the Ministry made it impossible for him to have a private audience to discuss these issues face to face. He combined defenses of his own behavior with less personalized critiques of the overall state of the United Society, focusing especially on the poor management of temporal resources, through extravagant spending and through allowing temporal officers, the deacons and trustees, far too much independence from supervision.

97. WR VII-B:124, pp. 30, 79–80.

98. Ibid., 80–86. Stewart is still demanding that the ministry, whom he accuses of sending him to Maine to "get rid of him," allow the child to be placed in the Second or First Order at New Lebanon, because of his moral and legal obligations to it and the Mother. He never uses a gendered pronoun in this discussion.

99. WR New Lebanon Corr IV-A:43, 13 October 1867, Philemon Stewart to the ministry.

100. "One of Philemon Stewart's Manifestoes to the Ministry," WR VII-B:124, p. 41.

101. Later he says he expected they might take the same course with him, but "as it happens, I am not afraid to show records for 40 or 50 years past, with any of

them so far as keeping good order, as it respects the opposite sex" (ibid., 44–45). Stewart had been unable to convince Elder Amos at the time of his version of the events, but he is "glad" Elder Amos later had to live as elder in the same family, and could realize the difficulty for himself. He also believes that "female influence" since he left undermined the confidence of the trustee, Jesse Lewis.

102. "Poland Book No. 1" (1870–74), entry for 2 April 1871, p. 29.

103. Ibid., 50–51.

104. Philemon Stewart, "Continued from Poland Book No. 1, by P. S" (Shaker Library at Old Chatham, #10,805), entry for 20 December 1874.

105. Once the western missionary venture had led to the establishment of several thriving communities far from the immediate surveillance of the eastern Shakers, a parallel system of lead ministry in the west was seen as increasingly desirable by the New Lebanon lead ministry. Although it was resisted by some, as discussed in the essay, the South Union, Ohio, ministry was designated as lead ministry in the west, with authority to oversee the affairs of the two Kentucky communities (Pleasant Hill and South Union) and the three other Ohio communities, Watervliet, North Union, and Whitewater. (West Union, Indiana, was abandoned in 1827.)

The Whirling Gift.

5 "Given by Inspiration": Visionary Expressions in Shaker Life and Art (1837 to 1859)

GERARD C. WERTKIN

Progressive revelation is at the heart of the Shakers' understanding of their history—a history that was born and nurtured in passion, revival, and religious ecstasy. According to Shaker tradition, the role that Ann Lee would play in the developing faith, her decision to lead a group of her disciples from England to America, the miracle that would save them at sea, their successful missionary efforts in the United States, and other significant events represented the unfolding of a divine plan, each occurrence being foretold through heavenly prophecy, voices, and visions. Taking place during the formative stages of the United Society's development, these phenomena became imprinted on the collective consciousness of the Believers and helped to define Shaker life and art. As a result, later Shakers were prepared to accept the veracity of spirit possession and other celestial gifts, which they held to be parallel to the experience of the first Christians at Pentecost, as described in the Acts of the Apostles.

The most significant Shaker growth occurred during the last decade of the eighteenth century and first two decades of the nineteenth. At the conclusion of this period of expansion, eighteen Shaker villages dotted the rural landscape from Maine to Kentucky. The requirements of larger-scale community organization brought order and regularity to Shaker life. Although significant visionary episodes continued to occur from time to time, the ecstatic nature of Shaker daily life and worship began to wane by the early 1830s. As Clarke Garrett has observed in his study of ecstatic religion, "the very orderliness of Shaker

life in the gathered communities made unlikely the spontaneous experiences of spiritual presence that had formerly occurred."[1] Moreover, without the charismatic leadership of Ann Lee or her immediate successors, all of whom were by then deceased, the Shakers of the 1830s drew fewer new seekers to their faith and witnessed a rising number of defections, especially among the young. According to many thoughtful Believers, this period was marked by spiritual stagnation and encroaching worldliness.

Then, in August 1837, a fourteen-year-old Shaker girl, Ann Mariah Goff, with Elleyette Gibbs and Clarissa Shoefelt, her young companions in the Second Family, or Gathering Order, at Watervliet, New York, fell into lengthy trancelike states (fig. 5-1). Apparently without prompting or provocation, they began to turn and shake and whirl. Observers heard them sing original songs, converse with invisible beings, and speak of wandering in beautiful fields, where they gathered fruits and flowers. The young visionaries and their visions were taken at face value by the leadership of the society, which saw them as part of an ongoing unfolding of divine revelation in the communities. Indeed, were it not for their familiarity with spiritual phenomena of this kind, it is unlikely that the Shaker leaders would have been so acquiescent. From August through the end of the year, there were few days at the Watervliet Second Family when spirit manifestations did not occur. In September Rufus Bishop, second elder in the New Lebanon ministry—the central leadership of the Shaker communities—recorded his impressions of these events:

Fig. 5-1. *The Whirling Gift.* Illustration from David R. Lamson, *Two Years' Experience among the Shakers* (West Boylston, [Massachusetts] 1848): 85. The Shaker Museum and Library, Old Chatham and New Lebanon, New York.

SHAKERS,
their mode of Worship.

Lith. of D.W. Kellogg & Co.
Hartford, Conn.

Fig. 5-2. *Shakers, Their Mode of Worship*. Hand-colored lithograph of Shaker dance, published by D. W. Kellogg & Co., Hartford, ca. 1838. The Shaker Museum and Library, Old Chatham and New Lebanon, New York.

For a number of weeks past the meetings have been wonderful, even to the astonishment of believers as well as unbelievers. In addition to the gifts of shaking, turning, bowing &c some souls seemed to be traversing the invisible world, at times viewing the happified state of the Saints in light, and when permitted, singing & dancing with them, some of whom had been their former companions in the gospel. Again one (after beholding the beauty & glory of the faithful & viewing their happy mansions) would be conducted down into dark and dismal dungeons to see the state of the wicked who seemed to be bound with chains and in awful distress—so great was their agony that the sight was too much to endure.[2]

Bishop reported the undeniable proof that the "work" was genuine when different visionaries reported the same visions separately to the elders. "Altho' some had doubts," he wrote, they no longer could be maintained.[3] The strange visionary experiences eventually came to be understood by the leadership of the United Society as signs of the divine, a heavenly call for the Believers to return to their founding principles after a period of spiritual "dullness" and loss.

In December 1837, Ann Mariah Goff received a vision of a "new manner" of labor, in which she saw 344,000 souls going forth in the dance—a practice at the heart of Shaker worship from the earliest days of the church that the Believers also called "exercising," "marching," or "laboring" (fig. 5-2). (The spirit of Mother Lucy Wright, for many years senior member of the New Lebanon ministry, was present and informed her of the number of dancers!) A few days later, the Shaker family "labored" in this manner before non-Believers at a public meeting, forming three circles, two abreast in each, the first and third turning to the left and the second to the right. It evidently was an impressive sight.[4] The ministry invited Joseph Hodgson, elder brother of the Second Family at Watervliet, to teach the new worship form at New Lebanon; it became known as the Heavenly March or Bowing Circle. Throughout the months of December 1837 and January 1838, several young sisters at Watervliet fell into lengthy trances and learned "through inspiration" still other forms of laboring, which the family incorporated into its religious services. So many visitors crowded into the village's meetinghouse during this period that it was increasingly difficult to conduct worship. The New Lebanon ministry was sufficiently impressed by the importance of these events to dispatch Isaac N. Youngs to Watervliet to record them.[5] For Rufus Bishop, the gifts were proof of the "condescending goodness of God." [6]

Soon similar manifestations were occurring in every Shaker village. The Believers called the period of the revival, which began in 1837 with Ann Mariah Goff's trance, the Era of Manifestations, also known as the Era of Mother's Work.[7] This era differed from earlier Shaker visionary episodes in its great intensity and in the astonishing variety and creativity of its expressions, but the earlier manifestations prepared the communities for what was to come. Bernhard Lang, in his comprehensive study of Christian worship, warns us that "Shaker emotion-

alism must not be thought of as an isolated matter." "By the end of the nineteenth century," he writes, "Protestantism had lived through various 'awakenings' and revivals of which the Shaker experience was only one example. Between 1800 and 1835—during the generation preceding the Shaker revival—Methodists, Presbyterians, and Congregationalists had their own revivals with emotional open-air preaching and the singing of hymns."[8] Lang correctly places the Era of Manifestations within the broader context of Christian revivalism—indeed, the participation of Shaker preachers in various frontier revivals resulted in substantial growth in the United Society—but the distinctive nature of Shaker ecstatic worship during the era should not be minimized. Not confined to church services, the varied expressions of Mother's Work touched virtually every aspect of life in the communities.

At first Mother's Work involved evocative visions of a heavenly state peopled with the spirits of departed leaders of the church, family members, and hosts of angels and saints. To the visionaries, heaven was an idealized Shaker village, and its inhabitants imparted simple messages of encouragement and reassurance. For example, on January 28, 1838, when John Whipple, a seventeen-year-old boy at the Enfield, Connecticut, Shaker community, awakened from a deep trance after turning for about an hour, he spoke of finding himself on an extensive plain, filled with light, in which a large assembly gathered for the worship of God. He recalled:

> I looked all around . . . and thought this place is Heaven. The spirits were singing quick songs the most beautiful I ever heard. They were turning, under the operation of the power of God, and stepping the notes of the tune, as they were turning. They all appeared to be filled and covered with the greatest and brightest light I ever saw. I now saw my sister Lucy, who had been dead about seven years. . . . She came out of this bright body, and took me by the hand, and asked me if I wanted to come into the happy meeting. I told her I did. . . .

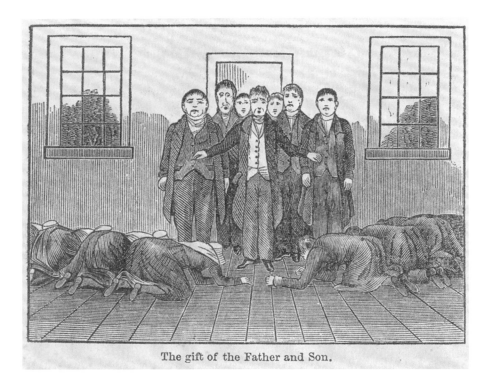

The gift of the Father and Son.

Fig. 5-3. *The Gift of the Father and Son*. Illustration from David R. Lamson, *Two Years' Experience among the Shakers* (West Boylston, [Massachusetts] 1848): 104. The Shaker Museum and Library, Old Chatham and New Lebanon, New York.

She then led me in with them; and that same bright light then covered me; and I never felt so happy before.[9]

Several days after John Whipple's experience, one of his companions at Enfield, the thirteen-year-old visionary Edward Lyman, saw Mother Ann "going forth in the worship of God with others." He also saw his deceased father. "I . . . told him I was thankful that he . . . got me in among Believers. And he said he was glad that he had." [10]

These dreamlike visions offered a private view of eternity to the visionaries, not unlike the visions often received by the Believers in the infant days of the church. Beginning in the spring of 1838, however, when the Era of Manifestations "opened" in its fullness at New Lebanon, the church as a whole became absorbed in a corporate vision, a tangible expression of the infinite apparently so real that almost every faithful Shaker was to share in it. Visionaries, "visionists," or "instruments," as they came to be known, now seemed possessed by the spirits that previously spoke to them only privately. As they walked among the brethren and sisters or addressed them in meet-

ings or at other gatherings, these spirit-possessed Shakers were believed to deliver divine messages and heavenly exhortations (fig. 5-3). A Shaker diarist recorded on January 1, 1840:

> It is now, in these days, a time of an abundance of manifestations from the spiritual world, particularly thro' instruments, by Inspiration. There is seldom a meeting without some communication, or message, from the spirits, mostly from our heavenly parents. There is also an abundance of written messages, consisting of instruction, love & admonition, and much in the way of reining us up to strict Church Order, as it was first established by Father Joseph.[11]

Perhaps the foremost of the New Lebanon instruments was Philemon Stewart (1804–1875), who with his brothers Charles and Amos had been placed with the Shakers in 1811, when he was six years old, and who was to be a leading personality throughout the Era of Manifestations. Stewart is an enigmatic figure. Although he was to serve as an elder later in his life at the Second Family, New Lebanon, and at Poland Hill, Maine, he was not in a position of authority during the revival period, except briefly in 1841–42 as second elder of the New Lebanon church under David Meacham. But as an instrument he wielded extraordinary influence for a span of ten years.

It was through Philemon Stewart, beginning in the spring of 1838, that the first leaders of the church, now deceased, were to speak to a generation of Believers that had not known them in the flesh. A New Lebanon diarist, writing in 1838, recorded that Christmas was blessed "with the presence of our first parents and elders in the gospel—Mother Ann, Fr. William, Fr. James and Mother Lucy—also with some of our deceased elders" and that "many beautiful gifts were administered."[12] Two days afterward, when Joseph Wicker (1790–1852), a leading instrument and elder at Hancock, with a group of sisters and brethren from the nearby Massachusetts community came to New Lebanon to learn some new spiritual songs that had been received through inspiration, "a precious message" of union and order was given to them by Father Joseph Meacham, through Philemon Stewart.[13]

As the events of the Era of Manifestations transpired, meetings for worship became increasingly animated. On December 9, 1838, as the New Lebanon Shakers gathered for religious services, Sister Hannah Blake (1811–1893) turned steadily in her place in the first rank. At the same time, she kept reaching down to the floor, until she lifted up "a golden ball out of Mother's box or treasure" for the Believers, one of many symbolic gifts that would later typify the spiritual presents of the era. There followed a "general outpouring of the power of God," as the young brethren became drunk with "Mother's Wine." We can only imagine the sights and sounds of that meeting, but for at least one Shaker observer, it was "like a mighty rushing wind."[14]

By 1839 inspiration was a daily feature of life in almost all of the Shaker villages, a commonplace to be recorded in family journals with other events of the day. "Jesus Christ attended our meeting," Russell Haskell wrote in a matter-of-fact manner at Enfield, Connecticut, late in the year.[15] A few months earlier, Haskell recorded Daniel Wilcox's vision of the biblical King David's visit to the Connecticut community. According to Wilcox, David entered the meetinghouse and wrote a message in two circular lines on the floor: "Bretheren [sic] and sisters," he wrote, "you will see and feel more of the power of God in this house for one year to come than you have seen and felt for the last eleven years that are past and gone."[16]

"This opening of the spiritual world into the earthly life of Believers," Anna White and Leila S. Taylor of the North Family, New Lebanon, New York, observed many years later, "was so actual and practical that it lifted the communistic toiler to the life of spirit spheres, and no longer was there a question of the possibility of angel communication. It was a natural, everyday fact."[17] Gifts could be received anywhere at any time. One afternoon in May, as the members of the ministry walked

through the bake room after dinner at Watervliet, New York, Saphrona Smith "was mightily shaken and whirled by the power of God." She told the venerable Ebenezer Bishop that Father Joseph was with him, while Father James was with Rufus Bishop, and Mother Lucy was with Aseneth Clark. The ministry elders were pleased by this affirmation of union from their predecessors.[18]

If they were pleased by these affirmations of divine notice, however, the leadership of the society was also concerned about the enormous number of visions. By mid-1839, inconsistencies were being noted among the instruments, resulting in a crisis in confidence. The necessity of "trying the spirits" to ascertain the authenticity and divine source of visions was earnestly discussed.[19] The ministry successfully asserted its right to judge the validity of the spirit manifestations, a position that was confirmed by prophetic utterance. In view of the emotional character of the era, however, this was a continuing problem. Inspired messages, oral and written, often warned instruments not to confuse true visionary experiences with their own private sentiments.

As we have seen, early in the revival period it had become apparent to the Shaker elders that the spirit manifestations had a solemn purpose. Whether that purpose was fostered by Philemon Stewart and the other instruments, or imposed by a leadership eager to encourage full-scale revival, is difficult to determine. But to the concerned Shakers who watched its development, it was a welcome phenomenon. Temporal prosperity had been achieved in many places, but the earlier zeal seemed to have been lost. Elders seeking to hold on to the loyalty of the young had made concessions to them "for more liberty and indulgence in their worldly tastes." Complacency was unwittingly engendered by a respected, if somewhat uninspired, central ministry, which had been in office for almost twenty years since the death of Mother Lucy Wright in 1821. "It appears that as a body, we have degenerated or fallen back considerably in many things," observed the church historian Isaac N. Youngs, writing of the events of 1840.

"Therefore, there is now an urgent call from the heavens for us to retrace our steps—to come more into order and under more restraint." [20]

At New Lebanon during the spring of 1840, instruments in the imposing roles of the first American-born leaders of the society, Joseph Meacham and Lucy Wright, "labored incessantly" to reestablish the "true primitive order" in which the church was founded.[21] The Believers were called upon to give up personal possessions and to repudiate the holding of private property, which had crept into the life of the communal Shaker villages and had been tacitly tolerated for some years. In particular, objects not conforming to the principles of the society and to its ideals of simplicity and utility were to be purged from the communities. Youngs noted that the changes were effected "with remarkable resignation and cheerfulness."[22]

A codification of rules and orders was undertaken on May 7, 1840, when Philemon Stewart, speaking for the spirit of Father James Whittaker, began the lengthy dictation of "A General Statement of the Holy Laws of Zion" to Seth Youngs Wells, the church's secretary and bookkeeper. One of several inspired rule books or codes of conduct introduced during the Era of Manifestations, "A General Statement of the Holy Laws of Zion" is a remarkable work, received by the Shakers of the revival period as an extract from a volume "written by the hand of God Himself." To be sure, there had been prior compilations of regulations, notably those adopted at New Lebanon on August 7, 1821, but these were not held to be the direct work of God. Despite their legalistic approach to almost every aspect of Shaker life, the "Holy Laws of Zion" are surprisingly flexible and compassionate; if their recital is solemn, it is not without a simple charm. For example, although the use of "ardent spirits" is discountenanced by the Holy Laws, cider in moderation is allowed to middle-aged and older Believers. The young "should train themselves to do without," but even for them, "a small beer" is permitted "in warm weather."[23]

Among other codes of conduct that were given by inspiration during the Era of Manifestations, the "Millennial Laws, or Gospel Statutes and Ordinances" of 1845 were perhaps the most influential, but even they were in force for only a limited period of time and by 1860 had been replaced by a simpler, more practical compilation of rules.[24]

The instructions with which the "General Statement" concludes specify that the laws were to be read to all Believers over the age of fourteen first on the second Sunday in July and then once in each of six succeeding years. Acknowledging the growing ritualism of the Era of Manifestations, the Holy Laws of Zion required the Believers "to bow low eight times" after hearing them read and, with three more bows, to repeat the words "I will keep—thy holy Laws—O Zion!" In the years immediately prior to the Era of Manifestations, religious ritual—with the notable exception of the dance or the march in worship—had a relatively minor place in Shaker life. By the early 1840s, however, the performance of rituals, which were often elaborate ceremonies and new forms of exercise, was a common feature of life in the Shaker communities.

For a full week in December 1841, a "chosen band of singers" daily passed and re-passed through all the dwelling houses at New Lebanon "to purify our habitations spiritually." This was reminiscent of the "gift of spiritual sweeping" that occupied some Shakers at Harvard, Massachusetts, for two weeks, very early in the history of the church. A similar ritual was enacted in 1842 at New Lebanon, "the work of sowing the seed of blessing," when many sisters and brethren "passed over all the principal lots and gardens" to sow spiritual seed. In his brief history of the revival period, Elder Henry C. Blinn (1824–1905) of Canterbury, New Hampshire, lists thirteen new worship forms received by inspiration and used at Canterbury during the era. The colorful names of these forms convey images of the Believers going forth in the dance: "Winding March," the "Cross and Diamond," "Elder Benjamin's Cross," "Moving Square," "Celestial March" and others.[25] Much of the elaborate ritual followed in the wake of the first appearance at New Lebanon on May 3, 1840, of Holy and Eternal Mother Wisdom, the feminine or maternal aspect of Deity as understood by the Shakers.

The "General Statement of the Holy Laws of Zion" and other visionary messages during the Era of Mother's Work placed great emphasis on "separation from the world." This renewed emphasis and the extravagance of rituals that may have subjected the Shakers to misunderstanding or ridicule led to the closing of the villages in the early 1840s and the cessation of public meetings. A "spiritual chain" was drawn between the World and the domain of the Believers at Watervliet, New York, and a sign forbidding entrance except for certain limited purposes was erected at the gate.[26] A similar notice placed at the entrance to the Enfield, Connecticut, village excluded the world from "consecrated ground" from December 24, 1841, to March 2, 1842, during which time the brethren and sisters were to be engaged in a work of "true repentance." In late 1841, the North Union, Ohio, Shakers "decided to close our meetings to the public for the outside world does not understand the manifestations of the Holy Spirit and crowd in out of curiosity to witness them. The notice of closing our meetings has been posted in all meeting places; this notice has been sent to the *Cleveland Herald* also."[27]

When the New Lebanon Shakers published advertisements in the local press in April 1842 advising that public meetings would be terminated, several written responses appeared at the village in May, challenging the Believers in biblical language not to hide their candles under a bushel but to let their light shine.[28] Whether these anonymous messages were placed by dissident Shakers who disagreed with the policy of insularity or a Worldly critic aggrieved by his inability to be entertained at Shaker meeting is not suggested by the Shaker account. Eventually, wooden crosses with forbidding messages inscribed on them were placed in the village to ward off visitors (fig. 5-4). This effort at more complete separation, however, proved unsuccessful, and before long the crosses were

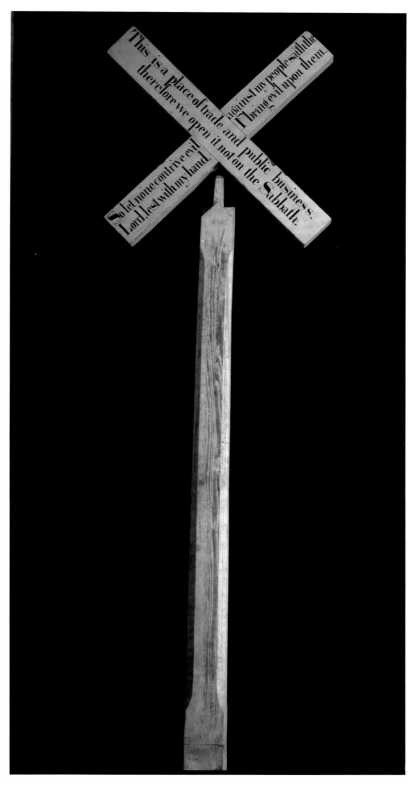

Fig. 5-4. Sign. New Lebanon, New York, 1842. Pine, black and white paint. Hancock Shaker Village, Pittsfield, Massachusetts. The sign in the form of a cross, restricting entry to the Shaker village. Photo: Paul Rocheleau.

removed and non-Believers were permitted to enter the village again except for periods of special introspection or spiritual work.

Another interesting development that reflects the heightened ritualism of the Era of Mother's Work was the revelation received in 1842 through Philemon Stewart for each community to clear a place for outdoor worship, a "Feast Ground" where a spiritual "fountain" was to be erected. Located in a secluded or protected place, frequently on high ground, the area was to be set apart as consecrated and was to be reserved solely for sacred use. On July 23, 1842, at New Lebanon, the gifted Shaker Brother Isaac Newton Youngs (1793–1865) finished engraving the following legend on a marble slab to be erected in that village's feast ground

THE WORD OF THE LORD

> Here is my Living Fountain,
> Saith the Holy One of Israel; and
> Here is where I shall set up my king-
> dom, forever more to reign.
> And From this place shall go forth
> my word and Holy Laws, to all
> nations of the Earth.
> And I say whomsoever shall
> presume to put their hands upon
> this stone, or step their feet
> within the spot where I have caused
> these posts to be set up,
> when their hands are unclean, and
> their hearts impure, shall in
> some day or other feel the rod
> of my severity, and fall under
> an awful curse, which I shall, in
> my own time, cause to come upon them,
> even I the Great I am, the Eternal,
> Almighty and Overruling Power of
> Heaven and Earth; My word is truth, Amen.[29]

On July 25, 1842, Philemon Stewart, his brother Amos, then first elder of the Second Order of the Church, Joel Turner and Isaac N. Youngs set the small "fountain stone" in place. Three days later the New Lebanon church family held its first meeting at the Holy Ground, in the presence of the ministry

of the communities at Harvard and Shirley, Massachusetts, Elder Grove Blanchard, Brother John Orsment, Eldress Betty Babbitt, and Sister Sally Loomis. Other Shaker communities were soon to set aside feast grounds for the placement of fountain stones. Groveland erected its stone, also engraved by Isaac N. Youngs, in May, 1843; Hancock, the same month; Harvard, its stone engraved by Elder Joseph Myrick, in November, 1843; and North Union in 1845. The fountain stone at Canterbury was not erected until 1848, the engraving completed by Elder Henry C. Blinn following the instructions of Joseph Myrick, who began the work. The wording on each stone, while similar in style and content to the one at New Lebanon, varied from village to village.

The Shakers' neighbors showed marked curiosity about the fountain stones. In October 1842, one of the brethren at New Lebanon discovered two "world's men" taking a facsimile of the writing. "And some wicked person has shot rifle ball against the face."[30]

In a diary kept by Sister Prudence Morrell (1794–1855) of a trip to the western Shaker communities in 1847, there is a detailed description of a worship service held at the feast ground at Union Village, Ohio, in which she participated. After assembling at the meetinghouse, where they sang an anthem, "danced a number of quick songs," and gathered "love from the holy angels," the Shakers marched to the "chosen square." There they bathed themselves symbolically, and "went forth in the dances of those that make merry," shaking off all pride, lust, self-will and "everything that goes to hinder a free circulation of the pure spirit of Mother." Many of the young people were especially expressive, being "filled to overflowing with the lovely gifts of God." "They shouted Glory to God in the highest, and sung many beautiful songs of praise."[31]

The exercises that Morrell described were typical of other rituals enacted during the Era of Manifestations throughout the Shaker communities, involving spirit possession, pantomime, symbolic gestures, and inspired songs and dances (see fig. 1-

19). It was during this period that the villages received the evocative spiritual names by which they became known—Holy Mount for New Lebanon; Wisdom's Valley for Watervliet, New York; City of Peace for Hancock; City of Union for Enfield, Connecticut, Chosen Land for New Gloucester or Sabbathday Lake, Maine, among others.

In keeping with the ritualistic emphasis of the revival period, the Shakers added new holy days to the calendar in the 1840s and placed greater stress on the observance of the major feast days of the Christian year. By prophetic utterance, February 29 or March 1 was to be commemorated as Mother Ann's birthday, to be kept "sacred as Christmas."[32] May 1 was celebrated as Passover and dedicated to the work of Holy Mother Wisdom, the feminine or maternal aspect of the one God, according to Shaker theology. June 1 was a day of Thanksgiving for "the ancients, Mother's first born." And August 6 was the anniversary of the arrival of the first Shakers in New York. Although the rites varied from year to year and from village to village, the observance of special days continued to be a feature of the Era of Manifestations through much of the period and in some cases became permanent elements of Shaker life.

In 1845 many Shaker communities celebrated especially elaborate Christmas rituals. The Christmas meeting at New Gloucester or Sabbathday Lake, Maine, saw the appearance through instruments of angels and prophets and saints, all imploring the brethren and sisters to persevere in the faith. "Then came an angel of the Lord," the record of the day relates, "in a very solemn, and striking appearance; and said that he was filled with the Holy Ghost; and bestowed his power on all in great measure." This impressive ritual, conducted in the small Shaker gambrel-roofed meetinghouse during a silent and cold Maine winter, opened with "one loud and solemn shout" by the Believers in unison, with uplifted hands to call forth the "holy and mighty Angels." The angels spoke through Sisters Maria Cummings, Harriet Adams, Adeline Jacobs, and Hannah Davis. Sisters Sarah, Abigail, and Sophia Mace were also active in

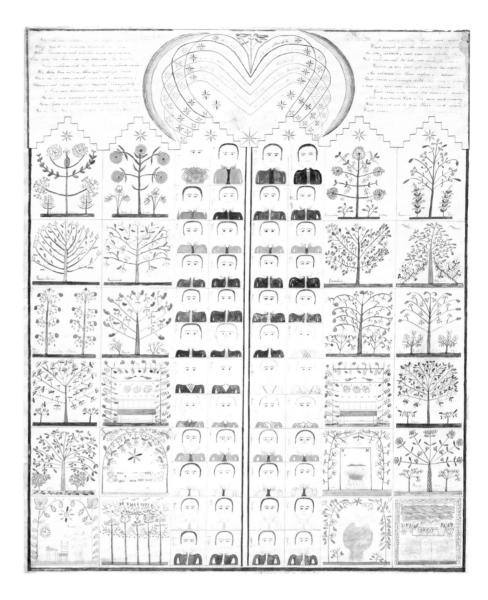

bringing forth gifts. So much happened during the lengthy meeting that the diarist could not record it all in detail. The account of the Christmas meeting ends with a moving summary of the unrecorded events of the day. "Add to this," the account states, "the almost innumerable exhortations to love, to zeal for the way of God, and the increasing work of the gospel; both from the old, and the young; from the visible, and invisible." [33]

The Shakers were diligent keepers of records; the journals, diaries, and correspondence of the era are replete with detailed and often animated

Fig. 5-5. Polly Collins (1808–1884). *An Emblem of the Heavenly Sphere*, 1854. Hancock, Massachusetts. Ink and watercolor on paper. Andrews Collection, Hancock Shaker Village, Pittsfield, Massachusetts.

descriptions of spiritual phenomena occurring in the villages. Thousands of such manifestations are described in the extant records. Shaker instruments were believed to speak in trance on behalf of divine figures, angels, and saints, as well as persons from Shaker and secular history. Soon after Mother's Work commenced, there were spirit visitations from deceased English and French kings and queens; Napoleon Bonaparte; Columbus; Lafayette; Sir Francis Drake; Eve, "our first mother"; John Calvin; and scores of other notables. In a letter written by inspiration at the Second Family, Watervliet, New York, on May 11, 1842, the spirit of George Washington admitted to the Shakers that during his lifetime he sought worldly honors of office and military victory rather than hear "what I must do in order to obtain eternal Life and peace, which is neither more nor less than taking up arms against ones self [sic]—But it is the most glorious warfare that mortals ever engaged in & brings the greatest victory that mortals ever won!"[34] Interestingly, in "An Emblem of the Heavenly Sphere," a drawing of 1854 by Polly Collins (1808–1884) of Hancock, Massachusetts, Washington is pictured in a celestial choir, which otherwise is composed entirely of figures from sacred and Shaker history (fig. 5-5).

In addition to the spirits of the famous and infamous, the Shakers received through inspiration a strange variety of "native spirits," initially in 1842 at Canterbury, New Hampshire. In August of that year, while the Canterbury ministry was visiting New Lebanon, "Indian" spirits took control of instruments at the parent community as well. Throughout the autumn these unruly spirits, which were particularly numerous among younger Shakers, disrupted life in several villages. Eventually the spirits of Africans, Arabs, Tartars, Chinese, and others were received in this manner. By November 1842, "taking in the spirits," as the practice was called, had become a serious enough problem for the leadership to give careful consideration to it. They reasoned that the ability of the Believers to accept the exuberant expressions as genuine was a mark of childlike faith and obedience, which should be encouraged. Also, "taking in the spirits" allowed the leadership to preach the message of the Shaker faith to those who had not known it in life. Eventually the ministry reasserted its right to judge the validity of all gifts. From time to time, the ministry discountenanced the practice of "taking in the spirits," but native spirits continued to take possession of Believers, at least on occasion. Their appearance has left a legacy of spirited gift songs, at least a few of which continued to be sung until well after the Era of Mother's Work had come to an end.

For the Shakers, all the manifestations of Mother's Work were "gifts." As in other examples of Shaker usage, the sense of the word is biblical in origin. According to the Epistle of James (1:17), "every good gift and every perfect gift is from above, and cometh down from the Father of lights." During the period of the revival, the Shakers believed that extravagant gifts, entirely invisible to the naked eye, were presented to them. "There is . . . an endless variety of gifts, and spiritual presents, bro't and given to us collectively & individually, much of which we do not fully understand & some of which we do understand as being signs and representations of divine things—such as lamps—doves—branches, balls of love, crosses &c &c."[35]

Occasionally symbolic gifts were received from the heavenly spheres in solemn rituals involving elaborate miming. David R. Lamson participated in the manifestations of Mother's Work for two years at Hancock until he left the society in 1845. He later wrote how curious it was to see the whole assembly reaching out to catch "balls of Mother's love" that were believed by faithful Shakers to be real, if not tangible to their natural senses.[36] Not infrequently the gifts were of symbolic food. "Mother's wine" and manna were distributed early in the era at New Lebanon, the young brethren acting "drunk" with new wine. In April 1842 at the New Lebanon meetinghouse, Jesus—through the mediumship of the inspired instrument Miranda Barber (1819–1871), with Polly Reed (1818–1881) as witness and "scribe"—offered gifts of peaches, oranges, pineapples, plums, and berries to the assembled Shakers. "Take freely," he assured them, for "there is a plenty."[37]

Were it not for the specific Shaker context, the matter-of-fact way in which the gifts frequently were described in the journals of the era would lead a casual reader to assume that they were being offered in actuality. This was rarely the case, however. Among other gifts were musical instruments, flowers and leaves, jewelry of gold and silver, emblems, stars, and lamps. In an interesting study of Shaker gifts, Virginia Weis concluded that they may be catalogued by function. "One small group of objects was meant to enlighten and clarify; a second, to heal; a third, to cleanse, a fourth, to clothe; a fifth, to nourish; a sixth, to regulate."[38] In their study of Shaker drawings, Edward D. Andrews and Faith Andrews refer to a contemporary manuscript in the hand of Elder David Austin Buckingham of Watervliet, New York, in which several typical gifts are listed with suggested meanings; apples, for example, signify "love," pearls "meekness," diamonds "peace and comfort," chains "union and strength," roses "love and chastity."[39] But, in fact, there does not appear to be a consistency of usage throughout the Era of Mother's Work in written or graphic references to gifts.

If some gifts were invisible, others were described in detail in written form. By 1841 written messages amounted to many hundreds, often contained in little booklets, detached sheets, and scraps of paper. In order to safeguard these gifts, the ministry appointed Seth Youngs Wells and Isaac N. Youngs to collate and record them for the first bishopric. Other copyists undertook this task elsewhere. So many spirit communications were collected that it took the conscientious recorders several years to complete the writing. In addition to public messages, there were also numerous private notices from the spirit world addressed to individual sisters and brethren, and these were retained by the individuals for whom they were intended. They are often striking examples of delicately wrought calligraphy.

At times the gifts were not wholly intangible but were objectified, as in an elaborate ceremony that took place at the Second Order, New Lebanon, on January 29, 1843, when an "angel" requested a box of seals, pen and ink, and five sheets of paper of varying colors: white, dark blue, light blue, and red.

> After singing a song of blessing, during which the white sheets of paper, & white cloths were waved around the Brethren & Sisters, Holy Wisdom's accompanying Angel came forward into the center of the room with all the writing utensils. Four lighted lamps were now brot & given to the Elders, with which they were requested to draw nigh the Angel who was about to write. They did so.
>
> The Instrument now took one of the sheets of white paper, & seemed to try hard to tear, by jerking it—it did not tear. She then carefully folded it & wrote upon it four lines, partly in English & partly in an unknown tongue, not clearly understood from the writing. . . . This was sealed up—& the red sheet was wrapped around it, & also sealed.

As the ceremony continued under the direction of Peter Long, as one of the leading angels, and Calvin Reed (1821–1900) and Orren Nathan Haskins (1815–1892), songs were sung, messages of warning and encouragement were given, and the sheets of blue paper were torn and scattered so that each Believer could have a piece. By the conclusion of the rite, the symbolism of the gifts was revealed. The four lamps represented four angels of judgment standing at the four corners of the earth. Their placement on the floor symbolized the need for the Shakers to "come very low, even bowing to the dust, to keep in the Light." The white color of the paper was seen as a representation of peace and union, which if kept pure cannot be torn or broken. The blue paper, a symbol of love, was divided and scattered like manna in the wilderness, a gift for everyone who would bow low enough to receive it.[40]

SHAKER GIFT DRAWINGS

Among the spiritual gifts offered at New Lebanon in 1842, there is a reference in a Shaker journal to likenesses, pictures and "representations of many things & scenes in the other world & ancient things

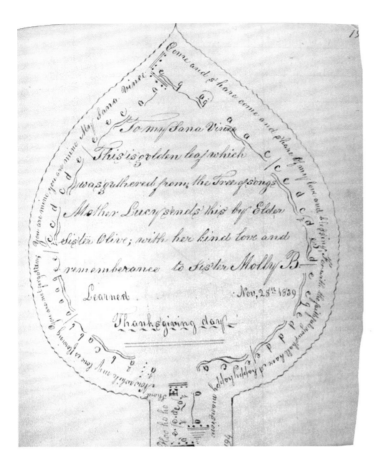
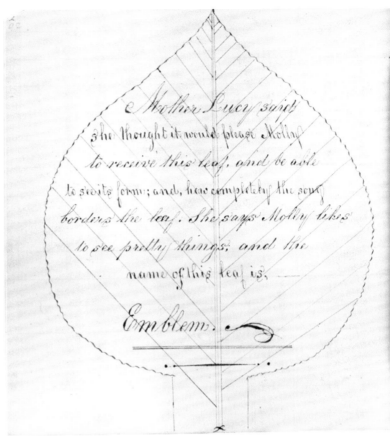

Fig. 5-6. Mary Hazard (1811–1899). Illustration from *A Collection of Songs of Various Kinds*, 1839. New Lebanon, New York. Blue ink on lined paper. Winterthur Library. Edward Deming Andrews Memorial Shaker Collection, Winterthur, Delaware, no. ASC 896. Showing drawing of leaf, recto and verso.

in this world." The following year the same journal records receipt of "certain mysterious sheets, containing many hieroglyphics, and generally more or less English, and abundance of mysterious writing in unknown characters. . . . These sheets," the entry concludes, "were written & given to individuals, with their names on them. They are said to contain much that will hereafter be revealed."[41]

These references are to a special category of gifts, which together are among the great spiritual and material legacies of the Era of Manifestations. Originally known to scholars and collectors as "spirit drawings," these graphic expressions of Mother's Work are more accurately called "gift drawings," or "gift images," following the terminology suggested respectively by Daniel W. Patterson and Sally M. Promey, each the author of a major study of Shaker drawings. The Shakers themselves did not categorize these gifts as drawings but

referred to them simply as "gifts," "sheets," "emblems," "rolls," or "presents"—terminology that was in common usage during the Era of Mother's Work to refer to oral and written gifts. But, as we have seen, terms such as "likenesses," "pictures," and "representations"—which recognized the visual nature of these manifestations—were also used by the Shakers to refer to gift drawings. Eldress M. Catherine Allen (1852–1922), a member of the society's central ministry, used the term "manifestation gifts" to describe the exquisite drawings of Polly Reed.

Patterson accounted for 192 gift drawings in 1983; perhaps a dozen or more have been discovered since then, but this number is small when compared to the thousands of surviving gift writings and songs. Although the drawings and paintings are far less commonly encountered than other Shaker gift expressions, they are simply extensions or elaborations of the oral and written phenomena and cannot be understood except in the same context. They derive from identical impulses and utilize equivalent symbolic language and imagery. The great majority of the extant examples are from New Lebanon or Hancock, and, with only a few exceptions, are the work of Shaker women.

Unlike the "automatic" or "spirit" writings or drawings of nineteenth-century American spiritualism, Shaker gift drawings, with some exceptions, were not generally believed to be the work of spirits guiding the hand of the medium or instrument. Catherine Allen, who did not live through the revival period herself, explained that Polly Reed "did the work by dictation of the medium to whom the message & the vision were given."[42] Although some Shaker instruments recorded visions that they had received themselves—Hannah Cohoon and Hester Ann Adams, for example—even then the work was rarely accomplished in a trance state. With the exception of certain communications in "unknown tongues," the Shaker drawings were carefully planned, composed and executed, and acknowledged to be the conscious act of their creators—the recording of a vision previously received. More often than not, they contain messages of consolation and encouragement intended for the Shaker brethren and sisters to whom they were addressed.

Drawing was a means of translating the symbolic gifts received during the Era of Manifestations into a more tangible form. In a small manuscript songbook compiled in 1839 by Sister Mary Hazard (1811–1899) of New Lebanon, for example, the words and melody of a song "gathered from the Tree of songs" are recorded on the edge of a carefully drawn two-sided, leaf, the first image of its kind in Mother's Work. The text explains that the intended recipient of the gift would be pleased "to receive this leaf, and be able *to see its form*" (fig. 5-6).

Some gift images were made even more substantial by being executed in the shape of the gift, as in the case of a series of small, meticulous, two-sided heart-and-leaf-shape cutouts drawn at New Lebanon in 1844 and 1845. Attributed to Sister

Polly Reed, one of the most accomplished Shaker instruments, each of these ink drawings is inscribed to an individual Believer. Of the heart-shape gifts, at least twenty-eight survive. Those that are dated invariably bear the year 1844, early in the eleven-year period in which Reed is known to have created gift drawings. At that time, her work was mainly textual in nature, although some of the emblematic figures that typify her later, more elaborate compositions—crowns, pillars, lamps, musical instruments, doves, trees, and flowers—may illustrate her texts or otherwise appear as elements in her heart-shape drawings.

Reed's heart-shape drawings were intended as gifts for the members of the First Order of the Church, the Shaker family in which the artist lived. Patterson has suggested that Reed may have created 148 of these exquisite drawings, equaling the number of Shakers, including children, residing in

Fig. 5-7. Polly Ann (Jane) Reed (1818–1881). *Gift Drawing for Eleanor Potter (verso)*, 1844. New Lebanon, New York. Ink on cut paper. American Folk Art Museum, New York, Promised gift of Ralph Esmerian, P1.2001.301B. Photo: © John Bigelow Taylor, New York.

Fig. 5-8. Polly Ann (Jane) Reed (1818–1881). *A Present from Mother Lucy to Eliza Ann Taylor*, 1849. New Lebanon, New York. Ink and watercolor on paper. Miller Collection, Hancock Shaker Village, Pittsfield, Massachusetts.

the First Order in 1844.[43] Almost half the extant heart cutouts are dated, and they all bear various dates in April 1844, except for one drawing, a gift for Eleanor Potter that, perhaps uniquely, has the date of June 2, possibly a final effort by Reed before the hearts were distributed to the members of the family later the same day.

A manuscript journal records that on Sunday morning June 2, 1844, the members of the First Order gathered in the family meeting room for a solemn ceremony. A table had been placed in the front of the room, spread with a white cloth on which "Hearts of Blessing" from "our Merciful, Holy & Heavenly Father" had been placed. "The writing was now accomplished—& the presents ready to be given out. The brethren and sisters then came forward, kneeling down & receiving the papers, in the form of a heart; beautifully written over with

words of blessing in the name of the *Father*"44 (fig. 5-7).

Among the more fully developed works by Reed, "A present from Mother Lucy to Eliza Ann Taylor" (1849) is one of the most complex. The work is pleasingly rendered in watercolor, its principal focus being a dwelling house with double front doors, as in a Shaker residence. With a tiny eye at the center of its roof and checkerboard tiles at its entrance,

the building is also reminiscent of a Masonic temple. Despite the great profusion of individual elements, the composition is exceedingly well balanced. In addition to Reed's more typical imagery, this drawing includes an Angel of Peace carrying a colorful "leaf of Peace" and wearing "a crown of plaited thorns." There are also an open book and a "breast plate from Socratees [*sic*]" (fig. 5-8).

Fig. 5-9. Polly Ann (Jane) Reed (1818–1881). *A Type of Mother Hannah's Pocket Handkerchief,* 1851. New Lebanon, New York. Ink and watercolor on paper. Andrews Collection, Hancock Shaker Village, Pittsfield, Massachusetts.

Fig. 5-10. Sarah Bates (1792–1881). *A Holy & Sacred Roll, sent from Holy & Eternal Wisdom*, 1846. New Lebanon, New York. Ink and watercolor on paper. Fruitlands Museums, Harvard, Massachusetts.

Fig. 5-11. Sarah Bates (1792–1881). *Untitled Sacred Roll*. New Lebanon, New York. Ink and watercolor on paper. Philadelphia Museum of Art, Philadelphia, Pennsylvania. Gift of Mr. and Mrs. Julius Zeiget, 1963. 1963-160-3.

"A type of Mother Hannah's pocket handkerchief" was completed by Polly Reed in 1851. Drawn for Jane Blanchard by the spirit of Father James Whittaker, the work is bolder than Reed's other major drawings. Its central image is a tiny "Lamb of Innocence," but lamps, flowers, and especially leaves are given visual emphasis. As in all of Reed's mature works, the individual elements of the drawing are specifically identified: "a dove of peace," "a trumpet from Moses," "a necklace from the Woman of Samaria," "a fan of Mother Hannah's, to blow away buffetings: the cruelest of foes" (fig. 5-9).

Several relatively large "sacred rolls" are attributed to Sarah Bates (1792–1881), Polly Reed's companion in the First Order of the church at New Lebanon. These drawings, a number of which bear dates of 1845–47, incorporate especially complex symbolic language through a display of image and text. Often a visual representation of "unknown tongues" frames the work and an image of a heart is

Fig. 5-12. Sarah Bates (1792–1881). *From Mother Ann to Amy Reed*, 1848. New Lebanon, New York. Ink and watercolor on paper. The Shaker Museum and Library, Old Chatham and New Lebanon, New York.

at its center. In each, the upper two-thirds of the composition is divided from the bottom third by a horizontal line, evidently a division between the heavenly and earthly spheres. Another, less apparent division is between male and female. Depicted at the top of each sacred sheet are the wings of the Heavenly Father on the right and the wings of Holy Wisdom on the left, representing the two aspects of deity, paternal and maternal, according to Shaker theology. The bottom register, or earthly sphere, often contains specific references from Shaker history. For example, in "A Holy & Sacred Roll" there are trees for each of the first leaders of the church (fig. 5-10). One of the drawings in this series is notable for having no text, but a composition and iconography that are directly appropriated from Masonic aprons or tracing boards—representations of the sun and moon; the all-seeing eye; the two Temple pillars, Boaz and Jachin; the mosaic floor; and other imagery[45] (fig. 5-11).

Sarah Bates's "sacred rolls" are rendered in blue or black ink, with perhaps a touch of red or brown. A closely related drawing by the artist in terms both of composition and theme is "From Mother Ann to Amy Reed" (1848). Drawn on blue paper and composed in a broader palette, this work is a colorful and lively version of the sacred rolls. As in the drawings of Polly Reed, the individual visual elements of Bates's sacred rolls are carefully labeled: A Rose Bush, A Heavenly Flower, Father William's Message-bearing Dove (fig. 5-12).

Several closely related drawings, which Patterson attributes to Semantha Fairbanks (1804–1852) and Mary Wicks (1819–1898) of New Lebanon, are composed entirely of cryptic messages in "unknown tongues." They may have been received by inspiration during a meeting for worship in March 1843. One example, identified on the reverse as "A sacred Sheet, sent from Holy Mother Wisdom, by her Holy Angel of Many Signs," is a gift to Fairbanks. This may place the attribution in question, although Shaker artists and scribes did record gifts intended

Fig. 5-13. Semantha Fairbanks (1804–1852) and Mary Wicks (1819–1898). *A sacred sheet sent from Holy Mother Wisdom, by her Holy Angel of many signs.* 1843. New Lebanon, New York. Blue ink on paper. American Society for Psychical Research, Inc. New York.

Fig. 5-14. Hester Ann Adams (1817–1888). *A Sheet prepared and written according to Mother Ann's directions,* 1845. Canterbury, New Hampshire. Ink and watercolor on paper. The United Society of Shakers, Sabbathday Lake, Maine. Photo: Luc Demers.

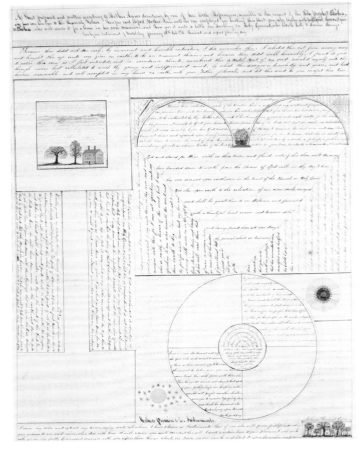

for themselves. "A sacred sheet," which is rendered in blue ink with four red seals, is geometric in format (fig. 5-13).

There is only one known gift drawing by Sister Hester Ann Adams (1817–1888) of Canterbury, New Hampshire. Adams, who was later to serve in the ministry of the Maine bishopric, used a ruler and compass to create a work in which geometric shapes dominate the composition. In addition to a heart, there are circles, squares, and rectangles, with a dense text running throughout the drawing. Adams also included several small watercolor illustrations, including one that depicts a staff from Jesus Christ, intended for Adams, "whereon to lean in tribulation." The drawing was "seen" on January 12, 1845, and "received" and "copied" the following day, "prepared and written according to Mother Ann's directions" (fig. 5-14).

Unlike gift drawings from New Lebanon, which typically include detailed symbolic displays of text and imagery, those from Hancock often (but not invariably) have a single, central emphasis, generally floral or arboreal in nature. Examples of New Lebanon drawings include Polly Reed's "A Present from Mother Lucy to Eliza Ann Taylor" (see fig. 5-8) and Sarah Bates's "Holy & Sacred Roll" (see fig. 5-10). Of the sixteen known drawings of Polly Collins of Hancock, several are dominated by tree imagery, including the "Tree of Comfort" (1859), a gift from Mother Ann to Eldress Eunice. Probably the last of Collins's gift drawings, the "Tree of Comfort" is among her most accomplished. The written text, partially in verse, states that the image is an emblem of Mother Ann's blessing, "directed by her hand." A member of a large natural family of Believers at Hancock, Collins was active as an instrument there (fig. 5-15).

A distinctive feature of some drawings by Collins is the construction of a grid of separate squares or rectangles, each of which contains stylized figures of trees, colorful flowering plants, and occasionally an arbor or other objects. The overall composition of these works and their individual elements suggest the design of album quilts (fig. 5-16). Despite their insularity, the Shakers were not immune from

influences from outside their villages. Not only were memories of the visual culture of the region retained, but new directions in design also found their way into Shaker communities through recent converts, publications, and the reports of Shakers who were charged with doing business with the non-Shaker world. Decorative bed coverings were not made or used in nineteenth-century Shaker villages, and album quilts had not become a popular form by the time Collins entered Hancock in 1820. When she created her drawings, however, album quilts were widely known and their influence cannot be dismissed.

Polly Collins's compositions are not as bold or direct as those of another Hancock Shaker, Sister Hannah Cohoon (1788–1864). Only five paintings by Cohoon survive, including the iconic and widely reproduced "Tree of Life" (1854) and two almost

Fig. 5-15. Polly Collins (1808–1884). *Tree of Comfort, or a gift from Mother Ann . . . To Eldress Eunice*, 1859. Hancock, Massachusetts. Ink and water-color on paper. The United Society of Shakers, Sabbathday Lake, Maine. Photo: Luc Demers.

identical versions of "The Tree of Light or Blazing Tree" (1845). The latter drawings, which depict a tree with burning leaves, call to mind the vision of Father James Whittaker, Ann Lee's disciple and successor (fig. 5-17). He was recalled to have said:

When we were in England, some of us had to go twenty miles to meeting; and we travelled nights on account of persecution. One saturday night, while on our journey, we sat down by the side of the road, to eat some victuals. While sitting there, I saw a vision of America, and I saw a large tree, and every leaf thereof shone with such brightness, as made it appear like a burning torch, representing the Church of Christ, which will yet be established in the land.[46]

Among the most appealing of Hannah Cohoon's drawings is "A Little Basket Full of Beautiful Apples for the Ministry" (1856) (fig. 5-18). The drawing depicts a highly stylized basket of apples, intended as a gift from two long deceased Shakers, Calvin Harlow and Sarah Harrison, through the spirit of Judith Collins. A chain that winds around the basket's handle "represents the combination of their blessing." The text that appears in the drawing's upper register is a simple greeting in verse, typical of spirit messages in gift drawings:

Come, come my beloved
And sympathize with me
Receive the little basket
And the blessing so free.

In the late revival period, as we have seen, visual imagery, rather than text, tends to be the dominant feature in Shaker drawings, although text is almost always present, if only in the form of "unknown tongues." Generally rendered in ink and watercolor, these drawings are colorful expressions of the spirituality of the Era of Mother's Work, but they often exhibit a simplicity, and even a whimsy, that contrasts with the solemn source of their inspiration and the portentous messages they convey. The iconography of the drawings is often drawn directly from the text of inspired gifts, as described in visionary communications. But sources from outside the immediate context of Shaker life may also be discerned. Symbols and motifs adapted from Masonic paintings and murals; design, composition, and thematic materials from ornamental needlework; and ideas bor-

rowed from popular prints (e.g., the widely-known "tree of life" by Nicholas Currier and other print-makers) are among these sources. It is not unlikely that some gift drawings also may bear a relationship to various New England watercolor traditions, such as decorated family registers, Valentine greetings, and rewards of merit, among others. But there is a quality that sets the Shaker drawings apart. Whatever their visual references, they are expressions of visionary manifestations, of the mystical and divine, and they do not yield to facile interpretation or understanding.

Gift drawings were intended to encourage and console their recipients. Although the idea of private property was abhorrent to Shaker ideals, personal articles were, in practice, held individually. It is assumed that most gift drawings were kept by the Shaker brethren and sisters to whom they were addressed. When Hester Ann Adams moved from Canterbury to New Gloucester, for example, she carried her drawing with her. Later, as interest in visionary phenomena waned, the drawings may

Fig. 5-17. Hannah Cohoon (1788–1864). *The Tree of Light or Blazing Tree*, 1845. Hancock, Massachusetts. Ink, pencil and gouache on paper. American Folk Art Museum, New York. Promised gift of Ralph Esmerian P2.1997.1. Photo courtesy Sotheby's, New York.

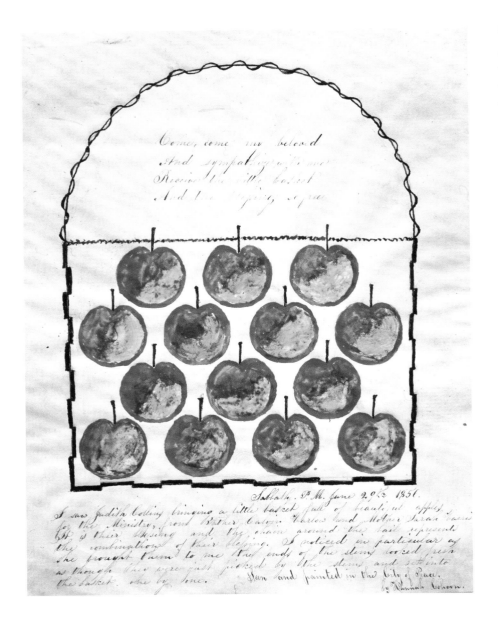

Fig. 5-18. Hannah Cohoon (1788–1864). *A Little Basket Full of Beautiful Apples for the Ministry*, 1846. Hancock, Massachusetts. Ink and water-color on paper. Andrews Collection, Hancock Shaker Village, Pittsfield, Massachusetts.

have been stored away. In the twentieth century, some Shaker leaders, eager to see them preserved, gave or sold gift drawings to libraries, historical societies, and other institutions. In his comprehensive study of Shaker culture, John T. Kirk illustrates a photograph (ca. 1913–17) of Eldress Miriam Offord at Mount Lebanon in which a framed gift drawing appears on the wall behind her.[47]

GIFT SONGS

Although there were relatively few gift drawings, the output of gift songs during the revival period was nothing less than prodigious. Summarizing the events of 1840, a New Lebanon diarist noted that the most remarkable features of the year were "in the line of spiritual manifestations, in visions, in speaking and writing by Inspiration and in a great flowing of new songs mostly sent to individuals." Daniel W. Patterson quotes Isaac N. Youngs's estimate that in the first ten years of the era there had been 300 new anthems, almost 1,000 "little anthem-like songs for use in the intervals between exercise and speaking" and more than 2,500 songs for exercise. The total of 3,850 songs was almost entirely from New Lebanon. Gifted brethren and sisters in other communities received hundreds of songs by inspiration as well. "Mother's Work unlocked floods of new songs," Patterson observes (fig. 5-19). "[N]o other period of Shaker song can compare with it in prodigality."[48]

Gift songs were a feature of Mother's Work throughout the Era of Manifestations and were received in every Shaker village. They might be given by inspiration at any time, day or night. Particularly gifted Shakers would put paper and pen near their beds when retiring so that the inspired verses could be remembered in the morning. Very soon after the revival period began at Enfield, Connecticut, Elder Joshua Bennett of the South Family had a vision in which he saw the brethren in one solid body dancing in complete harmony and singing the most melodic songs. "He then beheld a great company of angels gathering around them until they were completely surrounded. Then the angels began to sing new songs in a quick manner. The brethren and sisters were still, as to singing, for a few moments; then they would sing with them. The angels learnt them a number of songs, which were very beautiful." One of the songs given to Bennett that night was the following quick song:

O what pretty souls! All joind, heart and hand,
Singing on their way.
Angels guard the band. These are virgin souls,
Innocent and pure;
Standing in holiness: Unto the end endure.[49]

Communication with the spirit world was so fluid in the early 1840s that songs not only might be received by inspiration in *this* world, but also could be taught by Believers to spirits in the *other* world. The Shakers, at Enfield, Connecticut, for example, were fond of an anthem entitled "Acceptable Worship," which they wanted to teach the twelve Apostles. On Saturday evening April 11, 1840, by pre-rearrangement through the family's elder, the twelve Apostles—through their instruments—came to the village office and the anthem was presented to them. "Some of them read the anthem, and hummed it a little and spoke much in its recommendation. The virgin Mary said she would take the liberty to carry a copy of it to Jesus Christ; and said that Christ and the Apostles would sing this anthem a great deal; and when they sung it, they would think of the elders at Enfield."[50]

Shaker scribes duly recorded hundreds of gift songs in manuscript songbooks, often using the distinctive "letteral" music notation invented in the society to record melodies. An example of letteral notation may be seen in the hymnbook illustrated here (fig. 5-19). Gift songs were also included in the society's printed hymnals, most notably Elder Henry C. Blinn's *A Sacred Repository of Anthems and Hymns, for Devotional Worship and Praise*, published at Canterbury in 1852, which remarkably utilizes letteral notation in print. Sometimes the circumstances of the song's reception are noted, as with this anthem, which was "learned by inspiration" at New Lebanon in 1839 by Elder Sister Olive Spencer. She recalled that the song was sung "by the Angel of Light, which Mother Ann saw at the masthead," referring to the miracle at sea, when Ann Lee and her disciples journeyed to America.

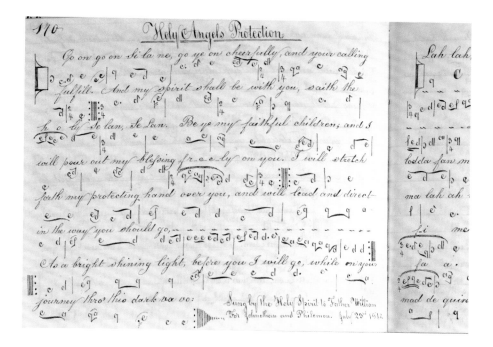

Fig. 5-19. Polly Ann (Jane) Reed (1818–1881), compiler and copyist. *A Collection of Songs, or, Sacred Anthems, mostly given by Inspiration, Beginning November 29th 1840.* Blue ink on paper, bound in leather. American Society for Psychical Research, Inc., New York. This volume is shown open to pages 170–71. Photo: Andy Dubeck.

TRUMPET OF PEACE

Know ye not that I am your guardian angel?
and by the hand of the Lord ye shall be
brought unto a land of freedom;
yea with an outstretched arm and a mighty
hand,
I will bring my chosen people to the land of
lib-er-ty.
Wars and tumults shall cease;
p—e—a—c—e shall be restored,
p—e—a—c—e shall be restored unto that
hap-py land;
and I will sound my trumpet loudly,
many people shall come from afar to receive
this gospel.
O happy day! Happy, happy day!
The angels of heaven shall rejoice and be glad,
for Columbia shall gain the vic-to-ry. [51]

Gift songs could sometimes be received in great numbers by a single Believer in a short span of time. At Watervliet, New York, young Elleyette Gibbs, who participated in the earliest manifestations there, fell into a trance that continued for about three hours. "She sang a number of beautiful songs, 2 of which seemed to be Father William's," referring to Ann Lee's brother and an early church leader. "She also sung some beautiful marches which she completely drummed with her fists on her knees, & at the same time with her feet on the floor as no mortal could do without supernatural power."[52]

Some Shaker songs utilized words in unknown tongues, either in whole or in part. One such song, given by inspiration in New Lebanon in 1839, was believed to have been sung to Mother Ann "when in Poughkeepsie jail in deep tribulation, by the holy angel that attended her."

THE COMFORTING ANGEL

Fear not, fear not, be not faint hearted nor
   dismayed,
for I am still, still with thee.
While surrounded by the shining host,
arm-ed with flaming swords,
how can the en-e-my prevail?
And I will guard thee, for a time and times,
and a half a time, till the time is fulfilled,
yea, the time that is spok-en,
when thou shalt rejoice with exceeding great
   j-o-y.
O si ne ne, O fan na na,
O si ne ne, O fan na na, ho———ly Se-lan;
O si ne ne O fan na na O si nene O fan na na,
h———ly Se-lan.
Re——joice, rejoice, O rejoice, for great shall
   be thy reward
O daughter of Zi-on! rejoice O re-joice, for
great shall be thy
   reward
O daughter of Zion; re-joice O rejoice, for
   great shall be thy reward.[53]

As we have seen, most of the work of inspiration was inner-directed and intended solely for the edification of Believers. However, the Shakers published two major collections of inspired writings during the Era of Manifestation that were directed to the world at large. Early on May 4, 1848, Philemon Stewart received a heavenly command through a vision from an angel: "Arise, O thou little one," the voice said, "and appear before the Lord,

on the Holy Mount; and as thou goest, kneel seven times, and bow low, seven times to the earth; for the Lord hath words for thee to write; and thou shalt kneel, or sit low, by the side of his Holy Fountain, and the words shall be revealed unto thee, in flames of fire." Stewart obeyed the command, and as he approached the fountain stone and seated himself to begin writing, "all became calm; and an inexpressible feeling, as of a consuming fire within, filled my mortal frame, and prepared me to write."[54]

So begins Stewart's work, *A Holy, Sacred and Divine Roll and Book; from the Lord God of Heaven, to the Inhabitants of Earth*, which he began writing in 1842 and which was printed at Canterbury and bound at Harvard in 1843. Before it was published, the book was the subject of intensive review and editing. Accompanied by Giles B. Avery of New Lebanon, Stewart visited several of the eastern societies to read the manuscript to Shaker elders, who considered it in the light of Shaker doctrine. It also received validation through many independent visions received by brethren and sisters in various communities, and these were printed as an appendix to Stewart's book. Upon publication, the volume was sent to heads of state and other world leaders.[55]

A Holy, Sacred and Divine Roll and Book is fundamentally a call to repentance and an exposition of Shaker religious thought. The other major publication of Mother's Work, *The Divine Book of Holy and Eternal Wisdom* by Sister Paulina Bates of Watervliet, New York, was published at Canterbury in 1849, nearer to the end of the Era of Manifestations. The book was edited by Seth Youngs Wells and Calvin Green from a lengthy series of divine communications received by Bates in the early 1840s. It was seen especially as a revelation "through the line of the female" of Holy and Eternal Wisdom, "the Bearing Spirit of all the works of God." During a period of great introspection, the Stewart and Bates works represented an attempt by the United Society to declare the message of Shakerism more universally. It was an attempt, however, that met with little success.

Remarkably, the Era of Mother's Work was a time of great productivity within the United Society. The attempt to reestablish the "primitive order" of the church resulted in a concentration of effort in all areas of the society's life. Shaker craftsmanship and design flourished, for example, because the emphasis on simplicity resulted in a refinement and paring down of furniture forms. The intent of the manifestations was to shore up the faithfulness of the communities and discourage defection from the ranks. In this the era may be judged a partial success. Certainly many of the most deeply respected and intelligent members of the society accepted the manifestations as genuine and were sustained in their faith by them. Others, no less thoughtful, found the phenomena of the period repugnant and left the Shakers in dismay and discouragement.

Several writers have suggested that the Era of Manifestations came to an end by a clearly delineated date, frequently given as 1848 or earlier. Although the intense emphasis on inspiration abated by 1848, however, the revival period continued with varying degrees of robustness in some communities for as many as ten years more. Some of the most impressive gift drawings and paintings, for example, were created in the late 1850s, the result of visionary experiences occurring at that time.

At New Lebanon, the enthusiasm of the early 1840s remained a potent force in the community as late as 1850. On July 16, four hundred Shakers marched four abreast—two brethren on the right and two sisters on the left—to the "Sacred Fountain" on the "Holy Mount," where they sang many songs, "danced with all their might," marched in circles around the fountain stone, heard testimonies, and "shook and shouted powerfully." Some Believers seemed to lose control of themselves and acted "much like the disciples did at the day of Penticost [sic] when they were accused of being drunk with new wine."[56]

By 1860, however, it was clear throughout the Shaker world that inspiration would no longer be a daily feature of life in the Shaker villages. The meeting grounds and fountain stones were abandoned and soon were desecrated by the world's people. On June 18, 1861, the New Lebanon ministry, together with the elders of the First Order of the Church, five other brethren, and one yoke of cattle went up to the Holy Mount to clean up the meeting place. Subsequently, Daniel Boler and Giles B. Avery, the elders of the New Lebanon ministry, buried the stone itself. After hiding this tangible symbol of the Era of Manifestations, Avery mused in his record book:

> Thus in nineteen years is there such a change in feeling in the Society as would not have been believed. Should this monumental relic bearing record of this eventful consecration of a meeting place on the top of the mountain remain there some hundreds or thousands of years and then be exhumed, to be wondered at by a people ignorant of the characters bearing the inscription, how wonderful and awful the thot [sic]. [57]

Fountain stones were buried or otherwise hidden in the other Shaker communities as well. But if the fountain stones were abandoned, the rituals of Mother's Work were not completely forgotten, especially in the more populous, active villages. The official New Gloucester (Sabbathday Lake), Maine, *Church Record*, for example, describes a solemn but beautiful "exercise meeting" on April 13, 1884, in the presence of angels. Eldress Mary Ann Gillespie, in whose hand the entry is written, notes that the "spirits of Our Dearly Loved Ones made themselves manifest." [58]

The *Church Record* contains an account of a gift received at New Gloucester by Anne Hurd on May 3, 1885, a "Ball of Gold Thread." Using symbolic language characteristic of gifts received during the Era of Manifestations, the Shaker sister is quoted as explaining that "each little good deed" will add to its beauty. "You can keep winding and winding . . . and this ball will continue to brighten until it shall look like pure gold. And it—will be the Gold of Truth, this will stand the Gospel fire."[59]

Songs also continued to be "given by inspiration" well after the revival period had come to an end. On March 26, 1910, at New Gloucester, the spirit of Eldress Mary Ann Gillespie taught Sister Ada Cummings a new song, intended for the girls in her Bible class. The following day was Easter Sunday, and the gift song was introduced to the Shaker family by Cummings and her girls in a meeting filled with spirituality and "food for the soul." [60]

Not surprisingly, even after the Era of Manifestations had ended, the Shakers continued to take an interest in mediumistic phenomena, observing the developing spiritualist movement in America from the self-assured position of pioneers and occasionally condescending to participate in it. Some of the leading mediums of the nineteenth century visited Shaker communities, and the Believers took part in séances and spiritualist camp meetings, as well as other demonstrations of spirit possession and mediumistic attainment. As the Shakers became known to Worldly spiritualists, their position as forerunners of the movement was increasingly recognized. In her 1870 study of modern American spiritualism, for example, Emma Hardinge referred to the Shakers as the "John the Baptists" of spiritualism, citing the "manifestations of spiritual presence" among them through visions, dreams, trances, and other phenomena.[61] Helena Petrovna Blavatsky, the founder of modern theosophy, was mirroring the opinion of others when she wrote in 1877 that spiritualistic phenomena in the modern period "first appeared among the ascetic and exalted Shakers whose religious aspirations, peculiar mode of life, moral purity and physical chastity, all led to the production of independent phenomena of a psychological as well as a physical nature."[62] The Shakers were pleased to accept this recognition, but in fact they had little direct influence on the development of American spiritualism or its institutions.

In August 1917, Dr. Walter F. Prince (1863–1934), a well-regarded researcher in the field of paranormal phenomena, visited the Shaker village at New Gloucester. He interviewed the resident Shakers individually and as a group, and he concluded that they were "thoroughly sincere and upright" and "intelligent considerably above the average." He noted that they had "no wish to apologize for the mediumistic experience of earlier days" and that they continued to accept the reality of spirit manifestation through apparition, dreams, and inspiration. Prince also discovered that spiritual gifts—symbolic and premonitory dreams and inspired music, among other phenomena—continued to be a feature of life in the community, even in the twentieth century.[63] This was still true two decades later when Sister Frances A. Carr, then a young Shaker girl attending Sunday worship, witnessed Sister Eliza Jeffers, "a gentle and unassuming Sister from Alfred [Maine]," suddenly leap "from her place in the second row and almost without touching the floor" begin "to whirl around in a small circle." For the gathered Believers, Sister Frances recalls, it was clearly "the manifestation of the Spirit."[64]

Many years after the Era of Manifestations had come to an end, Sister Aurelia G. Mace (1835–1910) of New Gloucester read an angelic message to the assembled members of her Shaker family, reflecting on the records of Mother's Work, by then stored in cupboards and drawers. Speaking for the angels, she said, "search your records, for laid away in your archives are thousands of messages, words of prophecy, of love, and of comfort, which we brought to you before we went abroad to do our work with the nations of the earth. We will come unto you again. In God's good time we will come."[65]

Mother's Work, a strange but creative chapter in the history of religion, has left a remarkable legacy of sacred drama, literature, music, dance, and visual art, very likely unparalleled by any other faith community of the size of the United Society. Known more widely for the elegant restraint of Shaker design, with its chaste but robust simplicity and rational sensitivity to the technological environment, the Shakers deserve to be better recognized for the fervently intense manifestations of spirituality that flourished during the Era of Manifestations and so vividly marked their culture.

1. Clarke Garrett, *Spirit Possession and Popular Religion: From the Camisards to the Shakers* (Baltimore: Johns Hopkins University Press, 1987): 234.

2. "A Daily Journal of passing events; Begun January the 1st 1830—By Rufus Bishop, in the 56th year of his age." [n.p., entry for 24 September 1837. New York Public Library, Shaker Manuscript Collection [NYPL], Reel 1, No. 1. An important souce, hereafter referred to as "Daily Journal" – (I).

3. Ibid.

4. "Daily Journal" – (I), entry for 24 December 1837.

5. "Records Kept by Order of the Church," [New Lebanon, N.Y.] entry for 5 December 1837, 140. NYPL, reel 2, no. 7. According to a note on page 156, this record book was kept by Seth Y. Wells until 9 January 1840. It was then "neglected" until January 1852, when Isaac N. Youngs brought it up to date and continued keeping it. It is an essential source for the Era of Mother's Work. Hereafter referred to as "Records."

6. "Daily Journal" – (I), entry for 1 October 1837.

7. Writing in 1877, David Austin Buckingham recalled that this "Movement of the Spirit" was called "Mother Ann's Work of divine Inspiration." "Copies of Letters and other Matters, On Various Subjects. By D.B.A.," vol 2 [Western Reserve Historical Society (WRHS) IV:B-33, 26]

8. Bernhard Lang, *Sacred Games: A History of Christian Worship* (New Haven: Yale University Press, 1997): 387.

9. "A Book of Visions and Divine Manifestations; The writing of which was commenced in January, 1838: wrote by Russell Haskell. Enfield, Connecticut," p. 22. New York: American Society for Psychical Research [ASPR], Shaker Manuscript Collection. Hereinafter referred to as "Visions."

10. "Visions," p. 21.

11. "Records," entry for 1 January 1840, 176. Reel 2, no. 7.

12. "Records," entry for 25 December 1838, p. 147.

13. "Records," entry for 27 December 1838, p. 147.

14. "Daily Journal" – (I), entry for 9 December 1838.

15. "Visions," p. 100.

16. Ibid.

17. Anna White and Leila S. Taylor, *Shakerism: Its Meaning and Message* (Columbus, Ohio: Press of Fred. J. Heer, 1904): 232.

18. "A Daily Journal of passing events begun May the 19th 1839 at Watervliet By Rufus Bishop in the 65th year of his age." Entry for 27 May 1839, p. 4. [NYPL, Reel 1, no. 2.] Hereinafter referred to as "Daily Journal – (II)."

19. Ibid.

20. "Records," entry for May 1840, p. 178. Reel 2, no. 7.

21. Ibid.

22. "Records," p. 179.

23. "A General Statement of the Holy Laws of Zion," p 93 [ASPR].

24. See Theodore E. Johnson, ed., "Rules and Orders for the Church of Christ's Second Appearing," *Shaker Quarterly* 11 (Winter 1971): 139–65.

25. Henry C. Blinn, *The Manifestation of Spiritualism among the Shakers, 1837–1847* (East Canterbury, N.H.: Shaker Society, 1899): 31.

26. "Records," p. 191.

27. Caroline B. Piercy, *The Valley of God's Pleasure* (New York: Stratford House, 1951): 107.

28. "Records," p. 197.

29. "Records," entry for 23 July 1842.

30. Philemon Stewart, "A Confidential Journal Kept in the Elders Lot, New Lebanon 1st Order, Commenced July 25, 1842, entry for October 7, 1842," p. 13 [WRHS B:136].

31. Theodore E. Johnson, ed., "Prudence Morrell's Account of a Journey to the West in the Year 1847," *Shaker Quarterly* 8 (Summer 1968): 56–57.

32. "Daily Journal" – (II), p. 313.

33. "Introduction to the Christmas Meeting of Dec. 25th 1845 on Chosen Land," *Shaker Quarterly* 7 (Winter 1967): 131.

34. "A Book of Rememberance [*sic*], Volume 2nd. Wilbur J. Phelps commenced writing this Book, Jan. 1876, Enfield, Conn. Copied from Alonzo G. Hollisters's Book," p. 18. [ASPR]

35. "Records," entry for 1 January 1840.

36. David R. Lamson, *Two Years' Experience among the Shakers* (West Boylston, Mass.: Published by the Author, 1848).

37. "Book of Spirit Voices, or Communications from Departed Spirits. Commenced October 10, 1873. Alonzo G. Hollister. Mount Lebanon, N.Y.," p. 75 [ASPR].

38. Virginia M. Weis, "Every Good and Simple Gift," *Shaker Quarterly* 13 (Fall 1973): 94.

39. Edward Deming Andrews and Faith Andrews, *Visions of the Heavenly Sphere: A Study in Shaker Religious Art* (Charlottesville, Va.: University Press of Virginia, 1969): 86–87.

40. Alonzo G. Hollister, "A Book of Vision and Prophesy." 1 March, 1873, p. 187 [ASPR].

41. "Records," p. 192.

42. Letter from Catherine Allen to W. H. Cathcart, 22 December 1917. Shaker Manuscript Collection IV: A-49, Western Reserve Historical Society, Cleveland.

43. Daniel W. Patterson, *Gift Drawing and Gift Song: A Study of Two Forms of Shaker Inspiration* (Sabbathday Lake, Me.: United Society of Shakers, 1983): 9.

44. "Records," entry for 2 June 1844. Quoted in Patterson, *Gift Drawing* (1983), and in Sally M. Promey, *Spiritual Spectacles: Vision and Image in Mid-Nineteenth Century Shakerism* (Bloomington: Indiana University Press, 1993): 18.

45. Illustrated in John T. Kirk, *The Shaker World: Art, Life, Belief* (New York: Harry N. Abrams, 1997): 168.

46. Rufus Bishop and Seth Youngs Wells, eds., *Testimonies of the Life, Character, Revelations and Doctrines of Our Ever Blessed Mother Ann Lee, and the Elders with her; through whom the word of eternal life was opened in this day of Christ's Second Appearing . . .* (Hancock, Mass.: J. Tallcott & J. Deming, Junrs., 1816): 66.

47. Kirk, *The Shaker World* (1997): 164.

48. Daniel W. Patterson, *The Shaker Spiritual* (Princeton: Princeton University Press, 1979): 317.

49. "A Book of Visions and Divine Manifestations; The writing of which was commenced in January, 1838; wrote by Russel Haskell. Enfield, Connecticut," p. 25 [ASPR].

50. Ibid., 106.

51. Henry C. Blinn, comp., *A Sacred Repository of Anthems and Hymns, for Devotional Worship and Praise* (Canterbury, N.H., Shaker Society, 1852): 105–6.

52. "Daily Journal" – (I), entry for 16 July 1850.

53. Blinn, *A Sacred Repository* (1852): 110–11.

54. Philemon Stewart, *A Holy, Sacred and Divine Roll and Book; from the Lord God of Heaven to the Inhabitants of Earth* (Canterbury, N.H.: Shaker Society, 1843): 1.

55. Robert F. W. Meader, "The Vision of Brother Philemon," *Shaker Quarterly* 10 (Spring 1980): 11.

56. "Daily Journal" – (1), entry of 9 December 1838.

57. "A Register of Incidents and Events Being a Continuation From other Records kept by the Ministry. Kept by Giles B. Avery. Commenced October 20, 1859,"entry for 19 June 19 1861 [New Lebanon, N.Y]: 76. NYPL

58. Mary Ann Gillespie, "Church Record," vol. 3, entry for 13 April 1884 (New Gloucester, Maine): 11. Sabbathday Lake, Maine, Shaker Library.

59. Ibid., 118.

60. Ada Cummings, [untitled Diary for 1910], entries for 26 and 27 March 1910. Sabbathday Lake, Me., Shaker Library.

61. Emma Hardinge, *Modern American Spiritualism: A Twenty Years' Record of the Communion between Earth and the World of Spirits* (New York, 1870): 27.

62. H. P. Blavatsky, *Isis Unveiled: A Master-Key to the Mysteries of Ancient and Modern Science and Theology*, vol. 2 (Pasadena: Theosophical University Press, 1976): 18.

63. Walter F. Prince, "The Shakers and Psychical Research: A Notable Example of Cooperation," *Journal of the American Society for Psychical Research* 12 (January 1918): 64–65.

64. Frances A. Carr, *Growing Up Shaker* (New Gloucester, Me.: The United Society of Shakers, 1994): 43–44.

65. Aurelia [G. Mace], *The Aletheia: Spirit of Truth* (Farmington, Maine: Press of Knowlton, McLeary & Co., 1899): 77.

The Fancy World

Plain Shakers, Fancy World

SUMPTER PRIDDY

The timeless quality of Shaker design can best be appreciated when the culture of the Believers is studied within a broader context. Much that we admire today about the Shakers' design aesthetic was the result of their opposition to the materialism that began its ascent in American life during the closing years of the eighteenth century, not long after the Shakers first arrived in the New World from England. By 1810, many well-to-do Americans lived in vibrant surroundings filled to capacity with color and pattern (fig. 6-1), and by the 1820s and 1830s, this approach had filtered into virtually every middle-class household. The new American style and the emotional approach to life that it reflected were referred to at the time with the progressive term "Fancy," and it provided a startling contrast to—indeed, the very antithesis of—Shaker simplicity and rational order.[1]

The word "Fancy" did not mean that furnishings and decorative objects were especially fine but rather that they were imaginative, the products of the imagination. With this word, Americans signaled their adherence to a new world view, one that provided a viable alternative to the restrained classical tastes that had dominated life through most of the eighteenth century (fig. 6-2).[2]

The Shakers' ingenuity has often been regarded as fresh and relevant to the American experience, their progressive vision and pared-down practicality a reflection of American ingenuity and straightforward character. One can also make the case that the proponents of Fancy were no less successful than the Shakers in applying their philosophy to the everyday objects they owned or used. Both of these divergent approaches—the understated order of Shaker aesthetics and the appealing whimsy of Fancy—influenced American design and left an impressive legacy. Together they provide intriguing insights into the contradictions that help to make nineteenth-century American culture so vital.

During the eighteenth century, most European and American philosophers, theologians, scientists, and educators viewed the mind as a polarized entity, much as we in the modern era distinguish between the left and right halves of the brain. On one side stood reason, which processed the hard facts of science, mathematics, and logic and pursued steadfast truth unclouded by emotion. The attributes of reason were embodied in a classical approach to designs in architecture and furnishings that alluded to ancient prototypes, whose proportions derived from measurable geometry. Such objects were seen to calm the passions, quietly engage the mind, and encourage a practical, understated approach to life.

Opposite the conservative stability of reason stood the temptations of the imagination or fancy, which processed life's momentary diversions, the fleeting amusements and indulgences that enliven everyday existence. In the eighteenth century, most conservative thinkers considered Fancy to be potentially corrupting, for it constantly threatened to undermine the stability of everyday existence. "A man may be reasoned into truth, but cheated into passion," as the writer John Dryden (1631–1700) had observed.[3] "We . . . must follow Reason as our guide,"[4] observed the noted English critic and lexi-

Fig. 6-1. Joseph Warren Leavitt. *Interior of John Leavitt's Tavern*, Chichester, *Merrimack County, New Hampshire*, ca. 1825. Watercolor, ink, and pencil on paper in original maple frame. Collection of the American Folk Art Museum, New York. Gift of Ralph Esmerian, 2005.8.5. Photo: © 2000 John Bigelow Taylor, New York.

cographer Samuel Johnson (1709–1784). Isaac Watts (1674–1748), the influential English pastor and hymn writer, warned his followers of the consequences of ingratiating the senses: "Fancy and humor, early and constantly indulged, may expect an old age overrun with follies."[5]

Pastors and physicians alike attributed a wide range of emotional and bodily illnesses to an indulgence in imaginative thinking. They advised pregnant women to keep their imagination in check, not only to prevent a similar fate, but also to avoid irreparably harming their unborn children. Depression, sometimes known as "the Blue Devils," was counted among its lesser reckonings, here illustrated by a print depicting a demented patient whose book, *The Powers of Imagination*, rests nearby. Imaginary fiends dance gleefully about his feet, scheming to wreak havoc on his mind (fig. 6-3).[6] The British painter, printmaker, and pictorial satirist William Hogarth (1697–1764) also illustrated Fancy's final reward in his engraving of London's principal madhouse, Bethlehem—or "Bedlam" as it was more commonly known. In the last of eight prints in his series entitled A Rake's Progress, his subject, the apprentice Tom Rakewell, embraces his

final destiny, as he grovels nude and in a maddened stupor on the asylum floor after a life dissipated in indulgence (fig. 6-4).[7]

Positive new outlooks toward Fancy began to emerge early in the eighteenth century and slowly escalated as the era progressed. At the time, Western culture was undergoing major changes, as the Industrial Revolution provided a host of material luxuries and decorative goods that had previously been available only to the wealthy, yet on the other hand it led to an uprooting of political, social, and economic life. This duality caused many to question whether the ideals of the Enlightenment and the techniques of science could, on their own, provide answers to the complex layering of rewards and demands that society now imposed on the individual. A new fascination with Fancy provided a means to understand this complex transition in emotional terms, and by mid-century Fancy would become one of the cornerstones for a movement later known as Romanticism. Proponents of this new aesthetic, which was grounded in an emotional approach to life, promoted it as an essential complement to restrained classical taste in architecture, literature, and the household arts.

Fancy provided a clear contrast to the reasoned designs of classicism, and it was expressed through ephemeral decorations that pleased the spirit but had few proven merits. The American essayist, poet, and philosopher Ralph Waldo Emerson (1803–1882) asked rhetorically late in the Fancy era: "In sculpture, did ever anyone call the Apollo a Fancy piece?" Certainly not in his time, or before.[8]

THE SHAKERS AND REASON

The eighteenth century is often labeled the Age of Reason, and the Shakers must be counted among the most ardent proponents of that era's fundamental principles. Their insistence on emotional restraint, their consistently orthodox approach to every aspect of life, and their emphasis on social order provided fundamental building blocks that insured the stability and prosperity of their society.

Fig. 6-2. Fancy Dome-top Box or Trunk, 1825–35. New England, probably Connecticut. Painted basswood, white pine, and iron hardware. Courtesy Elbert H. Parsons Jr. Photo: Astorino PhotoGraphics, Inc.

THE BLUE DEVILS!

Even with the rise of Romanticism, which applauded the roles of imagination and emotion, the Shakers advocated the dominance of reason, reserving the spiritual sphere as the principal arena for passion: "Hands to work; Hearts to God."

Within three decades of their arrival in America, the Shakers had clearly articulated their principles of order and efficiency. As the outside world slowly gravitated toward more liberal aesthetics, the Shakers further sharpened their focus and became even more orthodox in their culture and way of life, holding fast to what they believed was the word of God. Their conservative religious view helped them first to survive and then to thrive. It shaped their lives, molded their distinctive material world, and defined an emotional identity that was not simply distinct from the rest of the world but, in their eyes, separate from it.

The Shakers adhered strictly to biblical teaching, forging principles that not only reinforced their religious identity but also insured their prosperity. They looked upon the world and all that filled it as the gifts of God. Talents mastered through tremendous self-discipline were considered to be heaven sent—the gift of music and the gift of writing among them. Yet their most revered gift, expressed in the title of their most familiar hymn, was "The Gift to be Simple." Restraint permeated Shaker lives on every level, flowing from their beliefs into their actions and finally into their material expressions.

In the Shaker canon, superfluous decoration of any kind was unnecessary to the conduct of life, and served as a diversion from God's orderly plan. This belief was not just essential; it was God's Holy Law. Every object they made should be "plain and

Fig. 6-3 Richard Newton (English, 1777–1798). "THE BLUE DEVILS!" London, 1795. Copperplate engraving on paper with original watercolor, 14 ³/₄ x 10 in. Sumpter Priddy III, Inc.

Fig. 6-4 William Hogarth (English, 1697–1764). Plate VIII from *A Rake's Progress* (London, 1735). Copperplate engraving on laid paper. Colonial Williamsburg Foundation, Williamsburg. Virginia. 1967-566,8.

simple, and of . . . good and substantial quality . . . unembellished by any superfluities, which add nothing to its goodness or durability."9 To use emotional resources unwisely was an affront to God, no less contemptible than wasting material ones.

The Shakers gradually strengthened their resolve against excessive ornament and emotion in response to the social, economic, and political forces that seemed to be engulfing American culture. During their first decades in the New World, Shaker furnishings had much in common with the simple goods of the society beyond their gates and reflected the same practicality that was indigenous to most of rural America at that time. Even as late as 1821, when the Shaker elders first recorded the Millennial Laws, they felt little need to codify the details appropriate for their furnishings. Yet when the Fancy aesthetic prevailed across America during the 1820s and 1830s, the Shakers felt compelled to address the issue, to eschew almost everything that was propelled by this popular clamor. In 1845 the elders revised their laws and established clear guidelines that not only governed the appearance of Shaker furnishings, but also suggested the emotional behavior those furnishings were intended to elicit.

> Fancy articles of any kind, or articles which are superfluously finished, trimmed or ornamented are not suitable for Believers . . . marbled tin ware, superfluous paper boxes of any kind, gay silk handkerchiefs . . . [may not be used.]

> The following articles are also deemed improper, viz. Superfluously finished, or flowery painted clocks, Bureaus, and Looking glasses, also superfluously painted or fancy shaped sleighs . . . and many other articles too numerous to mention . . . are also deemed improper."

> Believers may not in any case or circumstances, manufacture for sale, any article or articles . . . which would have a tendency to feed the pride and vanity of men, as such would not be admissible to use among themselves, on account of their superfluity.

Beadings, mouldings, and cornices, which are merely for fancy, may not be used by Believers. Odd and fanciful styles of architecture may not be used among Believers.10

Another aspect of Shaker life demonstrates a parallel evolution toward greater order. During the early years, Shaker brethren and sisters often succumbed to rigorous, spontaneous shaking, whirling, and shouting when overcome by the Spirit—a practice that resulted, naturally, in the name "Shakers." Certainly, their sect was not alone in such expressions of rapture, which were common among evangelicals during the religious revivals that were becoming widespread in the Western world. The shaking was frowned upon by old-school religion for its abandonment of reason and excessive indulgence in "enthusiasm," and the Shakers eventually redirected their energies into more disciplined expressions of devotion. By the early nineteenth century, the last of the spontaneous shaking had given way to orderly group dances set to music, carefully choreographed so that the men remained apart from the women throughout the services and reflecting the careful sense of order by which they defined themselves.11

ORIGINS OF FANCY

The philosophical foundations of Fancy decoration can be traced to seventeenth-century Protestant England, well before the dawn of the Fancy style. At that time, Western culture had been guided for hundreds of years by the belief that humans were born with an inherently evil side, with a willful spirit that needed to be "broken" through stern discipline and then re-educated though the civilizing effect of Christianity. Revolutionary views opposing these medieval beliefs concerning human nature and education began to take root. One aspect of this new system of beliefs was first suggested by English philosopher Thomas Hobbes (1588–1679)12 and was subsequently explained in great detail by John Locke (1632–1704), who borrowed from the ancients a view of the mind as a *tabula rasa*, a clean slate that eagerly awaited impressions from the surrounding world.[13] Now the infant was seen not as a willful creature but as a neutral "bundle of nerves" that was constantly receptive to impressions, capable of learning virtually anything to which it was exposed.

Few individuals played a greater role in exploring Fancy's place in this new understanding of the mind's thirst for knowledge than the English politician Joseph Addison (1672–1719), whose essays on the "Pleasures of the Imagination" appeared in *The Spectator,* the most popular literary magazine among the intellectuals in London's coffee-house culture. Like many leaders in that rational age, Addison sought to advance Britain through education, but in contrast to the emphasis that others placed on reason, Addison suggested that nurturing imagination and emotion was also a viable means to expand one's intellectual horizons, refine taste, and elevate British culture.

Strongly impressed by the concept of the mind as a clean slate, Addison was fascinated by the crucial role that the eye and the emotions played in memory: "We cannot indeed have a single image in the fancy that did not make its first entry through sight," he noted and then observed: "The fancy must be warm to retain the print of those images it hath received from outward objects" (fig 6-6).[14]

Addison was curious about the seemingly insatiable human appetite for new experiences and the powerful impressions they make on the mind. He was particularly interested in the emotional power of these first impressions and their capacity to remain within easy reach of memory and imagination. He realized that each time an image was recalled or an object subsequently seen, it usually elicited the same emotional response as it did at the first encounter.[15] A negative first impression would elicit a negative response, whereas a positive impression would bring up a positive memory, regardless of whether it was recalled from memory or actually encountered again in real life. Essentially, he determined, first impressions play a powerful role in shaping one's response to an experience and thus one's inclinations and tastes.

The more Addison explored these ideas, the

more they seemed to suggest that Britain's strong emphasis on reason—and on carefully maintaining a stiff upper lip—was too narrowly focused for a maturing nation. Reason and restraint, he felt, would best serve British education if augmented by experiences in other realms. Consequently, Addison determined to explore these human inclinations and to discern how these might best be put to good use.

Later in the century, the Scottish educator Dugald Stewart (1753–1828) suggested the word *fancy* to describe the imaginative power that recorded images, connected them to the emotions of the moment, and recalled both with each subsequent memory of the event, thereby shaping one's preferences and, ultimately, one's personality. The phrase "It strikes my fancy" refers to this mental power and became widely used in the eighteenth century.[16]

Explorations of fancy caused a dilemma for conservative thinkers, who abhorred its potential to shape personal taste in ways that were beyond rational control. In 1771 the painter Sir Joshua Reynolds (1723–1792) lamented the public's inability to distinguish between the rational and the irrational influences that shaped their aesthetic choices: "We apply the term taste to that act of the mind by which we like or dislike, whatever be

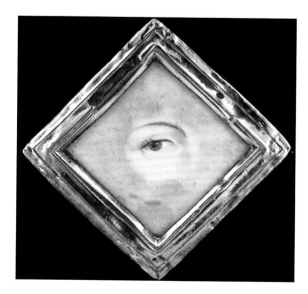

Fig. 6-5: Miniature Snuffbox, 1800–1820. England. Papier mâché, horn with gilt brass, and watercolor on ivory. Elle Shushan. Photo: Sumpter Priddy III, Inc., Gavin Ashworth.

Fig. 6-6: Robert Cukla (b. 1952). Sconce, 1995 reproduction of an original from 1825–35, Maryland. Tinned sheet iron and looking-glass plate. Paul Johnson. Photo: Gavin Ashworth.

Fig. 6-7 Fireworks. Courtesy Colonial Williamsburg Foundation, Williamsburg, Virginia. Photograph Hans Lorenz.

Fig. 6-8 Joggled Plate, 1750–80. England. Slip-decorated earthenware. Colonial Williamsburg Foundation, Williamsburg, Virginia.

the subject. Our judgment upon an airy nothing, a fancy which has no foundation, is called by the same name . . . [as] works which are only to be produced by the greatest efforts of the human understanding."[17]

It was the pragmatic French philosopher Voltaire (1694–1778) who offered a compromise for the dilemma that troubled Reynolds and his peers. In his *Essay on Taste*, Voltaire concurred that the time-honored arts of architecture, painting, and sculpture should be shaped by reason and the highest realms of emotion and defined with the term *taste*. Yet for the inconsequential realm of clothing and everyday objects, he offered another option, one that he found quite logical: "In this low sphere it should be distinguished, methinks, by the name of fancy; for it is fancy rather than taste that produces such an endless variety of new and contradictory modes."[18]

By separating the illustrious public arts from the lesser realm of everyday objects, and by accepting the inevitable and largely inconsequential role that fancy played in shaping individual choices, Voltaire provided British society with the capacity to understand the need for reasoned judgment in the public arena—and to accept the role of fancy and emotion in the personal realm. By separating these distinct arenas and identifying behavior admissible in each, Voltaire provided a logical compromise in answer to a question that had plagued the greatest minds in Britain. He inadvertently set into motion a revolution that would change the Western world.

Now that a major aspect of the debate had been resolved, discussions of everyday goods focused increasingly on their outward appearance and on their capacity to positively impact the mind and the emotions. Three characteristics in particular seemed to define the clothing and personal possessions that appealed to imagination: light, color, and motion (figs. 6-5, 6-7, 6-8). These lively visual stimulants played important roles in Fancy's process, for they caught the eye, awakened the mind, and provided the basis for dynamic mental activity. As Addison observed, "Colors paint themselves on the Fancy."[19]

Fig. 6-9 Attributed to Winthrop Chandler (1747–1790). Overmantel Painting, 1785–90. McClellan House, South Woodstock, Connecticut. Oil on panel. Shelburne Museum, Shelburne, Vermont, 27.1.6-10.

Unlike the indisputable facts that were said to fuel reason or the measurable attributes that helped to propel scientific investigation, the visual stimulants of light, color, and motion were ephemeral and ever-changing: "Light and colours, as apprehended by the imagination, are only ideas of the mind, and not qualities that have existence in matter," Addison wrote.[20] In practical terms, these three qualities varied according to the circumstances of the moment or the mood of the beholder. Therefore, every individual's fleeting experiences, and the personal preferences that derived from them, were distinct from ideas that were fueled by reason. Simply put, attitudes and tastes were personal and could not be disputed.

In addition to these three visual stimulants, Fancy objects inspired a range of psychological experience as well. Three stand out—novelty, variety, and wit—each with a corresponding range of emotional response. Novelty was widely held to elicit surprise; variety prompted delight; and wit induced smiles or laugher. These too are ephemeral experiences, sparked by the creativity of the maker and intended to elicit responses in the imagination of the viewer. As Dryden wrote, "It is the common effect of things unexpected to surprise us into a delight; and that is to be ascribed to the strong appetite, as I may call it, of the fancy."[21]

An overmantel painted about 1790 by the New England artist Winthrop Chandler (1747–1790) for the McClellan House in Woodstock, Connecticut, illustrates the whimsical attributes of Fancy (fig. 6-9), but, more importantly, it shows that one's perception of reality is not always what it appears to be. Chandler created a potentially engaging situation by painting a common New England feature, a bookshelf over a fireplace, in order to startle an unsuspecting visitor walking into the room. When one realizes that the painting is in fact a deception, the image becomes indelibly marked on the mind. The artist's creativity has awakened the mind, elicited delight and laughter, and caused the observer to be mindful of the limitations of individual perceptions. Unlike Shaker objects, which are meant to strengthen the connection between man and God and thereby to purify the soul, Fancy objects were meant to connect the imagination of the artisan to that of the beholder, and thereby to stimulate one's emotional and intellectual development.

Taken together, the ever-changing qualities of light, color, and motion and the fleeting pleasures of novelty, variety, and wit defined the nature of the Fancy experience. Increasingly, as the public came to grasp their importance, Fancy objects were seen as a desirable complement to the power of reason in the development of a well-rounded intellect.

Voltaire's suggestion of a viable realm for expressing fancy had barely filtered into London society when, in 1761, a savvy shopkeeper named Martha Wheatland happened on the clever idea to use the word *fancy* as an adjective in order to promote "all sorts of Haberdashery, and Fancy Millinery goods" for sale at her shop in Cheapside.[22] Her novel approach struck a chord with the public, and other merchants soon followed suit, initially relying on Fancy to promote colorful clothing intended for ladies. By the time the

Shakers landed on American shores in 1774, store-keepers here had already advertised a variety of Fancy goods: "True Italian Fancy caps," "Fancy Stomachers," and "Fancy French collars," to name a few. Sarah Pitt of Williamsburg, Virginia, was among the first to extend the concept beyond clothing when, in 1769, she offered "a very fancy assortment of paper boxes."[23]

After 1770, producers and consumers alike began to push the boundaries of Fancy beyond personal articles of clothing and small household ornaments and into the larger universe of material goods. Among the first were fancy ceramics, which were advertised in 1772 by New York City dealers Davis and Minnit, who offered "all kinds of earthenwares, and some curious fancy wares" (fig. 6-10) for sale in their shop.[24] In 1792 the first of an endless barrage of decorative objects that fell under the general category of "fancy goods" first sur-

Fig. 6-10 Vase, ca. 1820. England. Pearlware with polychrome enamels. Elbert H. Parsons Jr. Photo: Gavin Ashworth.

Fig. 6-11 "William Buttre's Fancy Chair Store." Advertisement in *Albany Advertiser*, Albany, New York. February 16, 1815; reprinted *Albany Register*, May 19, 1815. Albany Institute of History and Art.

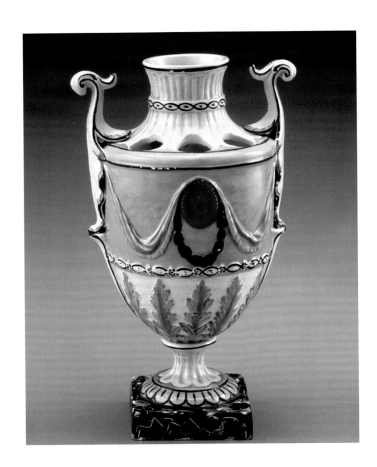

faced in the market when Boston merchant Jonathan Harris advertised in the *Columbian Centennial* that he had just received from Europe "a large and extensive assortment of staple and fancy goods of the latest fashion." Encompassing a variety of merchandise that included enameled boxes, tortoiseshell combs, painted fans, fine stationery, printed handkerchiefs, scented soaps, perfumes, and the like, Fancy had now expanded beyond clothing to an entire class of decorative objects. During the 1790s, the popularity of the Fancy style exploded.

Realizing its potential to attract customers and encourage sales, merchants and artisans everywhere used the word *fancy* in bold print on product labels and in newspaper advertisements, sometimes with woodblock illustrations of their merchandise to catch the eye and elicit the passions (fig. 6-11). Fancy quickly became the most ubiquitous word in all of advertising. Retailers placed Fancy products prominently in their store windows and illustrated their advertisements with small images that hinted at their enticing products.

Furniture makers soon embraced the concept. From the moment in 1797 when émigré artisan William Challen (fl. in America 1797–1820) first advertised "every article in the Fancy Chair line" for sale at his New York shop, there was something to satisfy everyone in every color of the rainbow.[25] There were Fancy side chairs, Fancy armchairs, Fancy benches and footstools, Fancy chairs for the infirm, and miniature Fancy chairs with chamber pots for children, to name but a few. Baltimore

Brothers John (1777–1851) and Hugh Finlay (1781–1831), whose establishment produced Fancy furniture from 1799 to 1837, must be counted among the earliest and most successful in the trade. Initially trained as carriage painters, the brothers attempted during their early years to provide original designs for each of their clients (fig. 6-12). However, they soon found themselves overwhelmed by market demands and eventually succumbed to standardized designs, which they produced by the hundreds to whet the public's appetite for the style. When the British author Frances Trollope (1780–1863) visited Baltimore in the 1820s, it was not surprising that she identified its character as one of "gaudy splendor."[26]

Nowhere was Fancy's impact more evident than in the lives of women. "Fancifulness seems most peculiar to the tastes of women," the cabinetmaker and designer Thomas Sheraton (1751–1806) observed in 1802, and everywhere one went, Fancy seemed to be expressed principally in women's possessions or in objects intended for the home.[27] Dugald Stewart was adamant that "Imagination is . . . the principal source of human improvement," and his ideals were widely applied by American instructors, especially for the instruction of young ladies in "fancy work."[28]

Fancy work encompassed an array of talents from watercolor painting to sampler making and embroidery, and progress in these realms was rapid at the turn of the century. In 1810 the author of an article in Ackermann's *Repository of the Arts*, a British journal with a large American following, was

Fig. 6-12. John and Hugh Finlay (act. 1799–1837). Window Cornice, 1828. Baltimore, Maryland. Painted tulip poplar. Mrs. R. Carmichael Tilghman. Photo: Gavin Ashworth.

particularly astute when he observed the "revolution" that had recently taken place: "Drawing and fancy work of endless variety have been raised on the ruins of the heavy, unhealthy, and stupefying occupation, needlework."[29] Instruction was also given to students in the fine skill of painting furniture, such as that expressed in a dressing table decorated by Elizabeth Lombard of Bath, Maine, in 1816. The table is covered with poetry and romanticized images of bridges and architectural ruins (fig. 6-13).

The importance of Fancy to female education was also manifested in albums and scrapbooks—the latter a new term that first appeared in 1825. These keepsake books, in which women permitted their best friends to create original poetry, artwork, personalized notes, or brief mementos, were carefully preserved for future recollection. An album cover (fig. 6-14) chosen by an anonymous New England schoolgirl shows a classically draped student, with a liberty pole in one hand and a cornucopia in the other, standing beneath the domed temple of American education. She symbolically empties her cornucopia, returning the fruits of imagination for the benefit and remembrance of her friends. Assembling an album, making a needlework picture, or sewing a quilt represented far more than mere schoolgirl exercises. These skills embodied the period's new emphasis on fanciful perception, whose ultimate goal was to carefully assemble the bits and pieces of experience into an accessible storehouse of imaginative ideas and emotions preserved for posterity.

Nowhere did society's embrace of Fancy provide a greater contrast to Shaker culture than in the realm of romantic love. By 1755, when the English lexicographer Samuel Johnson included *love* among his definitions for Fancy, the public had long since acknowledged the indelible power of first impressions in the realm of matchmak-

Fig. 6-13. Attributed to Elizabeth Lombard (b. 1793). Chamber Table, 1816. Inscribed in pencil on the drawer: Elizabeth Paine Lombard Feb 1816. Bath, Maine. Painted maple and white pine. Shelburne Museum, Shelburne, Vermont, 3.6-61.

Fig. 6-14 Kinsley C. Gladding. *Album*, 1826. Providence, Rhode Island. Watercolor and pen and ink on paper. Sumpter Priddy III, Inc.

ing.[30] In the late eighteenth century, an increasing number of families abandoned the old-fashioned concept of arranged marriages and embraced their impulse for romance: "Fancy only can inspire, a youthful heart to frantic fire," the young plantation tutor Philip Fithian of Virginia sent to his charge, Miss Priscilla Carter, in a playful Valentine poem that reflected his enchantment with the new mores. Then he further teased her: "Fancy whispered in my ear, that you would naught but nonsense hear."[31]

In American bedchambers, this new infatuation with Fancy brought on a tremendous shift in the character of bedsteads. After 1790 American consumers demanded larger mattresses and bolsters, taller posts with grander headboards, and elaborate hangings draped from end to end in a whimsical style (fig. 6-15). Some had painted posts capped by cornices with painted and gilded ornaments—symbolic "trophies" of music or love, such

Fig. 6-15 Bedstead with Fancy Hangings, ca. 1827. Boston, Massachusetts. Mahogany. Woodlawn Museum: The Black House, Ellsworth, Maine. Courtesy of The Magazine Antiques.

who had never read philosophy could comprehend the process, by experiencing first hand how an engaging swirl of light, color, and motion attracted the eye, impressed the imagination, and elevated the emotions.

In 1819 Brewster published A *Treatise on the Kaleidoscope*, in which he included a chapter on the "Application of the Kaleidoscope to the fine and useful arts."[33] The craze known as "Caleidoscopemania"[34] soon swept America, and visitors from abroad were surprised to discover that the "philosophical" instrument traditionally made in Europe of expensive brass was here constructed inexpensively of tin and given as playthings to children.[35] Never before had the American people been able to envision so rapid a succession of vivid first impressions.

The kaleidoscope's unprecedented and ever-changing images provided artisans with a new source of decorative detail and thereby established a new source for ornament. It was no longer necessary to look solely to Europe for inspiration, much less to borrow decorative details from the ancients or to copy the wondrous products of nature, such as leaves or shells. Instead, Americans simply pulled out the kaleidoscope and trusted their eyes and minds to interpret an endless trail of fleeting images. "It will create in a single house, what a thousand artists could not create in a year,"[36] boasted Brewster of his invention. Suddenly "huge, sprawling, and radiating devices"[37] appeared on a plethora of objects, from the expansive surfaces of quilts (fig. 6-17) and carpets to those of painted furniture. Yet the impact must be weighed in broader terms for, as we shall see, the unprecedented designs that emerged from the kaleidoscope reinforced the new Fancy aesthetic. Ornamentation inspired by the kaleidoscope could be measured not by objective standards but by the pleasure it brought to the eye and the inspiration it provided to the imagination, and as such, it sanctioned a new and completely personal standard for ornamentation. The kaleidoscope added a new expectation of spontaneity in the design process, resulting in images that were more visually stunning

as Cupid's bow, his quiver filled with arrows, or ornaments of cornucopia and luscious fruit. Eventually even middle-class households would replace old-fashioned bedsteads with posts that stretched toward the ceiling, fitted with cannonball turnings and brilliant paint and boasting a patterned Fancy coverlet or quilt. By contrast, every adult Shaker slept in a single bed with low posts, "painted green.—Comfortables should be of a modest color, not checked, striped, or flowered," as proscribed by their Millennial Laws. The Shakers used their beds solely for sleeping.[32]

BREWSTER'S KALEIDOSCOPE

No development had greater impact upon the Fancy style than the 1816 invention of the kaleidoscope by Scottish scientist David Brewster (1781–1868). Suddenly a capricious twist of the hand could transform colorful glass fragments into an ever-changing trail of pleasure and amusement (fig. 6-16). If philosophical discussions of Fancy had introduced educated Americans to the relationship between the eye and the mind, now even those

and more easily impressed upon the mind. The kaleidoscope inevitably came to epitomize our affirmation of the moment, for it heightened the relationship between emotion and material goods that today still plays such an important role in the American experience.

Few of the advances made in the Fancy era had a greater impact upon the appearance of the American home than the new craze for Fancy painting, defined by one artisan as "spirited and natural imitations of fancy wood."[38] Dazzling new colors,[39] heightened emotional expectations, and dynamic original painting techniques quickly transformed the appearance of the American home. By 1845 the artist Rufus Porter (1792–1884) estimated that in his native New England three of every four doors

Fig. 6-18. Attributed to the Matteson Family. Chest of Drawers, 1820–30. Shaftsbury, Vermont. Pine, brass, and paint. Shelburne Museum, Shelburne, Vermont, 3.4-37.

were imaginatively "grained," as were mantelpieces and wainscoting.[40]

Painted interpretations of exotic wood and rich marble were relatively inexpensive compared to the exotic originals sometimes chosen by wealthy patrons, yet to explain the phenomenon of Fancy painting purely in economic terms distorts the era's priorities, as paint offered a far greater variety and introduced a greater range of color and pattern than the original materials ever could. The principal intention of painter and patron alike was to animate the environment and to inspire the emotions: "Avoid somber hues," architect Alexander Jackson Downing (1815–1852) advised his readers. "The general effect should be lively and cheerful."[41]

In the early years, most examples of Fancy painting had relatively understated surfaces. The Matteson family of South Shaftsbury, Vermont, reflected this approach in a chest they made during the 1820s (fig. 6-18). Subtle suggestions of cross-banded veneers and delicately inlaid stringing suggest expensive materials and encourage a cautious approach. Seen across the room when new, the piece probably looked convincingly like mahogany. Only when one stepped up and tapped the surface could one appreciate the maker's intention or his deceptive skills.[42]

The whirling blend of light, color, and motion introduced by the kaleidoscope soon inspired artisans to paint furniture intended to elicit delight rather than to simply arouse curiosity. Fancy artisans increasingly juxtaposed their striking interpretations of wildly figured woods beside those of exotic marbles. Imitations of native species such as flame birch and curled maple were widely popular and provided superb contrast to imported exotics, such as shimmering satinwood or the ever-changing surfaces of mahogany. The artisan sometimes provided visual relief by using plain colors to offset the figured rarities or by choosing calm surfaces, such as cedar or cherry, as a foil to the busy patterns of exotic woods.

The parlor woodwork (fig. 6-19) of Cedar Level, a farmhouse built in Sussex County, Virginia, about 1835, offers a stunning example of one anonymous Southern artisan's interpretation of Fancy. He accented the moldings in contrasting shades of green and black and varied the marbled baseboards by alternating the veining on the mantel in black and red or gray and blue. For further effect, he highlighted the cupboard doors with a mahoganized surface. He reserved his greatest surprise, however, for the expansive doors and paneling, which was constructed of native yellow pine painted, oddly enough, to imitate yellow pine.

A New Hampshire tall clock constructed about 1830 reflects the advances in technology, as well as in furniture ornamentation, that were made during this Fancy period (fig. 6-20). In the eighteenth century, clocks were expensive because of their complex brass movements, which cost as much as twenty-five dollars each, making them accessible only to prosperous households. In 1806 the innovative Connecticut clockmaker Eli Terry (1772–1852) developed equipment to cut gears from inexpensive wood, and prices suddenly plummeted. By 1814 he reshaped the marketplace again by perfecting wooden gears for small shelf clocks, reducing his customers' cost even further. Consequently, by the late 1810s, almost every American family could afford the expense of a four-dollar parlor clock.[43]

One of the great pleasures of owning a timepiece was its ornamentation. Unlike the walnut and mahogany clocks of earlier days, many nineteenth-century examples were painted with abstract grain-

Fig. 6-19. Parlor Woodwork, ca. 1835. Cedar Level, Sussex County, Virginia. Pine and painted decoration. Bobbitt House Interiors. Photo: Gavin Ashworth.

Fig. 6-20. Tall Case Clock, ca. 1830. New Hampshire case, Connecticut works. Pine and paint. Shelburne Museum, Shelburne, Vermont, 3.10-3a-d.

Fig. 6-21. Chest with Three Drawers, ca. 1785, with marbled surface dating ca. 1835. North Carolina, Painted pine and poplar with brass and iron hardware. Robert and Michelle White.

Fig. 6-22. Kitchen Dresser, ca. 1835. Vermont. Pine and painted decoration. Private collection. Photo: © Christie's Images Limited 1995.

Fig. 6-23. Stillman Taylor (act. 1825–37), Stencil Box and Kit, 1825–35. Winchendon, Massachusetts. Stenciled on lid in gold powder: S.T. 1825–1840. Painted wood and mixed media. Shelburne Museum, Shelburne, Vermont, 2004-10.

ing, stenciled or gold leaf details, and brass or gilded finials. These decorative pieces embodied the "superfluously finished or flowery painted clocks" that so appalled Shaker sensibilities and that their elders specifically banned from dwelling houses in the 1845 Millennial Laws. The English novelist Charles Dickens (1812–1870) observed the trend when he visited a Shaker settlement in the 1840s: "We walked into a grim room, where several grim hats were hanging on grim pegs, and the time was grimly told by a grim clock."[44] To Dickens's heightened romantic sensibilities, *plain* sometimes meant uninspired or, worse yet, emotionally deadening, rather than straightforward and honest, as it did for the Shakers.

A dower chest made in North Carolina offers a

fine example of the Fancy style (fig. 6-21). Dated to the eighteenth century, the chest's original Prussian blue paint must have seemed dull by later standards, for in about 1830 the owner updated the surface with a dynamic combination of striated blue and white marble and green and white moldings, now visible on the exterior.

If some artisans preferred kaleidoscopic combinations of contrasting woods and unconventional colors, others took a different view of Fancy: "Avoid the fault of producing a caricature," warned one painter's manual, which instructed the practitioner to carefully emulate wood.[45] Such advice, however, had little impact on workers whose imaginative flare refused to be dampened and who pushed the limits of creativity to satisfy the public's rising passions for fancy. A kitchen dresser made about 1835 (fig. 6-22) is one of the most inventive examples of the craft. It embodies the ideals of Waldo Tucker (fl. 1830s), a seemingly irrepressible craftsman who in 1837 compiled a handbook entitled *The Mechanic's Assistant*. Tucker creatively advised his readers to use whiskey as a medium to mix their pigments and then urged them to "grain according to fancy."[46]

Painting such as this reflects the rising commitment of American artisans to aesthetic beliefs explained in Britain a generation before. The Scottish philosopher Thomas Reid (1710–1796), contemplating the capacities of Fancy, noted insightfully: "[Fancy] may enlarge or diminish, multiply or divide, compound and fashion."[47] The most innovative American painters clearly shared his perspective. Whether decorating a piece of furniture or ornamenting room after room of interior walls, they created a world that mimicked a giant kaleidoscope.

TAYLOR'S TOOLBOX

A Fancy box provides insight into the life of a "Fancy and Ornamental painter" named Stillman Taylor (active 1825–40) and suggests the work performed by other itinerant craftsmen of his profession (fig. 6-23). Taylor worked between Hampshire County, Massachusetts, and Cheshire County, New Hampshire, during the Fancy craze of the 1830s,

and he probably carried this box and its contents from town to town as he searched for work. He painted it a brilliant chrome green, a color that was first produced commercially in 1797 and had become affordable to the middle class. This green and the commercial chrome yellow—the most electrifying shade in the spectrum—revolutionized the painter's pallet, and with it the appearance of American interiors and furniture.

Interestingly, the Shakers adopted both colors, brushing them on as solid coats or employing them as stain on furniture or woodwork in their dwelling-house interiors. Here the similarities between Taylor's and the Shaker aesthetics end, however, for he ornamented his box in ways that would have seemed dishonest to the Believers. On the surface he displayed his talents by creating a lively interpretation of mahogany in a swirling blend of pigments, to which he added a coat of varnish and the initials "S T" to avoid any confusion as to his personal ownership of the box and its contents. The practice of identifying material possessions or the work of an individual's hands was a practice that was specifically discouraged by the Shakers in the 1845 Millennial Laws.

Taylor's box contains a dozen brushes in various sizes and textures, carefully wrapped in paper to protect the bristles and keep them straight.[48] He stored colorful powdered pigments and glittering metallic and gold powders in neatly folded papers to minimize any chance of loss. He employed velvet burnishers to polish and brighten the finished gilt surface and a sharp knife to cut the stencils. Also included was a flattened pewter plate covered with

Fig. 6-24. Stillman Taylor (act. 1825–37). Stencil 7, 1825–40. Winchendon, Massachusetts. Shelburne Museum, Shelburne, Vermont, 2004-10.

Fig. 6-25. Stillman Taylor (act. 1825–37). Stencil 6, 1825–40. Winchendon, Massachusetts. Shelburne Museum, Shelburne, Vermont, 2004-10.

Fig. 6-26. Militia Drum, 1775–1820. North Carolina. Wood and painted decoration. Guilford County Courthouse National Military Park, North Carolina. Photo: Gavin Ashworth.

Fig. 6-27. Fire Bucket, 1846. Salem, Massachusetts. Leather, paint, and iron with a rubber lining. Private collection. Photo: Sumpter Priddy III, Inc.

small cuts, which must have served as his cutting board.

The box also contains nearly one hundred of Taylor's stencils, which are cutout paper patterns (fig. 6-24) used for decorating furniture and walls. Although the process of creating pictures with stencils was perhaps more mechanical than creative, the practice was nonetheless referred to as "painting." Artisans usually applied each element in the design using a separate piece of paper. However, complex patterns, such as cornucopias filled with fruit, required that the artist compose the picture one layer at a time, by applying paint or metallic powder through the appropriate stencil and then removing it. The meticulous process was then repeated for each element—cornucopia,

grape cluster, leaves, apples, and so on—until the picture was complete.[49]

The resourceful Taylor cut most of his stencils from salvaged paper, including old letters and pages torn from ledgers and cipher books. Several surviving examples reveal his address during the mid-1830s as the village of Winchendon, in Worcester County, Massachusetts.[50] A militia document printed with an American eagle invites "S. Taylor" to his unit's "Independent Ball," held at James Garland's assembly room on July 3, 1835. After the ball, Taylor cut the eagle from the invitation so he could use it as a stencil pattern (fig. 6-25). He made other stencils from a letter dated June 19, 1833, in which he called his comrades to escort President Andrew Jackson through

Fig. 6-28. Table, 1820–30. Maine. Pine, maple, and paint. Shelburne Museum, Shelburne, Vermont, 3.6-92.

Worcester and signed it as "clerk" for the unit. Taylor noted that Captain Charles William Bigelow commanded the soldiers to "stand in readiness with arms equipment and uniform according to law."

Like many ornamental painters, Taylor likely played a role in decorating the militia equipment referred to in his letter—including perhaps the unit's flags or "colors," as they were known; a drum (fig. 6-26); or the colorful canteens, knapsacks, and other accoutrements that completed the company's uniforms. To be sure, Fancy ornamentation was a vital part of military ceremony during this period, thanks to the unprecedented emphasis on parades and ostentatious drills. At about this time, the nearby Shrewsbury Rifle Company formed a committee to select the uniforms and have these "trimmed according to their fancy."[51]

Some of the stencils bear initials or names instead of ornamental motifs, including one for "E. D. Weston" that contains the address "Weston Vt.," suggesting that Taylor, like many in his profession, traveled in search of work. The third line of Weston's stencil is incised "No. 2"—a feature commonly found on Fancy fire buckets (fig. 6-27).[52] Other tools inside Taylor's box reveal that the artisan mixed his pigments on a salvaged fragment of a feather-edged plate, since it still contains a range of pigment residue. He relied on a wooden-handled palette knife to blend the powders with oil and had a spare handle with three extra blades in reserve. A bone toothbrush—its bristles now missing—may have served to combine the pigments or to apply them over a painted surface to create a spatter design. The kit also contains two pieces of pumice stone, probably used to polish the top coat of varnish to achieve a luminous finish.

Taylor's kit is also equipped with six homemade leather combs of various sizes, and two flexible sheet-iron combs—one large and one small— which he used to emulate wood grain. Although the exterior surface of the box demonstrates that the artisan was adept at freehand interpretations of wood, the combs provided an alternate, particularly efficient method, for creating a similar effect. After applying a solid base color and allowing it to dry, he would add a second coat of a contrasting pigment that could be combed through while wet to reveal the color below. An ingenious artisan might use free-hand graining together with combing for maximum effect.

Combing was very popular after 1820, when, in addition to formal mahogany furniture, rosewood furniture gained commercial success. Fancy painters interpreted this exotic surface using a brilliant red background with deep black striations and flashy strips of yellow ocher or chrome yellow. Painters in northern New England were particularly fond of such combinations, especially in Maine, where a wide range of furniture was ornamented using this lively scheme (fig. 6-28).

WALL DECORATION

The size of Stillman Taylor's stencils suggest that he decorated relatively small furnishings, but other painters used larger ones to produce Fancy work for interior walls—often in emulation of the wood-block wallpapers that proliferated in America after the Revolutionary War. The plaster walls of the 1804 Stencil House in New York State (fig. 6-29)

Fig. 6-29. Interior of Stencil House, 1804. Stenciling, 1830. Sherburne, New York. Shelburne Museum, Shelburne, Vermont, 4.19.

Fig. 6-30. Box, 1815–25. American. Pine, iron, and leather. Shelburne Museum, Shelburne, Vermont, 3.4-39.

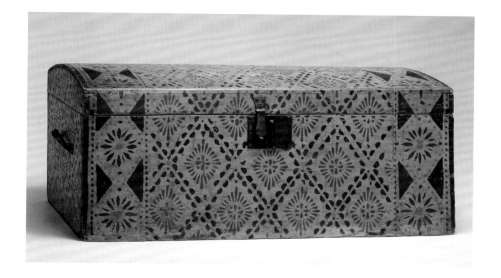

and the surface of an anonymous New England trunk (fig. 6-30) demonstrate the popularity of geometric designs during this period. To add further interest, some painters changed the decorative scheme from room to room, varied the colors, or alternated the border designs. Sometimes the artisan would stencil designs directly onto a painted floor or created a complementary floor cloth on canvas (fig. 6-31). Options for decorating with

stencils were almost limitless: "The practitioner will find in this . . . field . . . an infinite variety of beautiful fancy work," wrote the painter Rufus Porter (1792–1884) who published several booklets of instructions for ornamental brushwork.[53]

Painters who did stenciling often produced wall murals as well. About 1835 the ornamental artist Jonathan Poor (1807–1845) decorated a landscape mural over the mantel in Captain Dudley Haines'

Fig. 6-31. Floor Cloth Fragment, 1835–45. New England. Linen or jute with oil paint and varnish. Sumpter Priddy III, Inc.

Fig. 6-32. Jonathan Poor (d. 1845). Overmantel, ca. 1835. Readfield, Maine. Watercolor pigment on dry plaster. Shelburne Museum, Shelburne, Vermont, gift of the Saunders Manufacturing Co. Inc., 36.3-2.

parlor in Readfield, Maine (fig. 6-32). Poor often traveled with Porter, who was his brother-in-law, and following Porter's methods, Poor created the principal town buildings by painting through a set of stencils, although he relied on freehand brushwork for the trunks of the whimsical trees and finished the composition by sponging on feathery leaves. Flanking the chimney breast are two painted pots sprouting vines that meander up the walls. Scenery painted on plaster was more affordable than the imported French landscape papers then fashionable in urban households and was also more durable, for it was resistant to staining from moisture, smoke, and insects.

FANCY GOODS

After 1815 the heightened demand for whimsical ornamentation played a significant role in the marketplace, and retailers increasingly placed their Fancy products prominently in front windows and on accessible shelves. By 1820 the most astute businessmen had realized the advantage of specialized Fancy establishments, and Fancy stores (fig. 6-33) sprang up in urban centers across America. Some of these offered a broad range of merchandise for sale, whereas others focused on specialized lines—Fancy Hardware, Fancy Glass and China, Fancy Haberdashery, Fancy Chairs, and Fancy Groceries, to name but a few. In 1829 Ann Royall, a British visitor to America, was charmed when she stepped into a Baltimore Fancy Store that handled a wide range of merchandise: "I was not only gratified but astonished at the richness and brilliancy of the wares," she exclaimed soon after the experience.[54]

Producers on both sides of the Atlantic soon flooded the American market with inexpensive and highly ornamented goods, causing a revolution that reshaped the identity of American homes and bolstered Americans' sense of accomplishment by providing goods that only the wealthy could previously afford. With victory over England in the War of 1812 and inexpensive land out west beckoning to a burgeoning population, Americans everywhere felt a certain optimism that

simultaneously reflected, and reinforced, the new Fancy style.

British ceramic producers were rather astute concerning Fancy's potential and quickly set about producing goods geared to American tastes. Many of their products were ornamented with informal motifs that were also popular on furniture—leaves, birds, flowers, or grapevines (fig. 6-34). Some objects were highlighted with gilded or metallic

—ISAAC D'YOUNG'S FANCY STORE.—

Fig. 6-33. Isaac D'Young's Fancy Store. From Thomas Porter and James Mease, *Picture of Philadelphia* (Philadelphia, 1831). The Winterthur Library: Printed Book and Periodical Collection, Winterthur, Delaware.

accents that resembled the bronze ornamentation on furniture. The surfaces of other pieces were enhanced with finishes that gave the illusion of marble or agate.

Especially popular were the highly decorative examples that were widely known as Mochawares

(fig. 6-35). The name derived from a treelike ornament resembling agate, a semiprecious stone exported from the Yemini port of Mocha [al-Muhka] to London, where it was used in fashionable jewelry. Mocha stone lent its branched designs and its name to these popular new ceramic forms, which soon came to encompass a wider variety of ornament, including "wormed" motifs, images that resembled fans or feathers, and others that were similar to cats' eyes or children's marbles. Many of the Mocha patterns relate to those found on abstract painted furniture, perhaps because of the similarities between working wet paint over wood and applying liquid clay over the surface of a ceramic vessel (fig. 6-37). Not surprisingly, producers chose to use these whimsical Mocha patterns for informal ceramic objects, such as casual tea and dessert sets, punch bowls of various sizes, beer and cider mugs, and casters for sprinkling sugar or cinnamon on cookies, cakes, and syllabubs. Large dinner plates with Mocha motifs are virtually unknown,

as they were presumably not suitable for more formal occasions.

Among the most visually impressive of the Fancy ceramics was a group produced by Josiah Spode of Staffordshire, England. These objects were characterized by mottled grounds in shades of green, white, yellow, and black and were generally reserved for dessert plates. One of the most ambitious pieces currently identified is a remarkable compote that would have been used to best advantage when piled high with savory fruit or sweets and placed in the center of a dessert table (fig. 6-36).

The goods offered by Fancy stores or sold by specialty establishments also included colorful and

Fig. 6-36. Josiah Spode (1755–1827). Compote, 1805–20. Staffordshire, England. Pearlware with polychrome decoration. Shelburne Museum, Shelburne, Vermont, 2004-21. Photo: Sumpter Priddy III, Inc.

Fig. 6-37. Fancy Painted Chest, ca. 1825. Rhode Island. Painted white pine. Sumpter Priddy III, Inc. Photo: Astorino PhotoGraphics, Inc.

beautifully ornamented textiles for personal clothing and household use. The categories of Fancy carpets and Fancy coverlets offered exotic damask patterns at affordable prices, and these made it possible for middle-class consumers to cover their floors from wall to wall or to decorate their beds as never before. The new ornamentation was made possible when the French weaver Joseph Jacquard

(1752–1834) invented a simple computer-like device that could easily be attached to a loom. By feeding a series of punched cards into the mechanism, the operator automatically controlled the meticulous process of raising and lowering the warp threads in the necessary order to produce complex patterns. Suddenly weavers everywhere were incorporating the word *fancy* directly into their designs. "FANCY

WEAVER," "FANCY WEAVER AND DYER," "FANCY COVERLET," "LADY'S FANCY," "FARMER FANCY," "FANCY PATENT," and just plain "FANCY" (fig. 6-38) appeared in the signature blocks woven into the corners of these exciting new products. Wall-to-wall carpeting and multicolored patterned bed coverlets became affordable, and in 1841 the weaver Josiah Cass of Lodi, New York, boasted of the diverse goods he now offered his customers: "Having purchased looms for fancy and Ingrain carpeting, would inform his old customers, and the public generally, that he is now prepared to weave . . . Carpets and Coverlets of ever Description and Figure . . . many of which cannot fail to suit the taste of the most fanciful. . . . He has also made arrangements for Coloring Yarn for fancy Carpets."[55]

Few objects offered the public greater variety than Fancy chairs, which were now available in an ever-wider array of forms and colors. A whimsical Windsor armchair made for Union Lodge #2, the Free and Accepted Masons of Madison, Indiana, has an exaggerated shaped back and understated arms, which reflect the inherent tension and unconventional creativity so often found in works of Fancy (fig. 6-39). This chair may have been produced by James Huey (1805–1851), a Pennsylvania-born chair maker who worked near Pittsburgh before moving in 1828 to Zanesville, Ohio, where he established one of the most successful chair manufactories in the Midwest. With his shop well situated near the banks of the Muskingum River, Huey marketed his lively products up and down the Ohio River and its tributaries, where he advertised among his many products "Fancy Windsors and common Chairs, with a variety of Settees." The 1850 Census of Manufacturers for Ohio records that Huey employed twenty workmen, who turned out $8,000 worth of chairs annually—reflecting a degree of success rarely attained by any such establishment in the period.[56]

No form better reflected the new customs of the Fancy period than the rocking chair. Relatively scarce in the eighteenth century, these chairs were generally used by mothers with infants in the privacy of the bedroom. In the parlor, on the other

Fig. 6-39. Masonic Officer's Chair, ca. 1840. Ohio, possibly Zanesville. Poplar and maple with the original gilt and painted decoration. Elbert H. Parsons Jr. Photo: Gavin Ashworth.

Fig. 6-40. Child's Rocking Windsor Chair, ca. 1825. Virginia, possibly Abingdon. Yellow pine, poplar, maple, hickory, and painted decoration. Roddy and Sally Moore.

Fig. 6-41. Comb-back Rocking Chair, 1820–30. Probably New Hampshire. Maple ash, pine, and paint. Shelburne Museum, Shelburne, Vermont, 3.3-285.

hand, all other members of the household—adults and children alike—sat squarely in their seats, with their backs ramrod straight and their feet planted firmly on the floor.

In the nineteenth century, thanks to Fancy's more casual approach to life, Americans instinctively gravitated to rocking chairs, and manufacturers across the country produced them in astounding numbers—particularly those with painted decoration (figs. 6-40, 6-41). Conservative Europeans who visited the New World were aghast at the informality of American life, and the widespread use of rocking chairs only reaffirmed their disapproval. The British traveler Harriet Martineau, who recorded her observations of American manners, was nothing less than appalled at the "disagreeable practice," that was evident in the public

sphere: "In the inn parlors are three or four rocking chairs in which sit ladies who are vibrating in different directions and at various velocities. . . . How this lazy and ungraceful indulgence ever became general, I cannot image, but the nation seems wedded to it."[57] By contrast, the Shakers specified in their Millennial Laws that one rocking chair was sufficient in a retiring room, except where the aged reside.

FANCY FRENZY

Creative expressions in other media also flooded the marketplace, as publishers who had previously provided textbooks and biblical discourses competed with new offerings of inexpensive Fancy literature intended to entertain more than to instruct.

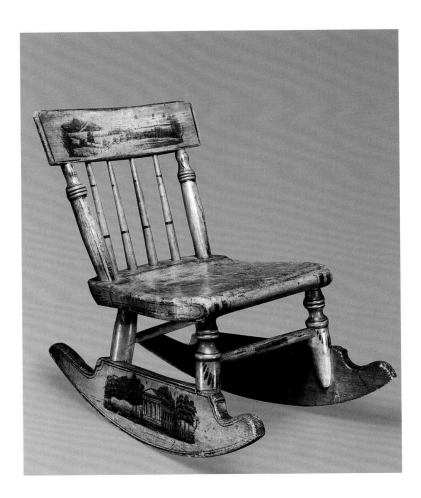

Amusing short stories, romance novels, titillating travelogues through exotic lands, and periodicals—some with lurid stories thinly veiled as tales of redemption—attained tremendous circulation.[58] In a parallel movement, composers and performers expanded their repertoire to include wide offerings of popular sheet music that publishers sold for pennies apiece out of the huge warehouses that now appeared in every major American city.

The Fancy aesthetic reached a feverish pitch in the economic boom of the mid-1830s, and eventually nothing seemed immune from its influence. No object was too small for ornamentation or too insignificant to merchandise. Within the course of the century, Fancy had moved from the province of philosophers to the parlors and schools of the wealthy, and finally into every aspect of the American experience.

Alexis de Tocqueville (1805–1859), the perceptive French historian who critiqued American culture in the 1820s, was impressed with the ingenuity of American manufacturers, yet he condemned the herculean efforts made here to give objects "attractive qualities which they do not in reality possess." De Tocqueville felt that the surfeit of ornamented materials inspired a certain frenetic character in the American consumer: "Besides the good things he possesses, he every instant fancies a thousand others," he complained.[59]

The economic boom fueled by the exuberance of Fancy came to an abrupt halt with the Panic of 1837, which precipitated the worst depression of the nineteenth century. Retailers found their stores overstocked and bankers faced overdrawn reserves. American consumers who had filled their houses with luxuries now looked into their wallets and purses to find them empty. When business in the Fancy realm shrank precipitously, the ornamental painter Stillman Taylor simply put away his toolbox for future historians to rediscover. He cut his last stencil from a letter dated 1836.

In 1839 the French scientist Louis Daguerre (1787–1851) invented a process that made it possible to record images of reality on shiny, silvered plates of copper. These new photographic portraits were small and reflective and required the viewer to focus intently in order to process the subtle details—a different skill from those needed to enjoy the fleeting images of the kaleidoscope. If the kaleidoscope helped to bring Fancy into the American consciousness, the camera effectively refocused the nation's attention on reality. The national mood was also shifting for other reasons, as regional tensions heightened over the unresolved issues of slavery and as America's artisans found themselves competing with a dehumanizing factory system. Emotions now turned inward as Americans grappled with seemingly irreconcilable conflicts.

Soon British reformers and the Transcendentalists of New England, inspired in part by Shaker aesthetics and morals, led a vocal onslaught against the very concepts of Fancy. Many felt that the mind should be deliberately directed toward higher realms that exalted the soul and not abandoned to Fancy for random nourishment or, worse yet, mere titillation. "The fancy sees the outside. . . . The imagination sees the heart and inner nature, and makes them felt,"[60] wrote the British architect and theorist John Ruskin (1818–1900). Ralph Waldo Emerson later offered a similar assessment: "Fancy amuses; Imagination expands and exalts us."[61]

Inspired by new standards, designers and artisans alike reconsidered their approach to decoration. "Bad decorators err as easily on the side of imitating nature, as of forgetting her" Ruskin noted and further clarified his remarks: "It is melancholy to think of the time and expense lost in marbling, and of the waste of our resources in absolute vanities, in things about which no mortal cares."[62] An American artisan named Walter Smith paraphrased Ruskin's observations when instructing his followers in the art of house painting: "The works of God are not built up. They are good throughout, from skin to the marrow; not surface and sham, but solid."[63] This same philosophy formed an essential part of the Shakers' belief system and was expressed in both the goods they made for their own use and the products they sold to the World's people.

Fig. 6-42. Trade Sign, 1840–60. Massachusetts. Pine and painted decoration. Hancock Shaker Village, Pittsfield, Massachusetts.

This new morality sought a different arena for expression, as the American preference for brilliant paints and wildly figured surfaces soon gave way to understated colors or simply varnished woodwork and to darkened rooms that inspired a reverential mood. In interior furnishings, a Bible was placed prominently on a table in the center of the parlor, where it set a tone and served as a focal point for family gatherings. Romantic landscapes were joined on walls by paintings or engravings that depicted parents tenderly holding children or children lovingly holding their pets. Schoolgirls contributed to the new environment by stitching sentimental sayings or biblical quotes on needlework panels, such as "Home Sweet Home" or "Honor thy Father and thy Mother."

The heartfelt emotions of this new Victorian imagination, and the subjects that appealed to it, differed markedly from the splashy displays and the outward jubilation that had characterized the whimsical imagination of the Fancy era. The new emphasis on noble pursuits that elevated one's

soul soon led to a rising interest in the Crusades and medieval literature, best fueled by the quiet realm of reading. A revived interest in the exploration of exotic lands, inspired a new generation of literary and architectural styles that were moralistic in tone—whether expressed in the new penchant for Gothic architecture or in novels such as Sir Walter Scott's *Tales of Ivanhoe*. The Victorian experience also led Americans in search of stylistic inspiration, not just to distant times and lands, but increasingly to realms that existed only in the imagination. Jules Verne's *Journey to the Center of the Earth* (1864) and Lewis Carroll's *Alice in Wonderland* (1865) helped contribute to a world of fantasy. Every mood, manner, and outlook found reinforcement in the complex world that defined the Victorian experience.

Although the Shakers identified with Henry David Thoreau's mantra to "simplify, simplify" and shared many of the values espoused by America's overtly religious reformers, there is nothing to suggest that they embraced larger society's increasingly layered emotions or material possessions. Their bright and sparsely furnished interiors seemed old fashioned compared to the cluttered rooms and veiled windows of America's Gothic architecture and its romantic, ivy-draped cottages. If the Shakers' practical approach to life and their functional design had helped to set a standard that would be assimilated by some of the most advanced thinkers in American industry and would eventually, in the twentieth century, find numerous admirers, their domestic lives at the time were increasingly out of step with the emotionality of mainstream America.

Shaker membership had peaked by 1850, and when the Civil War ended a decade later, the sect found its male population starting to dwindle. Always dependent upon converts, the Shakers eventually found themselves unable to sustain their extensive farming operations and their workshops. As the end of the century approached, Shaker women increasingly turned to handiwork to generate income to sustain the shrinking villages.

Never ones to let sound business opportunities pass them by, the Shakers found themselves accommodating the world as never before. This sign—"FANCY GOODS*FIR PILLOWS-and- MAPLE SUGAR FOR SALE HERE"—discreetly advertised Shaker goods for sale at a store in Massachusetts (fig. 6-42). Shaker baskets, satin-lined boxes with pretty bows, exotic "fancy Shaker seeds" for special farm produce, and a plethora of rocking chairs with colorful tape seats in every size and scale found an enthusiastic following in the world. These products did not reflect a major transition in Shaker philosophy but rather a shift in marketing tactics, a tacit acknowledgment of the Worldly appeal of material things, and the inevitable acceptance of the sect's shrinking financial security.

If the Shaker and Fancy approaches to design represent polar opposites in aesthetics and emotion, these disparate strands of American experience also have much in common. The two cultures coexisted at the dawn of the industrial era, and artisans in both found themselves pitted against competition from factories. Both eventually succumbed to forces beyond their control—the Shaker population decreasing as its members drifted back to mainstream culture or died, the Fancy aesthetic maligned as Victorian Americans gravitated toward quiet emotions and heartfelt sentimentality. The clarity and the intensity with which each culture articulated its creed—whether expressed in the restrained eloquence of the Shakers or the ephemeral nature of Fancy—can be counted among the nineteenth century's greatest legacies to the present. Indeed, their combined yet dissonant chorus seems more relevant today than ever, particularly so as post-modern Americans weigh the appropriate roles of spirituality and materialism in their lives.

The author is grateful to the following individuals for their assistance with this essay: Jean Burks, Laura Libert, Kory Rogers, and Ann Stewart.

1.   Interest in the concept of Fancy was reawakened by an exhibition and publication jointly sponsored by the Chipstone Foundation and the Milwaukee Art Museum between April 2004 and March 2005. For further insight, see Sumpter Priddy III, *American Fancy: Exuberance in the Arts 1790–1840* (Milwaukee: Chipstone Foundation in conjunction with the Milwaukee Art Museum, 2004).

2.   Samuel Johnson, *A Dictionary of the English Language,* 2nd ed. (London: W. Strahan, 1773), s.v. "fancy." The word does not enter the dictionary as an adjective defined as "ornamented" until Joseph E. Worcester, *A Dictionary of the English Language* (Cambridge, Mass.: H. O. Houghton, 1860), s.v. "fancy."

3.   John Dryden, "Preface, "*Religio Laici* (1682), in *The Oxford Authors*: *John Dryden*, ed. Keith Walker (Oxford and New York: Oxford University Press, 1987): 227.

4.   Samuel Johnson to James Boswell, undated (probably 19 March 1774) in *Letters of Samuel Johnson,* ed. Bruce Redford, vol. 2 (Princeton: Princeton University Press, 1994): 132–34.

5.   Isaac Watts, *The Improvement of the Mind, to which is added a Discourse on the Education of Children and Youth* (1741; 1847; repr. Kila, Mont.: Kessinger Publishing Co., 2004): 13.

6.   "The Blue Devils" also referred to despondency, depression, melancholy, and the apparitions seen during delirium tremens. The title of a popular London play, the phrase was in common use by the late 18th century. In 1787 the poet Robert Burns noted his "bitter hours of blue devilism."

7.   William Hogarth, *A Rake's Progress in Eight Plates* (London: Willliam Hogarth, 1735; retouched by the artist, 1763): pl. 8. For information concerning period attitudes toward women, imagination, and pregnancy, see Dolores Peters, "The Pregnant Pamela: Characterization and Popular Medical Attitudes in the Eighteenth Century," *Eighteenth-Century Studies* 14, no. 4 (Summer 1981): 432–51.

8.   Ralph Waldo Emerson, *Society and Solitude and Poems* (Boston and New York: Houghton Mifflin, 1929): 50.

9.   Quoted in Edward Deming Andrews and Faith Andrews, "The Holy Laws of Zion," in *Shaker Furniture* (New York: Dover, 1950): 49–50.

10.   Father Joseph Meachem, "Millennial Laws or Gospel Statutes and Ordinances," in Edward Deming Andrews, *The People Called Shakers* (1953; repr. New York: Dover, 1961): 271–72, 282–85.

11.   Scott T. Swank, *Shaker Life, Art, and Architecture* (New York: Abbeville, 1999): 60.

12.   Thomas Hobbes, *Leviathan* (1651: repr. New York: Penguin Books, 1985): pt. 1, p. 85.

13.   John Locke, *An Essay Concerning Human Understanding* (Oxford: Clarendon Press, 1924): bk, 2, p. 1.

14.   Joseph Addison, "Pleasures of the Imagination," *The Spectator* 411 (21 June 1712).

15.   Ibid. Addison and his contemporaries used the term *association* to identify the mental power that records these first impressions and then consistently recalls them precisely the same way each successive time. Addison observed that first impressions held other sway over the viewer, as well, causing one to experience the same sentiments when encountering situations, objects or persons that resemble one already impressed upon the memory. Say, for example, that one makes the acquaintance of an individual who resembles a trusted friend: Almost automatically— without rhyme or reason—one trusts such a stranger.

16.   Dugald Stewart, *Elements of the Philosophy of the Human Mind* (London: Printed for A. Strahan and T. Cadell in the Strand; Edinburgh: W. Creech, 1792): 477–78.

17.   Sir Joshua Reynolds, "Discourse VII," in *Seven Discourses on Art* (New York: Cassell, 1888): 268–70. The discourse was delivered 10 December 1771.

18.   [Francois Marie Arouet de] Voltaire, "Mr. De Voltaire's Essay on Taste," in Alexander Gerard, *An Essay on Taste* (1756, repr. New York: Garland Publishing, 1970): 212.

19.   Joseph Addison, "Pleasures of the Imagination," *The Spectator* 411 (11 June 1712): 324–25.

20.   Joseph Addison, "Pleasures of the Imagination," *The Spectator* 413 (24 June 1712).

21.   John Dryden, *Dramatic Essays*, ed. William Henry Hudson (London and Toronto: J. M. Dent; New York: E. P. Dutton, [1921]): 72–73.

22.   "Martha Wheatland & Sister, Millerners & Haberdashers," trade card, London, 1761, illustrated in Ambrose Heal, *London Tradesmen's Cards of the XVIII Century, An Account of their Origin and Use* (New York: Dover, 1968): 70.

23.   *Virginia Gazette* (Williamsburg), 30 April 1772; 14 October 1773; 19 April 1770; 26 October 1769.

24.   *New York Gazette Supplement*, 6 September 1772.

25.   *Gazette and General Advertiser* (New York), 22 February 1797.

26.   Frances Trollope, *Domestic Manners of the Americans*, vol. 2 (London: Whittaker Treacher, 1832): 99.

27.   Thomas Sheraton, Appendix, *The Cabinet-Maker and Upholsterer's Drawing Book,* 3rd ed. (1802; repr. New York: Dover, 1972): 3.

28.   Stewart, *Elements of the Philosophy of the Human Mind* (1792): 521.

29.   "Anonymous, "Observations on Fancy-work," in [Rudolph Ackermann's] *Repository of Arts, Science, Literature, Commerce, Manufactures, Fashions, and Politics*, no. 15 (March 1810): 192–95.

30.   Johnson, *Dictionary* (1773), s.v. "fancy." Shakespeare was among the first to explicitly link love to imagination and the joys of sight in *The Merchant of Venice*:

Tell me, where is fancy bred,
or in the Heart, or in the Head?
How begot, how nourished?
Reply, reply.
It is engendered in the eye.

31. Hunter Farish, *Journal and Letters of Philip Fithian, 1773–1774, A Plantation Tutor* (Charlottesville: University Press of Virginia, 1968).

32. Father Joseph Meachem, "Millennial Laws or Gospel Statutes and Ordinances," in Edward Deming Andrews, *The People Called Shakers* (1953; repr. New York: Dover, 1961): 271–72.

33. Sir David Brewster, *A Treatise on the Kaleidoscope* (Edinburgh: Archibald Constable, 1819).

34. A print entitled "Caleidoscope-mania, or the Natives Astonished" was published in London by S. W. Fores in 1818. A copy can be found in the Prints Division of the Library of Congress, Washington, D.C.

35. James Flint, *Letters From America, containing Observations on the Climate and Agriculture of the Western States, etc.* (Edinburgh: W. & C. Tart, 1822): 20.

36. Brewster, *Treatise on the Kaleidsoscope* (1819): 136.

37. Edgar Allan Poe. "Philosophy of Furniture," in *The Works of Edgar Allan Poe in One Volume*, ed. Hervey Allen (New York: P. F. Collier, 1927): 919–20.

38. Nathaniel Whittock, *The Decorative Painters' and Glaziers' Guide* (London: Isaac Taylor Hinton, 1827): 46.

39. For further discussions of pigments and historic paint colors, see Roger W. Moss, *Paint in America: The Colors of Historic Buildings* (Washington, D.C.: National Trust for Historic Preservation, 1994).

40. Rufus Porter, "Imitation Painting," *Scientific American* 1, no.17 (8 January 1846): 2.

41. A. J. Downing, *The Architecture of Country Houses* (New York: D. Appleton, 1850): 368.

42. For further insight into the breadth of the Matteson family skills, see Caroline Hebb, "A Distinctive Group of Early Vermont Painted Furniture," *Antiques* 104, no. 3 (September 1973): 458–61.

43. For further information on Eli Terry, see Kenneth D. Roberts, *Eli Terry and the Connecticut Shelf Clock* (Bristol, Conn: Kenneth Roberts, 1973); Leslie Allen Jones, *Eli Terry: Clockmaker of Connecticut* (New York: Farrar and Rinehart, 1942).

44. Charles Dickens, *The Life and Adventures of Martin Chuzzlewit* and *American Notes*, vol. 2 (Boston and New York: Houghton Mifflin, 1894): 56.

45. D. R. Hay, *The Laws of Harmonious Colouring Adapted to Interior Decorations, Manufacturers, and Other Useful Purposes* (1828; repr. Edinburgh and London: W. Blackwood and Sons, 1847): 134.

46. Waldo Tucker, *The Mechanic's Assistant* (Windsor, Vt., 1837): 38.

47. Thomas Reid, "Of Simple Apprehension in General," in *Essays on the Intellectual Powers of Man* (Edinburgh: John Bell, and London: G. G. and J. Robinson, 1785): 374.

48. The paper was also salvaged and has a printed label that reads "Rim'd coffee-pot tops" from "J. D. L & Co."

49. Taylor's stencils, like those of most artisans, included a broad range of designs, most of them relatively small in size, which suggests that he ornamented picture frames, chairs, boxes, and small pieces of furniture. Many of the motifs are naturalistic—birds, stars, leaves, flowers and the like—and some are geometric. "Allspice," the only stencil cut in script letters, was probably used to label a pantry box or storage canister. A particularly charming example consists of a profile of a man with a four-leaf clover or dogwood blossom suspended over his head. A cornucopia, two compotes, and fruit to fill them suggest that Taylor offered variations of these themes to many customers.

50. Winchendon records show that he didn't remain for long. In the U. S. Census for 1840, Taylor was living in the western Massachusetts college town of Amherst and by 1850 in Fitzwilliam, Cheshire County, New Hampshire.

51. Quoted in John Obed Curtis and William H. Guthman, *New England Militia Uniforms and Accoutrements—A Pictorial Survey* (Sturbridge, Mass: Old Sturbridge Village, 1971): 5.

52. Most New England townships required every household to place two such pails near the front door. In the event of a fire, townspeople would rally to the cause, contributing their colorful containers to a "bucket brigade" that formed at the nearest well, where they filled each receptacle and then passed it along the human chain to douse the blaze. To insure that the buckets were later returned to the right houses, each was identified with the owner's name and sometimes a number so that it could be accounted for.

53. Rufus Porter, "The Art of Painting: Ornamental Gilding and Bronzing," *Scientific American* 1, no. 9 (13 November 1845): 2.

54. Ann Royall, *Mrs. Royall's Pennsylvania, or Travels continued in the United States*, vol. 1 (Washington, D.C.: privately printed, 1829): 9.

55. *The Freeman and Messenger* (Lodi, N.Y.), 22 November 1841. Quoted in John W. Heisey, *Checklist of American Coverlet Weavers* (Charlottesville: University Press of Virginia, 1980): 45.

56. Nancy Goyne Evans, *American Windsor Chairs* (Manchester, Vt.: Hudson Hills Press, 1996): 614.

57. Quoted in Ellen and Burt Denker, *The Rocking Chair Book* (New York: Mayflower Books, 1979): 39.

58. For further information on popular literature in the period, see David S. Reynolds, *Beneath the American Renaissance: Subversive Imagination in the Age of Emerson and Melville* (New York: Knopf, 1988).

59. Alexis de Tocqueville, *Democracy in America*, ed. Andrew Hacker (New York: Washington Square Press, 1964): 150, 156.

60. John Ruskin, *Modern Painting* (1843), in *The Works of John Ruskin*, ed. E. T. Cook and Alexander Wedderburn, vol. 4 (London: George Allen; New York: Longman, Green, 1903): 253.

61. Ralph Waldo Emerson, *Poetry and Imagination* (1875), in *The Complete Writings of Ralph Waldo Emerson, Containing all of his inspiring Essays, Lectures, Poems, Addresses, Studies, Biographical Sketches, and Miscellaneous Works*, vol. 2 (New York: William H. Wise, 1929): 735.

62. Ruskin, *Modern Painting* (1843): 253.

63. Walter Smith, *Art Education, Scholastic and Industrial* (Boston: James R. Osgood, 1872): 191.

The Contemporary World

7 In the Spirit: Twentieth-Century and Contemporary Shaker-Inspired Design

KORY ROGERS

After almost two hundred years, the pared-down, functional forms of classic Shaker furniture continue to fuel the imaginations of craftsmen and designers around the world. Some are compelled to pay homage to the Shakers by faithfully reproducing their designs, while others are inspired to create modern adaptations that honor the spirit of the Shaker aesthetic. Any effort to define this influence accurately must rely on both historical evidence and supposition. Whether the associations are direct or implied, however, there is no doubt that Shaker furniture has had a substantial resonance. By considering a selection of Shaker-inspired approaches to design, this essay will explore the widespread appeal of Shaker furniture and how it has been interpreted and reinterpreted up to the present day. It considers the Shaker aesthetic—which Charles Dickens derided in 1842 as "grim"[1]— and the social and cultural factors that contributed to making it one of the most influential and widely imitated design vocabularies of the twentieth and early twenty-first centuries.

SPREADING THE WORD

At the beginning of the twentieth century, the Shakers were experiencing a dramatic decline in membership, as older Believers steadily passed away and the influx of new converts had all but stopped. As a result, many villages were closed and their remaining inhabitants were relocated and consolidated into other Shaker communities. By this time, the Shakers were not making furniture in large quantities for their own use but instead purchased whatever they needed from the outside World—a practical and cost-effective solution. One visitor to the community at Canterbury, New Hampshire, in 1917 recalled: "I remember how surprised Mother and I was [sic.] at our guestroom—no Shaker furniture, just modern things—probably like Grand Rapids furniture."[2]

Many factors contributed to the Shakers' relaxed enforcement of the Millennial Laws, which prohibited the use of Worldly furniture.[3] First and foremost was the dearth of skilled craftsmen. Always outnumbered by their female counterparts—sometimes by as much as two to one[4]—Shaker brethren trained in the furniture-making traditions were dying out at an alarming rate, taking their knowledge and experience with them to the grave. Secondly, the Shakers were engaged, rhetorically speaking, in a battle of public perception. It is ironic that the socially, technologically, and stylistically progressive Shakers believed their image inhibited conversions and strained their business interactions with the World.[5] In an attempt to shed their anachronistic reputation, the Shakers introduced into their interiors some fashionable furnishings that reflected the latest Worldly trends. They had come to realize that "unless we keep pace with the progress of the universe our individual progress will be an impossibility."[6]

Fear of the Shakers' impending extinction incited a small but dedicated group of collectors, dealers, scholars, and curators to work with the Believers, and they began in the 1920s to document Shaker history for the benefit of posterity.[7] Their concerted efforts led to the establishment of public repositories of Shaker artifacts and manuscripts, such as the Fruitlands Museum and the Western

Fig. 7-1. Kaare Klint (Danish (1888–1954). Church Chairs. 1936. Manufactured by Fritz Hansen A/S, Allerød, Denmark. Beech and papercord. www.fritzhansen.com.

187

Reserve Historical Society; the organization of groundbreaking exhibitions at venerated cultural institutions, such as the Whitney Museum's *Shaker Handicrafts* (1935); and the publication of countless books recording the Shaker way of life, including Edward Deming Andrews's *The People Called Shakers: A Search for the Perfect Society*.[8] This unprecedented preservation and promotional campaign ignited the twentieth century's fascination for and appreciation of all things Shaker, which continues to reverberate today. Indeed, recent scholarship reveals that this popularization also contributed to widespread commercialization of the name Shaker.

The husband-and-wife team of Edward Deming Andrews and Faith Andrews quickly distinguished themselves as the leading Shaker authorities. They organized dozens of exhibitions that traveled around the world and published numerous books and catalogues.[9] Their promotional efforts to link nineteenth-century Shaker furniture to twentieth-century Modernism, however, were of particular significance. By citing parallels that existed between the functionalist aesthetic of the Shakers and that of the European Modernists, they were able to "play on [Shaker furniture's] contemporary relevance."[10] They often wrote of the emphasis the Shakers placed on utility, using contemporary terms, such as functionalism, to make their point.

> The word functionalism was probably quite outside the vocabulary of Shakerdom. But what was "practical" and what was not, the Shakers understood better than most of their worldly neighbours. Untroubled by philosophies of style, they nevertheless held a very clear philosophy of craftsmanship. Whatsoever they built must serve a useful purpose; it must be so far as possible perfectly constructed, and must be devoid of all decorative embellishment. In the upshot, this meant that Shaker dwellings and Shaker furniture represented a virtually unconscious response to current styles and canons of proportion, which were in turn very consciously reduced to the ultimate of simplicity and subjected to further modification to meet the stern demands of utility.[11]

Such discussions stressing the Believers' emphasis on functionalism and their break with stylistic traditions set the stage for the comparison between Shaker and Modernism that has interested scholars ever since. Most comparisons, however, fail to recognize that the Shaker aesthetic was the by-product of a chaste, religious way of life, whereas Modernism was a deliberate attempt at cultural reform. Despite these fundamental differences in origins and intent, both approaches share physical and philosophical parallels.

THE QUESTION OF THE SHAKERS AND MODERN DESIGN

Aesthetically the Shakers seemed ahead of their time, which has made it difficult to resist the urge to compare Shaker design with European Modernism. Seventy-five years before the Austrian architect and critic Adolf Loos (1870–1933) described ornament as a crime,[12] the Millennial Laws (1845) denounced decoration as superfluous and prohibited Believers from using it in any way.[13] Indeed, the Shakers had stripped existing furniture forms of unnecessary elements a century before the expression "less is more" became associated with Mies van der Rohe (1886–1969).[14] The Shakers were making unconventional case furniture with asymmetrical drawer arrangements designed to meet the practical needs of their users decades before Louis Sullivan (1856–1924) declared that form follows function.[15]

Because the Shakers and many modernists shared a belief in economy of means, form, and decoration, it is tempting to declare the former as a source of inspiration for the latter. But even though the Shakers preceded Modernism chronologically, the early twentieth-century European designers were largely unaware of the existence of the religious sect and its nineteenth-century aesthetic philosophies. The primary exception to this was in Denmark, which is a focus of this study, although similar examples can also be found elsewhere in Scandinavia.

The Shaker aesthetic entered the Scandinavian

design lexicon via Denmark in 1927, when a #7 Mount Lebanon armed rocker (see fig. 7-2) with a cushion rail found its way onto an auction block in Copenhagen. There it caught the eye of the Danish architect, designer, and theorist Kaare Klint (1888–1954), an under-recognized contributor to twentieth-century design history.[16] As a co-founder of the furniture department at the Royal Danish Academy of Fine Arts (Kongelige Danske Kunstakademi) in Copenhagen, Klint became the main conduit through which the subsequent generation of Scandinavian designers discovered Shaker furniture and adopted many of its principles.

At the time he first saw the rocker, Kaare Klint was conducting pioneering research in the field of anthropometrics, the systematic study of human proportions and their correlation to historic furniture designs.[17] He collected the data for his research by instructing his students at the Royal Danish Academy to make detailed measured drawings of various furniture forms he considered to be classic ergonomic designs. Ostensibly because he admired the graceful proportions of the Shaker rocker, Klint commissioned one of his students, O. Brundum Christensen, to draft precise schematics of the Shaker chair's construction, from which he had a replica made to use as a teaching aide.[18] Klint was at first unaware of the chair's origins, believing it to be an "American rocking chair in the Colonial style—an example of a type which broadly speaking can still be used today."[19] In 1937 when the Andrews book *Shaker Furniture* appeared in Denmark, Klint discovered that it was a Shaker rocker.[20] Although he integrated certain aspects of the ladder-back chair into his Church Chair (fig. 7-1) of 1935, Shaker furniture had a more direct and pervasive impact on the work of the next generation of Danish furniture designers, many of whom became widely known in the United States.

Coincidentally, the Shaker rocker arrived in Denmark during the development of the Scandinavian social reform movement, which emphasized the societal relevance of good design in everyday life and the role of art and design as a vehicle for social change.[21] In 1927, when the

Shaker chair was auctioned in Copenhagen, Klint and other members of the Scandinavian cultural community campaigned for the social benefits of democratic design, believing that this would give every citizen access to well-designed, affordable furniture. They argued that one way to achieve this

Fig. 7-2. #7 Rocker, ca. 1870. Mount Lebanon, New York. Maple with woven cane seat. Skinner Inc., Boston and Bolton, Massachusetts.

goal was through the modernization of the region's outdated furniture industries, which still relied heavily on handcraftsmanship.[22]

In Denmark Børge Mogensen (1914–1972), a former student and protégé of Kaare Klint, contributed substantially to modernizing the country's antiquated furniture industry when he became head of the furniture design section of the Association of Danish Wholesale Cooperative Societies, a position he held until 1950.[23] He was given the challenging task of creating furniture for everyday use that would appeal to the country's agrarian population and could be easily mass-produced. To achieve this, Mogensen turned to the American Shakers for inspiration, adopting their low ladder-back dining chairs as the prototype for his J39 chair (fig. 7-3). Mogensen successfully designed seating well suited for mass production by simplifying the construction and reducing the number of back slats to one. First introduced in

1947, the J39 chair has been in continuous production for sixty years. Today it is considered a classic of Danish modern design, perfectly suitable "for seating ranging from canteens and conference rooms to churches and private homes."[24]

Børge Mogensen also created a trestle table (fig. 7-4) to complement his Shaker-inspired J39 Chair. He based the design on a nineteenth-century form from Hancock, Massachusetts, that he saw illustrated in *Shaker Furniture*. He modified the Shaker table by replacing the original single upright supports at each end with two thin legs, and he increased the structural stability by adding a second longitudinal stretcher. Mogensen echoed a distinctive detail found on the Hancock original by chamfering the corners of each leg.

Shaker influence is also visible in the furniture designs of Hans J. Wegner (1914–2007), one of the most gifted and widely praised twentieth-century Danish designers. Wegner most likely first

Fig. 7-3.
Left: Børge Mogensen (Danish, 1914–1972). J39 Chair. Designed ca. 1947, this example manufactured ca. 2006 by Fredericia. Beech and natural paper yarn. Bob and Aileen Hamilton. Photograph David Hollinger. *Cat. no. 152.*

Right: Low-back Chair, ca. 1860. New Lebanon, New York. Cherry with woven cane seat. Bob and Aileen Hamilton. Photograph David Hollinger

encountered the Shakers when he was a student at the Polytechnic in Copenhagen in the late 1930s.[25] The classes he took in joinery involved making detailed drawings of historic furniture on exhibit at the Danish Museum of Decorative Arts in Copenhagen, a display that included a #7 Shaker rocker.

Wegner's J-16 Rocker (fig. 7-5) combines Shaker elements with characteristics of Windsor seating. He enlarged the proportions of classic Shaker chairs for the J-16, increased the degree of the angled back posts, and replaced the traditional Shaker ladder-back with turned spindles typical of Windsor rockers. Wegner's CH44 Chair (fig. 7-6) is more recognizable as a modernized version of a Shaker ladder-back chair. Here he eliminated the minimally turned elements of the structural supports found in the Shaker original and again increased the degree of the angle of the reclining back posts for purposes of comfort.

PARALLELS IN JAPANESE AND SHAKER FURNITURE

The confluence of aesthetics and spirituality in the creation of objects for everyday life revealed in Shaker design may have been an anomaly in the West, but it had a counterpart in the beautifully restrained and minimalist designs of Japanese furniture. Although they developed independently on opposite sides of the world, the Shakers and the Japanese share a common design philosophy that emphasizes utility, simplicity, and reductive form, materials, and construction.[26] Both traditions are guided by a concept of functionality that is grounded in spiritual beliefs.

The parallel trajectories of Shaker and Japanese furniture traditions intersected in the mid-twentieth century in the work of George Nakashima (1905–90). The Japanese-American woodworker fused the aesthetics and techniques of his ancestral homeland with Anglo-American traditions, including Shaker.

Fig. 7-4. Børge Mogensen (Danish, 1914–1972). Shaker Table. Designed ca. 1947, this example manufactured ca. 2006 by Fredericia. Beech. Bob and Aileen Hamilton. Photograph David Hollinger. *Cat. no. 153.*

Fig. 7-5. Hans J. Wegner
(Danish, 1914–2007). J-16
Rocker. Designed ca. 1943, this
example manufactured ca. 2007
by Fredericia. Beech and natural
paper yarn. Shelburne Museum,
Shelburne, Vermont, 2007-2.
Photo: Andy Dubeck. *Cat. no.
151.*

Nakashima's furniture, like that of the Believers, embodies the spiritual beliefs of the maker, which in his case included the conviction that every tree possesses an inner soul, which is revealed in the natural beauty of the wood.[27] Indeed, the asymmetrical forms, exposed joinery, and figured wood of his furniture inevitably inspire comparisons between his work and that of the Shakers. According to Nakashima's daughter and protégée, Mira Nakashima-Yarnall, "Many people have mentioned the affinity with both Shaker and Japanese design to Nakashima. Conscious or not, simplicity and material must result in similar designs!"[28]

A visual comparison between Nakashima's bench (fig. 7-8) and the Shaker meetinghouse bench (see fig. 2-2) reveals certain parallels in design and construction. Both are modified variations of a traditional Windsor bench, which features a single plank seat and spindle-comb backrests. The tapered ends of the Nakashima crest rail are angled up and out in a manner characteristic of Asian furniture design. Instead of shaping the plank seat as the Shakers did, Nakashima allowed the organic shape of the black walnut to dictate the form of the slab seat. Both Nakashima and Shaker craftsmen exposed construction in their furniture, although for different reasons. For Nakashima, the use of a large, exposed butterfly joint was an aesthetic choice, whereas for the Shakers, the visible dovetailed construction found on some case furniture (see fig. 2-18) was done for reasons of economy.

Fully aware of the similarities between his work and that of the Believers, and deliberating choosing to align the cultural influences present in his own furniture design, Nakashima was known to call his work "Japanese Shaker."[29]

The distinguishing characteristics of traditional Japanese furniture produced during the Meiji (1868–1912) and Taisho (1912–26) eras are expressed in the work of Douglas Brooks, a contemporary Vermont-based woodworker trained in Japanese woodworking techniques and knowledgeable about historical Japanese forms. Brooks is articulate and precise when he acknowledges the spiritual essence of the Japanese aesthetic:

> The asymmetry of Japanese cabinetry can be linked to the twin pillars of Japanese spirituality: Shintoism and Buddhism. The Shinto reverence for nature—in which all objects are imbued by spirits, or kami—creates an aesthetic that reflects the randomness of the natural world. With its emphasis on contemplation, Zen Buddhism in particular influenced Japanese art and architecture by providing the context for responding to an object. Lack of balance and symmetry creates a question, inviting the viewer to engage with the piece at a deeper level. Beauty is not found in the piece

per se. In the Buddhist view, the beauty of the piece lies in the viewers' process of imagination, reflection and discovery.[30]

Brooks's work reveals the unexpected design parallels between traditional Japanese furniture and furniture made by the Shakers, both of which are inspired by religious beliefs and a reliance upon little or no applied decoration. But the most daring similarity is the deliberate avoidance of bilateral symmetry and the resulting emphasis on asymmetry—a concept unknown in Western furniture, but a logical result of the functional design espoused by both the Japanese and the Shakers.

Brooks's Chadansu (fig. 7-7) is a replica of a tea chest of the Japanese Meiji Period (1868-1912), a portable, freestanding storage case for specially blended teas and highly prized serving implements. The asymmetrical arrangement and varying size of each drawer and door suggest that traditional *chadansu* were designed to house specific implements used in the highly ritualized tea ceremony. The two sets of sliding doors located at the top and center right slide like shoji screens, and the larger center doors can be removed from their tracks to reveal a set of offset shelves holding teacups. The vertical hinged door at the left was probably designed to house the teapot.

THE COMMERCIALIZATION OF SHAKER DESIGN

During World War II, the American furniture industry curtailed production as factories realigned for war-related functions, and many Americans at home assisted in the war effort by rationing their consumption. After the war ended, the American furniture industry resumed production, as it was no longer competing with the military for materials. Many returning veterans, with the help of government loans, invested in new homes, which resulted in a boom for the housing and home-furnishings industries during the late 1940s and 1950s.

Some astute postwar designers such as Paul McCobb (1917–1969) tapped into the collective consumer psyche by appealing to the nation's

sense of pride and wide-eyed optimism and by developing "contemporary design(s) indigenous to this country and its living needs."[31] To achieve this, McCobb mixed historical elements with modern styling "to create contemporary home furnishings in the best tradition of the earlier noteworthy American artisans."[32] As he explained in a brochure for his Directional furniture line, McCobb borrowed freely from a roster of "American artisans," including the Shakers, whom he identified as an important model for his work. Creating a broad range of designs for the American market, McCobb focused on both economy, as revealed in the relatively affordable Planner Group (1950), and higher-end

Fig. 7-6. Hans J. Wegner (Danish, 1914–2007). CH44 Chair, 1951. Manufactured by Carl Hansen & Søn, Aarup, Denmark. Hardwood and papercord. Image courtesy of Carl Hansen. Photo: Søren Larsen.

production, including the Directional line (fig. 7-9) for Winchendon (1952). The latter series of "coordinated" furniture encouraged consumers to mix and match separate pieces in endless combinations. Although the long sideboard illustrated in figure 7-9 comprises three separate storage units, the drawer configurations in each of the three cabinets have their precedents in Shaker case pieces. In particular, the asymmetry of the central bar cabinet model number 7023 closely resembles the counter attributed to Brother Grove Wright (see fig. 2-5) from Hancock, Massachusetts. McCobb's modern version differs from its Shaker counterpart in that he graduated the bank of drawers on the right and replaced the three long drawers of the Hancock counter with a set of cupboard doors. In line with his characteristic "sleek simplicity," the cabinets are

supported on slender brass legs that run the height of the case.[33]

Although Paul McCobb's furniture designs represent the best of mid-century Shaker-inspired furniture, he is, sadly, an exception to the rule. Over the next fifty years, the American and international furniture industries produced an endless stream of uninspired furniture sold as "Shaker" but that had nothing to do with the original, being devoid of spiritual or aesthetic references. Virtually every major furniture company, including Ethan Allen, Lane, Ashley, and Ikea, has introduced Shaker-style lines intended to capitalize on the religious sect's popularity.

The commercialization and commodification of Shaker design, which began in the 1930s and continues unabated today, has diluted its original

potency and obfuscated its true nature. As a result, "Shaker" has become a brand name synonymous with inexpensive and inferior furniture. The sobriquet "Shaker-style" is liberally invoked to describe uninspired objects. The desire of many householders to own matching bedroom sets is responsible for the development of contradictory furniture forms such as "Simply Shaker" lingerie chests.[34]

Imitation has been a complicated and complex issue for the Shakers throughout their existence. Although Sister R. Mildred Barker (1897–1990) looked upon imitation as "the sincerest form of flattery,"[35] her nineteenth-century predecessors involved in the Mount Lebanon chair industry held the opposite opinion.[36] A victim of its own success, the lucrative Shaker furniture business became the target of competitors, including now venerated companies such as L. & J. G. Stickley, during the last quarter of the nineteenth century.[37] Attempting to capitalize on the Shaker reputation for integrity and high-quality goods, these unscrupulous opportunists either co-opted the Shaker name or copied their designs in order to market and sell knockoffs to unsuspecting consumers. In this instance, the normally pacifist Shakers refused to turn the other cheek and allow their good name to be tarnished. Instead, they launched an advertising campaign that warned consumers against counterfeiters and rebuked retailers who knowingly sold the fakes alongside authentic Shaker chairs. In order to safeguard against fraud and to guarantee authenticity, the Shakers adopted the use of "a Gold Transfer Trade

Fig. 7-8. George Nakashima (American, 1905–1990). Bench with Back, 1979. Walnut and hickory. Museum of Fine Arts, Boston, Massachusetts, Museum purchase with funds donated by the National Endowment for the Arts and the Deborah M. Noonan Foundation, 1979.275. *Cat. no. 154.*

Fig. 7-9. Paul McCobb (American 1917–1969). Directional Cabinet 7026, Bar Cabinet 7023, Chest 7025, 1952. Manufactured by Winchendon Furniture Company, Winchendon, Massachusetts. Image courtesy of Schiffer Publishing.

Mark" and counseled potential buyers to look for it "before purchasing—no chair is genuine without it."[38] This also implied they were codifying their own brand.

Furniture makers continue to imitate the Shakers today. Although some are motivated by respect and admiration, others are clearly intent on cashing in on the popularity of the Shaker "style." The Amish, for example, produce their own versions of "Shaker" furniture in varying degrees of verisimilitude. Most of the furnishings they advertise on the Web sites of their distributors are pastiches of varying styles, such as Shaker-Mission fusions.[39] The Amish aren't the only ones mixing Shaker with other designs; a quick Internet search brings up all types of hybrids and mutations, including "Rustic Shaker" armchairs and side chairs made of twigs and branches.[40]

Amidst the glut of inaccurate imitations and unimaginative interpretations, a number of contem-porary furniture makers and manufacturers honor the Shakers and their designs through faithful reproductions and creative adaptations. Some contemporary craftsmen, such as William Laberge (b. 1960) of Dorset, Vermont, hone their skills by meticulously replicating the functional forms, impeccable constructions, and quirky designs of nineteenth-century classic Shaker furniture. In one example (fig. 7-10), Laberge re-creates the asymmetry of the now familiar "upside-down" built-in cupboard (fig. 7-11) from the Shaker community of Enfield, Connecticut. Recent studies of the construction of the original case piece have revealed that it was displayed incorrectly—wrong side up—for decades. This conclusion is supported by the orientation of the internal locking mechanisms of the drawers, which suggests the tall cupboard shown here on the bottom (fig. 7-11) was meant to be on top.[41]

Thomas Moser (b. 1935) literally wrote the book

on how to make Shaker furniture.[42] As the founder of Thos. Moser Cabinetmakers, he made copies of Shaker pieces and later sold them in his retail galleries throughout the northeastern United States. As his career developed, Moser's approach to design changed. He began to experiment with historical designs, modifying them to improve their functionality. Moser even dared to improve upon a nineteenth-century Shaker design flaw commonly found in their long meetinghouse benches (see fig. 2-1), which were wobbly because they lacked a longitudinal stretcher connecting the two side stretchers. As Moser playfully explains: "I out-Shakered the Shakers"[43] when he redesigned the support structure of the Shaker settee form on his Deacon's Bench (fig. 7-12) by removing the stretchers and replacing them with arched, laminated ship's knee leg supports.[44]

FURNITURE OR ART?

Northwest Coast artist and craftsman Roy McMakin (b. 1956) designs and builds domestic furniture that obliquely references the Shaker aesthetic. Like the Shaker craftsmen before him, McMakin continually refines preexisting furniture forms by modifying them ever so slightly to create something new and thought provoking. McMakin disavows a direct Shaker influence on his latest work, believing that to "quote [the Shakers] has become a cliché."[45] Even though McMakin's pieces are the progeny of generic forms that do not belong to any specific style, vestiges of Shaker furniture are clearly present in his work, as evidenced by the asymmetrical surface treatment on his rectilinear Six Drawer Chest (fig. 7-13). Whereas the irregular drawer arrangement characteristic of Shaker case pieces is determined by user convenience, the uneven application of the enamel paint and the intentionally mismatched knobs on McMakin's chest are purely visual—playfully but falsely implying inferior quality, yet indirectly referencing Shaker asymmetrical design.[46]

Today most people encounter Shaker furniture in museum settings. With the exception of the institutions that occupy historic Shaker villages or have accurately re-created interiors, most museums display the furniture in sterile galleries out of its original context. By employing the standard museum practice of placing the furniture on pedestals, these institutions literally and figuratively elevate utilitarian artifacts to the level of fine art. This perception is further validated in the public's mind by the astronomical prices Shaker furniture commands at auction in the current market. Commenting on these prices, Brother Arnold Hadd (b. 1956) from the Sabbathday Lake, Maine, community says: "I think the market for Shaker antiques has gotten wholly out of control. It seems obscene to me for people to pay so much money, tens of thousands of dollars, for a piece of furniture, especially if it was made by a religious community that espouses Christian poverty."[47] Sister Frances Carr (b. 1927) made this poignant statement: "It always rains when they have these auctions—it's the old Shakers crying," in describing her personal opinion of the increasingly businesslike approach to Shaker design.[48] As a result, Shaker furniture has assumed a "precious" status and is viewed with the same reverence as a priceless piece of sculpture. Ostensibly there is nothing wrong with appreciating Shaker furniture for its impeccable craftsmanship and timeless design, but the prevailing attitude borders on the verge of idolatry. The idea of viewing their furniture as works of art would have been unthinkable to the Shakers, who originally lived, worked, and worshiped with these objects.

Roy McMakin blurs the lines between functional object and conceptual art in an untitled work from 2005 (fig. 7-14). Fusing a small Shaker-style table with a wide platform base, he has created a uniform object that seems both uncertain of its identity and self-conscious about its own importance. McMakin disguises the juncture at which the table meets the base beneath multiple layers of enamel, illustrating his perception of people's inability or disinclination to distinguish between furniture and art, as well as between structure and decoration.

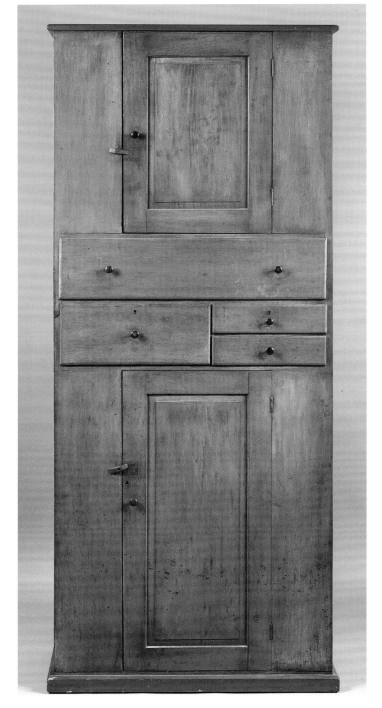

By intentionally placing the table out of arm's reach in the middle of the pedestal, McMakin subverts its practical utility—in the same way Shaker furniture has been separated from its origins by the art market and museum presentations.

Determining authorship and authenticity is often a complicated issue in assessing the work of contemporary designers whose work is modeled on Shaker forms. This is the case when one compares the AVL Shaker Chair (fig. 7-15) of the Dutch artist/designer Joep van Lieshout (b. 1963) to actual Shaker chairs. The simple form and bright red paint does form a connection between the AVL and its Shaker ancestors. However, the chair's conceptual origins are perhaps more important and interesting.

Joep van Lieshout operates outside the mainstream contemporary design world. His provocative sculptures push the boundaries of taste by tackling social taboos in a graphic way. Looking at the scope of his oeuvre reveals an affinity for loners, social outcasts, and people who dance to the beat of their own drum. His fascination with social misfits and peaceful separatists collided in 1998 in his The Good, The Bad, and The Ugly project for the Walker Art Center in Minneapolis. Van Lieshout originally designed the prototype for the AVL Shaker Chair for the Black House section of the project. The sparsely furnished Black House was conceived as the imaginary domicile of the Unabomber, the American terrorist who killed three people and maimed twenty-nine others with improvised incendiary devices from 1979 to 1995.[49] Ironically, van Lieshout turned to the pacifist Shakers as the source of inspiration for the furnishings of a deranged anarchist whose separation from the world led him to pathological violence.

Facing page:
Fig. 7-10. William Laberge (American, b. 1960). Enfield Cupboard, 2007. Painted poplar. William Laberge, Dorset, Vermont. *Cat. no. 156.*

Fig. 7-11. "Upside-down" Cupboard, 1820–50. Enfield, Connecticut. Polychrome pine and butternut. Skinner Inc., Boston and Bolton, Massachusetts.

Below:
Fig. 7-12. Thomas Moser (American, b. 1935). Deacon's Bench. Manufactured by Thos. Moser Cabinetmakers, Portland, Maine. Cherry and ash. Thos. Moser Cabinetmakers. Photo: Paul Rocheleau.

Van Lieshout has demonstrated that his fascination with the Shakers extends beyond superficial
formal comparisons to include their way of life. In
2001 van Lieshout successfully staged a peaceful
coup d'état in Rotterdam's harbor, when he transformed his studio into the AVL-Ville, a "free state."
Loosely patterned after the social structure and
self-sufficiency of Shaker communities, the AVL-
Ville was equally sociological experiment and performance art. Van Lieshout, along with thirty other
participants, lived under the governance of a written constitution and engaged in commerce using
their own printed currency. In addition to engaging
in artistic endeavors, the members of the AVL-Ville
experimented with agricultural practices, which produced food for the entire community.[50] Just as the
Shakers opened their worship to the scrutiny of
outside observers, van Lieshout invited spectators

to watch the activity of his workshop, where he
continued to develop his AVL Shaker furniture line.

SHAKER INFLUENCE IN THE TWENTY-FIRST CENTURY

At the beginning of the twenty-first century, three
remaining Shakers keep the faith alive in
Sabbathday Lake, Maine, the last active community.
Like their nineteenth-century predecessors, today's
Shakers openly embrace all the time-saving devices
that modern technology has to offer. They have
logged onto the Internet, where through the community's Web site they promote tourism for their
library and museum and engage in e-commerce,
selling their own proprietary blends of herbs, teas,
and potpourris.[51] A quick Google search for the
word *Shakers* results in an astonishing 9,400,000

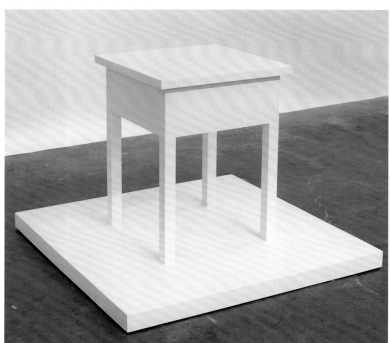

related hits, which include listings for museums, exhibitions, libraries, books, articles, furniture makers, dealers, and auction results, as well as condiment dispensers and cocktail mixers.[52] However, the Shaker online presence may be much larger than Google's complex algorithm is able to detect. A paper posted on the U. S. Department of Labor's Web site entitled "A Shaker Approach to Web Site Design" illustrates how the principles of Shaker design can be modified and applied to new technologies.[53] The author, Michael D. Levi, stresses three characteristics of Shaker furniture—simplicity, elegance, and quality—which if applied to Web page design will result in legible, user-friendly sites.

Contemporary designers are doing their part to ensure that the Shaker aesthetic continues in the twenty-first century. Although experiencing ebbs and flows in popularity, Shaker furniture has

secured its place in design history. In 2004 Brooklyn-based designer Portia Wells included an image of a Shaker ladder-back in her *Slipcover Chair Project* (fig. 7-16), in which she explored the concept "you are what you choose to sit on." To illustrate her point, Wells printed the silhouettes of four "iconic" chairs, including a high-style Chippendale side chair, the Eames's bent plywood DCW, a "ubiquitous" folding chair, and the Shaker ladder-back. Believing that each chair is a "cultural identifier," Wells suggests that individuals can manipulate the public image they project by merely changing the slipcover as circumstances dictate.[54]

Styling is an important tool in a designer's arsenal. Simply altering one aspect of an object's design can transform a centuries-old form into something new and exciting. Known for his ultra-modern, uber-chic furniture designs, Italian designer Antonio

Fig. 7-15. Joep van Lieshout (Dutch, b. 1963). AVL Shaker Chair, 1999. Manufactured by Moooi, Breda, The Netherlands. Lacquered beech. Shelburne Museum, Shelburne, Vermont, 2007-3. Image courtesy of Moooi. *Cat. no. 159.*

Fig. 7-16. Portia Wells (b. 1980). *Slipcover Chair Project*, 2004. Plywood, textiles, and acrylic paint. Courtesy Portia Wells, Brooklyn, New York.

Citterio (b. 1950) has recently applied his characteristic sleek styling to a Shaker cast-iron stove (fig. 7-17). Shaker stoves were acclaimed in the nineteenth century for their innovative two-chamber construction, which doubled the amount of heat produced.[55] No longer required to produce as much heat as its prototype, Citterio's modernized version consolidates the Shakers' stacked double-box construction into one tall open chamber. He utilizes the properties of heat-resistant glass to great visual affect, enabling observers to sit close to the fire on the attached bench.[56]

Occasionally a product emerges on the international scene that has its origins in the practical designs pioneered by the nineteenth-century Shakers. More than just an architectural element, the Shakers' innovative and ubiquitous peg rail was installed around the interior wall of every workshop and dwelling house. Everything from furniture and clothing was suspended from the peg railing to save space, maintain order, and make cleaning the rooms more efficient for the Shaker sisters. German designer Nils Holger Moormann's *Rechenbeispiel* system (fig. 7-18) is a contemporary version, which incorporates such luxury options as flocked-tipped

pegs to prevent your designer outerwear from being rubbed the wrong way. Catering to the current consumer desire for customization, Moormann's pegs are not permanently affixed like the original Shaker railing but rather are held in place magnetically, which allows the owner to adjust its appearance. The *Rechenbeispiel* comes with optional accessories, including modular storage units similar to the Shaker miniature cupboard (see fig. 2-1) and other modern forms, such as memo boards and key holders.[57]

It is impossible to predict with absolute certainty what the future will hold for the twenty-first-century Believers, but it is intriguing to speculate how they might influence generations to come. Perhaps the Shakers will become a model for Worldly growth. As American metropolises mutate into megalopolises, their increasing populations push city limits further away from their epicenters, contributing to longer commutes, higher gas consumption, and, ultimately, the production of environmental pollutants. Unchecked urban sprawl threatens to consume America's surrounding countryside, replacing beautiful vistas of grassy fields with impenetrable concrete and asphalt parking

lots, which prevent rainwater from collecting in underground reservoirs and leave urban areas without available potable water.

Having constructed nineteen self-contained communities, the Shakers were accomplished town planners, and their villages provide an ideal blueprint on which to base future planned communities (see Chapter 1 in this volume). Unlike the organic expansion of Worldly towns and cities, Shaker villages were carefully oriented to reflect heavenly order and neatness, which intrigued many outside visitors during the nineteenth century. Although they were not mirror images of each other, Shaker communities maintained a sense of "gospel order" by providing similar structures for their members, allowing of course for regional variances in the selection of available building materials.[58] By conveniently clustering their dwelling houses, laundry, infirmary, and power-generating facilities together, the Shakers were always within walking distance of any community or personal function. In order to maintain the order of their tight-knit communities, the Shakers often either relocated or dismantled buildings in disrepair, erecting their replacements on the same foundations—a labor-saving and cost-effective method of recycling.

If the town planners and civil engineers of tomorrow were to apply the common sense and the economical practices employed by the Shakers, they could curb, or at least constrain, and manipulate the advancement of suburban sprawl. By adapting the Shaker method of grouping buildings near large, open expanses of well-manicured agricultural fields, commuters would have shorter, more efficient travel to work, as well as access to locally grown produce. Realizing these simple concepts could have a positive impact on both the quality of life in future communities and the appearance of the suburban and rural landscape.

* * *

Fig. 7-18. Nils Holger Moormann (German, b. 1953). *Rechenbeispiel*, 2006. Manufactured by Nils Holger Moormann GmbH, Aschau im Chiemgau, Germany. Maple, birch plywood, flocking, and magnets. Nils Holger Moormann GmbH.

In striking contrast to the Shakers' dissident eighteenth-century beginnings and their steadily declining numbers over the past two hundred years, the aesthetic they created continues to have a broad international following. Sixty years ago, Shaker furniture had great appeal to Danish designers, among others, because of its reductive form and the integration of structure and decoration. Designers today continue to appreciate Shaker furniture for its minimalist sensibility. Regrettably, the commercialization of Shaker products is another aspect of their legacy. It is intriguing, however, to consider how the Shaker legacy might have a greater societal impact on contemporary design practice, such as finding solutions to sustainability and countering suburban sprawl. Indeed, Shaker design can be understood not only as a vital part of the history of American material culture but also as a potential model for resolving the pressing and complex problems that confront designers now and in the future.

1.   Charles Dickens, *American Notes for General Circulation* (London: Chapman & Hall, 1842), quoted in Flor Morse, *The Shakers and the World's People* (Hanover, N.H.: University Press of New England, 1980): 184.

2.   Letter from Mrs. Robert Reed, Madison, Wisconsin, to Bonnie Androski of Skinner Inc., Boston and Bolton, Massachusetts, April 15, 1991. Quoted in Jean M. Burks, "The Evolution of Design in Shaker Furniture," *The Magazine Antiques* (May 1994): 737.

3.   "Millennial Laws" (1845): pt. 1, sec. 4, no. 3; reprinted in Edward Deming Andrews, *The People Called Shakers: A Search for the Perfect Society* (New York: Oxford University Press, 1953): 282.

4.   These statistics are based on the demographics of compiled by Priscilla J. Brewer for the eleven eastern communities as published in John T. Kirk, *The Shaker World* (New York: Harry N. Abrams, 1997): 191.

5.   Burks, "The Evolution of Design" (1994): 734.

6.   Quoted in Robley Edward Whitson, ed., *The Shakers: Two Centuries of Spiritual Reflection* (New York: Paulist Press, 1983): 130.

7.   For a comprehensive list of the names of people involved in this group, see Stephen Bowe and Peter Richmond, *Selling Shaker: The Commodification of Shaker Design in the Twentieth Century* (Liverpool: Liverpool University Press, 2007): 13.

8.   For a comprehensive and unvarnished account of the early development of Shaker related institutions, see "Simple and Pure: The Early Promotion of Shaker Design in the United States of America" in ibid., 7–51.

9.   For a comprehensive list of books and articles written by the Andrews, see bibliography in ibid., 346–49.

10.   Ibid., 13.

11.   Edward Deming Andrews, "Shaker Home of Dr. and Mrs. Edward Deming Andrews in Pittsfield, Massachusetts, USA," in Milton C. Rose and Emily Mason Rose, eds., *A Shaker Reader* (New York: Universe Books, 1977): 77. Also quoted in Bowe and Richmond, *Selling Shaker* (2007): 13–14.

12.   Adolf Loos, "Ornement et Crimé," *L'Esprit Nouveau* 1, no. 2 (1920): 159–68.

13.   Millennial Laws (1845): 282.

14.   Philip C. Johnson, *Mies van der Rohe* (New York: Museum of Modern Art, 1947): 49.

15.   Louis Sullivan, *Kindergarten Chats* (1901), in Adrian Forty, *Words and Buildings: A Vocabulary of Modern Architecture* (London: Thames & Hudson, 2004): 178.

16.   John Vedel-Rieper, *An American Inspiration: Danish Modern and Shaker Design* (Glostrup, Denmark: Permild & Rosengreen, [1976]). The exhibition catalogue was issued as a poster, with the catalogue appearing on the verso. This exhibition was organized by the Danish Foreign Ministry for the USA '76 Committee in Denmark and the Smithsonian Institution Traveling Exhibition Service.

17.   Ibid.

18.   Ibid.

19.   Kaare Klint, "Om Undervisningen i Møbeltegning ved Kunstakademiet," *Arkitekten Månedshæfte* 30 (October 1930): 193–224. Illustrations of the Shaker rocker appear on pp. 204 and 205.

20.   Vedel-Rieper, *An American Inspiration* (1976): verso.

21.   David Revere McFadden, "Scandinavian Modern: A Century in Profile," in *Scandinavian Modern Design, 1880–1980* (New York: Harry N. Abrams, 1982): 17–18.

22.   Ibid.

23.   Mel Byars, *The Design Encyclopedia* (New York: John Wiley, 1994): 382.

24.   Vedel-Rieper, *An American Inspiration* (1976): verso.

25.   Charlotte and Peter Fiell, *Scandinavian Design* (Cologne: Taschen, 2002): 650.

26.   Ty and Kiyoko Heineken, *Tansu: Traditional Japanese Cabinetry* (New York: Weatherhill, 1981): 2.

27.   For further elaboration on Nakashima's work and spiritual philosophy, see George Nakashima, *The Soul of a Tree: A Woodworker's Reflections* (Tokyo and New York: Kodansha International, 1981).

28.   Timothy D. Rieman and Jean M. Burks, *The Complete Book of Shaker Furniture* (New York, Harry N. Abrams, 1993): 91.

29.   Christian Becksvoort, *The Shaker Legacy: Perspectives on an Enduring Furniture Style* (Newtown, Conn.: Taunton Books & Video, 2000): 18.

30.   E-mail message from Douglas Brooks to Jean Burks, 21 May 2007.

31.   Paul McCobb, *Fifties Furniture by Paul McCobb: Directional Designs* (Atglen, Pa.: Schiffer Publishing, 2000): 11. This publication reprints a 1956 brochure for the Directional Furniture Showrooms Incorporated.

32.   Ibid.

33.   Chris Ritter, "Interior View: McCobb's Modern Furniture," *Art Digest* 26 (September 1952): 19.

34.   www.thefurniture.com (accessed: 3 August 2007).

35.   Thomas F. Moser with Brad Lemley, *Thos. Moser: Artistry in Wood* (San Francisco: Chronicle Books, 2002): 48. This comment was made by Sister Mildred Barker of Sabbathday Lake, Maine, in response to Thomas Moser's request for a critique of his book *How to Build Shaker Furniture*, first published in 1977.

36.   For a more in depth discussion of the Shaker production chair industry at Mount Lebanon, see Stephen Miller's chapter "Designed for Sale: Shaker Commerce with the World," in this volume.

37.   See Appendix A, "The Imitators—Non-Shaker Chairs" in Charles Muller and Timothy D. Rieman, *The Shaker Chair* (Atglen, Pa.: Schiffer Publishing, 2003): 1–10. Appedix A appears after main text in this volume and the pages are numbered separately.

38.   Ibid., 186. This statement was originally published in an 1875 Shaker chair catalogue.

39.   www.amishdiningroom.com (accessed 6 May 2007).

40.   www.studiocrafts.com (accessed 6 May 2007).

41.   John T. Kirk, "Reappraising an Upside-Down Shaker Masterpiece," *The Magazine Antiques* (March 2004): 88–91.

42.   Thomas Moser, *How to Build Shaker Furniture* (New York: Sterling Publishing, 1977)

43. Moser and Lemley, *Thos. Moser* (2002): 89.
44. Moser, *How to Build Shaker Furniture* (1977): 172.
45. Telephone conversation with the author, conducted 12 March 2007.
46. Michael Darling, *Roy McMakin: A Door Meant as Adornment* (Los Angeles: Museum of Contemporary Art, 2003): 51.
47. Ken Burns and Amy Stechler, *The Shakers: Hands to Work, Hearts to God*, (Alexandria, VA: PBS Video, 1985). Brother Hadd spoke in the film. This documentary has been recently rebroadcasted as part of the *American Stories* series on public television, see http://www.pbs.org/kenburns/shakers/ (accessed 31 July 2007).
48. Ibid.
49. Jennifer Allen et al., *Atelier Van Lieshout* (Rotterdam: NAI Publishers, 2007): 87.
50. Ibid., 120–21.
51. www.Shaker.lib.me.us (accessed 31 July 2007).
52. www.google.com (accessed 31 July 2007).
53. Michael D. Levi, "A Shaker Approach to Web Site Design," http://www.bls.gov/ore/htm_papers/st970120.htm (accessed 5 May 2007).
54. www.portiawells.com (accessed 31 July 2007)
55. Robert F. W. Meader, *Illustrated Guide to Shaker Furniture* (New York: Dover, 1972): 101.
56. The stove is available from Wittus Fire by Design, see http://wittus.com.
57. www.moormann.de (accessed 10 May 2007).
58. See Chapter 1 in this volume.

Checklist

THE SHAKER WORLD

The United Society of Believers in Christ's Second Appearing, as the Shakers call themselves, is the most extensive, enduring, and successful utopian society. It was established in the eighteenth century and continues into the present. This dissident Quaker sect originated in Manchester, England, in the 1750s and, led by their charismatic leader Ann Lee (1736–1784), journeyed to America in 1774 to avoid persecution. After settling near Albany, New York, the Believers established eighteen more villages from Maine to Kentucky over the next fifty years. Nonbelievers derisively nicknamed them "Shaking Quakers" or "Shakers" for short—a term the group came to embrace—because of the ecstatic movements that accompanied their enthusiastic worship. The Shakers attempt to attain spiritual grace and to create their heaven on earth by leading simple, pure, and righteous lives patterned on the life of Jesus. This Christian sect practices regular confession of sin, communal ownership of goods, celibacy, and equality of the sexes. The Shakers are guided by utility, honesty, and order in both their work and their worship. This belief system has influenced the physical expression of the goods they have produced, both for use at home and for sale to the outside world, while they resided in communities established away from their rural neighbors, or "out of this world."

Communal Organization

For the sake of unity, Shaker communities sought to look, think, and act alike. Their system of government was established at the model community founded in 1787 at New Lebanon, New York, which became the home of the central ministry. Here men and women shared equally positions of spiritual and temporal responsibility. Reporting to the supreme authority of the central ministry at New Lebanon were two to four Shaker com-

munities in close geographic proximity that made up a bishopric. Each bishopric was governed by a quartet of branch ministry leaders—two elders and two eldresses—who traveled between their Shaker sites to ensure union in all things sacred and secular. Each village, in turn, was organized into several families of approximately fifty to one hundred and fifty people, which reflected a different level of commitment to the Shaker way of life, the most senior level being the "church family," which consisted of members who signed the Shaker covenant. Each family was administered by two elders and eldresses, who oversaw spiritual concerns; a staff of deacons and deaconesses, who supervised domestic operations; and trustees, who managed financial transactions with the outside World in the business office. Although the entire community worshiped together in one meetinghouse, each family was self-sufficient and equipped with its own dwelling house, workshops, and outbuildings.

Classic Shaker Design

Shaker furniture design as it gradually developed during the early nineteenth century combined two themes: the vernacular interpretation of the prevailing Chippendale and neoclassical aesthetic, and the elimination of unnecessary decorative details associated with the emerging Fancy style. As no one was born a Shaker, early craftsmen trained in the World before converting to the faith brought their taste, traditions, and technical skills with them when they joined the sect. The Shaker aesthetic that evolved during the period from the 1820s to the 1850s is a result of Worldly design traditions tempered by religious beliefs, institutional needs, and available materials. Shaker craftsmen were able to build unconventional and highly specialized furniture to suit their communal needs.

The resulting classic Shaker furniture is characterized by a combination of often subtle design elements. As they strove for functionality and simplicity, cabinetmakers

made striking use of symmetry by arranging drawers and doors in unconventional yet utilitarian combinations. Superfluous ornamentation in the form of carving, veneer, inlay, moldings, and hardware was eliminated. Instead, solid woods with natural graining and clear finishes, as well as brightly colored pigments, prevail. Opaque paints and transparent washes were used, depending on their availability, to create a neat and clean appearance. Chrome yellow, red ocher, bottle green, and Prussian blue dominated Shaker interiors, although scientific evidence shows that very few extant pieces of colorful Shaker furniture have undisturbed finishes today. Most of this disruption was certainly intentional on the part of the Shakers themselves, who removed or renewed the finish on their furniture over time, wanting it to remain neat and clean. Later Worldly owners influenced by the Arts and Crafts and Colonial Revival movements, which emphasized natural materials, deliberately stripped original paint surfaces to reveal the uncolored wood below.

1. Oval Storage Box

ca. 1830–40
Probably Canterbury, New Hampshire
Maple and white pine, with original yellow paint
Collection of Jane and Gerald Katcher

2. Oval Storage Box

Attributed to James Johnson (1776–1861)
ca. 1835–45
Canterbury, New Hampshire
Maple and white pine, with original reddish-orange paint
Collection of Jane and Gerald Katcher

3. Oval Storage Box

ca. 1840–60
Probably Alfred or Sabbathday Lake, Maine
Maple and white pine, with original blue paint
Collection of Jane and Gerald Katcher
(illustrated page 225)

The oval box is the single most recognizable form associated with the Shakers. Although not invented by the Shakers, oval boxes were manufactured in large quantities from the 1790s to the 1940s for sale to the World, as well as for Shaker use. Made in standard graduated sizes for storage of dry goods, the boxes were secured with distinctive wooden fingers, or laps, which helped control the natural expansion and contraction of the joints to prevent splitting; the fingers were reinforced with copper nails that would neither rust nor rot.

4. Side Chair

ca. 1840
Canterbury, New Hampshire
Maple, birch, and paint, with cotton seat
Collection of Canterbury Shaker Village,
Canterbury, New Hampshire, 2002.0237.1

The distinctive design of the Shaker chair evolved from the Shakers' dual position of being in the World and yet separate from it. They refined this New England ladder-back form by eliminating decorative turnings on the posts and stretchers and by often substituting a woven wool or cotton seat for the traditional splint or rush. The resulting design is an outward expression of the Shakers' internal concepts: simplicity, utility, perfection in craftsmanship, and cleanliness. When not in use, the chairs were suspended upside down from peg rails to prevent dust from settling on the seat.

Workshop Furniture

The Shakers' daily routine varied according to the time of year, the seasonal work at hand, and the skills of the individuals involved. The brethren were encouraged to master two or more occupations; this not only prevented boredom, but it also enabled the community to be less dependent on the contributions of a few key members of society. The range of these responsibilities was recorded by Brother Isaac Newton Youngs in his "Biography in Verse."

> I'm overrun with work and chores
> Upon the farm or within doors
> Which every way I turn my eyes;
> Enough to fill me with surprise.
> Of tayl'ring, join'ring, farming too,
> Almost all kinds that are to do,
> Blacksmithing, tinkering, mason work,
> When could I find time to shirk?
> Clock work, jenny work, keeping school
> Enough to puzzle any fool.
> An endless list of chores and notions,
> To keep me in perpetual motion.

The sisters were involved in a more systematic rotation of labor. They were responsible for traditional women's duties, which included monthly turns in the kitchen, bakery, laundry, and housekeeping departments, as well as in the dairy, spin shop, and herb house. The furniture in this section was made for brethren and sisters to complete textile-related activities and represents the variations in design found in different Shaker communities.

5. Case of Drawers

ca. 1840
Canterbury, New Hampshire
Pine with red paint
Collection of Canterbury Shaker Village,
Canterbury, New Hampshire, 1988.498

This chest, with its unusual grouping of shallow and deep drawers, was found in 1988 in the basement of a building at Canterbury Shaker Village, where the community's thriving textile industry was located during the twentieth century. Shaker trustees Emeline Hart (1834–1914) and Lucy Shepard (1836–1926) established a business called the Hart & Shepard Company during the 1890s to protect the Shakers' commercial interests from Worldly imitators. They successfully designed, produced, and marketed their famous cloaks and letter sweaters for

sale to the World (see cat. nos. 68–70, 72, and fig. 3-25). The shallow drawers are ideally suited to store flat pieces and the deep drawers to hold bonnets, although the original mid-nineteenth-century use of the chest is unknown. When the last sister died, this case was found by the Canterbury Shaker Village Museum, and it still contained a large number of paper patterns, cloak fabric, and related materials used in the textile business. The unidentified Canterbury cabinetmaker painted the case with an opaque red pigment that contrasts sharply with the unpainted drawer pulls.

6. Sewing Table with Add-On

Andrew Barrett (1836 or 1837–1917)
1830 (table), 1881 (gallery)
New/Mount Lebanon, New York
Written on top middle drawer of gallery: "Made by Andrew Barrett Feb 1881"
Cherry (table); cherry and pine, with porcelain knobs and brass pins (gallery)
Collection of Bob and Aileen Hamilton

This sewing table (fig. 2-21) is representative of the type commonly used at Mount Lebanon soon after mid-century. The design consists of a gallery fitted with several narrow drawers over a base that might contain one to three drawers on square tapered legs. This table's superstructure, which was added in 1881, shows the Shakers' belief in modifying and adapting existing forms to serve current needs. The drawer is inscribed and dated by the maker of the superstructure, Andrew Barrett, and fitted with commercially made porcelain knobs, which were readily available to the community. Although the 1845 Millennial Laws state that "it is not allowable for brethren to stamp, write or mark their own names upon any thing which they make for the sisters," signatures occasionally occur on furniture made after about 1860. Particularly interesting are the small brass pins that protrude from the table apron on the sides and back. One theory regarding their use is that they supported a fabric work bag underneath—a practice that was popular during the Federal period in America. A second theory is that a piece of material was suspended between the pegs to protect the seamstress from winter drafts.

7. Push-Pull Stand

ca. 1830
Hancock, Massachusetts
Cherry and pine
Collection of Robert and Katharine Booth

Traditionally, one- and two-drawer stands have been identified with sewing activities, although their actual nineteenth-century use is unknown. This example (fig 2-16) has two dovetailed drawers supported by simply fashioned cleats. The ingenious design allows two sisters working together to access each drawer by pushing or pulling the brass knobs situated at either end. Although not as common as stands with circular tops, those with rectangular tops and round corners are strongly associated with other documented pieces from Hancock in public and private collections. This stand is supported on a delicately turned cherry shaft and dramatic spider legs with a wide stance.

8. Miniature Hanging Cupboard over Drawers

1860–80
Canterbury, New Hampshire
Paper label affixed to inside of door with printed initials: "N.W.R."
Pine, cherry, iron, and brass hardware with traces of chrome yellow paint
Collection of Andrew D. Epstein
Provenance: John Keith Russell Antiques, Inc., South Salem, New York

This is an unusual scaled-down version of a free-standing Shaker cupboard over case of drawers (fig 2-1). Although the cupboard was clearly designed to hang from a peg rail or a wall, its exact purpose is still unknown. The knobs are turned with multiple concentric rings on each face, a feature exclusive to Canterbury, although the unidentified initials do not belong to a Canterbury Shaker. "N.W.R." may stand for a later owner at another community or simply refer to "North West Room" of the building where the piece was once located.

9. Sewing Case

ca. 1830
Hancock, Massachusetts
Cherry and pine with wrought iron and brass
Collection of Robert and Katharine Booth

Most of these small pieces of specialized work furniture for the sisters' sewing activities are scaled-down versions of a type of tailoring counter used by the brethren at Hancock. The desks may have drawers and doors of various sizes, numbers, and layout and can be supported either on square legs that taper toward the feet or on turned legs. Some sewing cases, including this one (fig. 2-9), are equipped with a drop leaf in the back and a swing-out forged iron support to extend the work surface. The two pull-out slides contained within a pine housing on either side may have been designed to hang additional sewing accoutrements or finished products near the work surface.

10. Sewing Desk

Attributed to Henry Green (1844–1931)
ca. 1860
Alfred, Maine
Birch and pine, with red paint and porcelain and metal pulls
Courtesy John Keith Russell Antiques Inc., South Salem, New York

The Shaker sewing desks from Maine and New Hampshire regularly display an asymmetrical layout. Here (fig. 2-6) the lower storage unit contains two unequal banks of three drawers—probably designed for utility to hold specific implements—while the gallery above is fitted with a central door flanked by six short drawers. An extra space-saving board pulls out in front to increase the work surface. These desks probably would have been used in a sisters' workroom along with up-to-date sewing machines. The design is complemented by the striking original red color—created from crushed cochineal insects—which has, remarkably, been preserved over time. Although exposure to air and light has flattened the surface patina considerably, the underside of the pull-out slide retains the original brilliant glossy finish.

11. Counter

Attributed to Grove Wright (1789–1861)
ca. 1830
Hancock, Massachusetts
Curly maple, cherry, and pine, with bone escutcheons
Collection of Bob and Aileen Hamilton

The quality of construction, the use of dramatically figured curly maple, and masterful proportions that convey a sense of grace despite the size of this piece (with a width of 5 feet) make this counter one of the masterpieces of Shaker design. The overall design represents an enlarged version of the typical small sewing case made for individual sisters at Hancock (see cat. no. 9 and fig. 2-9). This counter (fig. 2-5) exhibits the deliberate vertical and horizontal asymmetry of three drawers next to four drawers and a rear drop leaf that is supported by two wooden sliding supports. The presence of three bone escutcheons on the drawers indicates that locks were used. Although the Millennial Laws forbade the application of locks for private possessions, these fastening devices must have been considered necessary to secure the drawers, which may have held special tools or materials for the tailoring trade.

Dwelling House Furniture

Although men and women dined, met, and slept in the same building, they remained strictly segregated, passing through separate doors, staircases, and hallways. Written rules concerning furniture in retiring rooms as outlined in the Millennial Laws of 1845 suggest that they contained green beds, a table, several stands, one looking glass no larger than 12 by 18 inches, and only one rocking chair "except where the aged reside." No maps, pictures, or paintings were allowed to hang on the walls. In addition to innovative peg rails and storage units built into interior spaces, furniture consisted of moveable cases of drawers, lift-top boxes, specialized tables, washstands, and seating.

12. Washstand

ca. 1830
Hancock, Massachusetts
Cherry and pine with red wash
Collection of Robert and Katharine Booth

Because of the institutional requirements of communal living, this washstand (fig. 2-8) measuring 5 feet in length served the needs of several brethren or sisters simultaneously. It not only kept daily living neat and simple, but it also reflects a conscious awareness of pattern—the repetitive use of similar shapes, forms, and spaces to create unity and organization within a design. The alternation of two doors with three panels across the façade of the washstand creates an unusual yet harmonious rhythm that avoids the monotony of a flat surface.

13. WASHSTAND
ca. 1830
Enfield, New Hampshire
Pine with walnut knobs, yellow paint, and steel catch
Collection of Robert and Katharine Booth

With its original bold yellow paint, this washstand (fig. 2-7) undoubtedly contributed a major presence to whatever interior space it occupied. The maker exploited the asymmetrical balance between the large single door and the bank of three short drawers punctuated by solid walnut knobs against the bright surface pigment. The distinctly shaped legs, with a ringlike turning at the square-to-round transition in the leg, as well as the drawer fronts that are lipped on all four sides, are construction characteristics found on Enfield, New Hampshire, Shaker furniture.

14. BOX
ca. 1840
Canterbury, New Hampshire
Pine and maple with red paint
Courtesy John Keith Russell Antiques Inc., South Salem, New York

The stance of this 4-foot-square storage unit is notable (fig. 2-18). At first glance, the placement of the small central drawer appears to be a later addition, but closer inspection reveals that it is part of the original construction. Although one might expect to see a flat bottom when lifting the lid, there is instead a tunnel that extends from the front to the back of the case enclosing the drawer and exterior lock. Although the dovetailed bracket base is derived from Chippendale styling, the offset ogee profile is a distinguishing characteristic of Canterbury case pieces.

15. BOX
ca. 1830
Alfred, Maine
Pine with green paint and iron hinges
Courtesy John Keith Russell Antiques Inc., South Salem, New York

This simply but solidly built lift-top three-drawer box (fig. 2-13) displays a green color not seen on other Shaker furniture. The shaping and construction of the bottom rail, which is connected to the case sides with a rabbet joint to form a shallow cut foot, is a feature found on other Maine Shaker furniture.

16. BOX
ca. 1830
Enfield, New Hampshire
Written in ink on manila tag tied to key: "Key belongs to red Chest. Large"
Pine with hardwood pulls, red paint, iron hinges, iron lock, and brass escutcheon
Collection of Bob and Aileen Hamilton

The design of this piece reminds us that not all Shaker-made furniture is distinctly different from the country furniture of rural America. The chest-over-drawer form made throughout the eighteenth century in Colonial New England served as a model for this Shaker example. However, the absence of dovetailed construction and the addition of a paneled lid are not Worldly construction features. Judging from written Shaker documentation associated with a nearly identical but smaller two-drawer companion piece, both pieces were made by the same unidentified craftsman at the Enfield community in New Hampshire.

17. DOUBLE TRUSTEES' DESK
ca. 1850
Probably Watervliet, New York
Cherry and pine with yellow paint
Collection of American Folk Art Museum, New York, 2004.8.1

Each Shaker family had four trustees—two men and two women—who oversaw all business dealings with the World and were entrusted with all financial record-keeping activities. This impressive desk (fig. 2-17), was probably made for the trustees at Watervliet about 1850. The desk is fitted with cupboards containing shelves above, a slant front enclosing pigeonholes, and long drawers below. Both sides are identical to provide a similar workspace for both users.

Tables

18. TABLE
ca. 1840
Canterbury, New Hampshire
Birch, maple, and pine with red paint
Collection of Canterbury Shaker Village, Canterbury, New Hampshire, 1988.798

Tables with a deep, ogee-shaped apron tenoned into a turned or square tapering leg are a Worldly form that appeared in rural eighteenth-century New England vernacular furniture, especially in tea tables. A related example was signed by James Daniels (1767–1851), one of the founding members of the Canterbury Shaker Community, confirming the origin of this Shaker piece. Other typical construction characteristics include the drawer with a thumbnail edge on all four sides and a rectangular top with a deep overhang.

19. TRIPOD STAND
Attributed to Samuel Humphrey Turner (1775–1842)
1837
New Lebanon, New York
Stamped on underside of cleat: "SISTER ASENETH/ELD.S RUTH 1837"
Cherry with varnish
Collection of Robert and Katharine Booth

This piece (fig. 2-14) is remarkable for both its distinctive design and its documentation. Pedestal tables with simply turned shafts and arched spider legs are adapted from Sheraton prototypes and identified as originating at New Lebanon. These portable stands probably held candles initially; the 1845 Millennial Laws state that "one or two stands should be provided for the occupants of every retiring room." By the 1850s, however, the stands may have served to support lamps and probably also migrated into sewing rooms, seed shops, and kitchens.

The style of the inscription stamped on the rectangular cleat beneath the circular top relates this stand to the only known signed and dated piece of furniture by Samuel Turner, who assumed positions of leadership at the Pleasant Hill, Kentucky, community. "ELD.S RUTH" probably refers to Ruth Landon (1776–1850), appointed first female in the parent ministry at New Lebanon. Sister Aseneth Clark (1780–1857) was her assistant. This stand was clearly made in 1837 for these two leading figures, who likely shared a retiring room in the meetinghouse.

20. TRESTLE TABLE
ca. 1830
Watervliet, New York
Cherry and curly maple
Courtesy John Keith Russell Antiques Inc., South Salem, New York

Large, centrally positioned tables in monasteries and baronial halls were a medieval tradition in Europe. Such trestle tables, which were originally intended to be dismantled and stowed away at the end of the meal, were adapted by Believers for communal dining. Although they retained the same basic support system and overall size (up to 20 feet in length) to seat large groups of people, the Shakers moved the medial stretcher from its position just above the floor to just below the top in order to provide more leg room for the sisters and brethren. The Shakers' version was not disassembled but was used in a permanent location in the family dining room. Thomas Brown, a member of the Watervliet, New York, community, wrote in 1812: "The brethren and sisters generally eat at the same time at two long tables placed in the kitchen, men at one end and women at the other, during which time they sit on benches and are all silent." The short length of this table (fig. 2-3), which measures only 6 feet, suggests it may have been designed specifically for use of the four ministry leaders, who ate apart from the family brethren and sisters.

Chairs

Seating furniture was designed to serve specific needs in the meetinghouse, workshops, dining rooms, and retiring rooms. Depending on use, chairs were fitted with rockers, tilters, and arms and were seated with wood, cloth, or cane.

21. Dining Room Chair
Attributed to Micajah Tucker (1764–1848)
1834
Canterbury, New Hampshire
Birch and pine with red stain
Collection of Canterbury Shaker Village,
Canterbury, New Hampshire, 1982.113

The design of this distinctive chair (fig. 2-4) is derived from eighteenth- and nineteenth-century American Windsors, which are characterized by turned spindles; splayed, swell-tapered legs with four rungs; and shovel-shaped, undercut plank seats. They are strong, lightweight, and utilitarian, and they provide support for the lower back. According to written Shaker documentation on the history of the Canterbury community:

"Instead of chairs at the dining table, the first believers used long benches which accommodated some four or five persons each. They were not convenient, especially if one was obliged to leave the table before the others were ready. All were under the necessity of sitting just so far from the table. Elder Brother Micajah who was an excellent wood workman has now [1834] furnished the dining hall with chairs very much to the satisfaction of the family generally. At this date [1892] they are all in good order."

22. Meetinghouse Bench
ca. 1850
Enfield, New Hampshire
Birch and pine with cherry crest rail and spindles
The Shaker Museum and Library, Old Chatham and New Lebanon, New York

With their shaped plank seats and tapered comb at the top, Enfield's spindle-backed benches resemble Shaker dining chairs derived from Worldly Windsor models. Although inconvenient in dining rooms, benches functioned well in meetinghouses, where believers were not restricted by tables. They were light enough to be moved out of the way to make room for the dancing common during the Shakers' worship. The Enfield community produced settees in various sizes up to 12 ½ feet in length like this one (fig. 2-2). It has neither arms nor longitudinal stretchers, which results in an extremely delicate and structurally weaker design.

23. Armless Rocker
Freegift Wells (1785–1871)
ca. 1830
Watervliet, New York
Stamped on proper left front post: "FW"
Maple and yellow paint, with wool tape
Collection of Andrew D. Epstein

Freegift Wells recorded his daily turning, carpentry, and cabinetmaking activities in his "Memorandum of Events Covering the years 1812–1854," while he served both the Watervliet, New York (1803–71), and the Union Village, Ohio (1836–43), communities in various positions of leadership. More than any other craftsman, Brother Freegift provided documentation on the Shaker chair-making process. On May 22, 1819, he noted: "Made 26 chairs this week which is 10 short of a weeks work. It is a comfortable days work to make 6 chairs after posts & rounds

are turned and the backs bent. I have done it repeatedly." Several of his chairs retain original paint, including this example (fig. 2-12) with its striking chrome yellow pigment.

Candid Shaker historic photographs reveal how the armless rockers may have been originally used—as work seating rather than as chairs for leisure, which is how rockers are categorized today.

24. Armed Rocker
ca. 1830
Canterbury, New Hampshire
Maple or birch, cherry with red wash, varnish, and wool tape
Collection of Bob and Aileen Hamilton

Designed primarily for the elderly, Shaker-built rocking chairs (fig. 2-20) were not commonly made for children, although these small versions incorporate the form and details of adult models despite their size (this example is just over 3 feet high). The drop scroll arms and finials shaped like bowling pins with rounded tops and double shoulders are typical of rockers from Canterbury and Enfield, New Hampshire. The runners are short, which encourages gentle movement, and were practical in Shaker rooms, since the chairs could still be hung from wall pegs to save space.

Although tapes were used in the eighteenth and nineteenth centuries for clothing ties and carpet bindings, the idea of weaving cloth strips together to form a seat probably originated with the Shakers about 1830. The tapes had the advantage of being colorful, comfortable, durable, and easy to install. The earliest tapes like these were woven of homespun, home-dyed wool in a variety of colors on two- and four-harness looms. The resulting fabric tapes, called listing, were intertwined to create precise designs in checkerboard, basket-weave, or herringbone patterns. By 1860 the Shakers purchased commercially produced cotton tapes, which were readily available from the World.

25. Side Chair with Tilters
ca. 1850
New Lebanon, New York
Figured maple, cane seat, and pewter tilters
Collection of Andrew D. Epstein; formerly collection of Edward Deming Andrews and Faith Andrews

Probably no piece of furniture is more identified with Shaker design than the ladder-back chair. Although the form was derived from New England vernacular models, the Shakers simplified the process by using steam-bent slats and back posts, and they added distinctively turned finials, as well as a variety of seating materials. This example (fig. 2-11) is fitted with rattan cane, a natural fiber that contributes to its physical and visual lightness, delicacy, and portability. By about the 1840s, cane was replacing cattail rush as the primary seating material for these chairs.

The Shakers often took the realities of human behavior into consideration when making design decisions. They recognized the natural tendency for Believers to tip their straight chairs back on the rear posts and took pains "to prevent wear and tear of carpets and marking of floors" by adding tilting buttons or swivel feet to the hind legs.

26. PATENT MODEL FOR BUTTON JOINT TILTER

> George O. Donnell (1823–w. 1852)
> 1852
> New Lebanon, New York
> Bird's-eye maple and tape, with brass tilters and ferrules
> Collection of Jane and Gerald Katcher
> Photo: Bruce White

Always searching for new technologies to simplify their lives and streamline their work, the Shakers embraced change, unlike the Amish with whom they are often confused. According to Brother Elisha Myrick of the Harvard, Massachusetts, Shaker community: "Every improvement relieving human toil or facilitating labor gives time and opportunity for moral, mechanical, scientific, and intellectual improvement and the cultivation of the finer and higher qualities of the human mind." As a result of this overriding philosophy, Shaker brethren and sisters invented the flat broom, circular saw, revolving oven, commercial washing machine, chimney cap, window-sash balance and lock, metal pen nib, and permanent-press fabric, among other things. They believed that mechanical progress should be shared with the World and not be hoarded for a few people. However, experience taught them that patents were necessary to protect their economic rights and to certify their good name.

One example is the chair tilter invented by Brother G. O. Donnell of New Lebanon. This model (fig. 2-19) was submitted to the U. S. Patent Office in 1852. The ball-and-socket device was attached to the rear legs to allow "the chairs [to] take their natural motion of rocking backward and forward while the metallic feet rest unmoved: flat and square on the floor or carpet" without marring the finish. Although the wooden tilter is common in Shaker chairs, the metal variation is rare.

THE FANCY WORLD

The colorful objects in this section were not made by the Shakers. The ceramics, furniture, and wall and floor coverings shown here represent the Fancy style that was embraced by Americans from 1790 to 1840, a style the Shakers deliberately rejected in creating their own designs.

Fancy was based on an immediate visceral pleasure in activities or objects ranging from music and literature to cuisine and décor. The term implied not that an object was particularly fine or decorated but that it was a product of the imagination, that its first impression was what caught the eye and fueled the emotions. Light, color, and movement were perceived as strong stimulants that conveyed objects in the visible world to the viewer's imagination. The mind regarded Fancy objects as possessing novelty, variety, and wit, the building blocks of this popular movement.

Fancy provided a welcome alternative to the restraint of reason expressed in the neoclassical taste that had been popular in American life throughout most of the eighteenth century. The invention of the kaleidoscope by Scottish scientist David Brewster (1781–1868) in 1816 provided unexpected impetus to the popularity and proliferation of the style. The constantly changing bold colors and vivid patterns created by this optical device influenced designs for domestic furnishings and transformed an array of household goods in unexpected ways. The capricious twists and turns of glass fragments reflected by a series of mirrors placed inside a rotating cylinder fueled an emotional response generated by the moment. The kaleidoscope served as the ideal device to carry the nineteenth-century rational mind over the intellectual bridge into the new realm of ornamental abstraction.

Although expressed in pressed glass, textiles, and ceramics, the principal category of Fancy as it is recognized today comprises painted interior decoration and furniture.

Graining

Graining was popular in the early 1800s as a realistic attempt to copy mahogany, maple, and rosewood. The practice received widespread acceptance among middle-class households as an alternative to the prohibitively expensive fine woods used in furniture made for the affluent, such as the burled and highly figured woods in high-style furniture from urban centers.

Although the decorative surfaces of grained wood appear complex, most of them were simply and quickly achieved. Initially a coat of solid-colored paint—often a bright yellow, red, or orange—was applied and allowed to dry. The surface was then ready for graining. A thin layer of contrasting color dissolved in water, vinegar, or turpentine was applied with a brush, and the painter would immediately manipulate the wet coat, using combs, feathers, rags, paper or other unusual materials. Once the design was dry, a protective coat of transparent varnish or shellac would be applied; the surface could be further enhanced with colorful pigments or texturizing techniques.

Ingenious painters also sought to push the bounds of decoration well beyond polite imitation of true wood grain and moved toward highly imaginative and completely original designs. For Fancy painters committed to artistic exploration, the ultimate goal was to fill the eye with dazzling patterns and scenes and to provide the mind with a storehouse of bizarre or unconventional images.

27. TALL CASE CLOCK

ca. 1830
New Hampshire case, Connecticut works
Pine and paint
Collection of Shelburne Museum, Shelburne, Vermont, 3.10-3a-d

This neoclassical tall case clock from New Hampshire (fig. 6-20) is a very unusual example of a painted form. The whimsical surface treatment, executed only in black and yellow to resemble feathers, is highly innovative and must have succeeded in creating surprise and delight in the eyes of the nineteenth-century viewer.

28. BOX

ca. 1830
Northeastern United States
Pine and paint
Collection of Shelburne Museum, Shelburne, Vermont, 3.4-3

29. BOX

ca. 1840
Northeastern United States
Pine and paint
Collection of Shelburne Museum, Shelburne, Vermont, 3.4-44

With the exception of the feet, these two-drawer lift-top chests are similar in both form and decorative technique. Both chests feature a fanciful interpretation of faux burled wood, an effect achieved by applying a scumbled glaze over the completed design. In this technique, colorful pigments are mixed with varnish, and then a thickening agent known as megilp, a mixture of linseed oil and turpentine, is added to give the tinted finish extra body. This prevents the glaze from leveling out when it is drawn across the surface and allows it to remain thick and dark in some areas and thin and light in others. The colorful variegated glaze provides a transparent or semitransparent window to the layer of solid paint below.

30. BOX

ca. 1830
New Hampshire
Pine, brass, and paint
Collection of Shelburne Museum, Shelburne, Vermont, 3.4-42

Although the lift-top chest is an old form dating back to the Renaissance, the colorful surface makes this a very stylish piece. The one-drawer, lift-top pine box with bracket feet boldly uses brown and yellow paints to create the impression of large drapery folds—an urban neoclassical style of decoration that transforms a simple functional piece of rural New England furniture into a handsome work of art. The design is not defined by the structural divisions of the façade but serves to unite the upper box with the drawer below.

31. CHEST OF DRAWERS

Attributed to the Matteson Family
1820–30
Shaftsbury, Vermont
Pine, brass, and paint
Collection of Shelburne Museum, Shelburne, Vermont, 3.4-37

During the first quarter of the nineteenth century, various members of the Matteson family working in southwestern Vermont specialized in the exuberant decoration of simply constructed Federal-style case pieces, some of them like this one, with French feet (fig. 6-18). This conservative example of the Mattesons' painting technique clearly parrots high-style hardwood chests that date from the same period. Here the decoration is neatly confined by red banding, which is a reference to the expensive dark framing inlays and veneers of the period.

32. *Jane Henrietta Russell*

Joseph Whiting Stock (American, 1815–1855)
1844
Oil on canvas
Collection of Shelburne Museum, Shelburne, Vermont, 27.1.1-129

33. *Boy in Blue Dress with Whip and Dog*

Joseph Whiting Stock (American, 1815–1855)
ca. 1842–45
Oil on canvas
Collection of Shelburne Museum, Shelburne, Vermont, 27.1.1-50

Joseph Whiting Stock was born in Springfield, Massachusetts, in 1815. After he suffered a debilitating accident at the age of eleven, his physician encouraged him to study art. For instruction, he turned to Francis White, a student of Chester Harding, who was at the time one of the most prominent American portraitists. Stock remained largely self-taught, however, and developed his skills by copying famous paintings and making anatomical drawings. By his death in 1855, he had completed more than nine hundred paintings.

Stock incorporated a number of Fancy elements into many of his portraits. The colorful ingrain carpets that appear in both of these portraits are similar in pattern and style to cat. no. 42. Stock also surrounded each figure with lush velvet draperies and upholstered furniture, which in their material and excess are antithetical to the Shaker approach.

34. Box

A. B. Perkins
1838
Castleton, Vermont
Stenciled inside lid: "Castleton /Vt. / 1838"; sten-
ciled outside: "ABP"
Pine, iron, and paint
Collection of Shelburne Museum, Shelburne,
Vermont, 3.7.5-33

Figured maple was a readily available and popular wood for Vermont cabinetmakers who worked in the Federal style and a fash-ionable source of inspiration for Fancy painters. Maple could be simulated by using a yellow-brown glaze over a white ground color. Pushing the glaze into ridges of deeper color with a piece of cloth or leather created what was known as tiger figuring. Picking the wet glaze up into dots with a straw or stick gave the illusion of bird's-eye maple.

35. Box

ca. 1830
United States
Pine and paint
Collection of Shelburne Museum, Shelburne,
Vermont, 3.7.5-21

In the technique of sponge graining, a glaze is brushed over the ground color, and a piece of paper or leather is then pressed to create rows and circle patterns. The puckered effect caused by the glaze being gathered up by the leather is distinctive and reminiscent of burled maple.

36. Box

ca. 1830
United States
Poplar and paint
Collection of Shelburne Museum, Shelburne,
Vermont, 3.7.6-13

The painted surface of this box with a sliding top and drawer has been transformed to resemble mahogany, which was the favorite exotic wood for stylish furniture. Mahogany graining was often executed on a white-lead ground tinted pink by the addition of red pigment.

Stenciling

Painted decoration can also be achieved with stenciling, a technique in which a template of varnished paper, leather, or tin allows the exact duplication of a pattern when one paints through cutouts onto the surface below. Unlike freehand work, in which the paint is applied to a wet surface, stencils are applied to finished, dry areas of wood. Of all the ornamental techniques available during the early nineteenth century, stenciling proved to be the most efficient and assured the greatest measure of success. Stenciling was relatively easy and fast and, like most other forms of Fancy decoration, was inex-pensive to execute. It appeared on walls, fur-niture, textiles, and tin. Despite its simplicity, stenciling provided an astounding range of ornament.

37. Side Chair

William Page Eaton (1819–1904)
1830–50
Boston, Massachusetts
Painted at base of splat in black: "W. P. Eaton"
Maple, ash, and cane
Collection of Shelburne Museum, Shelburne,
Vermont, 3.3-444a

The popularity of cottage architecture, par-ticularly the designs of rural villas published by A. J. Downing in the 1840s, led to the making of country-style painted furniture such as this. Although the back of the rail and splat are grained to imitate rosewood, the front sides are stenciled with a pair of peacocks and leaves executed in gold and bronze powders. Eaton's templates for this chair and his account books still exist in the collection of Historic New England in Boston.

38. Box

1815–25
United States
Pine, iron, and leather
Collection of Shelburne Museum, Shelburne,
Vermont, 3.4-39

In American homes, ornamental painters commonly applied stenciling directly to plas-ter, where it functioned as a surrogate for boldly printed or painted wallpapers or bor-ders. This box (fig. 6-30) has an overall sten-ciled design of a diamond-and-rosette pattern executed in polychrome. The interior

is lined with Boston newspapers dated 1812 to 1816, which means that either old newspa-pers were used for the lining or that the stenciled decoration was added after the chest was made.

39. Stencil Box and Kit

Stillman Taylor (act. 1825–40)
ca. 1830
Winchendon, Massachusetts
Stenciled on lid in gold powder: "S.T."
Painted wood and mixed media
Collection of Shelburne Museum, 2004-10

Stillman Taylor was an itinerant stenciler who was active primarily in the region between Hampshire County, Massachusetts, and Cheshire County, New Hampshire, from 1825 to 1840. He carried this box (fig. 6-23) and its contents from town to town in search of jobs decorating a variety of objects, ranging from walls and furniture to trays and fire buckets, with his hand-cut stencils.

The unpredictable life-style and working conditions of a traveling artist for hire required Stillman Taylor to be resourceful. He collected both found objects and recycled materials as tools for his trade. He fashioned a cutting board out of a flattened pewter plate and used half of a broken pearl-ware plate as a palette to mix his paint. Almost half of the one hundred stencils in Taylor's repertoire were of his own design cut from personal letters and scraps of paper, as well as pages torn from account ledgers and arithmetic textbooks.

40. Double Drop Leaf Table

1820–30
New England
Pine, maple, and paint
Collection of Shelburne Museum, 3.6-92

By 1820 rosewood rivaled mahogany as the most sought-after imported wood for high-style furniture. It did not take long for artists to translate and improve upon its striking grains and flashy colors, using brown, red, and yellow to produce patterns that exagger-ated the natural appearance of rosewood (fig. 6-28).

41. Vase

ca. 1770–1800
England
Pearl ware with polychrome slip decoration
Collection of Shelburne Museum, Shelburne,
Vermont, 2005-17 a-b

This purely decorative vase was designed as fireplace garniture in direct imitation of the costly ornamental wares that Josiah Wedgwood (1730–1795) was manufacturing for England's elite during the last quarter of the eighteenth century. The urn-shape body and exuberant slip-decoration derive from Wedgwood's porphyry and jasper vases, which themselves were patterned after ancient Roman vessels uncovered at Pompeii and Herculaneum in the 1710s. The acanthus leaf handles and border, as well as the portrait medallions of unidentified Roman Caesars, also make reference to neoclassical taste.

42. Ingrain Carpet

1830–50
Northeastern United States
Plied wool yarns, Jacquard woven
Collection of Shelburne Museum, Shelburne,
Vermont, 9-F-110

During the nineteenth century, ingrain carpets were among the most common and affordable types of floor coverings in America. These colorful, flat-surfaced woven woolen rugs appear in many portraits and genre paintings (see cat. nos. 32, 33).

The jacquard mechanism patented in France by Joseph Jacquard (1752–1834) was a loom attachment that simplified the production of complex pictorial designs. Textiles that once required both a weaver and a draw boy to pull the cords that controlled the pattern warps could now be made by one person. The pattern was determined by a device that was programmed by punched cards, like those of an early computer, and it governed the raising and lowering of the warp threads in a predetermined sequence that created the Fancy design—in this case, rose tiles on a foliate background.

Ingrain was woven in strips of various widths that were seamed together to create wall-to-wall carpeting. It could be considered two carpets for the price of one, since it was reversible. Most ingrain has a double-weave structure, meaning it is made of two interconnected layers of cloth woven simultaneously. The result is cloth with the design on the front repeated on the back but with the colors reversed. This inexpensive new carpet helped working families cover still more surfaces with vibrant color and rich layered patterns that create a kind of woven pointillism.

43. Work Table

1810–20
Connecticut
Maple, pine, and glass with stenciled decoration
Collection of Shelburne Museum, Shelburne,
Vermont, 3.6-56

Theorems, or theorem paintings, were made by using stencils, even though the process of making pictures with them was called painting. The stenciling technique was actually more mechanical than creative and was easy to learn. Girls could fashion their own patterns and paint a composition by laying down one stencil at a time, applying color through its openings, and then removing it. The meticulous process was then repeated for each element until the picture was complete. Similar techniques were used to decorate furniture.

The exuberant decoration that fills the entire top of this work table includes a basket of flowers on each drop leaf and a central scene of a mother in a garden with five daughters. The table legs are covered with a scroll pattern produced by sponging paint onto the surface of the wood. The glass pulls and turned legs place this table in the Empire style.

44. Comb-back Rocking Chair

1820–30
Probably New Hampshire
Maple, ash, pine, and paint
Collection of Shelburne Museum, Shelburne,
Vermont, 3.3-285

The painted decoration virtually sings with an orange-red and black background, floral and leaf decoration in green, yellow, and bronze on both the rail and comb, and exuberant swirls on the seat (fig. 6-41).

45. Footstool

ca. 1840
Possibly Maine
Pine and paint
Collection of Shelburne Museum, Shelburne,
Vermont, 3.7.2-5

This footstool combines painting and stenciling techniques. The common red-and-black graining was executed with the dry technique, which was a simple and primitive method of decoration. After laying on the ground color with transparent varnish-based paints and letting it dry, the painter brushed on the top color in the desired pattern. The floral and geometric stencils were then applied with bronze powder.

46. Cradle

ca. 1810
United States
Wood and paint
Collection of Shelburne Museum, Shelburne,
Vermont, 3.5-15

This cradle is painted with an unusual continuous eye-with-eyelash motif in a free improvisational style that looks like the Fancy painter's version of doodling.

47. Box

ca. 1820
United States
Poplar, paint, and iron
Collection of Shelburne Museum, Shelburne,
Vermont, 3.4-64

The colorful sponging on this box was executed while the paints or glazes were still wet. Once dry, the decoration in green, yellow, and red was given a coat of varnish to give the surface a glossy finish.

48. Hearth Brush

ca. 1820
United States
Wood and paint
Collection of Shelburne Museum, Shelburne,
Vermont, 42.2-2

Even this small hearth brush did not escape the Fancy treatment. Every visible wooden surface is sponge decorated.

49. Hanging Shelf

ca. 1840
United States
Painted wood
Collection of Shelburne Museum, Shelburne,
Vermont, 3.7.4-24

This flight of shelves is remarkable for both its unusual form and its striking decoration. The edge is cut with a hand bow saw and consists of gentle curves at each end that become more angular and jagged at the center. Over the yellow ocher undercoat, the maker has fashioned a fantastic, unheard-of wood grain out of a darker brown that swirls diagonally across the uprights.

50. Selection of Mocha Ware

1800–1840
England
Slip-decorated creamware
Collection of Shelburne Museum, Shelburne, Vermont, 31.16.3-5, 31.16.2-32, 31.16.3-63, 31.16.3-20, 31.16.3-69

Some of the most stunning products available from Fancy stores in the early nineteenth century were whimsical and brilliantly painted ceramics (fig. 6-35). They were covered with vibrant colors and lively designs, and although they were utilitarian, they also served as vehicles for imaginative play. The term "Mocha ware" is derived from the design, which resembles agate, a semi-precious stone that was widely used in fashionable jewelry of the period. Agate was exported in great quantities from the port of Mocha (al-Muhka in Yemen) to London and was given the nickname "Mocha stone."

Most of these eye-catching ceramics were relatively inexpensive and featured ornamental techniques similar to those employed for Fancy furniture. The decoration of Fancy ceramics and furniture has an obvious parallel in the way the artisan worked wet slip over clay and wet paint over wood. The earthenware surfaces displayed here were enhanced to create faux finishes that gave the illusion of marble, agate, or granite. Abstract designs patterns called fan, cat's eye, and cable were also developed and seem to emulate grained or sponge-decorated wood.

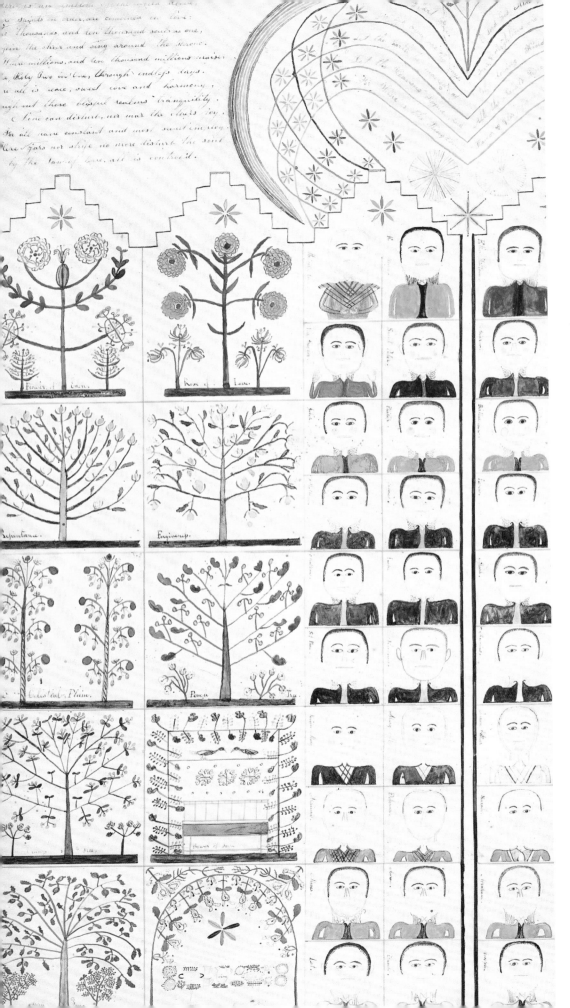

THE SPIRITUAL WORLD

The concept of spiritual gifts is a very important one to the Shakers. It is derived from the biblical idea that "every good gift and every perfect gift is from above, and cometh down from the Father of light" (James 1:17). For the Shakers, any spark of the divine is a gift, one that often provides guidance or moral direction in daily life. Gifts can be as simple, as sweeping, or as dramatic as whirling in place for hours on end. They can also relate to the practice of the Shaker faith, such as the gift for each community to receive a spiritual name, or for a "fountain stone" to be erected on a holy feast ground. Gifts can be oral or written communications.

Between 1837 and about 1859, during the brief period of intensive spiritual revival known as the Era of Manifestations or Mother's Work, elaborate drawings and emotional, instructive songs were received as gifts. Heavenly spirits, including biblical personages and deceased Shaker leaders, angels, saints, and even figures from secular history, such as George Washington and Christopher Columbus, were believed to appear to spiritually attuned Shaker mediums, known as instruments. These instruments were able to receive messages or gifts from the celestial sphere, and they or another person would transcribe them on paper.

Gift Drawings

Drawing was a means of translating the symbolic gifts received during the Era of Manifestations into a more tangible form. The great majority of the two hundred extant examples are from New Lebanon, New York, or Hancock, Massachusetts, and, with only a few exceptions, they are the work of Shaker women. To the third-generation Shakers who never knew Mother Ann personally, these communications from celestial correspondents confirmed her actual existence and provided insight into the next world.

The very existence of gift drawings reflects the Shakers' interest in the spirit world yet at the same time seems to contradict their rejection of art and decoration displayed on walls. It is not clear from surviving documents how the Shaker community viewed the gift drawings. The 1845 Millennial Laws state that "no maps, charts and no pictures or paintings shall ever be hung up in your dwelling rooms, shops, or office. And no pictures or paintings set in frames with glass before them shall ever be among you." This ruling suggests that gift pictures were not framed, glazed, or displayed on an everyday basis during the period of Mother Ann's Work. Instead, they may have been kept privately by the medium or by the spiritual leadership in the ministry and were revealed to Believers only on specific occasions.

Over time, the drawings were placed in storage and were occasionally forgotten by the Shakers until the early twentieth century, when they were rediscovered with renewed interest. Catherine Allen, an eldress at Mount Lebanon, sent a variety of Shaker materials, including gift drawings, to the Western Reserve Historical Society in Cleveland and the American Society for Psychical Research in New York City for safekeeping. Others are in the collections of the Shaker community at Sabbathday Lake, Maine, or institutions associated with Shaker sites, museums, and historical societies; many may be held privately.

51. HAND-COLORED LITHOGRAPH: *Shakers, Their Mode of Worship*

> Published by D.W. Kellogg and Co.
> ca. 1832–40
> Hartford, Connecticut
> Collection of Shaker Museum and Library, Old Chatham, New York, 10514

Unity of worship had made firm inroads into ecstatic-based worship by 1788, when Father Joseph Meacham learned, in a vision from angels dancing before the throne of God, the Square Order Shuffle, which is depicted here (fig. 5-2). In this pattern, Believers arranged themselves in rows, with women at one end facing men at the other. The two ranks advanced toward each other, turned around, and took three steps back to the place of beginning, then advanced up again and receded backward with the double step. Curious spectators from the World, seen at the left, were invited to observe the meetinghouse ritual. In 1832 a visitor to New Lebanon was impressed by the neatness of the building; the smooth floor; the sallow complexions of the sisters in contrast with the healthy, ruddy appearance of the brethren; and the presence of several African-Americans, both male and female, among the worshipers.

52. GIFT DRAWING, *I am the Lord Your God*

> 1843
> New Lebanon, New York
> Ink on paper
> Collection of Robert and Katharine Booth

With the exception of some communications in unknown tongues, Shaker gift drawings were not believed to be the work of a spirit guiding the hand of an artist. On the contrary, Shaker drawings were carefully planned, composed, and executed and were acknowledged to be the conscious act of their creators. Often they depicted a vision previously received—either by the artist or by another instrument. Shaker artists occasionally created more than one image of the same vision. Two virtually identical versions of this geometric drawing have survived.

53. GIFT DRAWING, *From Mother Ann Lee to her daughter, Eliza Ann Taylor*

> Eleanor Potter (1812–1895)
> 1847
> New Lebanon, New York
> Fan-shape cutout, ink, and watercolor on paper
> Collection of Shaker Museum and Library, Old Chatham, New York, 8129

In 1845 the New Lebanon domestic journals listed the employment of Eleanor Potter as "mender of the brethren's clothes"—an assignment that clearly demanded sewing skills. This drawing gives evidence that she was aware of stitches far more elaborate and fanciful than any she would have used in repairing clothing for members of the society. She bordered the edge of this fan-shape cutout with pen-and-ink strokes resembling the Fancy stitches that in secular culture would appear in a crazy quilt.

54. GIFT DRAWING, *From Holy Mother Wisdom to Sally Lomise*

> Sarah Bates (1792–1881)
> 1847
> New Lebanon, New York
> Circular cutout, ink, and paper
> Collection of American Folk Art Museum, New York, P1.2001.301d

GIFT DRAWING, *For Ursula Bishop*

> Polly Ann (Jane) Reed (1818–1881)
> 1844
> New Lebanon, New York
> Heart-shape cutout, ink, and paper
> Collection of American Folk Art Museum, New York, P1.2001.301a

GIFT DRAWING, *For Eleanor Potter* (FIG. 5-7)

> Polly Ann (Jane) Reed (1818–1881)
> 1844
> New Lebanon, New York
> Heart-shape cutout, ink, and paper
> Collection of American Folk Art Museum, New York, P1.2001.301b

GIFT DRAWING, *For Jane Smith*

> Polly Ann (Jane) Reed (1818–1881)
> 1844
> New Lebanon, New York
> Heart-shape cutout, ink, and paper
> Collection of American Folk Art Museum, New York, P1.2001.301c

These four drawings were executed by Sisters Sarah Bates and Polly Ann (Jane) Reed, companions in the First Order of the Church, a group of families that represents the highest level of commitment to the Shaker faith, at New Lebanon. Both were tailoresses, scribes, and expert calligraphers who also taught in the girls' school. Many of the same materials and skills that emphasized written composition and precise writing ability were required to produce this spiritual art. These sisters also had at their disposal an instrument of high quality—the silver-nibbed pen that the Shakers were manufacturing by the 1820s.

The meaning of the symbols they used is not always clear, although their ultimate source may have been in the language of the Bible. A Shaker diarist, commenting in 1840 on the phenomena of Mother Ann's Work, reflected this uncertainty: "There is . . . an endless variety of gifts, and spiritual presents, bro't and given to us collectively & individually, much of which we do not fully understand & some of which we do understand as being signs and representations of divine things—such as lamps—doves—branches, balls of love, crosses &c &c."

Among the emblems introduced by Sarah Bates in the circular cutout are two feathers, one from the wings of the Heavenly Father and the other from the wings of Holy Mother Wisdom. These references to God are expressed here in paternal and maternal terms in accordance with the Shaker conception of deity. Perhaps the most engaging symbols in this drawing are the fanciful lamp and the musical instrument. Imaginary machines of various kinds, often with wheels and pulleys, are not uncommon in the gift drawing tradition at New Lebanon, a reflection perhaps of the inventive spirit that animated life in the Shaker communities. The Bates drawing is inscribed to Sally Lomise (or Loomis), a member of the ministry of the Shaker villages at Harvard and Shirley, Massachusetts.

Some gift images were executed in the shape of the gift, as in the case of the three small, meticulous, two-sided heart-shape cutouts dating from 1844. Reed's heart-shape drawings were intended as tokens of encouragement and reward to each of the members of the Shaker family at New Lebanon, where the artist lived.

55. GIFT DRAWING, *A Holy & Sacred Roll, sent from Holy & Eternal Wisdom*

> Sarah Bates (1792–1881)
> 1846
> New Lebanon, New York
> Ink and watercolor on paper
> Collection of The Berkshire Athenaeum, Pittsfield, Massachusetts

Sacred rolls incorporate complex symbolic language through text and imagery. There is often a visual representation of unknown tongues that frames the work with a picture of a heart at its center. The upper two-thirds of the composition is separated from the bottom third by a horizontal line, which probably represents the division between the heavenly and the earthly spheres. Another, less apparent distinction is made between male and female. Depicted at the top of each sacred sheet are the wings of the Heavenly Father on the right and the wings of Holy Mother Wisdom on the left. The bottom register or earthly realm often contains specific references from Shaker history.

56. GIFT DRAWING, *A sacred sheet sent from Holy Mother Wisdom by her Holy Angel*

> Semantha Fairbanks (1804–1852)
> and Mary Wicks (1819–1898)
> 1843
> New Lebanon, New York
> Blue ink on paper
> Collection of American Society for Psychical Research, New York

Semantha Fairbanks grew up in the Church Family of New Lebanon and had become a deaconess by 1840. During the Era of Manifestations (1837–ca. 1859), she periodically entered a state of trance in order to receive and verbalize spirit communications. She is credited with the execution of six drawings that are categorized as sacred sheets. This example (fig. 5-13) rendered in blue ink with four red seals is geometric in format and composed entirely of cryptic messages in unknown tongues. It may have been received by inspiration during a series of meetings for worship between January and March of 1843. This gift to Fairbanks confirms that Shaker artists and scribes recorded gifts intended for themselves. Sacred sheets are some of the most mysterious and fascinating works ever produced by the Shakers.

57. GIFT DRAWING, *From Mother Ann to Amy Reed*

> Sarah Bates (1792–1881)
> 1848
> New Lebanon, New York
> Ink and watercolor on paper
> Collection of Shaker Museum and Library, Old Chatham, New York, 11520

Drawn on blue paper and composed in a wider palette than most, this work (fig. 5-12) by Sarah Bates is a colorful and lively version of the sacred rolls. The individual visual elements are carefully labeled: A Rose Bush, A Heavenly Flower, A Branch from Holy Mother's Weeping Willow, and Father William's Message-bearing Dove.

58. GIFT DRAWING, *A Table of Faith and Sweet Smelling Rose Bush from Seth Y. Wells*

> Attributed to Phebe Ann Smith (1817–1872)
> ca. 1846
> Watervliet, New York
> Ink and watercolor
> Collection of Canterbury Shaker Village, Canterbury, New Hampshire, 788

Roses are not uncommon symbols in gift drawings, but it is not clear that they had an overarching significance for the Shakers. Sometimes they are identified in the drawings by such names as Roses of Holy Wisdom's Approbation, Ever-Blooming Rose, or a Spiritual Rose Bush. An undated manuscript record in the Andrews collection by a Shaker brother, Elder David Austin Buckingham of Watervliet, New York, categorizes various symbols by their meaning. He states that roses signify love and chastity, which is in accord with their Worldly meaning.

59. GIFT DRAWING, *A Little Basket Full of Beautiful Apples for the Ministry*

> Hannah Cohoon (1788–1864)
> 1846
> Hancock, Massachusetts
> Ink and watercolor on paper
> Andrews Collection, Hancock Shaker Village, Pittsfield, Massachusetts, 1963.111.0001

Sister Hannah Cohoon's five paintings are among the boldest that survive. Unlike most other instruments, Hannah signed all of her known works. This drawing (fig. 5-18), which is among the most appealing, depicts a highly stylized basket of apples intended as a gift from two long-deceased Shakers, Calvin

Harlow and Sarah Harrison, through the spirit of Judith Collins. A chain wound around the basket's handle "represents the combination of their blessing." The text that appears in the drawing's upper register is a simple greeting in verse, typical of spirit messages in gift drawings: "Come, come my beloved/And sympathize with me/Receive the little basket/And the blessing for free."

60. GIFT DRAWING, *A Type of Mother Hannah's Pocket Handkerchief*

Polly Ann (Jane) Reed (1818–1881)
1851
New Lebanon, New York
Ink and watercolor on paper
Andrews Collection, Hancock Shaker Village,
Pittsfield, Massachusetts, 1963.126.0001

Polly Reed "did the work by dictation of the medium to whom the message & the vision were given." In this drawing (fig. 5-9), the gifts of the spirit are arrayed around the Lamb of Innocence, probably a reference to Jesus. Intended as a gift for Jane Blanchard, the drawing contains a text stating that the handkerchief belonged to Mother Hannah (d. 1816), the founding eldress of the communities at Harvard and Shirley, Massachusetts, and one of Ann Lee's missionary companions. It was said that Father James Whitaker, an English convert and early disciple of Ann Lee, actually painted the picture on the handkerchief. Mid-century Shakers would look back in time to recover the symbolic presence of an historical Ann Lee as they simultaneously looked ahead to a millennial future, when the gifts of the spirit would be distributed to members "of every nation, kindred, tongue and people."

Polly Reed's training as a tailoress at New Lebanon is suggested by the execution of this drawing. The creation of this large, intricate watercolor from individual motifs reflects her knowledge of sewing, working with remnants, and piecing fabric together. The gift drawings share similarities with such traditional feminine crafts in the outside world as appliquéd quilting and embroidered samplers and bedcovers.

61. GIFT DRAWING, *A Present from Mother Lucy to Eliza Ann Taylor*

Polly Ann (Jane) Reed (1818–1881)
1849
New Lebanon, New York
Ink and watercolor on paper
Miller Collection, Hancock Shaker Village,
Pittsfield, Massachusetts, 1963.106.0001

This is one of Polly Reed's most fully developed and complex works. Rendered in watercolor, the drawing (fig. 5-8) has as its principal focus a dwelling house with double front doors, like those of a Shaker residence. With a tiny eye at the center of its roof and mosaic tiles at its entrance, the building is also reminiscent of a Masonic temple. The imagery includes an angel of peace carrying a colorful leaf of peace and wearing a crown of plaited thorns. There is also an open book and a breastplate from Socrates.

Eliza Ann Taylor, the recipient of this drawing, arrived in New Lebanon in 1819. She attained the highest female rank within the Shaker church in 1869, that of First Eldress, a position she held until her death in 1891.

62. GIFT DRAWING FOR ASENETH CLARK, *The Word of the Lord Almighty Jehovah, To a Daughter of his Everlasting Love*

Polly Ann (Jane) Reed (1818–1881)
1844
New Lebanon, New York
Ink and watercolor on paper
Collection of Bob and Aileen Hamilton
(illustrated page xiii)

Polly Reed is assumed to have created a heart-shape cutout for every member of the First Order of the Church at New Lebanon. This example, which measures 4½ by 4⅝ inches, is somewhat larger than the others, which are closer to 4 by 4 inches. The increased size of this gift drawing may reflect the position of Aseneth Clark (1780–1857) in the lead ministry. Her elevated stature is also suggested by the tripod stand (see cat. no. 9) that is stamped with her name and attributed to cabinetmaker Samuel Humphrey Turner. Perhaps Aseneth kept her gift heart in a special place in her room in the ministry dwelling near the tripod stand.

Gift Songs

Although about two hundred gift drawings have been accounted for, this number is small when compared to the ten thousand surviving songs that were received in every Shaker village by brethren and sisters alike throughout the Era of Manifestations. According to Brother Isaac Newton Youngs (1793–1865), there were three hundred new anthems produced in the first ten years of the revival period, nearly one thousand "little anthem-like songs for use in the intervals between exercise and speaking and over 2500 songs for exercise."

Gift songs were sometimes received in great numbers by a single Believer in a short span of time, and especially talented Shakers kept paper and pen near their beds while they slept so that the inspired verses could be remembered in the morning. Shaker scribes duly recorded hundreds of gift songs in manuscript songbooks to be circulated and sung by the community at large during regular worship. The songs were also integrated into new rituals that emerged during the period, such as Walking the Narrow Path or the Cleansing Gift, which included fasting, singing, and cleaning. Unlike the drawings, Shaker songs were gifts shared among Believers, and they played an important role in bringing the community into union and order and in strengthening the Believers' faith.

63. *A Short Abridgement of the Rules of Music*

Isaac Newton Youngs (1793–1865)
1843
New Lebanon, New York
Ink on paper, bound in leather
Collection of Shaker Museum and Library, Old
Chatham, New York, Op-3

Brother Isaac Newton Youngs pursued a variety of interests, including cabinetmaking, tailoring, and clockmaking, but he was especially passionate about music and worked continuously to develop and refine Shaker music theory. This text explains the system of using the distinctive "letteral" music notation invented by the Shakers, which was an efficient and accurate method of recording melodies. This process used a central pitch, for instance C in the natural major mode, as the focus for a song. The central pitch was placed in the middle of a blank space or along the center line of a section of lined paper. Pitches were then denoted with letters (D, E, F, G, A, B, C) placed either above or below the C to indicate whether the note lay in the octave above or below. This ingenious system allowed people with no formal musical training to read and even write music more easily. The efficiency of the system provided for the quick notation of inspirational songs, which came at the rate of hundreds per year during some particularly ecstatic periods.

64. Music Staff Writing Pen and Box
Isaac Newton Youngs (1793–1865)
1820
Etched in brass: "L. W." (possibly Mother Lucy Wright, 1760–1821)
Cherry, brass, and paper
Collection of Bob and Aileen Hamilton

This five-pointed pen was designed by clockmaker Isaac Newton Youngs to save time writing music—one pull across the page and the whole musical staff was complete. The paper label inside the case bears Youngs's initials and reads: "This pen may be used either side up—but if it will not make good lines without bearing on too hard, it needs some repair." According to recent research conducted by Shaker scholar Steve Paterwic, this pen may have been given by Brother Isaac to Shaker leader Mother Lucy Wright, who was one of Mother Ann's successors at New Lebanon. Based on the written inscription that accompanies the pen identifying subsequent ownership, Paterwic surmises that it may have traveled from New York to the Enfield, New Hampshire, community with two Shaker sisters in 1874. They made the journey to learn how to play the organ from Brother James Russell just months before a great fire destroyed eight buildings, including the dwelling house, of the Church Family at Mount Lebanon.

65. Hymnal, *A Sacred Repository of Anthems and Hymns, for Devotional Worship and Praise*
Henry Clay Blinn (1824–1905), compiler
1852
Canterbury, New Hampshire
Ink on paper, bound in leather
Collection of Shaker Museum and Library, Old

Chatham, New York, 8792

Anthems were spontaneous, rhapsodic songs with each line set to music that does not repeat, a technique that suited the free-flowing format of the inspired message. Similar in nature to gift drawings, anthems had wandering melodies and exalted language. Hymns, on the other hand, were characterized by multiple stanzas using the same melody in a repetitive verse structure (often AAB); they were doctrinal in nature, often describing events or religious ideas in narrative form. From about 1805 to the 1820s, hymns were learned, rehearsed, and integrated into the worship ritual.

Gift songs were included in the society's printed hymnals, most notably Elder Henry Blinn's *Sacred Repository of Anthems and Hymns*, which is remarkable because it utilizes letteral notation in print. Sometimes the circumstances of the song's reception are noted, as with this anthem "Trumpet of Peace," which was "learned by inspiration" at New Lebanon in 1839 by Elder Sister Olive Spencer. She recalled that the song was sung "by the Angel of Light, which Mother Ann saw at the masthead," referring to the miracle at sea when Ann Lee and her disciples journeyed to America.

66. Manuscript, *A Collection of Songs, or Sacred Anthems, mostly given by Inspiration . . .*
Polly Ann (Jane) Reed (1818–1881), compiler and copyist
1840–42
New Lebanon, New York
Bound manuscript; blue ink on paper, bound in leather
Collection of American Society for Psychical Research, New York

The gift songs in this 279-page manuscript volume (fig. 5-19) were recorded during 1840–42, the heart of Mother Ann's Work. They were compiled in the First Order of the Church at New Lebanon by Polly Reed and copied in her meticulous handwriting, using Shaker letteral notation. Several songs are rendered in unknown tongues, such as "Jana de Tan molia."

67. *Millennial Praises, Containing a Collection of Gospel Hymns . . .*
Seth Youngs Wells (1767–1847), compiler
1813
Printed at Hancock, Massachusetts by Josiah Tallcott Jr.
Book
Ink on paper, bound in leather
Collection of Shaker Museum and Library, Old Chatham, New York, 5100

Millennial Praises is a book of hymns and anthems without notation that marked the acceptance of the hymn as a more useful form of devotion than the early chants and wordless solemn songs. The texts received the general approval of the leadership of the church and contain doctrinal statements that made the Shaker teachings more accessible to new converts who were still coming to grips with Mother Ann's message.

The preface to *Millennial Praises* warned the society against regarding these compositions as eternally useful, "for no gift or order of God can be binding on Believers for a longer term of time than it can be profitable to their travel in the gospel." It is ironic that these hymns, which contrasted the church and the outside World, were sung to tunes largely borrowed from the World.

THE COMMERCIAL WORLD

The Shakers interacted with the outside world through many successful entrepreneurial ventures to support their communal way of living. From the 1790s to the present, the Believers have developed, marketed, and sold a wide variety of goods to customers outside the United Society. These products of Shaker lands and Shaker hands—ranging from packaged seeds to poplarware destined for sale to the World, as they put it—are represented here.

From their early years, Shaker communities sold the surplus food and goods they had made. With the money they earned from these endeavors, the Shakers purchased raw materials or merchandise they could not produce themselves, such as metals, glass, ceramics, and brick. In this way, the Shaker villages developed an economic system that supported their communal life-style. Without these industries, the Shakers could not have survived as a religious society living apart from mainstream America.

Accustomed to making for themselves large quantities of chairs and brooms, pails and storage boxes, cheese and dried sweet corn, the Shakers easily applied their skills to mass-producing these goods—and many others—for sale to the World. Trusted brethren and sisters were designated to sell their merchandise in nearby towns and later in shops within Shaker villages. They also developed a sophisticated mail-order system. Today the Sabbathday Lake family successfully markets its herbs over the Internet.

Thus, the Shakers came to know the World and the World came to know them. Their products became widely known for exceptional quality, as the sect developed a reputation for honest business dealings, trustworthiness, and fairness. All this helped to overcome the early suspicion, even hostility, faced by what was viewed as a peculiar sect. Simon Atherton, trustee at the Harvard Shaker community (1829–1888), summarized this philosophy with a motto: "A good name is better than riches." This statement was echoed by all of the communities with various implied guarantees of quality.

In the last two decades of the 1800s, it was primarily Shaker sisters in the Maine and New Hampshire communities, and at Mount Lebanon, New York, who met the challenge of keeping the movement alive—through strong leadership and by providing economic support to their villages through the products of their hands. Both factors prevailed throughout the twentieth century.

Hart & Shepard

Sometime during the 1890s, Shaker trustees Emeline Hart (1834–1914) and Lucy Shepard (1836–1926) of Canterbury formed a company (Hart & Shepard) to market textile products, such as sweaters, cloaks, wool stockings, and yarn dust mops, to the World.

68. DARTMOUTH GREEN TURTLENECK LETTER SWEATER
Label: "Hart & Shepard"
ca. 1910
Canterbury, New Hampshire
Wool and leather
Collection of M. Stephen and Miriam Miller

69. WHITE COAT SWEATER WITH SHAWL COLLAR
Label: "Hart & Shepard"
ca. 1910
Canterbury, New Hampshire
Wool and pearlized buttons
Collection of M. Stephen and Miriam Miller

70. BLUE COAT SWEATER WITH SHAWL COLLAR
Label: "Hart & Shepard"
ca. 1910
Canterbury, New Hampshire
Wool and pearlized buttons
Collection of Canterbury Shaker Village, Canterbury, New Hampshire, 1988.2393.0001

In 1901 Hart & Shepard registered as a trademark the name "Shaker Sweater" with the state of New Hampshire in order to protect their industry from imitators. Their designs included machine-knit woolen turtleneck letter sweaters for Harvard (fig. 3-25), Princeton, Yale, and Dartmouth students and jacket sweaters with V-neck and shawl collars for popular use. The sweaters were sold wholesale and also retail in department stores until 1922. Although the name "Shaker Knit" remains popular today, the cotton crew-neck and raglan-sleeve cardigan versions made by mail-order companies such as L. L. Bean and Lands' End have little to do with the Shakers' original design.

71. RULER
ca. 1890
Probably Canterbury, New Hampshire
Maple
Collection of M. Stephen and Miriam Miller

Although no manuscript documentation is known, the numbers and provenance of surviving wooden rulers suggest that they were made at Canterbury and probably intended for sale. These measurement devices range from 6 inches to over 4 feet in length and are marked with meticulously hand-stamped numbers. With their interest in precision, the Shakers made their own rulers, each suited to a specific task. This example, which is 54 inches long, was used in the cloak-making industry.

72. THE DOROTHY CLOAK
Design attributed to Eldress Dorothy Durgin (1825–1898)
ca. 1925
Canterbury, New Hampshire
Wool and silk
Collection of Canterbury Shaker Village, Canterbury, New Hampshire, 2002.258.3

Another important sales item, a cloak called "The Dorothy," is attributed to Canterbury Eldress Dorothy Durgin, who based her unique design on a raincoat she owned and found to be exceptional in design and function. An excellent tailor, she dismantled the coat to provide a pattern for a woolen cloak she made for herself. Large-scale production began in the 1890s. In 1903, The Dorothy cloak was granted trademark protection. Made from fine French broadcloth with a silk lining and ribbons, this opera-style cloak with pleated hood and pockets was available in sizes from doll to adult size and was successfully marketed around the world. Fashionable as well as functional, a "Genuine Shaker Cloak" was worn by Grover Cleveland's wife to his second inauguration in 1893.

Fancy Goods

The last Shaker textile industries fall under the broad category of "fancywork," a term rejected in the 1845 Millennial Laws and later embraced in the twentieth century to successfully market products that included brushes and dusters, pincushions in various shapes and sizes, and an innovation called poplarware. During the Victorian era, the Shakers deliberately incorporated design and taste trends of the period into their products. Although some critics may accuse the Shakers of selling out to the World in designing their fancywork, this enterprise was a tangible symbol of the Shakers' ability to adapt to changing times in order to survive.

These colorful, portable, and whimsical fancy goods were inexpensively produced in various Shaker villages and were sold to supply the tourist trade with mementos of a visit. The enterprising sisters themselves also peddled these items, first by wagon and then by car, to resort hotels and vacation spots from Maine to Florida. As the number of Shaker brethren declined, fancywork assumed an increasingly heavy share of the income-producing burden. Eventually, sales trips were curtailed and the gift stores at the villages provided the last venue for Shaker textile products. The last remaining community, at Sabbathday Lake, Maine, continues this tradition of handcrafted work into the twenty-first century.

73. THE CANTERBURY GIFT SHOP
Probably photographed by Brother Irving Greenwood (1876–1939)
ca. 1910
Canterbury, New Hampshire
Shaker Museum and Library, Old Chatham, New York

In the 1890s, Shaker communities began operating souvenir shops to sell mostly small handmade items to tourists. These shops were located inside the trustees' offices, where the public was welcomed. Many of the types of items pictured in this 1910 view at Canterbury, such as spool stands, tomato and bureau cushions, and wool dusters, are included in the exhibition.

74. WOOL DUSTERS

ca. 1910
Mount Lebanon, New York, or Canterbury, New Hampshire
Maple and dyed wool
Collection of M. Stephen and Miriam Miller

Two communities made this style of duster in large numbers (see fig. 3-31). Strands of different colored wool were fastened to the turned wooden handles with wire, and a hanging string was fitted to the other end.

75. BRUSHES

Attributed to Ada Cummings (1862–1926)
ca. 1920
Sabbathday Lake, Maine
Maple with natural horsehair and varnish finish
Collection of M. Stephen and Miriam Miller

Considering their total commitment to spiritual and physical cleanliness, it is not surprising that nearly every Shaker community produced brushes and full-size brooms during the nineteenth century. Images of sweeping away sin appear in several of the most sacred expressions of their faith—their hymns.

These delicate twentieth-century examples (see fig. 3-31) were generally referred to as hat or clothing brushes and were made at both Sabbathday Lake and Canterbury communities. Sister Ada Cummings was in charge at Sabbathday Lake, and her brushes featured a pinked velvet "skirt" between the bristles and the turned handle. Available in two sizes, all brushes were made with a means for hanging, either a drilled hole or a turned knob to accommodate a string or ribbon tie.

76. SCREWBALLS

late 19th century
Canterbury, New Hampshire
Maple, wool, ash rickrack, and fabric
Collection of M. Stephen and Miriam Miller

Nineteenth-century Canterbury sisters called these table-clamped pincushions "screwballs." Although no two cushions are identical, the basic design and materials are always similar: two pieces of maple turned on a lathe by brethren and then covered with a variety of fabrics, filled with wood shavings, and finished with rickrack or braid by sisters.

77. BUREAU CUSHION

1900–1910
Canterbury, New Hampshire
Turned maple, velvet, brass feet, and ash rickrack
Collection of M. Stephen and Miriam Miller

This type of pincushion was designed to sit on top of a dresser (see fig. 3-27).

78. SEWING CASE

Painted by Cora Helena Sarle (1867–1956)
ca. 1930
Canterbury, New Hampshire
Linen and felt with paint
Collection of M. Stephen and Miriam Miller

This foldout fabric sewing case with accoutrements displays both machine and hand stitching. This example is special because of the painted flowers, which are probably the work of Sister Cora Helena Sarle, an amateur painter best known for two volumes of watercolor drawings of the flora at Canterbury.

79. SCALLOP-SHELL PINCUSHION

ca. 1880
Sabbathday Lake, Maine
Shell, velvet, and wood shavings
Collection of M. Stephen and Miriam Miller

Although this pincushion was never illustrated in their catalogues, individual sisters at the North Family, Sabbathday Lake, Maine, made these scallop-shell cushions for sale (see fig. 3-27).

80. SPOOL STANDS

1910–20
Canterbury, New Hampshire
Pine and cherry (pink), pine and maple (white), with velvet and poplar
Collection of M. Stephen and Miriam Miller

This tomato-shape pincushion came equipped with an emery bag in the form of a strawberry for sharpening needles; a wax cake to strengthen the thread; and a needle case of felt or woven poplar attached to a turned hardwood stand. The base is fitted with metal pins to hold commercial spools of thread (fig. 3-27). The printed cardboard packaging clearly indicates that the stand was manufactured at Canterbury. Several communities manufactured stands that were nearly identical to these, among them Alfred, Mount Lebanon, and Sabbathday Lake.

81. TOMATO PINCUSHION AND BOX

ca. 1930
Canterbury, New Hampshire
Cotton blend and cardboard
Collection of M. Stephen and Miriam Miller

Pincushions in the shape of heirloom tomatoes were produced in large quantities by the Canterbury sisters. Many examples are displayed hanging in the photograph of the Canterbury gift shop (cat. no. 73).

Poplarware

The poplarware industry—a Shaker innovation—combined an abundant natural resource, poplar trees, with two well-developed skills—weaving and handwork. The brethren felled poplar trees, an almost useless material for furniture making or firewood, and kept them outdoors in winter. The frozen wood was shaved into curled, paper-thin strips that were then flattened, dried, and split into narrow pieces measuring only $\frac{1}{16}$ inch wide. The sisters wove the strips of dried poplar wood into different patterns on looms warped with cotton thread. The finished cloth was backed with paper for additional strength, cut into pieces that were wrapped around pine bases, and then tacked into place. The edges of the poplar cloth were protected with a thin band of white kid leather. The boxes were lined with an array of colored silks, and matching silk ribbons secured the lids and held sewing implements in place. These were designed for many uses, including storage for handkerchiefs, calling cards, and bureau accessories, such as beads and buttons. Canterbury is the only community that packaged its fancywork in cardboard boxes, such as the examples below.

82. SQUARE WORK BOX WITH CARDBOARD BOX

1920
Canterbury, New Hampshire
Poplar, silk, kid leather, and cardboard
Collection of M. Stephen and Miriam Miller

83. OCTAGON WORK BOX WITH CARDBOARD BOX

ca. 1940
Canterbury, New Hampshire
Poplar, silk, kid leather, and cardboard
Collection of M. Stephen and Miriam Miller

84. CARD TRAY WITH CARDBOARD BOX
ca. 1940
Canterbury, New Hampshire
Poplar, kid leather, and cardboard
Collection of M. Stephen and Miriam Miller

85. HEART NEEDLE CASE
ca. 1940
Canterbury, New Hampshire
Poplar and kid leather
Collection of M. Stephen and Miriam Miller

86. ROUND PINCUSHION
1920
Enfield, New Hampshire
Poplar, velvet, silk, and kid leather
Collection of M. Stephen and Miriam Miller

This assortment of boxes shows the variety of poplarware made by several Shaker communities (see fig. 3-26).

87. BELL-SHAPE WORK BOX
1908
Alfred, Maine
Poplar, silk, wax, and kid leather
Collection of M. Stephen and Miriam Miller

As described in the 1908 *Catalogue of Fancy Goods* (cat. no. 88), this bell-shape work box (fig. 3-26, bottom right) is furnished inside with a strawberry emery and a wax cake and fitted on the outside with a needle case.

88. CATALOGUE OF FANCY GOODS
1908
Alfred, Maine
Paper and ink
Collection of M. Stephen and Miriam Miller

The bell-shape work box pictured in the upper left hand corner of this catalogue (fig. 3-28, left) is identical to catalogue number 87.

89. BUREAU BOX
ca. 1920s
Alfred, Maine
Poplar, silk, and kid leather
Collection of M. Stephen and Miriam Miller

Also pictured in the 1908 catalogue from Alfred (cat. no. 88), this diamond-shape open box was used by women to hold pins, combs, and other hair-dressing accoutrements.

90. CATALOGUE, *Products of Intelligence and Diligence*
1908
Mount Lebanon, New York
Paper and ink
Collection of M. Stephen and Miriam Miller

This catalogue (see fig. 3-28, right), produced at Mount Lebanon, pictures a variety of products the Shakers sold to the World. The various Shaker villages bought extensively from each other, and the appearance of items pictured does not necessarily mean that they were made at Mount Lebanon.

Woodenware

The Shakers at Mount Lebanon began crafting woodenware for sale as early as 1800. These endeavors, which would ultimately bring enduring renown to the sect and would survive in some form into the twenty-first century, began with the manufacture of dippers, oval boxes, and cooperage (staved wooden vessels).

91. OVAL BOXES
1840–60
New Lebanon, New York
Maple and pine
Collection of M. Stephen and Miriam Miller

Oval boxes are probably the most immediately recognizable products of Shaker hands (fig. 3-9). Although made and sold by many communities, only at New Lebanon were the sizes standardized, ranging from #1—the largest, measuring 15 inches—to #12, the smallest. The external joints were formed of a series of "finger" or "swallowtail" laps, which let the wood expand and contract across the grain without splitting. Although not invented by the Shakers, this form of construction allowed the sides of the boxes to be very thin, as well as visually appealing. These containers, however, were made to be used and not to be admired as art objects.

92. OVAL BOX PRICE LIST
1875–80
Mount Lebanon, New York
Paper and ink
Collection of M. Stephen and Miriam Miller

This is the only freestanding broadside that the Shakers issued to advertise oval boxes that were sold in graduated nests (see fig. 3-

9). The broadside was clearly intended for the wholesale market, as all prices are "per dozen" and range from $3 to $9.

93. TABLE SWIFTS
1850–70
Hancock, Massachusetts
Maple with metal rivets and string
Collection of M. Stephen and Miriam Miller

Beginning in the 1840s, Elder Thomas Damon (1819–1880) developed a type of table yarn winder at Hancock, Massachusetts, that became the community's signature crafted item and continued in use for thirty years (fig. 3-14). Available in five sizes, these umbrella swifts were clamped to a table or a countertop and could be expanded for use or folded up for storage.

A skein of yarn was placed over a partially opened swift and then the sliding lower piece was raised and tightened with a thumbscrew, expanding the slats. As the skein unwound, a ball was formed that was placed in the cup on top of the shaft. Knitters find that yarn taken from a ball is much less likely to tangle.

94. METRIC MEASURES
Designed by Granville Merrill (1839–1878)
1870–1900
Sabbathday Lake, Maine
Ash and unknown wood
Collection of M. Stephen and Miriam Miller

A completely new style of dry measure was developed about 1877 by Brother Granville Merrill at Sabbathday Lake, Maine. He produced forms and patterns from which a series of ten graduated measures could be made (see fig. 3-15). They ranged in size from 20 liters to 1/10 liter. In the 1870s, "Winchester" measures (pint, quart, gallon, etc.) were the norm, and the metric system—authorized for use by Congress in 1832 and again in 1866—was regarded as relatively progressive. Metrics—a product of the French Enlightenment movement in the 1790s—were very much in keeping with the Shaker ethic of applying the latest, most scientific ideas to their own industries. Although the concept never took hold, the mill was in operation until World War II, producing parts for metric measures.

95. Dipper

before 1840
New Lebanon, New York
Maple and pine with iron and copper hardware
Collection of M. Stephen and Miriam Miller

This type of dipper, made to scoop dry materials, was constructed from thinly planed and steam-bent strips of maple, seamed with copper tacks and attached to circular pine disk bottoms. These were among the first craft items made at New Lebanon and were produced until about 1840 (see fig. 3-8).

96. Carriers

William Perkins (1861–1934) and Lillian Barlow (1855–1947)
1920s
Mount Lebanon, New York
Gumwood and pine with stain, varnish, and copper hardware
Collection of M. Stephen and Miriam Miller

The transition from oval box to "carrier" was a short step, as the Shakers needed to add only a handle. This particular style was made of stained gumwood, fitted with a lid, and was offered in four sizes, ranging from 7½ to 11½ inches long.

97. Photograph of Brother Delmer Wilson (1873–1961)

1923
Sabbathday Lake, Maine
Collection of M. Stephen and Miriam Miller

The Shaker community of Sabbathday Lake was the leader in producing sewing carriers—oval boxes fitted with a pivoting handle and four sewing accessories (see fig. 3-30). They were available in four sizes and were made between the 1890s and 1950s. This photograph was taken of Brother Delmer in his workshop, together with the machinery he is credited with designing and making. By late spring of 1923, he had finished making his annual supply of carriers for the summer tourist trade—1,083 by his own count. It was this level of productivity that earned him the title "Dean of the Carrier Makers."

98. Carriers

1920–40
Sabbathday Lake, Maine
Cherry, maple, pine, copper, silk, wax, and felt
Collection of M. Stephen and Miriam Miller

Sisters lined and outfitted the boxes for sale with four sewing accoutrements—a pincushion, a strawberry emery bag, a wax cake, and a needle case. Each of these accessories was secured to the sides of the carrier with a silk ribbon (fig. 3-30).

Production Chairs

From the end of the eighteenth century, the Shakers made furniture for their own use that exhibited distinctive design and construction details particular to the community where they were made. Starting in the 1860s, however, the Mount Lebanon Shakers developed an industry of chairs for sale to the World. The chief difference between communal and production seating is that the latter used uniformly interchangeable parts, put together in assembly-line fashion—true hallmarks of an industry. The Shakers' acceptance of machine technology allowed for the standardization of components, and the division of labor made mass-production possible.

In 1863 the South Family, under the direction of the shop deacon, Elder Robert Wagan (1833–1883), was responsible for developing the fledgling chair industry. Four years later, Mount Lebanon issued its first broadside and, in 1872, built a factory dedicated to chair manufacture. The Shakers set up a booth at the 1876 Centennial Exhibition in Philadelphia and won a Certificate of Award there.

This business venture was so successful that imitations started flooding the market. The Shakers had a product and a reputation they had to protect. Consequently, in 1875, they trademarked a logo and affixed a gold transfer decal to every genuine Shaker chair in order to proclaim its true origin. Their sales and marketing strategy paid dividends for them, both literally and figuratively, for years to come. Having survived the death of its founder, Elder Robert Wagan, in 1883, and the complete loss of the factory to fire in 1923, the chair business continued under the direction of two sisters, Eldress Sarah Collins (1855–1947) and Sister Lillian Barlow (1876–1942), until it finally closed about 1940.

99. #1 Rocker

1900–1925
Mount Lebanon, New York
Maple and stain, with original tape seat
Collection of Shelburne Museum, Shelburne, Vermont, 3.3-336

100. #5 Side Chair with Cushion Rail

1900–1925
Mount Lebanon, New York
Figured maple and stain, with replaced cotton tape seat
Collection of M. Stephen and Miriam Miller
(FIG. 3-17)

101. #7 Armed Rocker with Cushion Rail

1900–1925
Mount Lebanon, New York
Maple and stain, with replaced cotton tape seat
Collection of Hancock Shaker Village, Hancock, Massachusetts

102. Chair Catalogues

1874–81
Mount Lebanon, New York
Paper and ink
Collection of M. Stephen and Miriam Miller

The earliest bound chair catalogue was issued in 1874, and eight more were produced before about 1881. Although the colors, typefaces, and border decorations varied, the format was always similar and included many illustrations of chair types, with prices and descriptions of the numerous options available to the buyer (see fig. 3-20).

In addition to a choice of eight graduated sizes, from #0 (smallest) to #7 (largest), customers could select: straight or rocking models; with or without arms; with slatted or taped backs; and with finials on top or a cushion rail (designed to hold the ties of a back pillow). In addition to these choices, chairs were also available in a range of finishes, from "natural" (clear varnish) to a dark ebony stain, and with a variety of seating tape colors.

Pails and Tubs

Many Shaker villages made cooperage—staved and hoop-bound wooden wares to hold liquids—for their own use. After about 1860 the New Hampshire communities of Canterbury and Enfield produced pails and tubs for sale. They used specialized machines to form the edges of staves into V or U shapes, respectively. These configurations increased the surface area of contact and ensured a snug fit, which was made even more secure with exterior metal bands.

103. Covered Pail
1870–90
Canterbury, New Hampshire
Pine, birch, and iron with red paint
Collection of M. Stephen and Miriam Miller

104. Pail
1870–90
Canterbury, New Hampshire
Pine, birch, and iron with dark blue and red paint
Collection of M. Stephen and Miriam Miller

The blue paint that covers and protects the exterior of this pail, now oxidized to blue-black, is the same color as the original woodwork on the two upper floors of the 1792 meetinghouse at Canterbury.

105. Covered Pail
1870–90
Canterbury, New Hampshire
Pine, birch, and iron with mustard paint
Collection of M. Stephen and Miriam Miller

At Canterbury the brethren almost always used diamond-shape bail plates to secure the handle and to prevent excessive wear to the wood (fig. 3-6).

106. Wash Tub
ca. 1880
Enfield, New Hampshire
Stamped into bottom: "N F Shakers / Enfield, NH"
Pine, birch, and brass with clear varnish
Collection of M. Stephen and Miriam Miller

The North Family at the Enfield, New Hampshire, community had an industry that specialized in making sap buckets and larger pieces of cooperage, such as this tub, for sale (fig. 3-6). The containers were often stamped on the bottom. In addition to the

diamond-shaped bail plates, the Enfield Shakers used tear drop, tombstone, and simple rectangular shapes.

Food Products

No other Shaker commercial endeavor accounted for a wider range of goods than food production. As large collective farm villages, the Shakers converted a "family business" into a profitable industry as early as 1828. Although few financial records have survived, the business must have been sufficiently cost-effective to justify the time, the effort, and the purchase of specialized machinery (such as shelling and drying devices) and additional ingredients (including sugar and vinegar), as well as the packaging materials (firkins, barrels, and glassware) necessary to carry it out successfully. The list of prepared and processed foods that were important sources of revenue at a variety of communities include apples—for cider in barrels and sauce in firkins; string, lima, and butter beans, which were boiled and canned; dried sweet corn and baked beans in cardboard boxes; honey put up in jars; tomatoes made into catsup; and sugared nuts.

107. Dairying Box
1880s
Enfield, Connecticut
Pine with blue paint and iron
Collection of M. Stephen and Miriam Miller

Dairying was an important enterprise at every Shaker community, and large quantities of milk, cream, and butter were produced for home consumption as well as for sale. Richard Van Deusen (1829–1893) served as trustee of the dairy industry at the Enfield, Connecticut, Shaker community from 1867 until his death. This sturdy yet colorful box was supposedly used to transport butter to Worldly customers.

108. Fresh Apples Label and Shaker Fruit Labels
1880s
Mount Lebanon, New York
Paper and ink
Collection of M. Stephen and Miriam Miller

Nearly every Shaker village at some time in its history had orchards of some kind. The Shakers grew apples plums, pears, and

peaches and prepared cider, jams, jellies, and sauces for sale. The tradition continues today at Sabbathday Lake, where thirty-five acres of apple orchards are still harvested annually.

109. Dried Green Sweet Corn Display Sign
ca. 1890
Mount Lebanon, New York
Paper and ink
Collection of M. Stephen and Miriam Miller

Because DeWitt Clinton Brainard (1828–1897) served as a trustee at Mount Lebanon for many years, his name appears on various products put up there in the 1880s and 1890s. The community stopped selling dried sweet corn in 1910.

110. Lemon Syrup Broadside
ca. 1861
Mount Lebanon, New York
Paper and ink
Collection of M. Stephen and Miriam Miller

Elder Benjamin Gates (1817–1909) of Mount Lebanon was another trustee of the society for many years, and he was always looking for new ways to produce income. On a business trip in 1861, he purchased "5 barrels of sugar, 6 gross of bottles & lemon oil & citric acid . . . preparatory to making Lemon Syrup for the [East] family to sell." The broadside boasts: "One tablespoonful of the syrup in a tumbler of water, furnishes a superior lemonade at one-twelfth the cost of lemonade commonly made at Hotels."

111. Candy Box
late 19th century
Mount Lebanon, New York
Cardboard and ink
Collection of M. Stephen and Miriam Miller

112. Candy Box
ca.1890
Canterbury, New Hampshire
Cardboard and ink
Collection of M. Stephen and Miriam Miller

113. Candy Box
1900–2000
Sabbathday Lake, Maine
Cardboard and ink
Collection of M. Stephen and Miriam Miller

Candy making provided a steady source of revenue for three communities in the twentieth century: Mount Lebanon, Canterbury, and Sabbathday Lake. Homemade sugared nuts, flag root, orange and grapefruit peel, butternut, peanut clusters, preserved ginger, chocolate peppermints, and stuffed dates were sold at the gift shops as well as outside each village. The industry at Sabbathday Lake began in 1883 and remains active today under the direction of Sister Frances Carr. Many boxes still carry a sketch of their 1794 meetinghouse.

114. String Bean Can

ca. 1890
Mount Lebanon, New York
Tin and paper
Collection of M. Stephen and Miriam Miller
(illustrated page 62)

The canned vegetable industry was primarily confined to the Shaker communities in Mount Lebanon and Watervliet, New York. The business began in the early 1880s and lasted at Watervliet until the 1930s.

115. Brick Oven Baked Beans Box

ca. 1930s
Canterbury, New Hampshire
Cardboard and ink
Collection of M. Stephen and Miriam Miller

During the 1930s, several sisters at Canterbury started a new business of preparing, packing, and selling baked beans and brown bread on a retail basis. The cardboard carton depicts the Shaker-built brick revolving oven, invented and patented by Sister Emeline Hart (1834–1914) in 1876. It was outfitted with rotating steel shelves that evenly distributed heat to bake many loaves of bread simultaneously.

116. Applesauce Firkin

Made by George F. Lane & Son
ca. 1870s
Canterbury, New Hampshire
Wood
Collection of M. Stephen and Miriam Miller

All containers for packaging the products of Shaker food industries—whether glass, cardboard, tin, or ceramic—were made outside the communities. George F. Lane & Son of East Swanzey, New Hampshire, supplied the wooden firkins used by several communities for applesauce. The firkins came in two sizes and were shipped six to a crate.

117. Dried Green Sweet Corn Box

ca. 1890s
Enfield, Connecticut
Cardboard and Ink
Collection of M. Stephen and Miriam Miller

The Shakers at Enfield, Connecticut, packed their products in these cardboard boxes and offered them for sale until the community closed in 1917. Rarely was a female trustee's name used on a product of the fields that was associated with the work of the brethren. Miriam R. C. Offord (1846–1917), however, assumed this leadership role in 1899. Although there were eligible males at Enfield at the time, none of them apparently was qualified to serve in this position.

118. Green Sweet Corn Can

ca. 1875
Hancock, Massachusetts
Wood, tin, paper and ink
Collection of M. Stephen and Miriam Miller

The Hancock community packaged its dried sweet corn in cylindrical containers made from thin bent wood, with tin rims reinforcing the lid and bottom. Instructions printed on the label direct the user to "Put the corn to soak for two hours previous to cooking in warm water, place it to cook one hour before eating in the same water" (fig. 3-33).

119. Catsup Jug; Pickles, Horseradish, Onions, and Olive Bottles

Bottled and sold by E. D. Pettengill, Co.
ca. 1890
Portland, Maine
Glass, paper, and ink
Collection of M. Stephen and Miriam Miller

In the 1870s, the Shakers at Sabbathday Lake developed a relationship with a Worldly merchant, Edward D. Pettengill of Portland, Maine. They supplied him with a variety of foods and condiments that he bottled, labeled and sold—using the word *Shaker* as a trademark—from 1885 until the early 1900s (fig. 3-34).

120. Lemon Syrup Bottle

ca. 1880
Sabbathday Lake, Maine
Glass, paper, and ink
Collection of M. Stephen and Miriam Miller

Elder Giles Avery (1817–1909), of Mount Lebanon, started the production and sale of lemon syrup in 1861. The formula was based on materials purchased by Brother Benjamin Gates (1817–1909) during a business trip to Buffalo and included sugar, lemon oil, and citric acid. In addition to its culinary use, lemon oil also had a medical application. According to the 1881 issue of the Shaker newspaper called *The Shaker Manifesto*, lemon syrup "is suitable to all stomach diseases; is excellent in sickness."

Garden Seeds

The raising and selling of garden seeds was the first of the many Shaker commercial industries. By 1790 the community at New Lebanon had initiated a business of selling seeds in bulk to neighboring farmers. A few years later, for the first time anywhere, Shakers began to sell their seeds in small paper envelopes at a retail level. This enterprise, more than any other, was the main economic engine at New Lebanon until the 1850s.

The business involved a substantial commitment of all of the Shakers' resources: land, time, manpower, cash reserves, and marketing ability. In addition to planting and harvesting, the process involved printing labels, invoices, and advertising materials; shipping and retrieving products; collecting money, and eventually developing a large mail-order business. For their ephemera, the Shakers used the latest printing technologies as they evolved, both inside and outside their communities. The Civil War and its aftermath had an impact on every facet of American society, and competition to sell garden seeds on a retail basis increased markedly. In the 1880s, for the first time, Mount Lebanon began using commercially printed papers with the saturated colors of lithography as a competitive necessity. For a group that was already progressive in the business world, this was accepted as a natural transition. However, it did not help to postpone the collapse of the Shakers' seed industry, which came to an end at Mount Lebanon in 1888.

121. DISPLAY POSTER, *Shakers' Garden Seeds*

> 1840s
> Probably New Lebanon, New York
> Paper and ink
> Collection of M. Stephen and Miriam Miller

This is the earliest known surviving seed poster or display sign. It would have hung on a merchant's wall or in a window, and it reflects the way the Shakers were viewed by the World's people—simple, solid, bold, and straightforward. It also suggests, in its appealing lack of sophistication, the fact that the Shakers were probably still unchallenged in the seed business by outside competitors.

122. DISPLAY POSTER, *Shakers' Garden Seeds*

> ca. 1860
> New Lebanon, New York
> Paper and ink
> Collection of M. Stephen and Miriam Miller

When the Shakers began to face competition from seed merchants in the world, in the 1860s, they responded with advertising that for the first time used color, ornamental borders, and more elaborate typefaces (fig. 3-2). This display poster, printed outside the community some time before 1861, when the community changed its name from New Lebanon to Mount Lebanon, is the first evidence of this shift in marketing strategy. It was most likely intended to be hung on the wall of a country store, where the Shakers left seeds for sale on a consignment basis.

123. SEED-BOX LABEL, *Shakers' Genuine Garden Seeds*

> 1860–70
> Mount Lebanon, New York
> Paper and ink
> Collection of M. Stephen and Miriam Miller

This is an early style of illustrated label that the Shakers used inside their seed boxes. Both New Lebanon and Mount Lebanon are mentioned as the community of origin, indicating that the label dates to the period of transition between the two—1860 to 1870. Root vegetables, such as beets (with nine varieties), turnips, and radishes (with six varieties of each), dominate the inventory.

124. SEED-BOX LABEL, *Shakers' Genuine Vegetable & Flower Seeds*

> 1880s
> Mount Lebanon, New York
> Paper and ink
> Collection of M. Stephen and Miriam Miller

This is the type of label that was pasted under the lid of the box in catalogue number 125. When placed on the merchant's counter, the box was left with the lid open so that the illustrations of flowers and vegetables could attract the eye of potential customers. The listing on the lower half of the label was filled in by the Shakers by hand, in ink, before the box was left on consignment. This allowed for a quick and accurate calculation of the merchant's commission when the box was retrieved at the end of the selling season. The name of longtime trustee D. C. Brainard (1828–1897) appears on the label as an implied warranty.

125. SEED BOX

> 1880s
> Mount Lebanon, New York
> Wood and paper
> Collection of Shelburne Museum, Shelburne, Vermont, 1949-117.36

The Shakers filled these wooden boxes with seed "papers" over the winter and delivered them to Worldly merchants in the spring. Each fall a Shaker seed peddler returned to retrieve the boxes, along with any unsold envelopes, and would pay the dealer a 33 percent commission for the seeds sold. Defined seed routes were agreed upon among Shaker communities to avoid intra-society competition.

126. SEED-BOX LABEL, *Shakers' Choice Vegetable Seeds*

> late 1880s
> Mount Lebanon, New York
> Paper and ink
> Collection of Shelburne Museum, Shelburne, Vermont,1949-117.44

In about 1883, the Shakers reorganized their foundering seed business as the Shaker Seed Company. Illustrated here (fig. 3-5) is the last of the interior seed-box labels—which is arguably the most attractive—with rich colors and an inviting wedge of watermelon. This was, however, the last gasp of their one-time flagship industry. In order to conform to the later boxes, which were longer and nar-

rower, the list of contents—now significantly reduced to sixty-two varieties—was shifted to the side. Companies in upstate New York, which had sprung up along the Erie Canal, from Albany to Buffalo, produced this and all of the other color lithographs for Mount Lebanon.

127. SHAKER SEED BOX

> 1870s
> Mount Lebanon, New York
> Wood and paper
> Collection of Shelburne Museum, Shelburne, Vermont, 1950-219

128. ASSORTED SEED CATALOGUES

> 1843–86
> Mount Lebanon, New York
> Paper and ink
> Collection of M. Stephen and Miriam Miller

The Gardener's Manuel (*sic*), published in 1843 (see fig. 3-4), first issued in 1835, includes many recipes for cooking, pickling, and preserving vegetables. Beginning in 1877 and continuing until 1883, Shakers published a series of books called Shakers' Descriptive and Illustrated Catalogue and Amateur's Guide to the Flower and Vegetable Garden. These hefty booklets ran from sixty to eighty-four pages and were filled with wood or metal plate cuts of vegetables and flowers, along with detailed descriptions and planting instructions. The last two catalogues, dating from 1885–86, were printed for Mount Lebanon after the reorganization of the industry into the Shaker Seed Company. There is no indication that consumers were charged for these.

129. PHOTO REPRODUCTION OF *Catalogue of Flower Seeds*

> ca. 1850
> Enfield, Connecticut
> Paper and ink
> Collection of M. Stephen and Miriam Miller

The history of the seed industry at Enfield, Connecticut, is the most enigmatic of all the Shaker businesses. At its height in the mid-1850s, with one hundred acres of seed plants under cultivation, it was second in size only to New Lebanon, New York. But with the onset of the Civil War, the business vanished without a trace. *The Catalogue of Flower Seeds*, shown here, lists ninety-five specimens.

130. FLOWER SEED ENVELOPES

1840–60
New Lebanon, New York
Paper and ink
Collection of M. Stephen and Miriam Miller

The vast majority of seeds sold by New Lebanon were for vegetables, but after about 1850 the community began to offer a modest number of flowers and other ornamental varieties. This may have been a response to a growing interest in the World (and among the Shakers themselves) in alternative forms of medicine, some of which used material from flowering plants for therapeutic purposes. For flower seeds alone, New Lebanon's Second Family used a rainbow array of colored papers.

Today almost all consumer goods are "branded" with visual devices, such as defined colors combined with distinctive typography, trademarked names, or corporate/product logos, all meant for instant public recognition. For the Shakers, "D.M." was printed on each seed package—the initials of New Lebanon's beloved first trustee or business manager, David Meacham Sr. Although he died in 1826, invoking his legacy of trustworthiness and fairness imparted an implied guarantee of quality for a wide range of products at New/Mount Lebanon throughout the nineteenth century. "D.M." was used on seed envelopes until 1888, when this business closed.

131. VEGETABLE SEED ENVELOPES

1884–88
Mount Lebanon, New York
Paper and ink
Collection of M. Stephen and Miriam Miller

These envelopes (fig. 3-3) represent the final variation of a form that had begun some eighty-five years earlier. The vivid colors and the technique called vignetting (stippling) were made possible with color lithography. These envelopes were only made for a short period, and few have survived. Yet even this final effort to attract buyers was doomed to failure before 1890, for the diminished community at Mount Lebanon could not match the lower prices charged by its competition.

Medicinal Remedies and Herbs

The Shakers' medicinal herb industry, which included both raw packaged products and the preparations derived from them, was enormous and had a huge financial impact on the communities that adopted it to help support their economy. During the seventy-five years when it was at its peak (1825–1900), the business at just five Shaker communities averaged an aggregate gross of $150,000 annually. With their reputation for quality, the Shakers' remedies—whether taken internally or applied externally—enjoyed a high level of respectability with the general public.

132. BROADSIDE, *Fresh Herbs*

ca. 1840
Enfield, Connecticut
Paper and ink
Collection of M. Stephen and Miriam Miller

This medicinal herb broadside is the largest that the Shakers ever used for any purpose. It includes 221 different items, available in various forms, with a total of more than 300 items listed. Enfield may have bought some of these herbs from other Shaker villages to supplement their own harvest.

133. DISPLAY CARD, *Shakers' Tooth-Ache Pellets*

ca. 1910
Mount Lebanon, New York
Paper and ink
Collection of M. Stephen and Miriam Miller

The pellet consisted of a wad of cotton fiber impregnated with chemicals, which was placed directly on the painful tooth to relieve discomfort. "The novelty of the thing is in having the pellets already for use which saves time, trouble & are convenient to carry." This display card for the Shakers Tooth-Ache Pellets included a portrait of Sister Mary Hazzard (1811–1899)—a marketing tactic that was calculated to link the product with the idea of "Shaker purity."

134. DISPLAY SIGN, *Tisane Americaine des Shakers*

Manufactured by A. J. White
ca. 1910
Lille, France

Paper and ink
Collection of M. Stephen and Miriam Miller

By 1890 A. J. White, the Worldly distributor for the Mount Lebanon Shakers, had developed flourishing manufacturing facilities in Canada, England, and France. He used these to produce and market products with the Shaker name. Mother Siegel's Syrup, the name used for the product outside the United States and France, also came packaged for the World market in pill and pellet forms, as featured in this broadside.

135. BOTTLE AND BROADSIDE, *Imperial Rose Balm*

1861
Mount Lebanon, New York
Glass, paper, and ink
Collection of M. Stephen and Miriam Miller

Imperial Rose Balm was a thick liquid made from soap, alcohol, and chemical oils, which, according to the broadside, was capable of curing pimples, chapped hands, and spongy and sore gums. Although the origin of the formula is unknown, in 1861 Brother Benjamin Gates (1817–1909) initiated and developed the business at Mount Lebanon.

136. BOTTLE AND BROADSIDE, *Shaker Hair Restorer*

1886–90
Mount Lebanon and Watervliet, New York
Glass, paper, and ink
Collection of M. Stephen and Miriam Miller

According to the label and package insert, this preparation (fig 3-21) "restores gray hair to its original color, beauty and softness. An excellent preparation to free the hair from dandruff." Despite these exaggerated claims, the product was sold only between about 1886 and 1890 and did not generate a great deal of income for the Shakers. However, the name of longtime trustee D. C. Brainard (1828–1897) appears on the label—again as an implied warranty.

137. HERB EXTRACT BOTTLES AND CYLINDERS

1840–60
New Lebanon, New York
Glass, cardboard, and ink
Collection of M. Stephen and Miriam Miller

The introduction of the vacuum pan by

Brother Alonzo Hollister (1830–1911) in the 1840s revolutionized the medicine business at the New Lebanon community. For the first time, liquid extracts could be obtained in concentrated form by being cooked at a relatively low temperature in a vacuum pan. In 1850 a specialized, four-story extract house was built, and a pamphlet was published in 1861 listing 135 extracts with the common name, botanical name, and cost per bottle.

138. Culinary Herb Tins

Sage (Harvard, 1870–1900), Sweet Marjoram, (Harvard, 1850–60), Summer Savory (New Lebanon, 1840–60), and Marshmallow Root (Sabbathday Lake, 1980); Tarragon, Sage, Basil, Rose Hips, Herbal Blend (Sabbathday Lake, 2007)
Tin and paper
Collection of M. Stephen and Miriam Miller

Many Shaker villages sold culinary herbs, but usually in only four varieties: summer savory, sage, sweet marjoram, and thyme. They were packaged in small, cylindrical tin cans (fig. 3-35). Harvard had the largest culinary herb business, and it lasted the longest, under the direction of Brother Simon Atherton, who served as trustee there for fifty years, until his death in 1888. The herb industry at Sabbathday Lake had been inactive for nearly ninety years when Brother Theodore Johnson (1931–1986) arrived in the 1960s. It continues today, with most sales by mail and through the community's Internet site.

139. Containers and Package Insert, *The Shaker Asthma Cure*

ca. 1890
Mount Lebanon, New York
Glass, cardboard, paper, and ink
Collection of M. Stephen and Miriam Miller

The Shaker Asthma Cure was manufactured in the 1880s and 1890s. Although the Shakers never published their formula for this preparation, testimonials printed on advertising broadsides attest to the newfound ability of asthmatics to sleep well.

140. Box with Vials and Photo Reproduction of Broadside, *Shakers' Toothache Pellet*

Probably manufactured by J. V. Calver & Co (1842–1913)
ca. 1900
Mount Lebanon, New York

Glass, paper, cotton, cork, cardboard and ink
Collection of M. Stephen and Miriam Miller

James Valentine Calver joined the society at New Lebanon in 1850, at the age of eight, and he remained there until 1871. Nine years after he left, he graduated from the Baltimore College of Dental Surgery and established a practice in Washington, D.C. He stayed in contact with his former Shaker family and offered them an idea for a topical toothache medicine that contained pure wood creosote, oil of eucalyptus, and oil of cloves. Trustee Benjamin Gates (1817–1909), at Mount Lebanon, agreed to manufacture, package, and wholesale this formula, returning a percentage of the profits to Calver. The product was launched in 1890 and was eventually produced by Calver himself (and later his wife), first in Washington and then in Los Angeles, until 1922 (fig. 3-22).

141. Corbett's Syrup of Sarsaparilla

Thomas Corbett (1780–1857)
ca. 1910
Canterbury, New Hampshire
Glass, paper, and ink
Collection of M. Stephen and Miriam Miller

142. Corbett's Wild Cherry Pectoral Syrup

Thomas Corbett (1780–1857)
ca. 1890
Canterbury, New Hampshire
Glass, paper, and ink
Collection of M. Stephen and Miriam Miller

143. *Catalogue of Medicinal Plants and Vegetable Medicines*

Thomas Corbett (1780–1857)
1854
Canterbury, New Hampshire
Paper and ink
Collection of M. Stephen and Miriam Miller

The name Thomas Corbett is synonymous with the medicinal business at the Canterbury Shaker community. In 1813 he was directed by the ministry to become the community's first trained physician. Although he did not earn a formal degree, he was apprenticed to a Worldly doctor, studied with several herbalists, and took classes at one or two medical colleges. When he returned to Canterbury, he cultivated medicinal plants and herbs, from which he processed extracts

for complex compounds. His best-known cure-all—Syrup of Sarsaparilla—contained ten herbs and claimed to be useful for fourteen different disorders. The compound was highly respected by many Worldly physicians and was awarded a U.S. Patent in 1886. The formula for Wild Pectoral Syrup, which treated coughs and congestion, was patented by Canterbury in 1883.

144. Herb Cakes: Peppermint, Lobelia, Skullcap, Snakehead

1870s–1880s
Harvard, Massachusetts
Paper, herbs, and ink
Collection of M. Stephen and Miriam Miller

145. Herb Broadside

1889
Harvard, Massachusetts
Paper and ink
Collection of M. Stephen and Miriam Miller

The medicinal herb business at Harvard began in 1820. Unlike other communities, the Harvard Shakers formed most of their dry herbs into one-pound bricks, using a hydraulic press to apply tremendous pressure. Trustee Simon Atherton oversaw the business for fifty years. It started to decline after his unexpected death in 1888, and finally closed around 1910 (see fig. 3-13).

146. Wrapped Herb Cakes

1840–60
Watervliet, New York
Paper and herbs
Collection of M. Stephen and Miriam Miller

147. *Catalogue of Medicinal Plants and Vegetable Medicines*

1833
Watervliet, New York
Paper and ink
Collection of M. Stephen and Miriam Miller

Dried herbs were used primarily in the form of infusions or teas. A piece of the one-ounce herb cake was broken off and placed in boiling water, and after the herbs were strained, the liquid was poured and sipped.

148. Shaker Extract of Roots
ca. 1880
New York and London
Glass, cardboard, and paper
Collection of Shelburne Museum, Shelburne,
Vermont, 1949.117.40ab, 41ab, 43ab

149. Mother Siegel's Curative Syrup
ca. 1880
New York and London
Glass, cardboard, and paper
Collection of M. Stephen and Miriam Miller

In the mid-1870s, Mount Lebanon Trustee Benjamin Gates (1817–1909) struck a deal with a Worldly opportunist, Andrew Judson White (1824–1898), to distribute mostly Shaker-made remedies. The Shakers agreed to create and bottle White's preparation called the Shaker Extract of Roots, using their herbs, which he would purchase and market. White's formula borrowed heavily from the drug firms where he had previously worked. It consisted of sixteen ingredients designed to "purify the blood" by the elimination of waste products, but it was simply another laxative in a market already saturated with them. Renamed Mother Siegel's Curative Syrup, this single medicine was the most widely distributed and, most likely, the best-selling remedy in the world at the end of the nineteenth century.

150. *Shaker Almanac*
Published by A. J. White
1884
New York City
Paper and ink
Collection of M. Stephen and Miriam Miller

A. J. White issued a series of almanacs between 1875 and 1918, printed in French, German, and English. They prominently featured either the Shaker Extract of Roots or Mother Siegel's Syrup, along with a host of other advertising gimmicks ranging from tiny thimbles to large brass clocks.

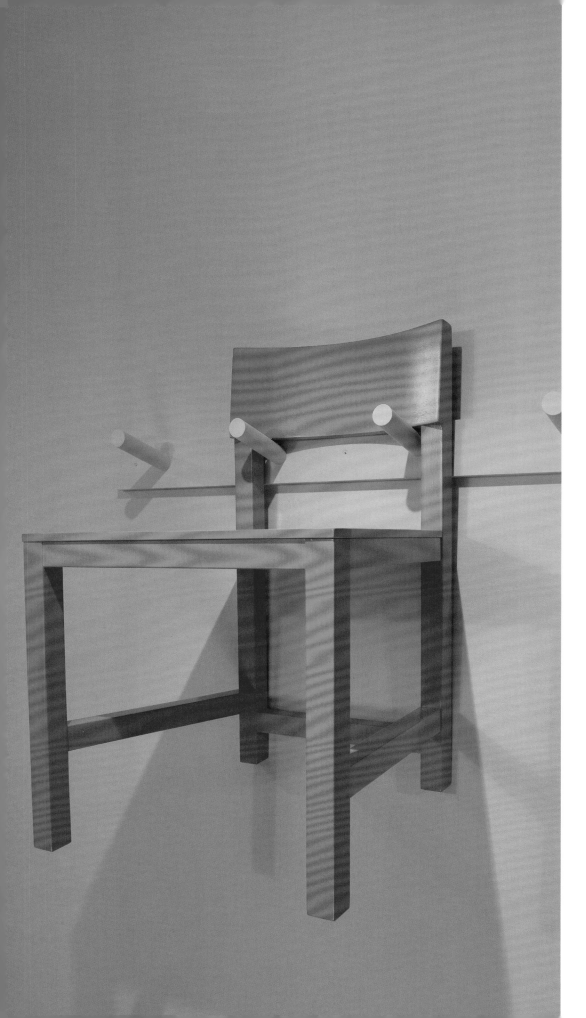

THE CONTEMPORARY WORLD

Furniture from Scandinavia, Japan, and America shows the continuing influence and widespread appeal of nineteenth-century Shaker design. Some of these pieces, which date from 1943 to 2007, are faithful replications of Shaker examples; others are modern reinterpretations, and still others are products of cultures that were completely unaware of the Shakers' existence but shared certain characteristics.

The Shakers and Scandinavian Design

The Shaker aesthetic was exported from the United States to Denmark in 1927, when a #7 Mount Lebanon rocker with arms and a cushion rail found its way to Copenhagen. There it attracted the attention of the influential Danish designer Kaare Klint (1888–1954), who was conducting a pioneering investigation into anthropometrics, the study of human proportions and their relationship to furniture design. As the foundation of his research, Klint directed his students at Copenhagen's Royal Danish Academy of Fine Arts to execute detailed measured drawings of chairs from around the world that he considered to be examples of proven ergonomic designs. Inspired by the Shaker rocker's graceful proportions, Klint commissioned one of his students to draft schematics and make a sample to serve as a teaching aid. Klint was originally unaware of the chair's origins, believing it to be an "American rocking chair in the Colonial style—an example of a type which broadly speaking can still be used today." He eventually discovered the rocker's true identity when *Shaker Furniture,* a book by Edward D. Andrews and Faith Andrews, was published in 1937. Klint is considered the father of Danish Modernism, and his appreciation of Shaker design resonated with the following generation of Danish furniture makers, including Hans J. Wegner (1914–2007) and Børge Mogensen (1914–1972), both of whom went on to produce Shaker-inspired furniture during their illustrious careers.

151. J-16 Rocker

Hans J. Wegner (Danish, 1914–2007)
Manufactured by Fredericia
Designed ca. 1943, this example manufactured ca. 2007
Denmark
Beech and natural paper yarn
Collection of Shelburne Museum, 2007-2

Considered to be one of the greatest Danish designers of all time, Hans J. Wegner most likely first encountered the Shakers as a student at Copenhagen's Polytechnic in the late 1930s. Wegner's lessons in joinery involved making detailed drawings of historic furniture on exhibit at Copenhagen's Museum of Decorative Arts, which included a #7 Shaker rocker.

Wegner's J-16 Rocker (fig. 7-5) blends Shaker elements with characteristics of Windsor seating. He enlarged the proportions of classic Shaker chairs for J-16, increased the degree of the angled back posts, and replaced the traditional Shaker ladder back with turned spindles typical of Windsor rockers.

152. J39 Chair

Børge Mogensen (Danish, 1914–1972)
Manufactured by Fredericia
Designed ca. 1947, this example manufactured ca. 2006
Denmark
Beech and natural paper yarn
Collection of Bob and Aileen Hamilton

The Association of Danish Cooperative Wholesale Societies commissioned Børge Mogensen to design attractive and affordable furniture for everyday use that would appeal to the agrarian tastes of Danish farmers. A student and former colleague of Kaare Klint, Mogensen turned to America's Shakers for inspiration, adopting their low, ladder-back dining chairs as the prototype for his J39 Chair (fig. 7-3). By reducing the number of back slats to one, Mogensen successfully designed a chair well suited for mass production. First introduced in 1947, the J39 has been in continuous production for sixty years. Today the J39 has become a classic piece of Danish Modern furniture, perfectly suitable "for seating ranging from canteens, and conference rooms to churches and private homes."

153. Shaker Table

Børge Mogensen (Danish, 1914–1972)
Manufactured by Fredericia
Designed ca. 1947, this example ca. 2006
Denmark
Beech
Collection of Bob and Aileen Hamilton

Børge Mogensen designed this trestle table (fig. 7-4) to complement his Shaker-inspired J39 Chair. He based his design on a nineteenth-century model from Hancock, Massachusetts, which he saw pictured in the book *Shaker Furniture* by Edward Deming Andrews and Faith Andrews. Mogensen modified the table by replacing the original single upright supports at each end with two thin legs, and he increased its structural stability by adding a second longitudinal stretcher. Mogensen also chamfered the corners of each of the four legs—a distinctive detail found on the Hancock original.

The Shakers and American Design

154. Bench with Back

George Nakashima (American, 1905–1990)
1979
Walnut and hickory
Museum of Fine Arts, Boston, Massachusetts, Museum purchase with funds provided by the National Endowment for the Arts and the Deborah M. Noonan Foundation, 1979.275.

The furniture of Japanese-American woodworker George Nakashima, like that of the Shakers, embodies the spiritual beliefs of the maker. According to Nakashima, every tree possesses an inner soul that is revealed in the natural beauty of the wood. The asymmetrical forms, exposed joinery, and figured wood of Nakashima's furniture inspire comparisons between his work, which he described as "Japanese Shaker," and that of the Shakers themselves. A visual comparison between this bench (fig. 7-7) and the Shaker meetinghouse settee (see cat. no. 22, fig. 2-2) reveals significant parallels in construction and design. Both are modified variations of a traditional Windsor bench, characterized by a single plank seat and spindle-comb back rests. However, instead of shaping the plank seat as the Shakers did, Nakashima allowed the organic grain of the wood to dictate the form of the slab seat

155. Chadansu

Douglas Brooks (American, b. 1960)
2007
Courtesy Douglas Brooks, Vergennes, Vermont

Although the Shaker and Japanese furniture-making traditions developed independently on opposite sides of the world, they share a common design philosophy that emphasizes simplicity, honesty, and utility. Both traditions incorporate the concept that form follows function, an idea that is reflected in the asymmetry of their respective case furniture. Literally translated as "tea chest," *chadansu* are portable, free-standing storage cases used to house specially blended teas and serving accoutrement (see fig. 7-8). The asymmetrical arrangement and varying size of each drawer and door suggest that they were designed to house specific implements used as part of the highly regimented tea ceremony.

156. Enfield Cupboard

William Laberge (American, b. 1960)
2007
Courtesy William Laberge, Dorset, Vermont

The simple forms, impeccable craftsmanship, and quirky designs of nineteenth-century Shaker furniture continue to inspire and challenge talented contemporary cabinetmakers like William Laberge of Dorset, Vermont. Here (fig. 7-10) Laberge faithfully re-creates the asymmetry of the famous "upside-down" built-in cupboard (see fig. 7-11) from the Shaker community of Enfield, Connecticut. Recent examinations of the cupboard's construction have revealed that the original case piece has been displayed incorrectly—wrong side up—for decades. This conclusion is supported by the orientation of the internal locking mechanisms of the drawers, which suggests the tall cupboard shown here on the bottom was originally intended to be on top.

157. Six-Drawer Chest

Roy McMakin (American, b. 1956)
2003
Painted maple and enamel, holly
Courtesy Mathew Marks Gallery, New York

West Coast artist and craftsman Roy McMakin designs and builds domestic furniture that obliquely references the Shaker aesthetic. Like the Shakers before him,

McMakin continually refines preexisting furniture forms by tweaking them ever so slightly to create something new and thought-provoking. Even though McMakin's pieces are the progeny of generic forms that do not belong to any specific style, Shaker DNA is clearly present in the genetic makeup of his furniture, as evidenced by the asymmetrical surface treatment on this rectilinear chest (fig. 7-13). Although the irregular drawer arrangement characteristic of Shaker case pieces is determined by user convenience, the uneven application of the enamel paint and the intentionally mismatched knobs on McMakin's chest are purely visual, playfully but falsely implying inferior quality.

158. UNTITLED

Roy McMakin (American, b. 1956)
2005; edition 1 of 3
Eastern maple with enamel paint
Courtesy Mathew Marks Gallery, New York

Today most people encounter Shaker furniture in a museum setting, displayed on tall pedestals that literally and figuratively elevate the utilitarian objects to the level of fine art. This perception is enhanced by the escalating prices that Shaker furniture commands at auction. As a result, Shaker furniture is viewed with the same reverence as a priceless piece of sculpture, not at all compatible with the attitude of the Shakers, who lived, worked, and worshiped with these artifacts. Roy McMakin blurs the lines between functional object and conceptual art in this untitled work from 2005. Fusing together a small Shaker-style table and a wide platform base, he creates a uniform object that seems both uncertain of its identity and self-conscious about its own importance (see fig. 7-14). McMakin disguises the juncture at which the table meets the base beneath multiple layers of enamel, illustrating our culture's inability or disinclination to distinguish between furniture and art. By placing the table out of arm's reach in the middle of the pedestal, McMakin subverts its practical utility—a very non-Shaker concept.

159. AVL SHAKER CHAIR

Joep van Lieshout (Dutch, b. 1963)
Manufactured by Moooi
1999
Lacquered beech
Collection of Shelburne Museum, 2007-3

Dutch artist and designer Joep van Lieshout designed the prototype for the AVL Shaker Chair (fig. 7-15) in 1999 for the Black House section of his interactive environment *The Good, The Bad, The Ugly* for the Walker Art Center in Minneapolis. The sparsely furnished Black House was conceived as the imaginary domicile of the Unabomber, the American terrorist who killed three people and maimed twenty-nine others with his improvised incendiary devices from 1979 to 1995. Ironically, van Lieshout turned to the pacifist Shakers as the source of inspiration for the decor of a deranged isolationist whose separation from the world led him to pathological violence. Joep van Lieshout's fascination with the Shakers extends beyond aesthetics to include their way of life. In 2001 van Lieshout transformed his Rotterdam studio into the *AVL-Ville*, a self-sufficient "free state" loosely patterned after Shaker communities. Complete with its own constitution and monetary system, the *AVL Ville* was part sociological experiment and part performance piece. In addition to engaging in artistic endeavors, the members of the *AVL-Ville* experimented with agricultural practices, which produced sustenance for the entire community. Just as the Shakers opened their worship to the scrutiny of outside observers, van Lieshout invited spectators to watch the activity of his workshop, where he continued to develop his AVL Shaker furniture line

BOOKS AND ARTICLES

Allen, Jennifer, et al. *Atelier Van Lieshout*. Rotterdam: Nai Publishers, 2007.

Andrews, Edward Deming. *The Community Industries of the Shakers*. Albany: University of the State of New York, 1933; reprinted Charlestown, Mass.: Emporium Publications, 1971.

Andrews, Edward Deming. *The People Called Shakers: A Search for the Perfect Society*. New York: Oxford University Press, 1953; reprinted New York: Dover Publications, 1963.

Andrews, Edward Deming, and Faith Andrews. *Shaker Furniture: The Craftsmanship of an American Communal Sect*. Albany: University of the State of New York, 1937.

Andrews, Edward Deming. *A Shaker Meeting House and its Builder*. Pittsfield, Mass.: Shaker Community, 1962.

Andrews, Edward Deming, and Faith Andrews. *Visions of the Heavenly Sphere: A Study in Shaker Religious Art*. Charlottesville: University Press of Virginia, 1969.

Andrews, Edward Deming, and Faith Andrews. *Work and Worship*. Greenwich, Conn.: New York Graphic Society, 1974.

Anonymous. "An Ancient Witness," *The Shaker Manifesto* 11, no. 2 (February 1881): 45.

Anonymous. "A Barn," *Ohio Farmer and Mechanics Assistant* (15 July 1854): 1, 109.

Anonymous. *The Manifesto* 17, no. 3 (March 1887): 57–58.

Anonymous. *The Manifesto* 29, no. 9 (September 1899): 134.

Anonymous. "Rambles Among the Shakers," *Illustrated News*, New York, 29 October 1853, p. 245.

Anonymous. *A Summary View of the Millennial Church, or United Society of Believers (Commonly Called Shakers)*. Albany; Packard & van Benthuysen, 1823.

Bainbridge, William Sims. "Shaker Demographics 1840–1900: An Example of the Use of U. S. Census Enumeration Schedules," *Journal for the Scientific Study of Religion* 21, no. 4 (1982): 352–65.

Barber, John Warner, and Henry Howe. *Historical Collections of the State of New York*. New York: S. Tuttle, 1841.

Bauer, Cheryl, and Rob Portman. *Wisdom's Paradise: The Forgotten Shakers of Union Village*. Wilmington, Ohio: Orange Frazer Press, 2004.

Beale, Galen, and Mary Boswell. *The Earth Shall Blossom: Shaker Herbs and Gardening*. Woodstock, Vt.: The Countryman Press, 1991.

Becksvoort, Christian. *The Shaker Legacy: Perspectives on an Enduring Furniture Style*. Newtown, Conn.: Taunton Books & Video, 2000.

Bentley, William. *The Diary of William Bentley, D.D.*, vol. 2. Salem, Mass.: The Essex Institute, 1907.

Blakeman, Elisha. *The Youth's Guide in Zion and Holy Mother's Promises*. Canterbury, N.H.: Shaker Society, 1842.

Blinn, Henry C., comp. *A Sacred Repository of Anthems and Hymns, for Devotional Worship and Praise*. Canterbury, N.H.: Shaker Society, 1852.

Blinn, Henry C. "Autobiographical Notes." In *In Memoriam: Elder Henry C. Blinn 1824–1905*. Concord, N.H.: The Rumford Press, 1905, p. 28.

Blinn, Henry C. *The Life and Experience of Mother Ann Lee*. Canterbury, N.H.: Shaker Society, n.d.

Bowe, Stephen, and Peter Richmond. *Selling Shaker: The Commodification of Shaker Design in the Twentieth Century*. Liverpool: Liverpool University Press, 2007.

Brewer, Priscilla J. *Shaker Communities, Shaker Lives*. Hanover, N.H.: University Press of New England, 1986.

Brown, Thomas. *Account of the People Called Shakers: Their Faith, Doctrines, and Practice*. Troy: Parker and Bliss, 1812.

Buchanan, Rita. *The Shaker Herb and Garden Book*. Boston and New York: Houghton Mifflin Company, 1996.

Buck, Susan. "Bedsteads Should be Painted Green: Shaker Paints and Varnishes." *Old-Time New England* (Fall 1995).

Buck, Susan. "Interpreting Paint and Finish Evidence on the Mount Lebanon Shaker Collection." *Shaker: The Art of Craftsmanship*. Alexandria, Va.: Art Services International, 1996.

Buck, Susan. "Shaker Painted Furniture: Provocative Insights into Shaker Paints and Painting Techniques." *Painted Wood: History and Conservation*. Los Angeles: Getty Conservation Institute, 1994.

Burks, Jean M. "The Evolution of Design in Shaker Furniture." *The Magazine Antiques* (May 1994): 737.

Byars, Mel. *The Design Encyclopedia*. New York: John Wiley, 1994.

Cooper, James Fenimore. *Notions of the Americans, Picked up by a Travelling Bachelor*. Philadelphia: Carey & Lea, 1828.

Cummings, Henry. "A Sketch of the Life of Caleb M. Dyer." *Enfield Advocate* 30 (December 1904).

Curtis, John Obed, and William H. Guthman. *New England Militia Uniforms and Accoutrements—A Pictorial Survey*. Sturbridge, Mass: Old Sturbridge Village, 1971.

Darling, Michael. *Roy McMakin: A Door Meant as Adornment*. Exh. cat. Los Angeles: Museum of Contemporary Art, 2003.

Denker, Ellen. *The Rocking Chair Book*. New York: Mayflower Books, 1979.

Dickens, Charles. *American Notes for General Circulation*. London: Chapman & Hall, 1842.

Downing, A. J. *The Architecture of Country Houses*. New York: D. Appleton, 1850.

Elkins, Hervey. *Fifteen Years in the Senior Order of Shakers*. Hanover: Dartmouth Press, 1953.

Emlen, Robert P. "The Great Stone Dwelling of the Enfield, New Hampshire, Shakers." *Old-Time New England* 69 (Winter–Spring 1979): 69–83.

Emlen, Robert P. "Raised, Razed, and Raised Again: The Shaker Meetinghouse at Enfield, New Hampshire," *Historical New Hampshire* 30, no. 3 (Fall 1975).

Emlen, Robert P. "The Shaker Dance Prints." *Imprint: The Journal of the American Historical Print Collectors Society* 17, no. 2 (Autumn 1992): 14–26.

Emlen, Robert P. *Shaker Village Views: Illustrated Maps and Landscape Drawings by Shaker Artists of the Nineteenth Century*. Hanover, N.H.: University Press of New England, 1987.

Estes, J. Worth. "The Pharmacology of Nineteenth-Century Patent Medicines." *Pharmacy in History* 30 (1988): 3–18.

Estes, J. Worth. "Shaker-Made Remedies." *Pharmacy in History* 34 (1992): 63–73.

Estes, J. Worth. "The Shakers and their Proprietary Medicines." *Bulletin of Historical Medicine* 65 (1991):162–84

Evans, Nancy Goyne. *American Windsor Chairs*. Manchester, Vt.: Hudson Hills Press, 1996.

Farish, Hunter. *Journal and Letters of Philip Fithian, 1773–1774, A Plantation Tutor*. Charlottesville: University Press of Virginia, 1968.

Fiell, Charlotte, and Peter Fiell. *Scandinavian Design*. Los Angeles: Taschen, 2005.

Flint, James. *Letters From America, containing Observations on the Climate and Agriculture of the Western States, etc.* Edinburgh: W & C. Tart, 1822.

Foster, Lawrence. *Religion and Sexuality: Three American Communal Experiments of the Nineteenth Century*. New York: Oxford University Press, 1981.

Garrett, Clarke. *Spirit Possession and Popular Religion: From the Camisards to the Shakers*. Baltimore: Johns Hopkins University Press, 1987.

Gifford, Don, ed. *An Early View of the Shakers: Benson John Lossing and the Harper's Article of July 1857*. Hanover, N.H.: University Press of New England, 1989.

Goodwillie, Christian, and Mario DePillis. *Gather Up the Fragments: The Andrews Shaker Collection*. New Haven and London: Yale University Press (in press).

Goodwillie, Christian. "Coloring the Past: Shaker Painted Interiors." *The Magazine Antiques* (September 2005): 80–87.

Gordon, Beverly. *Shaker Textile Arts*. Hanover, N.H.: University Press of New England, 1980.

Grant, Jerry V. 'Forty Untouched Masterpieces of Shaker Design." *The Magazine Antiques* 135, no. 5 (May 1989): 1226–37.

Green, Calvin. "Biographical Account of the Life, Character, & Ministry of Father Joseph Meacham" (1827) Reprinted in *Shaker Quarterly* 10, 1 (Spring 1970): 21–102.

Ham, F. Gerald. "Shakerism in the old West." Ph.D. dissertation, University of Kentucky, 1962.

Hawthorne, Nathaniel. "The Canterbury Pilgrims" (1832). Reprinted in Hyatt H. Waggoner, ed., *Nathaniel Hawthorne: Selected Tales and Sketches*. New York: Holt, Rinehart and Winston, 1970, pp. 466–71.

Hawthorne, Nathaniel. Letter to Louisa Hawthorne, 17 August 1831. Quoted in Seymour L. Gross, "Hawthorne and the Shakers," *American Literature* 29 (January 1958): 458.

Hawthorne, Nathaniel. "The Village of the United Society of Shakers, in Canterbury, N.H." *The American Magazine of Useful and Entertaining Knowledge* 2 (November 1835).

Hay, D. R. *The Laws of Harmonious Colouring Adapted to Interior Decorations, Manufacturers, and Other Useful Purposes*. London, 1828; reprinted Edinburgh and London: W. Blackwood and Sons, 1847.

Hayden, Dolores. *Seven American Utopias: The Architecture of Communitarian Socialism, 1790–1975*. Cambridge, Mass.: MIT Press, 1976.

Hebb, Caroline. "A Distinctive Group of Early Vermont Painted Furniture." *The Magazine Antiques* 104, no. 3 (September 1973): 458–61.

Heineken, Ty, and Kiyoko. *Tansu: Traditional Japanese Cabinetry*. New York: Weatherhill, 1981.

Heisey, John W. *Checklist of American Coverlet Weavers*. Charlottesville: University Press of Virginia, 1980.

Hill, Isaac. "A Grand Edifice." *The Farmer's Monthly Visitor* 1, no. 9 (20 September 1839): 142.

Hill, Isaac. "The Shakers." *Farmer's Monthly Visitor* 2 (31 August 1840): 113. Reprinted in T. E. Johnson, ed., "Canterbury in 1840," *Shaker Quarterly* 4 (Summer–Fall 1964): 85.

Humez, Jean M., ed. *Mother's First-Born Daughters*. Bloomington: Indiana University Press, 1993.

Humez, Jean M. "'Weary of Petticoat Government': The Specter of Female Rule in Early Nineteenth-century Shaker Politics." *Communal Societies* (1992): 1–17.

Humez, Jean M. "Ye Are My Epistles: The Construction of Ann Lee Imagery in Early Shaker Sacred Literature." *Journal of Feminist Studies in Religion* 8, no. 1 (Spring 1992): 83–103.

Johnson, Theodore E. "Life in the Christ Spirit: Observations on Shaker Theology, Being in Substance Remarks Delivered at the Shaker Conference, Hancock, Massachusetts, September 7, 1968." *Shaker Quarterly* (Fall 1968). Reprinted in Morse, *The Shakers and the World's People* (1987): 182, 184.

Johnson, Theodore E., ed. "The 'Millennial Laws' of 1821," *Shaker Quarterly* 7 (Summer 1967): 35–58.

Jones, Leslie Allen. *Eli Terry: Clockmaker of Connecticut*. New York: Farrar and Rinehart, 1942.

Kennedy, Gerrie, Galen Beale, and Jim Johnson. *Shaker Baskets & Poplarware*. Stockbridge, Mass.: Berkshire House Publishers, 1992.

Kern, Louis. *An Ordered Love: Sex Roles and Sexuality in Victorian American Communes*. Chapel Hill: University of North Carolina Press, 1981.

Kirk, John T. "Reappraising an Upside-down Shaker Masterpiece." *The Magazine Antiques* (March 2004): 88–91.

Kirk, John. *The Shaker World: Art, Life, Belief.* New York: Harry N. Abrams, 1997.

Lamson, David R. *Two Years' Experience among the Shakers.* West Boylston, Mass: David Lamson, 1848.

Lang, Bernhard. *Sacred Games: A History of Christian Worship.* New Haven and London: Yale University Press, 1997.

Levi, Michael D. "A Shaker Approach to Web Site Design," http://www.bls.gov/ore/htm_papers/st970120.htm

Lossing, Benson John. *Benson John Lossing and the Harper's Article of July 1857.* Ed. by Don Gifford. Hanover, N.H.: Hancock Shaker Village with University Press of New England, 1989.

Marshall [Dyer], Mary. *A Portraiture of Shakerism.* 1822; reprinted New York: AMS Press, 1972.

McCobb, Paul. *Fifties Furniture by Paul McCobb: Directional Designs.* Atglen: Schiffer Publishing, 2000.

McFadden, David Revere. *Scandinavian Modern Design, 1880–1980.* New York: Harry N. Abrams, 1982.

Meader, Robert F. W. "The Vision of Brother Philemon." *Shaker Quarterly* 10 (Spring 1980): 11.

Meader, Robert F. W. *Illustrated Guide to Shaker Furniture.* New York: Dover, 1972.

"Millennial Laws of Gospel Statutes and Ordinances Adopted to the Day of Christ's Second Appearing." Revised and reestablished by the Ministry and Elders, October 1845. Reprinted in Andrews, *The People Called Shakers* (1953).

Miller, Amy Bess. *Shaker Medicinal Herbs: A Compendium of History, Lore, and Uses.* Pownal, Vt.: Storey Books, 1998.

Miller, M. Stephen. *From Shaker Lands and Shaker Hands: A Survey of the Industries.* Hanover, N.H.: University Press of New England, 2007.

Montgomery, Charles F., and Patricia E. Kane, eds. *American Art: 1750–1800 Towards Independence.* Boston: New York Graphic Society, 1976.

Montgomery, Charles F. *American Furniture: The Federal Period in the Henry Francis du Pont Winterthur Museum.* New York: Viking Press, 1966.

Morin, France. *Heavenly Visions: Shaker Gift Drawings and Gift Songs.* Minneapolis: University of Minnesota Press, 2001.

Morse, Flo. *The Shakers and the World's People.* Hanover, N.H.: University Press of New England, 1987.

Moser, Thomas. *How to Build Shaker Furniture.* New York: Sterling Publishing, 1977.

Moser, Thomas F., with Brad Lemley. *Thos. Moser: Artistry in Wood.* San Francisco: Chronicle Books, 2002.

Moss, Roger W. *Paint in America: The Colors of Historic Buildings.* Washington, D.C.: National Trust for Historic Preservation, 1994.

Muller, Charles R., and Timothy D. Rieman. *The Shaker Chair.* Winchester, Ohio: The Canal Press, 1984; reprinted Atglen, Pa.: Schiffer Publishing, 2003.

Nakashima, George. *The Soul of a Tree: A Master Woodworker's Reflections.* Tokyo and New York: Kodansha International, 1981.

Nicoletta, Julie. "The Architecture of Control: Shaker Dwelling Houses and the Reform Movement in Early-Nineteenth-Century America." *Journal of the Society of Architectural Historians* 62, no. 3 (September 2003).

Nicoletta, Julie. *The Architecture of the Shakers.* Woodstock, Vt.: Countryman Press, 1995.

Nordhoff, Charles. *The Communistic Societies of the United States.* New York: Harper & Brothers, 1875.

Noyes, John Humphrey. *History of American Socialisms.* Philadelphia: Lippincott, 1870; reprinted New York, Dover, 1966.

Ott, John Harlow. *Hancock Shaker Village: A Guidebook and History.* Hancock, Mass.: Shaker Community, 1976.

Patterson, Daniel W. *Gift Drawing and Gift Song: A Study of Two Forms of Shaker Inspiration.* Sabbathday Lake, Me.: Shaker Society, 1983.

Patterson, Daniel W. *The Shaker Spiritual.* Princeton: Princeton University Press, 1979.

Pearson, Elmer R., and Julia Neal. *The Shaker Image.* 2nd ed. Pittsfield, Mass.: Hancock Shaker Village, 1994.

Peladeau, Marius. "The Shaker Meetinghouses of Moses Johnson." *The Magazine Antiques* 98 (October 1970): 594–99

Philadelphia Museum of Art. "The Shakers: Their Arts and Crafts." *Philadelphia Museum Bulletin* 57 (Spring 1962): 95.

Piercy, Caroline B. *The Valley of God's Pleasure.* New York: Stratford House, 1951.

["Pilgrim"], "The Shaker Community," *The Augusta Rural Intelligencer* 1, no. 37 (15 September 1855): 293.

Poe, Edgar Allan. "Philosophy of Furniture." In Hervey Allen, ed., *The Works of Edgar Allan Poe in One Volume.* New York: P. F. Collier, 1927, pp. 919–20.

Porter, Rufus. "Imitation Painting." *Scientific American* 1, no.17 (8 January 1846): 2.

Porter, Rufus. "The Art of Painting: Ornamental Gilding and Bronzing." *Scientific American* 1, no. 9 (13 November 1845).

Priddy, Sumpter III. *American Fancy: Exuberance in the Arts 1790–1840.* Exh. cat. Milwaukee: Chipstone Foundation with Milwaukee Art Museum, 2004.

Procter-Smith, Marjorie. *Women in Shaker Community and Worship: A Feminist Analysis of the Uses of Religious Symbolism.* Lewiston: Edwin Mellon Press, 1985.

Rathbun, Reuben. *Reasons Offered for Leaving the Shakers.* Pittsfield, Mass: Chester Smith, 1800.

Reid, Thomas. "Of Simple Apprehension in General." In *Essays on the Intellectual Powers of Man.* Edinburgh: John Bell, and London: G. G. and J. Robinson, 1785.

Richards, David L. *Poland Spring: A Tale of the Gilded Age, 1860–1900.* Durham: University of New Hampshire Press, 2005.

Richmond, Peter and Stephen, Bowe. *Selling Shaker: The Commodification of Shaker Design in the Twentieth Century.* Liverpool: Liverpool University Press, 2007.

Richmond, Colin Becket. *A Collection of Shaker Thoughts.* Oneida, N.Y.: Colin Becket Richmond, 1976.

Rieman, Timothy D., and Jean M. Burks. *Encyclopedia of Shaker Furniture.* Atglen, Pa.: Schiffer Publishing, 2003.

Rieman, Timothy D., and Jean M. Burks. *The Complete Book of Shaker Furniture.* New York: Abrams, 1993.

Ritter, Chris. "An Interior View." *Art Digest* 26 (September 1952): 19.

Roberts, Kenneth D. *Eli Terry and the Connecticut Shelf Clock.* Bristol, Conn: Kenneth Roberts, 1973

Rose, Milton C., and Emily Mason Rose. *A Shaker Reader.* New York: Universe Books, 1975.

Royall, Ann. *Mrs.Royall's Pennsylvania, or Travels continued in the United States,* vol. 1. Washington, D.C.: privately printed, 1829.

Schorsch, David A., ed. *The Photographs of William F. Winter, Jr. 1899–1939.* New York: David A. Schorsch, 1989.

"Shaker Portfolio, a Picture Record of an American Community," *US Camera Magazine* (March/April 1939).

Silliman, Benjamin. *Remarks Made on a Short Tour Between Hartford and Quebec in the Autumn of 1819.* New Haven: S. Converse, 1820.

Smith, Walter. *Art Education, Scholastic and Industrial.* Boston: James R. Osgood, 1872.

Somer, Margaret Frisbee. *The Shaker Garden Seed Industry.* Orono: University of Maine, 1966.

Sprigg, June. *By Shaker Hands.* New York: Knopf, 1975.

Sprigg, June. *Shaker Design.* Exh. cat. New York: Whitney Museum of American Art, 1986.

Sprigg, June. *Shaker: Original Paints & Patinas.* Exh. cat. Allentown, Pa.: Muhlenberg College for the Arts, 1987.

Sprigg, June, ed. *Kindred Spirits—The Eloquence of Function in American Shakers and Japanese Arts of Daily Life.* San Diego: Mingei International, 1995.

Stein, Stephen J., ed. *Letters from a Young Shaker: William S. Byrd at Pleasant Hill.* Lexington: University Press of Kentucky, 1985.

Stein, Stephen J. *The Shaker Experience in America.* New Haven and London: Yale University Press, 1992.

Stewart, Philemon. "'Petticoat Government' Issues and Later 19th century Shakerism." *The Shaker Quarterly* 22, no. 4 (Winter 1994): 122–52.

Stewart, Philemon. *A Holy, Sacred and Divine Roll and Book; from the Lord God of Heaven to the Inhabitants of Earth.* Canterbury, N.H.: Shaker Society, 1843.

Swank, Scott T. *Shaker Life, Art, and Architecture: Hands to Work, Hearts to God.* New York: Abbeville Press, 1999,

Tucket, Waldo. *The Mechanic's Assistant.* Windsor, Vt., 1837.

Weis, Virginia M. "Every Good and Simple Gift," *Shaker Quarterly* 13 (Fall 1973): 94.

Wells, Seth Youngs, compiler. *Testimonies of the Life, Character, Revelations and Doctrines of Mother Ann Lee.* 2nd ed. Albany, N.Y.: Weed-Parsons Printing Company, 1888.

Wergland, Glendyne. *One Shaker Life, Isaac Newton Youngs, 1793–1865.* Amherst: University of Massachusetts Press, 2006.

Wergland, Glendyne. *Sisters in the Faith: Shaker Women, 1780–1900* (forthcoming).

Wertkin, Gerard C. *The Four Seasons of Shaker Life.* New York: Simon & Schuster, 1986.

White, Anna, and Leila Taylor. *Shakerism: Its Meaning and Message.* Columbus, Ohio: Fred J. Heer, 1904.

Whitson, Robley Edward, ed. *The Shakers: Two Centuries of Spiritual Perfection.* New York: Paulist Press, 1983.

Whittock, Nathaniel. *The Decorative Painters' and Glaziers' Guide.* London: Isaac Taylor Hinton, 1827.

www.moormann.de

www.Shaker.lib.me.us

MANUSCRIPT COLLECTIONS

Andrews Shaker Collection, Western Reserve Historical Society, Cleveland, Ohio [WR].

Canterbury Shaker Village Archives, Canterbury, New Hampshire.

Edward Deming Andrews Memorial Collection, Winterthur, Delaware.

New York Public Library, Shaker Manuscript Collection, New York, New York [NYPL].

Shaker Library, Sabbathday Lake, Maine.

Shaker Museum and Library, Old Chatham, New York.